Flying a Floatplane

TAB PRACTICAL FLYING SERIES

Other books in the TAB PRACTICAL FLYING SERIES

Flying a Floatplane

Third Edition

C. Marin Faure

McGraw-Hill

New York San Francisco Washington, D.C. Auckland Bogotá
Caracas Lisbon London Madrid Mexico City Milan
Montreal New Delhi San Juan Singapore
Sydney Tokyo Toronto

McGraw-Hill

A Division of The McGraw·Hill Companies

©1996 by **The McGraw-Hill Companies, Inc.**

pbk   1 2 3 4 5 6 7 8 9 FGR/FGR 9 0 0 9 8 7 6

Library of Congress Cataloging-in-Publication Data
Faure, Marin.
    Flying a floatplane / by C. Marin Faure.—3rd ed.
        p.   cm.
    Includes bibliographical references and index.
    ISBN 0-07-021304-6 (pbk.)
    1. Seaplanes—Piloting.   I. Title.
TL711.S43F38 1996
629.132'5247—dc20   96-646
                                          CIP

McGraw-Hill books are available at special quantity discounts to use as premiums and sales promotions, or for use in corporate training programs. For more information, please write to the Director of Special Sales, McGraw-Hill, 11 West 19th Street, New York, NY 10011. Or contact your local bookstore.

Acquisitions editor: Shelley IC. Chevalier
Editorial team: Robert E. Ostrander, Executive Editor
               Norval G. Kennedy, Book Editor
Production team: Katherine G. Brown, Director
                Donna K. Harlacher, Coding
                Rose McFarland, Desktop Operator
                Linda L. King, Proofreading
                Jodi L. Tyler, Indexer
Design team: Jaclyn J. Boone, Designer   0213046
             Katherine Lukaszewicz, Associate Designer   PFS2

Contents

Introduction

BEFORE MY VERY FIRST flying lesson back in 1971, my instructor recommended that I read a book called *Stick and Rudder*, by Wolfgang Langewiesche.

"It won't teach you to fly," my instructor said, "but you'll understand the theory. You'll know what you're *supposed* to do. The rest of it's just practice and experience."

I read the book, and on my first flight I understood why the plane took off, why it stayed up, and how I could make it climb and descend and turn. Doing it properly was another matter—flying is a learned skill—but as my instructor predicted, I understood the theory, and that pretty much took care of any sense of mystery, confusion, or fear I might have felt otherwise.

I don't pretend to be in the same league as Mr. Langewiesche, but I've tried to follow in his footsteps with this book. It won't teach you to fly a floatplane, but you'll certainly know what to expect when you step onto the dock for your first lesson.

I've made the assumption that the reader already knows how to fly, so I've concentrated only on those procedures and techniques that apply to floatplanes. The book is organized along the same lines as a typical floatplane course, introducing you first to the airplane itself, and then progressing through the basic procedures to finish up with advanced techniques and cross-country work.

Change seems to be the common thread running through industry today, and the floatplane business is no exception. In the six years since the second edition of this book was published, there have been numerous changes just in the part of the world where I fly. Some of the big floatplane operators have disappeared, replaced by other operators who've grown even bigger. The ultralight craze has given way to the kitplane, a sensible move as far as I'm concerned, as you can actually carry something and go somewhere in a kitplane. Turbine power has arrived in a big way with conversion kits breathing new life into de Havilland's venerable Turbo Beaver and single-engine Otter. Operators from Seattle to Anchorage are discovering the advantages of turboprops, and more and more docks are sporting brand-new Jet-A pumps next to their battered and worn avgas dispensers.

Of course, as the years go by, people change, too. Neil Ratti, who is at the controls of the Beaver pictured in the chapters on technique, is now a captain for Alaska Airlines, as is Kevin Nelson, who indoctrinated me into the world of amphibious floats. Tom Eldridge, the guy fighting the fish in chapter 1, is now with the FAA in Alaska.

But not everything has changed. The Inside Passage to Alaska is as spectacular as it was the first time I flew it. The satisfaction that follows a perfectly executed docking hasn't changed. The excitement of landing amid the eagles, fishing boats, and floatplanes in Ketchikan's windy harbor hasn't changed. And the perfection of a glass-calm evening deep in the solitude of the Coast Range hasn't changed.

When I was approached to produce a third edition of this book, my first reaction was to say I couldn't think of anything to add. It's not that I thought I'd written the perfect book: far from it. There are lots of aviation writers far more talented than myself, and the list of better and more experienced pilots would fill volumes. I just felt I'd covered the subject about as well as I could cover it. But after bouncing the idea around for awhile, and talking to a few of my more critical friends, I decided there were some things I could do that would reflect some of the changes that have occurred in the floatplane industry, while adding value to the book at the same time.

I'd been introduced to turbines in time to include some brief operational information in the second edition, but as I watched the growing number of turboprops whistle in and out of Seattle's downtown floatplane base, I decided they deserved a chapter of their own. Anyone interested in flying floatplanes for a living has a pretty good chance of eventually ending up in a turbine, so I thought it might be helpful to give him or her a head start.

Fortunately, I have access to one of the best turbine pilots in the business. Bill Whitney, Kenmore Air's chief pilot, pioneered that company's use of turbine Beavers and has spearheaded its move into turbine Otters. He's had the guts to sit in the right seat while I flew Kenmore's reengined Turbo Beavers and Vazar Dash-3 Otters, both million-dollar machines *without dual controls*. While I might have written the words in chapter 18, it's really Bill's chapter. He spent a lot of time with me, turning his tens of thousands of hours of ex-perience into explanations and descriptions I could understand.

I can't think of anyone who knows more about floats and floatplanes than Jay J. Frey, who runs the EDO Corporation's Float Division. Jay has never hesitated to give me the benefit of his experience and expertise, starting with the first edition of this book back in 1984. I asked him for a few photos of modern floatplanes mounted on EDO floats. He sent me what I asked for, plus dozens of other pictures he thought I might find interesting. Thanks to his initiative and enthusiasm for the subject, the chapter on floatplane history is much more complete than I ever imagined it could be.

When it came time to start thinking about a third edition, I called Jay and asked him what I could do to make the book better. "Put in a chapter on maintenance," came the immediate reply. "The fleet's 25 to 30 years old now, and maintenance is more important than ever."

"I'm not a mechanic," I answered. "What I know about maintenance wouldn't fill half a page."

"I'll help you," Jay replied, and he did. In the same way that the turbine chapter is really Bill Whitney's, chapter 20 belongs to Jay.

The chapter on history benefited from the help of two other aviation experts. Walter J. Boyne, aviation author and former director of the National Air and Space Museum at the Smithsonian Institution, took time from his busy schedule to see that I received the photos I'd requested, as well as articles written by people who worked on and flew Supermarine's remarkable racing floatplanes. Captain Richard C. Knott, naval historian and author, provided valuable information about the designer and builder of the world's first floatplane, Henri Fabre.

I did not teach myself to fly a floatplane. Whatever value this book has, it's due to the efforts of some outstanding instructors. The late, and very respected, Lana Kurtzer made sure I deserved the single-engine sea rating on my ticket.

Neil Ratti helped me fulfill my dream of learning to fly a de Havilland Beaver, while Kevin Nelson gave me a thorough checkout in the Cessna 185 "amphib" pictured in chapter 17. Scott Spengler indoctrinated me into the hows and whys of cross-country float flying. Tom Eldridge put some polish on what Neil started, and did his best to keep me out of trouble in the turbulent world of saltwater float flying.

Most recently, I've had the benefit of learning some of the finer points of back-country float flying from two of the most competent pilots I've ever known: Brent Robinson and Jim Kastner. Their expertise extends far beyond the cockpit. Brent, who used to run a string of pack horses for a living, can fit more stuff into a Beaver than anyone, including its designers, would have thought possible. And if the mountain men of the 1800s had needed a pilot, they couldn't have done any better than Jim. The more rugged the country, the more at home Jim is in it.

However, it is to the owners of Kenmore Air Harbor—Bob, Ruth, Gregg, and Leslie (Banks) Munro—that I owe the greatest debt of gratitude. It was a checkout in one of their immaculate Beavers that inspired me to write my first magazine article, so you could say that the Munros are responsible for the very existence of this book. Not only do they run a first-class operation, but they have gone out of their way to accommodate my seemingly endless requests for new experiences and new pictures. My flights to southeast Alaska would not be possible without their cooperation.

There are times when I might not have *found* southeast Alaska had it not been for my wife. Ruth has a real aptitude for finger-on-the-map navigation, along with a pair of eyes that can spot a landmark through a drizzly haze that has the seagulls thinking seriously about investing in GPS. If I've learned one thing from flying, it's that you can't go wrong if there's a good navigator in the right seat. Thanks, Ruth, for keeping us on course.

1
Flying floats

THE RAIN-STREAKED SIGN on the side of the dilapidated floating hangar read, "Kurtzer Flying Service: Seaplane Charters since 1928," so I went in and asked about lessons. A white-haired gentlemen whom I took to be Mr. Kurtzer stood behind the counter scribbling notations on an old rotating calendar. The drumlike device squealed shrilly as he turned it, so thinking that it might have drowned out my request, I loudly repeated my desire to take floatplane lessons. The squealing stopped abruptly.

"Why?" asked Mr. Kurtzer.

I hadn't expected this. "Why?"

"Why do you want a sea rating?"

I didn't know what to tell him. I'd seen my first floatplane a few years before while vacationing in Alaska. It had rumbled slowly over our campsite, its triple silhouette of floats and fuselage dark against the evening overcast. It was the end of my first day in Alaska, the realization of a dream that had been a long time in the dreaming. As I watched the plane drone off toward the silver horizon, I was overcome by the mood of the north: the overpowering sense of space and solitude, anticipation, and wonder.

That first trip to Alaska was filled with images, but the only one that didn't fade with time was that of a solitary floatplane winging its lonely way across a vast, gray bowl of northern sky. Back home in Hawaii, while my friends admired the latest retractable offerings from Piper, Beech, and Cessna, I would walk through the weeds that rimmed the south side of Honolulu International Airport to the cracked concrete ramp that was home to a pair of old Army Beavers. There they sat, leaking oil and baking in the tropical sun, far from the bush country that had inspired their design. By squinting just so, I could add a set of floats and turn the remorseless sky overhead to a cool silver-gray. I could almost relive that moment in the campground when I saw that first floatplane.

I don't know when I made the decision to move to the northwest. It might have been as I watched that floatplane grow smaller against the brooding Alaskan overcast. It might have been later, on the deck of the *Queen of Prince Rupert* as we slid through the emerald and granite canyons of the Inside Passage on our way south to Seattle. But the decision was made, and so I stood in the cluttered office of Kurtzer's Flying Service and tried to think of a convincing reason why I wanted to get a seaplane rating.

For an instant, I considered telling Mr. Kurtzer about the plane that flew over the campground, and about the Beavers baking on the ramp in Honolulu. I considered telling him that the floatplane had come to stand for everything I loved about the northwest, but I didn't think a pilot who had started his flying career 20 years before I was born would be impressed by such romantic foolishness. So I muttered something about wanting the rating because I thought it might help me get work up north. I didn't tell him I already had a job as a film producer for The Boeing Company.

Mr. Kurtzer stared at me a moment longer and then licked the tip of his pencil as the calendar resumed its infernal squealing. "When do you want to start?"

Lana Kurtzer is gone now, but my mind still goes back to the question he barked at me over the top of his antique calendar so many years ago. *Why fly floats?* Romance is certainly part of it, but there's more to it than that. There's the challenge— the challenge of learning to do something new, and the unending challenge of trying to master something that never stays the same. Every takeoff, every flight, and every landing is different. The fact that you flew the identical route yesterday is immaterial. Today the wind will be different, the water will be different, the number of planes at the dock will be different. A floatplane pilot never stops learning.

Floatplanes offer a unique view of the world, a view you just can't get up at 10,000 or 20,000 feet, surrounded by squawking radios and blinking readouts. Microwave landing systems, satellite navigation, collision avoidance systems, category-something-or-other approaches: Aviation grows more complex and intimidating each year. Floatplanes aren't totally immune from high technology—the Beaver I fly now sports an encoding altimeter, dual VHF radios, and a loran in place of the single, scratchy com radio it had for years—but the high-tech gear tends to take a backseat to the view out the window. Floatplane pilots seem to see things a little differently. They talk about the pod of killer whales they saw on their most recent flights, or about the fabulous fishing they had at a lake with a name they've conveniently forgotten (Fig. 1-1).

Fig. 1-1. *Fishing access to remote lakes is just one of the activities a floatplane makes possible. Beaver pilot Tom Eldridge is fighting a nice cutthroat trout on a lake in Alaska's Misty Fiords National Monument.*

A few years ago my wife and I took a de Havilland Beaver to Bakewell Lake in southeast Alaska. The morning we were to leave, we found huge, dog-like footprints all around the floats of our plane. We'd been visited by a wolf, and his tracks made it obvious that he'd climbed up onto the floats and had a look around. We never heard or saw him, but now, years later, when I sit in meetings struggling with the global politics and complexities of the aerospace industry, the knowledge that we shared a lake with a wolf helps me keep the world in perspective.

I've always been sorry I didn't tell Lana Kurtzer the real reason I wanted to get my sea rating. I think he would have understood. For over 50 years, he pushed seaplanes up and down the foggy raincoast of Washington and British Columbia. It can be a miserable job; he must have loved it dearly.

A UNIQUE EXPERIENCE

What makes flying a floatplane such a unique and rewarding experience? Certainly part of the answer lies in the opportunity to observe nature's never-ending panorama from a ringside seat (Fig. 1-2).

Fig. 1-2. *Hole-in-the-Wall Passage, near Desolation Sound, British Columbia.*

Thin, curving lines of low-water sand stretch ahead of you along the shores of a deep, narrow fjord, faced on one side by steep, sandy bluffs topped by dense stands of spruce and fir. The opposite shore rushes up out of the blue-green water to meet the near-vertical slopes of a glacier-draped mountain range. The shoreline below the mountains is broken by countless streams and rivers whose headwaters lie in the snowfields and blue glacial ice 8,000 feet above. The sandbars are dotted with the black, white, and gray shapes of ravens, gulls, and herons.

A sudden swirl of water a few yards offshore marks the presence of a harbor seal, and as the bubbles subside, you can see the seal's sleek form twisting gracefully beneath the surface in pursuit of a salmon. The seal had better keep a wary eye turned toward the deeper water of the sound, however, for Orca, the killer whale and the seal's mortal enemy, is a frequent visitor. In fact, a mile or so up ahead, a feathery plume of spray and a six-foot dorsal fin announce Orca's arrival. As you pass overhead, the powerful animal does a half-roll onto its side to keep an eye on you, revealing the telltale white markings on its streamlined black body. You hope the seal has seen the fin, too.

Another few miles up the sound, you come to a large sawmill, with the little town that grew up around it neatly arranged on a hill overlooking the water. Even at 500 feet, the heady aroma of fresh-cut cedar is strong. Along one side of the inlet near the mill are rafts of logs that have been towed down from the log dumps up north. The rafts are dotted with the gray shapes of seals that have hauled out to sun themselves on the warm logs. Although they're safe from Orca, the seals keep a sleepy eye on the little round boom boat that's noisily butting logs into position to be pulled up the jackslip into the saws.

A few miles more, and another fjord comes in from the east. The resulting tide rips are popular with sport fishermen, and as you sweep past the motley collection of boats jockeying for position around the point, several of the fishermen look up from their tangle of lines and wave. One even holds up a good-sized fish. At least somebody's catching something besides his neighbor's tackle.

Ahead, the sound takes on a pewter cast in the low afternoon light, and the silver sheet of water is dotted with the dark silhouettes of islands, the first of an unbroken chain stretching north for hundreds of miles (Fig. 1-3). Your destination lies somewhere among those islands. It could be a re-

Fig. 1-3. *Approaching Roche Harbor in Washington's San Juan Islands.*

mote beach sheltered in a secluded bay, or perhaps a fishing resort nestled between the green mountain walls. Maybe you're headed for one of the coastal towns that promise adventure even in the sound of their names: Bella Coolla, Ketchikan, Sitka, Wrangell, Skagway, Yakutat. The country that the floatplane calls home is invariably beautiful because it is invariably remote. Whether you're flying in the mystical myriad of islands and fjords of southeast Alaska, the rugged interior of British Columbia, the vast distances of the Canadian arctic, or the brooding expanse of forest and lakes that stretches from Minnesota to Hudson's Bay, beauty and isolation go hand in hand.

And therein lies the challenge of flying floats: You're on your own. Even if you're landing in the crowded harbor at Vancouver, British Columbia, or on the East River in New York City, you're on your own. There are no marked runways, no glideslopes, no localizers, no radars, and probably no wind socks. I know of only two seaplane bases in North America that have formal control towers. A few others have unicom frequencies, but most of the time your radio will be silent.

Contrary to what you might think, however, one of the greatest satisfactions of flying floats is the fact that you *are* on your own. Seaplanes offer one of the last chances for a pilot to be truly independent. *You* determine the wind direction, *you* determine the safety of your landing site, *you* designate your runway, *you* plan your approach, and *you* figure out how to get your floatplane to the dock. And after your plane is safely tied to that dock, you can take pride in what you've accomplished because you've done it by yourself.

Federal Aviation Regulation (FAR) 91.3 states that "The pilot in command of an aircraft is directly responsible for, and is the final authority as to, the operation of that aircraft." I've talked to student pilots who believed the final authority governing the operation of their aircraft lay not with themselves, but with air traffic control. The students were wrong, of course, but considering the ever-increasing amount of airspace regulation

and control facing pilots today, I could understand why they felt their flying was being controlled from the ground.

However, there are a few areas where FAR 91.3 is still considered aviation's First Commandment. It's the primary insurance policy for the pilots of crop dusters, water bombers, aerobatic and experimental aircraft, bushplanes, and seaplanes. No other type of flying offers pilots the same chance to so completely control their own fate. To this opportunity to be one's own master in the air, the seaplane adds the beauty of its environment. It's an unbeatable combination.

THE WORLD OF SEAPLANES

So why isn't everyone out flying seaplanes, if they're so great? Before answering that question, I think we should run through some definitions. You might have noticed that all of a sudden I've started using the term seaplanes instead of floatplanes. While this book is about floatplanes, I don't want to suggest to any readers who might be flying-boat pilots that they don't experience the same independence, freedom, and beauty enjoyed by those of us who fly floatplanes. They do, for these privileges are enjoyed by all water fliers.

The terms seaplane, floatplane, flying boat, and amphibian all refer to airplanes that can operate on the water, and it's important that you understand the exact meaning of each to avoid confusion. A *seaplane* is any airplane that can land on, and take off from, the water. Floatplanes, flying boats, and amphibians are all seaplanes. Seaplanes can be either single-engine or multiengine, and the engines can be reciprocating, turboprop, turbojet, fanjet, or some future powerplant as yet undiscovered. The ratings added to a pilot's private, commercial or ATP certificate are for this class of aircraft (i.e., "single-engine sea" and "multi-engine sea").

A *floatplane* is a seaplane that is supported on the water by one or more separate floats, or *pontoons* (Fig. 1-4). A *flying boat* is a seaplane whose

Fig. 1-4. *The two-place tandem-seat Piper Super Cub is popular both as a trainer and as a bushplane. Equipped with a 150-horsepower engine, the Super Cub can lift heavy loads out of small lakes.*

fuselage is also the "hull" that supports the airplane on the water. Unlike conventional airplanes, the bottom of a flying boat's fuselage is designed for maximum efficiency in the water, having a V-shaped keel, one or more planing "steps," spray rails, and so forth. Most flying boats also have small, pylon-mounted wingtip floats to keep the plane on an even keel when it's on the water (Fig. 1-5).

Fig. 1-5. *This Grumman Widgeon is a typical boat that also happens to be an amphibian. Many Widgeons have been updated with modern, horizontally opposed engines, but this one still has its original in-line Rangers.*

An *amphibian* is any seaplane that can operate from both land and water. Amphibians can be flying boats or floatplanes. Amphibious flying boats have landing gear that retracts into the fuselage or wings, while the landing gear of an amphibious floatplane retracts into the floats (Fig. 1-6).

Fig. 1-6. *A huge floatplane to begin with, the de Havilland Otter becomes even bigger when fitted with amphibious floats.*

So, back to my question: Why isn't everyone out flying seaplanes? As we will see in the next chapter, the seaplane was a popular design during the early years of aviation because while runways and airports were scarce, protected bodies of water were not. These "seadromes," as they came to be called, were plentiful and free. Many of today's commercial transport designers consider landing gear the most critical element in the overall design of an airplane. Since seaplanes are supported by water, not wheels, they were not limited in size by the primitive landing gear technology of those early years. In fact, the problem was not supporting the big flying boats that were built in the 1920s and 1930s, but getting the monsters to fly. The Dornier Do-X, built in 1929, needed no fewer than 12 engines to get off the water (Fig. 1-7).

Even as late as the 1940s and 1950s, landing gear and runway technology was not capable of supporting such floating giants as the Hughes H-4 Hercules (wingspan: 320 feet), the Martin JRM Mars (200 feet), or the Saunders Roe SR-45 Princess (219 feet). By contrast, the Boeing 747 has a wingspan of "only" 195 feet, 8 inches.

Unfortunately, seaplanes—particularly flying boats—have several built-in disadvantages. Compared to landplanes, they are very expensive to build. The fuselage of a landplane can be relatively lightweight and simple in design since its

Fig. 1-7. *The Dornier DO-X, built in 1929, needed no less than 12 500-horsepower Siemens Jupiter engines to get off the water. During flight, mechanics could crawl out to the engine pylons through tunnels in the massive wing and service the accessory groups at the rear of each engine.* Smithsonian Institution

main function is to provide aerodynamic streamlining to the passengers, cargo, and pilots carried inside. The fuselage of a flying boat, on the other hand, must be strong enough to withstand the terrific pounding it will receive as it slams through the water during takeoffs and landings. The complex shape of the hull, with its watertight bulkheads and compartments, is costly to design and construct.

Two other factors that contributed to the demise of the large commercial seaplane were its inefficient aerodynamic shape and its high maintenance costs. Advances in landing gear technology allowed landplanes to grow in size, and retracting the gear made for higher speeds and longer ranges. World War II spurred the development of long-range land-based bombers, and it was only natural that some of these designs evolved into passenger airplanes. The world's first four-engined pressurized airliner, the Boeing Model 307 Stratoliner, was derived from the Boeing Model 299, also known as the B-17 Flying Fortress. After the war, the Boeing B-29 Superfortress acquired a double-deck fuselage and became the Model 377 Stratocruiser. The era of the big commercial seaplane was over.

There might be a future for medium-to-large seaplanes in island countries such as Japan, where there is precious little land to spare for airports, but for the most part, the seaplane has been pushed back by the advance of asphalt and concrete, until today its environment is limited to those places where landplanes dare not tread.

So to answer my question, the reason for the seaplane's limited popularity today is due to its relatively remote environment and specialized design. Seaplanes are not for everyone.

However, in those parts of the world where airports and roads are scarce, but lakes, rivers, and bays are plentiful, the words "survival" and "seaplane" are often synonymous. In addition to carrying food, mail, medicine, machinery, and everything else that's needed in a remote community, seaplanes are often required to assist in the preservation of life itself through mercy flights. Seaplanes are used for mineral exploration, fish spotting, law enforcement, game management, forest fire protection, and the multitude of interesting—and occasionally odd—tasks that fall under the general heading of "charter flying."

Seaplanes play an important recreational role, too. Each year, the best fishing, camping, and hunting spots seem to be a little farther away, and often a seaplane is the only way to reach them (Fig. 1-8). Many fishing and hunting resorts now have their own seaplanes, and most of them provide docking facilities for city-dwelling guests who like to use their own airplanes to get away from it all for a few days.

The most popular and economical type of seaplane today is the floatplane. Modern floatplanes are production landplanes that have been modified to accept a pair of floats in place of the landing gear. This system has several advantages. The floats can be removed and the wheels reinstalled if the owner wants to use the airplane on land for awhile. Many northern operators use the same planes year-round by installing floats during the summer and changing to wheels or skis for the winter.

Fig. 1-8. *A nice catch of silver salmon taken near Big Bay Resort, on Stewart Island, British Columbia. The only access to the island is by boat or seaplane.*

Most floatplanes are high-wing airplanes and, unlike flying boats, do not require wingtip floats. This makes a floatplane easier to dock, since its high wing will clear many obstacles that would catch the wingtip floats of a flying boat. High-wing floatplanes are generally easier to load and unload, too, thanks to their large side doors, which extend down to the floor of the cabin. Heavy cargo can be slid directly into or out of the plane. The doors of flying boats are often too small for bulky cargo, and as a rule are mounted fairly high because the cabin floor is usually below the waterline.

Floatplanes come in all sizes and shapes, from tiny ultralights to the massive single-engine de Havilland Otter. Some floatplanes have two engines, such as the Beechcraft Model 18 "Twin Beech" (Fig. 1-9) and the de Havilland Twin Otter.

Turbine-powered floatplanes are becoming popular, especially in noise-sensitive areas and in underdeveloped countries where there is usually a plentiful supply of cheap kerosene (Fig. 1-10). For pilots who love that turbine whine, there is a growing range of airplanes, from the original de Havilland Turbo Beaver (Fig. 1-11) to the meteorlike Turbine Maule.

Fig. 1-9. *A Beechcraft Model 18 "Twin Beech" on EDO floats.* EDO Corp.

Fig. 1-10. *The turboprop de Havilland Twin Otter is the largest floatplane in use today. This one, operated by Air B.C., is taxiing in after landing in Vancouver Harbor, British Columbia.*

Fig. 1-11. *The original de Havilland Turbo-Beaver was powered by a 550-shaft-horsepower turbine Beaver. This one, modified by Kenmore Air Harbor, is powered by a 750-shp Pratt & Whitney PT6A-135 turbine. Its sea-level rate of climb is 1,800 feet per minute.*

Before we tackle the techniques of flying a floatplane, however, let's take a brief look at its colorful history. It's the story of two men who were determined that flight from the water was possible. It's the story of a floatplane that launched a company that today is the world's leading manufacturer of jetliners. It's the story of a little racing floatplane, and how it was largely responsible for an entire country's survival in a world war. It's a story of discovery, exploration, and adventure.

It's a story that deserves more than just one chapter in one book. In fact, it would take several books to properly document the floatplane's place in history, but for now, we'll examine some of the headlines in the chronicle of events that has resulted in this wonderful machine—a machine that carries us to the challenging, rewarding, and beautiful world of wings, water, and floats.

2
The historical floatplane

THE SEED of the family floatplane tree was planted in 1906, when Henri Fabre, the son of a French shipowner, started work on what he hoped would be the world's first successful seaplane. Four years later, the seed pushed up an ungainly little sawhorse of an airplane called the Hydravion (seaplane).

It was a high-wing monoplane with a rear-mounted engine and a pusher propeller. The "fuselage" of the Hydravion consisted of two long beams running fore and aft, one about five feet above the other. The wing was mounted on the aft end of the upper beam, just ahead of the engine. The pilot sat in front of the wing, and the horizontal stabilizer was in front of him, giving the skeletal machine a canard configuration (Fig. 2-1).

The elevator was a separate horizontal surface that sat several feet above the stabilizer. Twin vertical rudders were mounted on the elevator and moved with it. The pilot, who sat astride the upper beam in a sort of wicker tractor seat, gripped two tiller bars that ran forward to control the elevator-rudder assembly.

The pilot's feet dangled down into a pair of pedals that were attached to the wing-warping mechanism. Like the Wright brothers before him,

Fig. 2-1. *Henri Fabre's Hydravion in its original configuration with the rudders mounted up forward.*
Genevieve Fabre

Fabre achieved roll control by wing warping; there were no ailerons.

The wing itself had a unique design. The single main spar also served as the leading edge and consisted of a massive wooden truss that extended the entire length of the wing. The spar sat, fencelike, on top of the wing. Nobody seems to understand why this arrangement didn't act like a full-span spoiler and kill the wing's lift completely. One possible answer is that Fabre's wing developed most of its lift on the underside, like a kite. Gracefully curved ribs extended aft from the spar, and the wing itself was constructed of light canvas, which could be detached from the ribs and furled against the spar, like a sail.

After experimenting with long, catamaran-style floats, Fabre decided to use short, wide, flat-bottom floats instead. Its three floats had curved upper surfaces to produce additional lift once the plane was airborne.

One float was mounted up forward on the lower end of the same vertical strut that carried the stabilizer and elevator. The other two floats were mounted on storklike legs extending down from the main wing spar. The float arrangement was not unlike today's tricycle landing gear, complete with a steerable forward float that provided some degree of directional control of the water.

Fabre's previous seaplane design, built in 1909, used three 12-horsepower Anzani engines linked together to drive a single propeller. This arrangement did not develop enough power to get the craft off the water, so Fabre went in search of a more powerful engine for the Hydravion. He settled on the Gnome seven-cylinder rotary engine, which produced 50 horsepower at 1,100 rpm and swung an 8½-foot propeller. One advantage of the rear-engine configuration became apparent the first time the Gnome was started up. Like all early aircraft engines, the little rotary threw oil all over the place, but Fabre was safely out of the line of fire in his wicker chair up forward.

On March 28, 1910, Fabre conducted some high-speed taxi tests of his floatplane off the town of La Mede, France, near Marseilles. The Hydravion handled well, and Fabre, who had never flown an aircraft of any kind before, decided to attempt his first flight that afternoon. He later described the experience:

"I started at a great speed. For a long time I continued this fast hydroplaning without opening entirely the throttle and, thus, risking a takeoff. My machine had been built to be stabilized automatically. The weather was so calm, I knew I should be able to fly it without moving the controls.

"With my hand on the throttle, I let the airplane increase speed. One of the rear floats started to lift up; I slowed down and was able to equalize the wings by neutralizing the throttle. I accelerated again; this time, both rear floats lifted at the same moment. The hydroplane was balancing on the front float, which, in turn, began to rise above the water. I was airborne, totally stable, gliding over this glassy water, or buzzing a few meters above the surface. The feeling was the same.

"Pulling on the throttle, I soon saw the front float touching gently the surface of the water, leaving a thin trail like a diamond on glass. Again, I took off. My flights lasted longer and longer. I was making wide turns. Never a sudden move, never a hard landing. I had the greatest confidence in my hydroplane.

"When I returned, the spectators thought I had a great machine whose moves were so smooth that they shouldn't cause any anxiety."

And so the world of water flying was born. The following day, Fabre flew the Hydravion from La Mede to Martigues, a distance of about four miles, thus completing the world's first cross-country seaplane flight.

Fabre continued to make improvements to his machine. He moved the rudders aft, and also added little water rudders to the rear floats for better directional control on the surface (Fig. 2-2).

Fig. 2-2. *Fabre's Hydravion in flight, after the rudders were moved aft. Note the small water rudders attached to the rear of the main floats.* Genevieve Fabre

On May 18, 1910, Henri Fabre, the world's first pilot of the world's first seaplane, became the world's first victim of the phenomenon that has probably caused more seaplane accidents than any other: glassy water. While demonstrating the Hydravion to a prospective financial backer, Fabre misjudged his height above the water, and landed too fast and too hard. The machine broke apart, throwing Fabre into the water. The fact that he was not hurt led him to the immediate conclusion that seaplanes were safer than landplanes. As we will learn in a later chapter, he was right.

The Hydravion was repaired and exhibited later that year at the second Salon de l'Aeronautique in Paris. Among the visitors to the exhibition was the American aviation pioneer Glenn H. Curtiss, who met with Fabre and discussed his experiences with the little seaplane. Curtiss had been experimenting with the concept of taking off and landing on water since 1909, but so far he had been unsuccessful.

In March 1911, Fabre hired pilot Jean Becue to demonstrate the Hydravion during a motorboat exhibition at Monaco. The first flight was successful, but after the second, the spindly floatplane got caught in the surf and was destroyed. Becue was unhurt, and the remains of the airplane were pulled from the water. Years later the airplane was rebuilt, and today Henri Fabre's Hydravion hangs in the Musse de L'Air in Chalais-Meudon, near Paris.

Fabre himself, having accomplished what he set out to do, did not build any more seaplanes, although he constructed floats for other seaplane manufacturers. He died on June 29, 1984, at the age of 101.

THE PRACTICAL FLOATPLANE

Meanwhile, on the other side of the Atlantic, Glenn Curtiss was still trying to get an airplane off the water. His biggest problem seemed to be one of float design. Curtiss' approach was to take an airplane that had successfully flown as a landplane and mount it on floats. His first attempt was made with the Aerial Experiment Association's Loon in 1908.

The Loon never had a chance. The engine only produced about 30 horsepower, and the bottoms of the long, twin floats were completely flat. While the Loon did manage to plane across the surface of Lake Keuka at Hammondsport, New York, the engine simply did not have the power to overcome the suction of the water on the flat float bottoms, and the airplane refused to become airborne.

In his next attempt, Curtiss decided to stick with proven designs. He mounted a standard Curtiss Model D on a canoe. This didn't work either, but it convinced Curtiss that a single-float design handled better on the water than the twin-float, or catamaran, design.

Finally, in 1911, Curtiss got it right. Again using a Model D, he replaced the main wheels of the tricycle-geared airplane with a single large float similar in design to one of Fabre's floats. The nosewheel of the Model D was replaced with a small scowlike float, and a hydrofoil was mounted in front of *that* to keep the forward float from digging in when power was applied. Curtiss successfully flew his float-equipped Model D from San Diego Bay on January 26, 1911 (Fig. 2-3).

Fig. 2-3. *Glenn Curtiss's first practical floatplane, the Model D.* Smithsonian Institution

He then replaced the rather complicated tandem float arrangement with a single long, narrow float. Three weeks after his first successful seaplane flight, Curtiss flew his plane across the bay to the *U.S.S. Pennsylvania*. After landing next to the cruiser, the Model D was hoisted aboard by one of the ship's cranes. An hour later, it was lowered back into the water for the return flight to North Island.

The Navy was intrigued, and in July 1911, it commissioned the airplane under the designation Curtiss Hydroaeroplane, Navy A-1. It was the first of the Navy's long line of shipboard scout planes.

Glenn Curtiss was responsible for at least two more innovations that have become standard design features of all the seaplanes flying today. In May 1911, Curtiss was flying a single-float Model D from Lake Keuka when the float sprung a leak. The weight of the water that entered the float did not prevent him from taking off, but when he pitched the plane down to begin his landing descent, the water rushed to the front of the float, causing the airplane to nose-dive into the lake. Curtiss was not seriously injured, but the airplane was destroyed.

From then on, all his floats contained bulkheads that divided the float into several watertight compartments. Not only did this prevent any water that might be present from running freely from one end of the float to the other, the results of which Curtiss had just experienced, but the watertight compartments would ensure that the floatplane would not sink if the float sprung a leak or was damaged while on the water. This design practice was later applied to flying boat hulls as well.

Curtiss is generally given credit for another important innovation in seaplane design. In the summer of 1911, he was testing his first true flying boat. The machine failed to get off the water for the same reason that his first floatplanes refused to fly: Its long, flat bottom could not be pulled free of the water's suction. Curtiss came up with the idea of wedging, or stepping, the bottom at the airplane's center of gravity, so the seaplane could be rocked back and forth to break the suction.

This is usually considered to be the first appearance of the step-hydroplane bottom that has been used on every floatplane, flying boat, and high-performance speedboat since. Henri Fabre, however, in his book about his aviation experiences, makes reference to a racing boat named *Ricochet*, which was designed by a Monsieur Bonnemaison in 1905. The *Ricochet* had a step-hydroplane bottom, so perhaps Curtiss' real contribution was the first use of a hydrodynamic step on a seaplane.

Although the floats used by Curtiss and his contemporaries incorporated the hydrodynamic step, the bottom sections were still flat in cross section. This flat bottom allowed the floats to quickly assume a planing attitude after takeoff power was applied, but in anything other than absolutely calm water, the airplane was subjected to a terrific pounding. Rather than cut through the waves, the flat-bottom floats simply slammed into them, throwing spray in all directions and drenching the pilot, to say nothing of putting a tremendous strain on the airframe.

In an effort to solve these problems, float designers developed the wave-cutting, spray-deflecting, V-shaped bottom that is used on almost every float manufactured today.

THE FLOATPLANE THAT LAUNCHED A JETLINER

From Glenn Curtiss and sunny San Diego, we move up the coast to the rain-swept forests of the Pacific Northwest and a wealthy timber baron who thought it would be fun to build an airplane. His name was William E. Boeing.

Born to a family who had acquired vast holdings of timber and iron ore in Minnesota's rich Mesabi Range, William Boeing decided to strike out on his own when he was 22. The Pacific Northwest, with its apparently endless forests of spruce, hemlock, cedar, and fir, seemed to be a promising destination for a young man who was looking to make his fortune in the lumber business, and Boeing eventually settled in Seattle, Washington.

In January 1910, the first international aeronautical tournament held in the United States took place near Los Angeles. There were balloons and dirigibles, and airplanes built by Bleriot, Farman, and Curtiss. The airplanes competed in endurance and cross-country events before a crowd of 25,000 spectators. One of the 25,000 was 29-year-old William Boeing.

He was fascinated by the airplanes and tried to get a ride with the pilot of a Farman biplane. Although the pilot agreed, either an upcoming event or a local dignitary who wanted a ride always seemed to take priority over Boeing's request. He returned each day of the tournament and waited patiently for his turn to fly, but it never came.

At the end of the air meet, the Farman was disassembled, crated, and shipped away. Boeing returned to Seattle disappointed, but intrigued with the idea of air travel.

A few years later, Boeing met Conrad Westervelt, a naval officer and engineer who was assigned to the Moran Shipyard in Seattle. Back in 1910, nine months after Boeing had attended the air show in Los Angeles, Westervelt had represented the Navy at a similar tournament held at Belmont Park, New York. Like Boeing before him, Westervelt came away with a tremendous enthusiasm for the airplane, and he recommended in his report that the Navy pay close attention to the rapid advancements taking place in the field of aviation.

Westervelt and Boeing, who had studied engineering at Yale before moving west, shared a common interest in anything mechanical, and they soon became good friends. When a pilot named Terah Maroney arrived in Seattle with a Curtiss seaplane and began selling rides, it was only natural that Boeing and Westervelt were among his first customers. On the Fourth of July 1914, Boeing finally got his first airplane ride.

One day, after another ride in Maroney's Curtiss, Boeing remarked to Westervelt that they could probably build a better airplane than the flimsy pusher Maroney was flying. Westervelt, ever the engineer, obtained all the information he could about airplanes—their stability and control, the types of stresses to which they were subjected, what kinds of motors were available, and so forth. He did some strength calculations using his naval engineering tables and the dimensions of the structural members in Maroney's plane and reached the startling conclusion that the strength of the parts in the Curtiss was just about equal to

the load they supported in flight. There was no margin of safety. Westervelt couldn't understand why Maroney's airplane hadn't fallen apart a long time ago.

Boeing became intrigued with the idea of building a sport airplane he could use himself. He also felt that the war raging in Europe would eventually envelop the United States, and he was concerned that the United States was falling behind in the field of aviation.

In 1915, Boeing and Westervelt organized a small group of craftsmen and set about building two airplanes, which would be given the name "B & W" for Boeing and Westervelt (Fig. 2-4). Before construction began, however, Boeing went to Los Angeles to learn to fly. When he returned, he brought with him a Martin seaplane, which the group used to determine some of the dimensions for their own airplanes.

Fig. 2-4. *This little biplane is the direct ancestor of the Boeing 747. Called the "B & W," the wood and fabric floatplane was the first airplane built by William E. Boeing.* The Boeing Co.

Each B & W would be a floatplane, partly because the Martin seaplane that Boeing brought home was a floatplane, and also because there weren't any airfields in the mudflats that lay at the base of Seattle's steep hills. There were plenty of lakes, however, and the protected bays and coves of Puget Sound offered countless landing sites.

The airplanes' components would be constructed at Boeing's shipyard, located in the maze of sloughs and tideflats south of the city. Upon completion, the components would be taken to a boathouse on Seattle's Lake Union and assembled.

Ed Heath, who ran the boatyard, was put in charge of building the twin floats for each airplane. They were beautifully crafted out of thin wood, and at one point, after being cautioned by Boeing for the hundredth time to keep the floats light, Heath reported that they were already so light he was afraid to open the door for fear that the floats would blow out.

Unlike the scowlike floats used by Glenn Curtiss on his early airplanes, Boeing's floats were similar in appearance to the floats used today. They utilized a step-hydroplane bottom, which had a shallow V-shape. The tops of the floats were gently curved to reduce drag. There were no water rudders, so the only directional control was from the airflow over the vertical rudder.

An interesting feature of the B & W was the small tail float that occupied the same position as the tail skid used on land planes. Although this float did not help support the airplane while it was on the water, it might have been installed to keep the tail surfaces from striking the water during takeoff and landing. The tail float was not used on later Boeing floatplanes.

The B & W was a two-place airplane, with a wingspan of 52 feet and a length of 27 feet, 6 inches. The plane had a gross weight of 2,800 pounds and was powered by a water-cooled, 125-horsepower Hall-Scott engine, which gave it a top speed of 75 miles per hour and a cruising speed of 67 miles per hour. (During the years covered by this chapter, speed was generally measured in miles per hour. I have elected to continue this tradition for historical purposes. Airspeeds described throughout the rest of the book are in knots.)

Conrad Westervelt was transferred back to an assignment on the East Coast before the first B & W was ready to fly, so on a June day in 1916, Boeing worked to get the airplane ready for its first flight. The pilot, Herb Munter, was late, so Boeing finally took the airplane out himself. After a taxi test, he lifted the B & W off the water for a short, straight flight before returning to the boathouse. For the next several days, Munter performed more taxi tests until making the B & W's first real flight from Lake Union to Lake Washington.

With his first airplane flying successfully, Boeing became convinced that, someday, the airplane would become an accepted means of transportation. He decided the future was bright for a commercial airplane company, so on July 15, 1916, he incorporated the Pacific Aero Products Company. The company's first order was from the Navy, for 50 Model C seaplanes. The Model C was a much-refined version of the B & W, and was used by the Navy as a trainer. The two B & Ws were sold to the New Zealand government, where they were used for many years as trainers.

On April 26, 1917, Pacific Aero Products became the Boeing Airplane Company. I wonder if even William Boeing himself could have conceived of what was to follow.

WOODEN FLOATS

When Boeing decided to build his own airplanes, he set about putting together a team of the best local craftsmen he could find. Seattle had become the busiest port city on Puget Sound, so it was only natural that he look to the shipyards for the experienced men he needed.

One of the greatest challenges facing the designers and builders of the first floatplanes was to reduce the weight and bulk of the floats themselves. Boeing decided to find someone who could design a lighter, stronger float than the ones he'd used on the B & W.

His search took him to the University of Washington, where he was introduced to George Pocock. George, together with his brother, Dick, were building lightweight racing shells for the university's rowing team, and as Boeing inspected the beautifully crafted, eight-oared shells in Pocock's shop, he decided that this was how he wanted his floats made.

The Pocock brothers did not immediately accept Boeing's offer of employment. A short time later, however, the university ran out of funds to keep the Pococks busy building racing shells, so they decided to go to work for the newly formed Pacific Aero Products Company.

Their first assignment was to design and build a lighter, stronger float. After outlining the general specifications for the new float, Boeing's chief engineer asked George Pocock for a rough weight estimate.

"One hundred and fifteen pounds," was the immediate reply. The chief engineer was skeptical, and said he would buy Pocock a new hat if the float came in under 125 pounds. The two brothers went to work, and when the first float was finished, it weighed in at a fraction over 114 pounds. Presumably, George got his new hat.

The Model C was the first airplane to use the new float, and after the first two planes passed inspection at Pensacola, the Navy ordered 50 more. The Pocock floats were made entirely of wood and were built around a longitudinal keel. There were four watertight compartments (Fig. 2-5). Lightweight bulkheads and stringers supported the thin outer planking, which was applied diagonally for extra strength. Also, like the racing shells that came before them, Pocock's floats were beautifully streamlined (Fig. 2-6).

Despite the improvements, however, wooden floats still had several drawbacks. For one thing, their elaborate construction made them expensive to manufacture (Fig. 2-7). In addition, the thin wooden skin, while strong enough for normal operations, was easily damaged upon hard contact with a dock or ramp.

Fig. 2-6. *Side view of a Boeing float, showing off its beautiful lines.* The Boeing Co.

Fig. 2-7. *The interior of the Boeing float shop in 1918. Note the complex forming jig in the foreground.* The Boeing Co.

After World War I, the increasing use of floatplanes for both military and civilian purposes created a demand for floats that were stronger, lighter, and cheaper. In 1925, a World War I veteran named Earl Dodge Osborn set out to design just such a float.

EDO'S ALL-ALUMINUM FLOAT

Osborn was interested in seaplanes, and he began building and testing both airframes and floats. In 1925, he used his initials to name his new firm, which became the EDO Aircraft Corporation. Shortly afterwards, the company introduced the first practical aluminum float, and it became an immediate success.

The advantages of building in aluminum were many. It made for a lighter and less cumbersome float, yet one that was stronger and more damage-resistant than the old wood floats. An aluminum float was easier to build and did not require a work

Fig. 2-5. *The underside of one of George Pocock's wooden floats, showing the central keel and watertight bulkheads.* The Boeing Co.

force of skilled cabinetmakers to assemble. Aluminum is easier to shape than wood, and EDO was able to develop a very efficient fluted bottom for its floats. The fluted bottom develops maximum hydrodynamic lift while giving a smooth ride over the surface and minimizing spray.

The best thing about EDO's new aluminum floats was that they could be fitted to many of the popular landplanes of the period. The company offered the floats in several sizes, and they were attached in place of a plane's landing gear by a relatively simple system of aluminum struts. All sorts of airplanes began showing up on floats, including the boxy Ford Tri-Motor, the Army's Martin B-12 bomber, and even Beechcraft's sleek new Model 17, which quickly acquired the nickname "Staggerwing Beech" (Figs. 2-8 through 2-10).

Aerial exploration became popular during the 1920s and 1930s, and many of the expeditions to the undeveloped areas of the world required the use of a seaplane. All you had to do to get one was to purchase a proven landplane design, fit it with a set of EDO floats, and you were ready to go.

In the early 1930s, Admiral Richard E. Byrd explored the shores of Antarctica in a Curtiss Condor, a large, twin-engined biplane that had been fitted with EDO floats. In 1931, Colonel Charles Lindbergh and his wife, Anne, explored Alaska and the Aleutian Islands on their way to Japan in a Lockheed Sirius, also mounted on EDO floats (Figs. 2-11 and 2-12). In 1935, the American polar explorer Lincoln Ellsworth and his Canadian pilot, Herbert Hollick-Kenyon, made a 2,300-mile

Fig. 2-9. *A Martin YB-12 bomber fitted with EDO Model 15750 floats for coastal defense.* EDO Corp.

Fig. 2-10. *EDO's aluminum floats could even be installed on the beautiful Beechcraft Model 17, or "Staggerwing Beech." This one is resting on a special dolly for moving the plane around on the ground.* EDO Corp.

Fig. 2-11. *Admiral Richard E. Byrd's Curtiss Condor near a supply ship during his Antarctic expedition. Powered by two Wright Cyclone supercharged engines developing 725 horsepower each, the plane was fitted with EDO Model 16800 floats.* EDO Corp.

Fig. 2-8. *A Ford Tri-Motor on EDO Model 14060 floats.* EDO Corp.

Fig. 2-12. *Charles and Anne Lindbergh pose for photographers in front of their Lockheed Sirius mounted on EDO Model 6235 floats.* EDO Corp.

flight across Antarctica in a Northrop Gamma they named the *Polar Star*. The big Northrop was fitted with EDO floats, which enabled the plane to land on the snow-covered surface of the continent when necessary (Fig. 2-13).

Fig. 2-13. *Lincoln Ellsworth's sleek Northrop Gamma, mounted on EDO Model 7080 floats.* EDO Corp.

Some aircraft manufacturers of the period saw a market in the export of airplanes that could be converted to military uses by overseas customers. Because arms control laws forbade the export of aircraft that were actually fitted with armament, the planes were sold as "reconnaissance" models, but they were designed to be easily converted to fighters and bombers by the customer. In order to appeal to as many countries as possible, some manufacturers offered their customers a choice of either conventional landing gear or EDO floats (Fig. 2-14).

Fig. 2-14. *A Bellanca Model 77-140 export bomber mounted on EDO Model 15750 floats. The plane was powered by two 715-horsepower Wright Cyclone radials. Note the gunner's position on the nose.* EDO Corp.

Osborn's aluminum float probably did more to spur the popularity of floatplanes than any other development, and for years the EDO enjoyed a monopoly in the manufacture of twin aluminum floats. EDO floats were available for the two-place Piper Cub, the 10-passenger Twin Beech, and just about everything else in between (Fig. 2-15). The largest floatplane in the world was created when EDO designed and built amphibious floats for the C-47, the military version of the famous Douglas DC-3. Each massive float had a displacement of 29,400 pounds, and the landing gear retracted into wheel wells complete with gear doors. The plane flew quite well, but the Army canceled the order after only two had been built (Fig. 2-16). One set of the massive floats survived, parked in the weeds beside an East Coast airport. In the early 1990s, the surviving floats were restored and mated with a DC-3 to make one of the most impressive air show exhibits ever.

Fig. 2-15. *The popular little Piper J-3 Cub mounted on a pair of EDO floats.* EDO Corp.

Fig. 2-16. *EDO designed and built special amphibious floats for the Douglas C-47 (DC-3) during World War II. Each float displaced a whopping 29,400 pounds to make this the largest floatplane in the world. Although the plane performed quite well, only 10 were built.* EDO Corp.

EDO has some competition today, but it remains the world's foremost supplier of aluminum floats. Its current line of "straight" (no wheels) and amphibious floats are certified for many of today's popular landplanes, from the two-place Cessna 150 to the big de Havilland DHC-2 Beaver (Fig. 2-17).

Fig. 2-17. *Quite a contrast to the float-equipped C-47, the Cessna 150 also can be fitted with EDO floats, the Model 1650. This popular two-place airplane performs well on floats, but does not have quite enough power to make it a satisfactory floatplane trainer.* EDO Corp.

THE FLOATPLANE THAT SAVED A NATION

Today's float-equipped de Havilland Beaver has a cruising speed of about 110 miles per hour, but

back in September 1931, there was a floatplane zipping around in excess of 400 miles per hour. Its pilot, Flight Lieutenant George Stainforth of the British Royal Air Force, became the first man in history to break the 400-mile-per-hour limit. The world's fastest airplane was a floatplane.

It is unlikely that Hermann Goering, World War I fighter ace and soon to be the head of German Chancellor Adolf Hitler's powerful Luftwaffe, had more than a passing interest in the record-shattering speed runs being made by the little silver- and-blue floatplane across the channel in England in 1931. He should have paid more attention, for the song thundering from the floatplane's exhaust stacks was destined to become the death knell for Germany's invincible air armada nine years later.

How could a single airplane—and a floatplane at that—affect the outcome of a World War? In December 1912, Jacques Schneider, heir to steel and munitions factories in France, announced he was offering a new international trophy race to promote the development of seaplanes. It would be a closed-course race, and any country winning the trophy three times within five consecutive contests would keep it, ending the competition forever. The trophy itself was a rather elaborate affair featuring a nude, winged woman flying over, and kissing, an ocean wave with the face of a man. It was officially called the *Coupe d'Aviation Maritime Jacques Schneider.* The English aviators who competed for it called it the "Flyin' Flirt," and the race itself became known simply as the Schneider Race.

One of the English entries in the 1925 Schneider Trophy race was the beautiful Supermarine S-4, designed by R.J. Mitchell. It represented quite an advancement over the other racing planes of its day, being a midwing monoplane with extremely clean lines (Fig. 2-18). In tests, it had broken every existing record, exceeding 226 miles per hour at only ¾ throttle. Unfortunately, it crashed during a trial run just before the race. The pilot escaped with only a broken wrist, but the plane was destroyed.

Fig. 2-18. *R.J. Mitchell's revolutionary Supermarine S-4, designed and built for the 1925 Schneider Trophy race.* Smithsonian Institution

The design of the S-4 set the stage for the next three planes from Mitchell's drawing board. The S-5 won the 1927 race, the S-6 took the 1929 contest, and in 1931, Supermarine rolled out the magnificent S-6B, which permanently retired the "Flyin' Flirt" to England (Fig. 2-19).

Fig. 2-19. *The Supermarine S-5, winner of the 1927 Schneider Trophy race. It was the last of designer Mitchell's racing planes to use the 12-cylinder "broad-arrow" Napier Lion engine.* Smithsonian Institution

All three airplanes were low-wing monoplanes, with a fuselage profile similar to the S-4. The S-4 had been constructed entirely of wood, with an aluminum engine cowling, while the S-5 combined wooden wings with an aluminum fuselage. The S-6 and S-6B were of all-aluminum construction.

Mitchell had used the 700-horsepower Napier Lion engine in the S-4, and a geared version developing 875 horsepower was used in the S-5. The Lion was unusual in that its 12 cylinders were arranged in three banks of four cylinders each. From the front, the engine looked like a broad arrowhead pointing down.

Although the S-5 had roared to victory in the 1927 race, it became obvious to Mitchell that he had gotten everything he could out of the Lion. The United States, France, and Italy were all determined to recapture the trophy, and in order to stay competitive, Mitchell knew he needed a bigger engine.

It was provided by Sir Henry Royce, who guaranteed that his company, Rolls-Royce, would deliver an engine developing 1,500 horsepower. While Mitchell set about designing an airplane around the promised engine, the Rolls-Royce engineers set about designing the engine itself. It was called the Rolls-Royce "R" engine at first, and its development was surrounded by the utmost secrecy. Ten years later, however, a derivative of the big V-12 would become a household word. It would be called *Merlin.* Sir Royce's engine delivered 1,900 horsepower at 2,900 rpm and weighed only 1,530 pounds.

On Saturday, September 7, 1929, to the cheers of more than a million spectators, Flight Officer Waghorn's S-6 blasted across the finish line to give England her second consecutive win. Waghorn's course speed was 328.63 miles per hour (Fig. 2-20).

After the 1929 race, the British Air Ministry decided not to underwrite the development and construction of any more Schneider Trophy airplanes, nor would RAF personnel be allowed to fly in the race. If it were not for the generosity of

Fig. 2-20. *This is the Supermarine S-6 that won the Schneider Trophy for England in 1929. It was the first use of the Rolls-Royce R engine, a big V-12 that led to the development of the Merlin engine used in the Supermarine Spitfire.* Smithsonian Institution

a remarkable woman, Goering's Luftwaffe would have had an easier time of it in the skies over England in 1940.

Lady Houston was indignant over the government's decision to abandon the race for glory, so she offered to put up 100,000 pounds to finance the British effort. The offer was accepted, and the government also rescinded its order banning RAF personnel from flying in the Schneider race. Mitchell went back to his drawing board, and the Rolls-Royce engineers went back to theirs. The result was the magnificent S-6B (Fig. 2-21).

Fig. 2-21. *The magnificent S-6B. The S-6B won the 1931 Schneider race and permanently retired the trophy to England. Note the oil cooler running the length of the fuselage and the massive fixed-pitch propeller.*
Smithsonian Institution

The S-6B was a refinement of the S-6 design. The plane was 28 feet, 10 inches long, and had a 30-foot wingspan. The engine cowl was closely fitted around the V-12's two long cylinder heads, and the fuselage itself was no wider than the engine block. The 24-foot aluminum floats were joined to the fuselage by a pair of streamlined A-frames, which carried the full-length engine supports.

The engine was a Rolls-Royce R-29. The original R engine had been boosted to an amazing 2,350 horsepower by increasing the engine speed, the size of the air intake, and the supercharger gear ratio. The R-29 delivered its maximum power at 3,200 rpm, and the engine was designed to hold together at this speed just long enough to win the race. It turned a huge, two-bladed fixed-pitch metal propeller.

One of the greatest challenges facing Mitchell was the problem of providing enough cooling to keep the engine running for the duration of the race. The wing skins were actually radiators, made by riveting together two thin sheets of aluminum separated by $\frac{1}{16}$-inch spacers. The radiator panels were fastened directly to the wing spars and ribs and formed the actual aerodynamic surfaces of the wings. Hot engine water was pumped to the wings for cooling and then returned to the engine.

This arrangement had worked quite well on the S-6, but wing radiators alone were not sufficient to dissipate the tremendous amount of heat generated by the R-29. Mitchell solved the problem by covering the entire upper halves of the floats with radiators as well. The floats did double duty by serving as the fuel tanks for the thirsty V-12. The starboard (right) float carried considerably more fuel than the port float in an attempt to balance out the tremendous torque developed by the engine.

The oil cooling system was ingenious. From the engine, the oil passed through cooling tubes faired into the sides of the fuselage and up to the top of the vertical tail. The hot oil was sprayed onto the tinned-steel inner skin of the tail, where it ran down to a collection tank and filter. It was then pumped back to the engine via more cooling tubes under the fuselage. After much experimentation, it was found that by placing small vanes in the cooler oilways, the hot oil could be kept in constant contact with the outer surfaces, thus increasing the efficiency of the cooling system by 40 percent. Even so, the pure castor oil used by the Rolls-Royce engine disappeared at the rate of 14 gallons per hour.

The most important instruments in the cockpit were the engine temperature gauges, for these determined how far the pilot could open the throttle. The races were flown with the engine at its maximum temperature, a factor that undoubtedly contributed to its short life.

Italy, France, and the United States all had built floatplanes to compete in the 1931 contest, but none of them were ready in time. At two minutes after 1 o'clock on Sunday, September 13th, a single Supermarine S-6B was launched from its barge on the Solent in England, and Flight Lieutenant John Boothman flew unopposed around the triangular course at an average speed of 340 miles per hour, winning the Schneider Trophy for England once and for all.

You have to have tremendous respect for the pilots of these fast, but relatively crude machines. I've had the privilege of experiencing first hand the narrow, cramped cockpit of Boothman's S-6B. With virtually no visibility forward between the massive rocker covers and pummeled by the V-12's blistering heat and shattering noise, the Schneider pilots exhibited the same skill and fortitude we see in our carrier pilots today.

A few days after the 1931 race, the same S-6B was prepared for a crack at the world speed record. Rolls-Royce had developed a special sprint version of the R-29 engine, but it had an unnerving tendency to explode when full power was applied, so a reconditioned and slightly modified Schneider Race engine was used instead. It burned an exotic, foul-smelling, methanol-based fuel, and turned a special propeller designed specifically for the record attempt.

On September 29, 1931, Flight Lieutenant George Stainforth made his successful assault on the world speed record, raising it above 400 miles per hour for the first time in history. He made five runs over the 3-kilometer course, and his official average speed was 407.5 miles per hour.

The floatplane Boothman flew to victory and Stainforth flew into the record books, Supermarine S-6B number S1595, is on display in the Science Museum in London. A few yards away, the next and last design to come from R.J. Mitchell's drawing board hangs from the ceiling. Though a landplane, its racing floatplane heritage is obvious in the sleek lines of its fuselage, its gracefully rounded wingtips, and the powerful V-12 nestled in its nose.

Mitchell's new plane also was designed to win races, but they were races with death. The dark clouds of war were beginning to gather over Europe, and the excitement of the Schneider races would soon be forgotten as England struggled for her very life. Her survival would come to depend in large part on a little airplane Mitchell conceived in the thunderous exhaust and blurring speed of his Schneider floatplanes. His new plane was called Spitfire.

THE ULTIMATE FLOATPLANE

The Italians had hoped to wrest the Schneider Trophy away from the British in 1931 with a truly awesome machine. Called the Macchi-Castoldi MC-72, the bright red plane might well have won the race, but it wasn't ready in time. Italy asked for a postponement, but it was refused since a similar request by England had been turned down by the Italians only a few months earlier.

The MC-72's powerplant consisted of two Fiat V-12 engines in tandem driving a pair of coaxial, counter-rotating propellers. The 24-cylinder engine was 11 feet long and developed a staggering 3,100 horsepower (Fig. 2-22).

Fig. 2-22. *On June 2, 1933, Warrant Officer Francesco Agello drove this Macchi-Castoldi MC-72 to a new world speed record of 440.67 miles per hour. Note the radiators mounted on the floats and the counter-rotating propellers.* Smithsonian Institution

Having lost out on their bid to recapture the Schneider Trophy, the Italians set their sights on Lt. Stainforth's speed record. On April 10, 1934, Warrant Officer Francesco Agello piloted the MC-

72 to a new world speed record of 423.82 miles per hour. Eighteen months later, he broke his own record by averaging 440.68 mph on two runs over Lake Garda. The racing landplanes of that same year were over 100 miles per hour slower. Although this speed record was soon broken by the fast fighters that were being developed as a result of World War II, Agello's record has never been equaled by any propeller-driven seaplane. That this speed was achieved by a floatplane in 1935 is even more remarkable in light of the fact that the record speeds flown around the racecourse at the Reno Air Races today are only about 40 mph faster than the MC-72's record.

WORLD WAR II AND BEYOND

We have seen how the development of long-range land-based bombers during World War II rendered the large flying boat obsolete, but the Navy hung onto its floatplanes for a while longer.

From the day Glenn Curtiss had droned across San Diego Bay to the *U.S.S. Pennsylvania* in his floatplane, the Navy had been intrigued with the concept of using airplanes as aerial observation platforms for its surface ships. The perfection of the steam catapult meant that planes could be carried right on the ships and launched off the stern or even off the tops of the gun turrets.

Launching an airplane was one thing; getting it back again was something else. One of the Navy's first retrieval schemes called for the pilot to simply crash his plane in the water, climb out, and wait for a lifeboat to come fetch him back to his ship. While easy enough to execute, this method proved to be rather expensive, since a new airplane had to be purchased after each flight. The obvious solution was to use a seaplane of some sort and do what Glenn Curtiss had done. After landing on the water next to the ship, the airplane could be hoisted back aboard with a crane and used again. After much experimentation, this method proved successful, and catapult-launched floatplanes became standard equipment on the Navy's large surface ships until the end of World War II.

The retrieval of the floatplane was an interesting process. Prior to the airplane's arrival, a landing mat would be rigged from a long pole extended out from the ship's side and parallel to the water. The ship would then make a sweeping turn to an upwind heading, which flattened out the waves and created a stretch of smooth water for the pilot to land on. After touchdown, the pilot would taxi up over the landing mat and cut the power. This caused the airplane to settle onto the mat, which was constructed in such a way as to snag the float keel at the step. The plane was then pulled along by the landing mat until the hook on the ship's crane could be attached to the lifting fixture on top of the fuselage.

Lifting the plane back aboard to a catapult shoehorned in among the masts and funnels was not always an easy task, especially if the ship was rolling in a heavy swell. Most of the battleships and cruisers designed during World War II had their catapults mounted on the stern. When the planes returned, they simply landed in the ship's wake and taxied up under the fantail, where an aft-mounted crane picked them up.

Almost all of the floatplanes used by the U.S. Navy were of the single-float design, and they had to be extremely rugged to withstand the tremendous pounding received during open-ocean operations. One of the most popular of the ship-launched floatplanes was the Vought OS2U Kingfisher (Fig. 2-23). This versatile reconnaissance plane earned the affection of many a downed airman who was plucked from the ocean by the two-man crew of one of these sturdy seaplanes.

One of the best-looking catapult-launched floatplanes ever designed came from the drawing boards at EDO during the closing days of World War II. The airplane, called the XOSE-1, used the new, air-cooled, inverted V-12 Ranger V-770 engine. Only the prototype of this single-float scout-observation plane was built, and the project was canceled at the end of the war (Fig. 2-24).

The Japanese produced a handsome floatplane version of the famous Mitsubishi A6M Zero-sen called the Nakajima A6M2-N. Code named "Rufe"

Fig. 2-23. *A formation of Vought OS2U Kingfishers, one of the most popular catapult-launched observation planes used by the U.S. Navy during World War II. The large rear cockpit canopy was designed to afford the observer maximum visibility.* U.S. Navy

Fig. 2-24. *EDO built this handsome floatplane, the XOSE-1, during the closing days of World War II. Designed to be launched from shipboard catapults, the airplane was intended to use the new inverted V-12 Ranger engine.* EDO Corp.

by the Allies, the single-float plane was designed to defend remote island outposts that didn't have landing strips.

As the United States carried the war deeper into the Western Pacific, the Navy decided it needed a similar float-equipped fighter. Plans were made to fit 100 Grumman F4F Wildcat fighters with twin EDO floats, but the program was canceled when it was found that the Navy's Sea Bee construction crews could build airstrips as fast as the Marines could secure a beachhead. Only two of the planes, nicknamed "Wild Catfish," were ever built.

We've looked at just a few of the historical highlights of the floatplane's development. There's much more to the story, and some of the books on the subject that I've found particularly interesting are listed in the resources at the end of this book.

The modern floatplane has a rich and colorful heritage, and as you taxi away from the dock, listen carefully. You can almost hear the clatter of Henri Fabre's little rotary engine, the echoing thunder of a Schneider racer, or the hissing boom of a steam catapult as it flings a rugged, single-float observation plane into the sky.

3

The modern floatplane

THE VOUGHT KINGFISHER and the Curtiss Seahawk of World War II marked the end of an era. They were the last catapult-launched floatplanes to be produced for the U.S. Navy, and they were the last production airplanes to be designed exclusively as floatplanes. Since the close of World War II, virtually all floatplanes have been landplane designs adapted for use on floats.

One exception was the Noorduyn Norseman, nicknamed the "Thunderchicken" by the pilots who flew it (Fig. 3-1). Originally designed in 1935 to meet the rugged demands of Canadian bush flying, its production was continued after the war by Canadian Car and Foundry. The Norseman was designed primarily for use on floats or skis, but wheels were necessary to bridge the period between winter's solid ice and the open water of summer. The landing gear designed for the Norseman had the look of an afterthought about it, and the massive, single-engined plane looked rather comical squatting on its tiny wheels.

CURRENT FLOATPLANE MODELS

Today's floatplane is generally a high-wing, single-engine landplane fitted with twin floats. The single-float configuration favored by the U.S. Navy has virtually disappeared. Landplanes that

Fig. 3-1. *A rare shot of a Noorduyn Norseman "Thunderchicken" in U.S. military markings.* EDO Corp.

have become popular as floatplane conversions include the Cessna 150, 172, 172XP, 180, 185, and 206; the Champion Citabria and Scout; the de Havilland Beaver and Otter; the Helio Courier; the Maule M-5, 6, and 7; the Piper Super Cub; the Aviat Husky, and the Taylorcraft.

Some of the higher-powered models in the Piper Cherokee line of low-wing airplanes are certified for floats, but their popularity is limited due to the difficulties imposed by the low wing when docking and loading the airplane (Fig. 3-2). Twin-engined landplanes occasionally found on floats include the venerable Beechcraft Model 18 Twin Beech and a modified Piper Aztec called the Nomad (Fig. 3-3).

Turbine-powered floatplanes are becoming quite popular, especially among commercial oper-

Fig. 3-2. *Some low-wing airplanes can be mounted on floats, such as this Piper Cherokee Six, but the low wing makes for difficult docking and loading. The plane pictured here has been fitted with EDO Model 3430 floats.* EDO Corp.

Fig. 3-3. *A Piper Aztec, as modified by Huntsville Air Service, mounted on a pair of EDO Model 4930 floats.* EDO Corp.

Fig. 3-4. *The Cessna 208 Caravan is powered by a Pratt & Whitney PT6A turbine, and it can carry up to nine passengers. This one is fitted with Wipline Model 8000 amphibious floats.* Robert Murray

Fig. 3-5. *One of the many ultralights that can be mounted on floats. While its behavior on floats is similar to conventional airplanes, the ultralight's small size and light weight restrict it to use on relatively calm water and in light winds.* Lightning Floats

ators (Fig. 3-4). Turbines aren't cheap, but they offer reduced noise, higher performance, and enhanced reliability. The same techniques that apply to piston floatplanes apply to turbines, although reversing propellers give turbines an added element of control on the water. Turbine operations are discussed in detail in chapter 19.

At the other end of the scale, floats are available for many of the ultralights and kitplanes that are becoming so popular today (Fig. 3-5). Ultralights offer a relatively inexpensive way to get into the air, and while a pilot's license currently is not required, the FAA has set some basic design parameters for the little planes. Part 103 of the Federal Aviation Regulations limits the empty weight of an ultralight to no more than 254 pounds. Top speed is limited to 55 knots, and no more than five gallons of fuel can be carried on board. A set of ul-

tralight floats cannot weigh more than 60 pounds, or 30 pounds per float, bringing the maximum allowable empty weight of an ultralight floatplane to 314 pounds. Ultralight floats are available in aluminum and fiberglass, and there is also a line of inflatable floats on the market (Fig. 3-6).

The flying characteristics of an ultralight are considerably different from those of a conventional airplane, and as each ultralight model is unique, I don't want to go into a long discussion about their individual handling and control quirks. Suffice it to say that most of them have a completely different

Fig. 3-6. *An ultralight on Full Lotus inflatable floats owned by Fred Paulsen in Petersburg, Alaska. Paulsen often can be seen on calm mornings flying over the harbor and exploring the network of channels and bays that surround the town.*

Fig. 3-7. *Fred Paulsen, an accomplished shipwright, felt his ultralight would be easier to maneuver in the tight confines of Petersburg's harbor if it had water rudders, so he designed and fabricated his own. They are patterned after the rudders used on full-size floatplanes, with steering linkages to the air rudder and a retraction system.*

"feel" in comparison to general aviation airplanes, and *no one, including experienced pilots, should attempt to fly an ultralight without receiving some instruction first*. On the water, the operation of a float-equipped ultralight and a conventional floatplane are quite similar, so most of the techniques and procedures described in this book apply equally to both types of airplanes.

Size is an ultralight floatplane's greatest limitation. Water conditions that would merely bounce a Piper Super Cub around a little bit could easily overstress an ultralight; however, ultralight floats are surprisingly strong for their size, and many of them are filled with foam, making them virtually unsinkable. Most ultralight floats are not equipped with water rudders, as the airplane's light weight makes it fairly easy to steer with the air rudder alone. If you're going to be operating in breezy conditions, however, or in an area with swift tidal currents, you might want to fabricate a set of steerable and retractable water rudders for more positive control (Fig. 3-7).

With a gross weight of only 500 pounds or so, an ultralight is very susceptible to wind, and while it might be able to survive the choppy water conditions brought on by a strong breeze, a sudden gust could quickly put the plane on its back. If

you're planning to fly a float-equipped ultralight, pay special attention to the sections of this book that describe the wind's effects on a floatplane and how to deal with them. If you should encounter strong winds and rough water while flying an ultralight, it's essential that you follow the proper procedures to avoid flipping the plane.

If operations are restricted to relatively calm water in light or no-wind conditions, float-equipped ultralights are a lot of fun, and in many ways they capture the true feeling of water flying far better than the closed-cockpit, multi-instrumented floatplanes most of us are used to. Sitting exposed to the elements, it's easy to imagine oneself as Henri Fabre or Glenn Curtiss, taxiing a prototype floatplane out for its first flight.

Kitplanes are a fast-growing category of airplanes. Larger and heavier than ultralights, kitplanes often look like conventional airplanes with enclosed cockpits and covered fuselages. While they are not simply scaled-down copies, many kitplanes resemble Piper Cubs or Taylorcrafts and, as such, tend to have pleasing lines and snappy performance. A pilot's license is required to fly a kitplane, some of which can carry two, three, or even four people. Some of the smaller kitplanes use engines identical to those used in ultralights, but the larger kitplanes can use engines developing up to 200 horsepower.

The floats made by traditional manufacturers such as EDO and Wipaire are too large and heavy for most kitplanes, but there are several companies that specialize in smaller floats designed specifically for kitplanes. Like ultralight floats, kitplane floats are available in aluminum, fiberglass, or as inflatables. Some kitplane floats have one or two water rudders, and some have none. Generally, the heavier the plane, the more it will benefit from water rudders. There are even amphibious floats for kitplanes complete with hydraulic gear retraction, and some manufacturers offer useful features like baggage hatches and rubber nose bumpers.

Kitplanes handle more like conventional airplanes than do ultralights. This book is written for the pilots of conventional floatplanes because that is what I fly, but virtually all the procedures and techniques I'm going to describe apply equally to the pilots of kitplanes; for the most part, a kitplane is just a small conventional floatplane. Kitplanes such as the Avid Flyer, the Kitfox, the Zenair STOL, and the Murphy Rebel have earned excellent reputations as floatplanes, and their popularity is increasing rapidly (Fig. 3-8).

Fig. 3-8. *A Murphy Rebel mounted on Murphy amphibious floats. The two-place kitplane can be fitted with up to a 160-horsepower Lycoming engine, which gives it a climb rate of 1,200 feet per minute and a cruise speed of 120 knots. The all-aluminum plane has a range of up to 880 miles, depending on the engine selected. Murphy offers kits for both amphibious and straight floats, complete with baggage compartments. The company is located in Chilliwack, British Columbia.* Murphy Aircraft Mfg.

While kitplanes don't have the carrying capacities and rough water capabilities of conventional floatplanes, they also don't have the high costs of conventional floatplanes. Some companies offer partially or completely built-up kitplanes and floats if you don't feel you're up to the task of putting them together yourself. On the other hand, kitplanes have been around long enough for the manufacturers to refine their parts and instructions, so most of them will be more demanding on your time than your skill. If you're mainly interested in local-area recreational flying, or cross-country flying with lightweight camping gear, a kitplane on floats might be just the thing. Don't let anyone tell you that kitplanes aren't real floatplanes. They require just as much skill from their pilots as their Cessna and de Havilland brothers; in fact, at regional seaplane fly-ins, kitplane pilots are starting to outperform the "heavy iron" pilots of conventional floatplanes in the landing accuracy and takeoff contests.

FLOAT INSTALLATION

Converting a landplane to floats is a little more involved than simply removing one undercarriage and bolting on another. Before the floats can be installed, there are several modifications that must be made to the airplane itself. The number and type of modifications required varies from model to model. Some airplanes are designed from the outset to accommodate floats. The de Havilland Beaver, for example, was designed and built to be used on wheels, floats, or skis, and most of the mounting hardware required by these systems was built into each airplane on the assembly line. A Cessna 206, on the other hand, might spend only a portion of its life on floats. If the airplane is to be used on wheels only, there's no point in wasting fuel and useful load by dragging around a bunch of unused attachment hardware.

There is also the matter of expense. The modifications required to provide attach points for the floats (adding strength to the fuselage) and protect the airplane from corrosion are collectively referred to as "float kits" by most manufacturers, and float kits are not cheap. Today's airplanes are expensive enough as it is, so why spend money for equipment that's not going to be used?

Actually, there are occasions when it might be wise to add the expense of a float kit to a new airplane, even though the owner might never intend to install floats. If the landplane being ordered is also popular as a floatplane, a factory-installed float kit will considerably increase the airplane's resale value. The Cessna 185, for example, is very popular among commercial floatplane operators, so it's not uncommon to find used 185s with factory-installed float kits that have never been attached to a pair of floats.

A good example of the modifications required to prepare a landplane for a life on the water is the float kit offered by Cessna for the Model 206 Stationair (Fig. 3-9). (At the time of this writing, Cessna had announced intentions to resume manufacturing the 206, and will presumably be once again offering a float kit as a factory-installed option.)

First, additional fuselage hardware is added to provide attach points for the float struts. This attachment hardware must be strong enough and mounted securely enough to transmit the entire weight of the airplane to the float structure.

Fig. 3-9. *The Cessna 206 is a popular workhorse, and it is made even more versatile when mounted on floats. Both straight and amphibious floats are available for the 206, and the spacious cabin has room for six adults or a lot of bulky freight. This one has been fitted with EDO Model 3430 floats.* EDO Corp.

A V-brace is installed inside the cabin, between the upper corners of the windshield and the cowl deck, adding torsional stiffness to the fuselage.

Because the nosewheel will not be needed, removable panels are installed over the nosegear opening. The stall sensor is relocated so it will not be affected by turbulent air coming off the floats, and the left-hand forward fuselage static source is deleted to ensure proper airspeed system calibration.

To improve directional stability, the standard vertical tail is replaced by a tail that has been redesigned to accommodate a larger rudder, and a ventral fin is installed below the tailcone. The new tail necessitates the use of a different tail "stinger," as well as a redesigned flashing beacon installation. The position of the ventral fin requires replacement of the single tail tie-down ring with a dual-ring assembly.

A new nose cap with revised engine baffling is fitted, and special cowl flaps, cowl flap side extensions, and cowl flap controls are installed to provide proper engine cooling.

Hoisting rings are attached to the top of the wing center section, and the wing flap limit switch is adjusted to restrict the maximum flap extension to 30 degrees. (The flaps on the 206 normally have a maximum extension of 40 degrees.)

The elevator trim tab rigging is changed to increase the maximum down travel, and the rudder trim bungee is replaced by a bungee with a lighter spring. The airframe receives a lot of additional corrosion protection, especially on the inner surface of the fuselage, and stainless steel control cables are used throughout the plane. Finally, to aid in fueling the floatplane, steps and assist handles are mounted on the forward fuselage, and steps are mounted on the wing struts.

Floatplanes are subjected to a lot of pounding, and on some models, the float kit includes additional strengthening of the engine mount attach points.

Many float kits—particularly those for planes that use fixed-pitch propellers—include a special seaplane prop. In order to overcome the tremendous drag created by moving a float through and over the water, a floatplane needs every bit of horsepower it can get. Horsepower is a function of rpm, so these special "water props" are longer and flatter-pitched to let the engine spool up to its maximum allowable rpm, thus developing maximum horsepower during the takeoff run. This is why a floatplane makes so much noise when it takes off. It's not the engine you're hearing, but the howl of that long, flat prop as the blade tips approach the speed of sound.

Although it allows the engine to develop maximum horsepower, a fixed-pitch seaplane propeller does not take as big a "bite" of air in cruise as does a cruise prop, so for a given power setting, a seaplane prop won't pull an airplane along as fast, or as far, as a cruise prop.

A good example of the effect a propeller can have on a floatplane's performance is the experience the British had in 1931 with their entry in that year's Schneider Trophy race. The airplane was the Supermarine S-6B, which, as we learned in the previous chapter, was a further refinement of the 1929 race winner, the Supermarine S-6. The S-6 had been fitted with a Rolls-Royce V-12 engine that developed 1,900 horsepower and swung a 9½-foot propeller. For the 1931 race, Rolls-Royce managed to get 2,350 horsepower out of its big V-12, and the engine was fitted with a new, shorter, coarser-pitched propeller, making the airplane potentially capable of over 400 miles per hour. When Wing Commander A.H. Orlebar took the S-6B out for its first test flight, however, the plane wouldn't lift off the water, but instead went plowing around in circles. The engine ran beautifully, but the airplane simply refused to take off. During the frantic testing that followed, someone suggested they try fitting the S-6B with one of the old, longer propellers from an S-6. This was done, and the S-6B's takeoff and water-handling problems disappeared. Despite the engine's 2,350 horsepower, the new, short, coarse-pitched "cruise" prop couldn't develop enough power to overcome the water's drag on the floats. The pro-

peller would have worked beautifully once the floatplane was in the air, but it wasn't flat enough to power the plane off the water. The Schneider Trophy racers all used fixed-pitch propellers, and a constant-speed (or at least a variable-pitch) propeller would have solved a lot of problems—as they do today.

A plane manufactured without a float kit can have the necessary modifications installed at a later date, but because the airplane has to be partially disassembled before the work can be done, the cost will probably exceed that of a factory-installed kit. If there's any chance the airplane will be used on floats sometime in the future, or if the installation of a float kit will enhance the plane's resale value, it's probably worth having the manufacturer install the kit on the assembly line.

The float kit prepares an airplane to receive a float system, which is composed of two basic groups; the attachment hardware and the floats themselves (Fig. 3-10).

ATTACHMENT HARDWARE

Each float is positioned properly underneath the airplane with forward and aft vertical struts. These struts connect the float to the fuselage, and a diagonal strut, installed between the top of one vertical strut and the bottom of the other one, provides fore and aft stiffness. The de Havilland Beaver uses twin V-struts to attach each float to the fuselage, and there are other strut arrangements as well, but in each case the purpose is the same—proper positioning of the float, and fore and aft stiffness.

The floats are held the correct distance apart from each other by the front and rear spreader bars. Both the struts and the spreader bars are streamlined in cross section; one manufacturer even gains a little lift by giving its spreader bars an airfoil shape.

Additional stiffness is provided by the bracing wires, which might run diagonally between the left and right vertical struts or the front and rear spreader

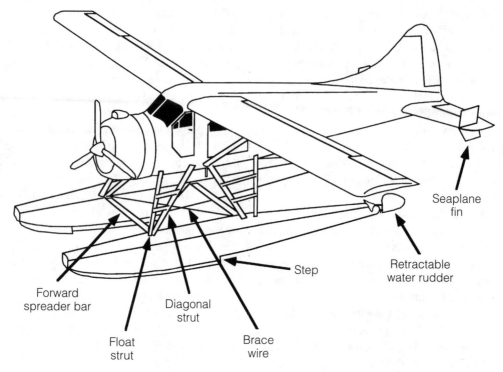

Seaplane
fin

Step

Retractable
water rudder

Forward
spreader bar

Diagonal
strut

Float
strut

Brace
wire

Fig. 3-10. *A typical floatplane and the components of its float system.*

bars. While they are called wires, they are usually streamlined stainless steel rods with tension adjustments at each end. Their purpose is to further stiffen the float system and distribute the stress encountered during water operations among the various attachment components.

THE FLOATS

The other major components of a float system are, of course, the floats themselves (Fig. 3-11). Several companies manufacture floats that are available in aluminum and fiberglass. The model number of a float usually indicates its water displacement in pounds, and float sizes range from the 16-foot Capre Model 1500 for the Piper J-3 Cub, to Wipaire's Model 13000, a 31-foot amphibious monster for the de Havilland DHC-6 Twin Otter.

The de Havilland Beaver pictured throughout this book is mounted on EDO 4930 floats; each float displaces 4,930 pounds of water. The two floats together have a total displacement of 9,860 pounds. Nearly 10,000 pounds seems a little like overkill when you consider that the gross weight of a Beaver is only 5,090 pounds; however, the floats are required by law to have a combined buoyancy of at least 180 percent of the airplane's gross weight, which in the case of the Beaver comes to 9,162 pounds.

An individual float is required to have at least four watertight compartments and must continue to support the airplane with any two compartments flooded.

Most floats have a V-shaped bottom to help cut through the waves, soften the impact of landing, and provide some degree of spray control. An exception to this configuration was the inverted V-bottom used on the fiberglass floats manufactured by the Fiberfloat Corporation. The theory behind the reverse-V shape was that the air being scooped

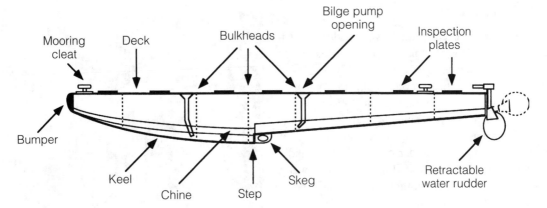

Fig. 3-11. *The components of a typical float.*

Labels (from diagram): Mooring cleat, Deck, Bulkheads, Bilge pump opening, Inspection plates, Bumper, Keel, Chine, Step, Skeg, Retractable water rudder

into the "tunnel" underneath each float would help lift the plane onto the step faster, assisted by the upward force of the spray deflected into the tunnel. (The "step" is defined in chapter 10's subsection on the "planing phase" of a takeoff.)

Spray control

Float designers try very hard to minimize the amount of spray thrown off by their floats. Besides impairing the pilot's vision and thoroughly soaking down the airplane, spray can be very damaging to a propeller. Its effect on a high-revving prop is very much like shot-peening, and it can cause serious pitting on the propeller's leading edge.

Spray is not really a problem when the floatplane is either moving very slowly through the water, or very rapidly over it. At low speeds in smooth water, there isn't any spray, and at high speeds the spray is thrown well aft of the propeller arc. The problem occurs just after takeoff power is applied. As the floatplane accelerates, the floats begin to mush through the water prior to achieving a planing attitude. A lot of spray is generated at this point, and because of the floatplane's low forward speed, the spray remains in the general vicinity of the propeller.

There are several ways to control this spray. One is to contour the bottom of the float in such a way as to deflect the spray out to the side. This is

accomplished by designing the float with a flared V-bottom and hard chines where the bottom meets the sides of the float. An alternative to this is the inverted-V bottom that was used by Fiberfloat, which deflects much of the spray into the tunnel under the float.

Another spray control device is the spray rail, attached to the forward section of the float chines (Fig. 3-12). These metal strips act as extensions of the chines and deflect the spray out and down. The disadvantage of spray rails is that, like any additional surface, they create aerodynamic drag. For this reason, and to prevent them from snagging and bending on docks, most operators install spray rails on the inboard sides of the floats only, where they are quite effective in keeping spray away from the propeller.

Fig. 3-12. *A spray rail as fitted to an EDO Model 4930 float on a de Havilland Beaver.*

Water rudders

At the aft end of each float is a water rudder, which is used to steer the floatplane at low speeds on the surface. The water rudders are linked by cables to the floatplane's vertical air rudder and are controlled by the rudder pedals in the cockpit. Before takeoff and while sailing or beaching the floatplane, the water rudders must be pulled up, so an additional set of cables connects each rudder to a retraction handle on the floor of the cockpit (Fig. 3-13). The water rudders are held down by their own weight, and in the case of larger floatplanes such as the Beaver, a healthy tug on the retraction handle is necessary to lift the heavy rudders clear of the water.

Unlike conventional landing gear, the water rudders do not lock down when they are lowered. Since the only thing keeping them down is their own weight, the rudders are free to "kick up," like an outboard motor, if they hit the bottom, or an underwater obstacle (Fig. 3-14).

It is very important that the water rudders be retracted before takeoff. Water rudders that are left down during takeoff could cause the airplane to veer to one side and possibly overturn. And because the rudders don't lock down, they will begin to bang up and down as the floatplane's speed across the water increases. This can damage the rudders and weaken the stern of the float, causing the seams to open up and leaks to develop.

Getting the water out

Even though a float is divided into four or more watertight compartments, this does not ensure that it will remain dry on the inside. There are many ways that water can leak into the float compartments. Rainwater and spray can seep in around the access and inspection plates, the seams in the float can begin to work open with use, and moist air can condense on the inside of the float.

The resulting water trapped in the float must be removed before each flight, and the float manufacturers have provided a couple of ways to accomplish this. The deck covering each watertight compart-

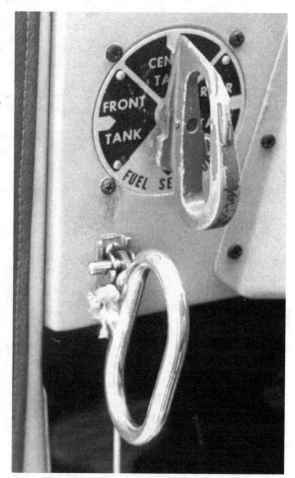

Fig. 3-13. *The water rudder retraction handle on a Beaver. The handle is attached to the water rudders by the line shown extending toward the floor of the cabin. When the handle is in its bracket, as shown here, the water rudders are up. Lifting the handle out of its bracket and lowering it to the floor lowers the rudders.*

ment contains one or more access hatches. The covers over these hatches can be removed, allowing any water present to be swabbed out with a large sponge. This method works best on small floats because of the difficulty involved in reaching the bottom of a large float through the access hatches.

The most efficient way to remove water from the compartments of larger floats is with a bilge pump. These lightweight handpumps can be in-

serted through an open access hatch, or applied to the deck openings of special bilge pump down-tubes. The down-tubes extend from the deck to the bilge of each watertight compartment and act as bilge pump extensions. The end of the pump is inserted into the recessed down-tube fitting in the deck of the float. When the pump is activated, any water present in that compartment is sucked up the down-tube into the pump, and thrown overboard (Fig. 3-15).

Fig. 3-15. *Pumping the floats on a Beaver. The most efficient way to remove water from the float compartments is with a manual bilge pump. The water is discharged on the upstroke of the pump. Make sure you aim the opening at the top of the pump away from yourself and your passengers.*

Float accessories

The bow of each float usually has a rubber bumper to absorb shock if the airplane contacts a dock nose first. Mooring cleats are mounted fore and aft on the deck of each float, and many floats have provisions for carrying a paddle on the inboard side (Fig. 3-16). A nonskid surface is often applied to the float decks for better footing.

Fig. 3-14. *The water rudder on an EDO Model 4930 float shown in the retracted position (top) and the lowered position (bottom). The cable attached to the top of the rudder blade on each float goes to a yoke under the fuselage from which a single line runs to the retraction handle in the cockpit.*

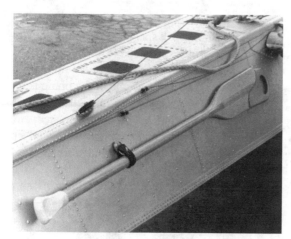

Fig. 3-16. *A paddle can come in very handy, and it should be easy to reach in a hurry. Many floats are equipped with exterior paddle brackets like these, which are mounted on an EDO Model 4930 float.*

Some manufacturers use the center watertight compartment for additional baggage space, and offer large, hinged hatch covers for easy loading and unloading. EDO even offers a six-gallon gas can that fits into the center compartment of some of its float models.

These float compartments can come in very handy. During the production of a marketing film for Boeing, I was faced with the necessity of shooting both underwater and aerial sequences, with very little time to do either one. The solution to my problem came in the form of a de Havilland Beaver. The bulky scuba tank, along with wetsuits, flippers, masks, and towels, fit nicely in the port (left) float compartment, leaving the cabin free for cameras, accessory cases, and the film crew. We flew to our first location in Puget Sound's San Juan Islands, tied a diving flag to the propeller, and shot the underwater sequence, using the Beaver as a diving barge. We then stowed all the scuba equipment back in the float compartment, removed one of the main doors, stashed it in the back of the cabin, and proceeded to film the aerial sequences. By using a floatplane, what would have been a two-day job was completed in four hours.

Most floatplanes have mooring lines permanently attached to each float. They are usually six to eight feet long, and in flight they lie quietly on top of the floats; there's no tendency for them to wave about in the breeze. Most operators also fasten three- or four-foot-long grab-lines to the end of each wing. These lines are used to pull the floatplane up to a dock, or as handholds while turning the airplane around. In flight, they stream back against the lower side of the wing.

HOW FLOATS WORK

The floats support the airplane while it's on the water. This is obvious enough, but actually this support is rendered in two ways: water displacement and hydrodynamic pressure.

When the floatplane is at rest on the water or moving slowly through it, the floats act like two boats and support the airplane's weight by displacing an equal weight of water. Put another way, if the amount of water displaced by the two floats could be weighed, it would be found to weigh exactly as much as the airplane. As weight is put into the plane in the form of passengers or cargo, the floats will sink lower into the water because they have to displace an additional pound of water for every pound of weight added to the airplane.

Support by water displacement works fine up to a point. The problem occurs when you try to accelerate the floats to a higher speed through the water. The water exerts a tremendous amount of drag on the partly submerged floats, and it's simply not possible to accelerate beyond a certain speed, called *hull speed*. Because the hull speed of an aircraft float is much slower than the speed required for flight, a method had to be found of reducing the hydrodynamic drag on the floats while still allowing them to support the airplane on the water until the plane could become airborne.

The answer was to design the floats to *plane*, or *skim*, across the surface of the water when a certain speed was achieved. Once the floats are riding on top of the water instead of driving through it, the hydrodynamic drag is considerably reduced, and the airplane can accelerate to liftoff speed.

When the plane is at rest or taxiing slowly, the entire length of each float is used to support the airplane by water displacement. As power is added and the floatplane accelerates, the hydrodynamic pressure on the bottom of the floats increases, lifting them up until they are planing across the surface.

As we saw in the previous chapter, some of the early floats built by Glenn Curtiss refused to lift from the water, even though they were driven fast enough to achieve a planing attitude. Their long, flat bottoms, which were necessary to support the floatplane at rest, were unable to break free of the water's suction. The solution to this problem was the single-step hydroplane bottom, which is the configuration used on all floats today. The *step*, or break, in the bottom of each float allows air to flow in under the afterbody, eliminating the suction problem that so plagued Curtiss. As the speed across the water increases, the hydrodynamic pressure on the bottom of each float also increases, forcing them to ride higher and higher. Eventually, the only wetted surface of each float is that portion of the bottom just ahead of the step. This small surface is all that's necessary to support the weight of the floatplane, and hydrodynamic drag is drastically reduced.

Also, don't forget that the wing starts developing lift as the airplane accelerates. As far as the floats are concerned, the faster the plane goes, the less it weighs, and the less support it will require from the floats. Eventually the wing's lift will be equal to the weight of the floatplane, and there will be nothing left for the floats to support. At this point, the airplane can be taken off the water completely.

This sequence of weight transfer will occur in reverse order when the floatplane lands. The plane will first touch down and run along on the step for a short distance before settling back into the displacement mode of support.

Numerous attempts have been made over the years to reduce the hydrodynamic drag on the bottoms of floats (and the hulls of flying boats) so they will accelerate faster during the takeoff run. Thin strips of metal have been attached along the length of a float between the keel and the chine. Floats were built with multiple steps in place of the conventional single step. (This did work on flying boats, and most of the larger ones incorporated two and sometimes even three steps in their hull designs.)

Most of these experiments met with limited success, but there has been a recent development that seems promising. Called *riblets*, this low-drag surface first came to the public's attention when it was applied to the hull of the 12-meter racing sloop *Stars and Stripes* for the successful recapture of the America's Cup from Australia in 1986.

Marketed by the 3-M Company, this surface covering is available in tape form, and seems to be quite effective in reducing the hydrodynamic drag on airplane floats. In one documented case, low-drag tape was applied to the bottoms of a pair of EDO Model 2870 floats that were installed on a Cessna 180. During the test, the tape reduced the takeoff runs by 18 to 30 percent. A note of caution, however: The low-drag tape also increases the landing run after touchdown. Anyone deciding to apply low-drag tape to float bottoms should be aware that the airplane will now "coast" farther before it comes to a stop. Most of the time, this won't present a problem, but it's something that should be taken into consideration before landing in a crowded harbor or on a small lake.

However, before we discuss the specific techniques for takeoffs, landings, and everything else in between, let's set the stage by examining the most important floatplane technique you'll ever practice—the technique of floatplane safety.

4

Floatplane safety

THE PILOT of the six-place floatplane was tired after his long cross-country flight and was in a hurry to land. He was behind a larger floatplane as he began his final approach toward shore. Witnesses said later he appeared to be following the first airplane too closely and was caught by wake turbulence just before he touched down. Others thought the pilot might have felt he was going to overshoot the landing area and tried to force the plane onto the water too soon. Still others thought he might have hit a boat wake. Whatever the cause, the result was disastrous. Digging one float into the water, the plane tipped up on one wing and cartwheeled over onto its back. Thanks to the quick action of nearby boaters, the occupants were saved from drowning as the overturned plane settled into the mud at the bottom of the lake. There were no injuries.

The pilot of the small, two-place floatplane was taxiing downwind on a blustery day prior to taking off. When the strong tailwind started to weathercock the plane around, the pilot attempted to "catch it" with a burst of power and opposite rudder. The added power made the downwind float dig in, and the plane turned over. There were no injuries.

The pilot of the eight-place floatplane began his takeoff run close to shore in the lee of a small island. The area is notorious for its nasty, swirling winds, and commercial pilots always taxi out into open water before beginning their takeoff runs. As the plane accelerated out from behind the island, the wind caught the plane and swung it into a sharp turn. The pilot tried to power his way out of trouble as he shoved the downwind rudder pedal to the floor. The plane slammed into the rocks and broke apart. There were no injuries.

These three accidents had two things in common. In each case, there were no injuries, which says something about the safety of floatplanes, and in each case, poor judgment on the part of the pilot was the direct cause of the accident.

Actually, this entire book is about floatplane safety. It's a subject you'll find woven into the description of every technique I discuss. But no matter whether you're about to take a short spin around the locai lake or embark on a thousand-mile journey, there are some basic rules you should put into effect the moment you step onto the dock.

RULE ONE: Exercise proper judgment

Poor judgment is probably the single greatest cause of aviation accidents. Whether on the part of a pilot, an air traffic controller, or a mechanic, the results of poor judgment are often irreversible. Floatplanes are not dangerous. In fact, in many ways they are much safer than their wheeled counterparts, but because of their unique and constantly changing environment, proper judgment is absolutely essential to floatplane safety.

As I noted earlier, the pilot of a floatplane is pretty much on his or her own. At least landplane pilots have their landing sites defined for them. Not only do floatplane pilots have to choose their own runways for each landing, but they also have to determine if they're safe. Are there any floating logs or deadheads lurking just beneath the surface? Is the water too shallow? Too rough? What about boat traffic?

Then there's the wind. Which way is it blowing? How hard? Is it gusty? Will you be able to taxi to the dock, or will you have to sail the plane in backwards?

If all this sounds too complicated to master, relax. The techniques for obtaining the answers to all these questions are easily learned. The important thing is what you do with the information once you've obtained it. If you think the water looks too shallow, should you attempt a landing anyway? The obvious answer is no, but what if that's where your passengers are paying you to take them? Or maybe the weather is deteriorating, or it's getting dark. What do you do then?

All you can do is use your best judgment, based on the pertinent facts of the situation, your own experience, and what you have been taught. If this sounds like a time-consuming procedure, it can be, which brings us to the next floatplane safety rule.

RULE TWO: Don't allow yourself to be rushed into making a decision

There's nothing wrong with overflying a landing site several times until you're sure you can land safely. There are a lot of things to look for, especially if you're unfamiliar with the area. You don't want to be in such a hurry that you overlook a power line, or a floating log, or some rocks just below the surface. Take your time. At least you won't have a tower controller constantly squawking orders at you on the radio.

RULE THREE: Think through the consequences of each action

This is a good rule to follow for any type of flying, but it is particularly applicable to flying floats. For example, while floatplanes come to a stop quickly, they can take a long time to become airborne. If you find a small lake you'd like to visit, make sure you'll be able to take off again before you land. You don't want to end up having your plane lifted off the lake by a helicopter. In chapter 19, we'll look at a method of determining the length of a lake while flying over it.

If you operate a floatplane in coastal waters, don't forget the tide (Fig. 4-1). I know of at least one pilot who beached his airplane and left it, only to find several hundred yards of mud between the plane and the nearest water when he returned. The tide had gone out, and my friend was faced with a six-hour wait for its return. At least he still had his airplane, which he probably wouldn't have had if he had beached it during low tide!

Even the simplest of maneuvers can have dire consequences if you aren't alert. I once tied a Cessna 172 floatplane to a dock that was several feet higher than the docks I normally used. When it was time to leave, I followed the standard procedure of turning the airplane out 90 degrees from

Fig. 4-1. *A Cessna 172 that has been tailed into a beach on the Hood Canal in Washington's Puget Sound. While this scene looks innocent enough, the tide was ebbing rapidly, and the plane had to be moved every 15 minutes to keep it from becoming stranded.*

the dock. Just as I was about to step onto the rear of the left float and walk forward to the cockpit, I realized that my weight would force the tail of the plane down and slam it onto the planking. Fortunately, I was able to move the floatplane to the end of the dock and depart from there, but had I not anticipated the consequences of my original plan, I could have damaged the tail.

RULE FOUR: Plan ahead

This is probably the most important rule to follow when flying a floatplane. Remember, you're driving a machine that has no brakes, no reverse, and somewhat vague steering. As soon as you untie it, it's at the mercy of the wind. You won't get into trouble, however, if you plan each course of action well in advance.

I have a friend who spends a lot of his time flying floatplanes up and down the Inside Passage along the coasts of British Columbia and Alaska. While describing the constantly changing weather and water conditions with which he has to contend during each trip, he remarked that no matter what the forecast was, he always prepared for the worst. "That way," he said, "I'm never surprised."

RULE FIVE: When in doubt, don't

If you think you saw a log under the surface, don't land there. If the water looks like it might be too shallow, stay out of it. If it looks like the beach could be too rocky, stay off of it. If you think that sailboat might tack back across your path, stay away from it. If you're not sure that the water is smooth enough for your floatplane, land somewhere else. If you have doubts about the weather, don't go.

RULE SIX: Know your own limitations

It's vitally important that you be constantly aware of your own limitations. Don't take on anything you're not sure you can handle. For example, floatplanes are regularly landed on snow and ice by experienced pilots. They know their airplanes' performance and are experts at picking just the right surface conditions that will safely allow such operations. The slightest miscalculation can destroy the floatplane, to say nothing of endangering the lives of the occupants. The procedure is surprisingly easy. The hard part is deciding when and where to make the landing and deciding in your own mind whether or not the risks are too great. These are decisions that can only be based on experience—a lot of experience—and it cannot be acquired from a book or a few "hangar flying" sessions.

Another good example is docking a floatplane. It always looks so easy. You just slide up alongside the dock, step gracefully out, and gently pull the airplane to a stop. You'll soon find out there's much more to it than that. A smoothly executed docking is a combination of good planning, good timing, and good judgment, all of which take some time to acquire. My initial floatplane instruction took place at a flight school that operated off a ramp. Ramping was simple. You just hit the thing head on, slid up it a short ways, and stopped. When I started flying at a facility that used docks instead of ramps, it took a couple of sessions with an instructor before I felt competent enough to try docking the floatplane myself, and even then I had some nervous moments. I still do.

If you already know how to fly, you know enough not to take on weather conditions that are beyond your abilities. The aviation publications are full of stories every month about people who tried unsuccessfully to push the weather. Floatplanes—like cars, bicycles, skis, scuba equipment, and landplanes—can get you into trouble only if you take on something you can't handle. Build your experience gradually and safely. Above all, don't fall into the trap of thinking that flying with an instructor after you've obtained your rating is demeaning, or shows incompetence on your part. I, for one, would not want to take on the potential dangers of landing on rivers or small, high mountain lakes without the benefit of some instruction from a pilot experienced in these advanced techniques.

In summary, floatplane safety is really just another term for plain, ordinary, common sense. While it might seem that the constantly changing wind and water conditions throw an almost insurmountable bunch of variables at you, the challenge of successfully coping with these variables is what makes flying floats so rewarding. To prepare you to meet this challenge safely, a thorough course of flight instruction is absolutely essential.

5
Floatplane instruction

LET'S ASSUME you've decided to give float flying a try. Great! Now, how do you go about doing it? Obviously, you'll have to get some flight instruction, and the question that immediately comes to mind is, "How much flight instruction?"

There is no minimum hour requirement specified by the FAA if you are simply adding a seaplane rating to your existing pilot's certificate. If, however, you plan to receive your primary flight instruction in a floatplane, you'll have to meet the same requirements the FAA has defined for all student pilots, including a written exam and a flight test. A written exam is not required if you are merely adding a seaplane rating to your existing pilot's certificate, but you will have to pass a flight test designed to demonstrate your floatplane proficiency.

On the average, it should take 10 to 12 hours of instruction to receive a single-engine sea rating at a good flight school. Some places claim to be able to qualify pilots for the rating in less than half that time, but I would question the quality of their instruction, even though it represents a considerable monetary savings. Ten to 12 hours is little enough time as it is, and you have a lot to learn.

A thorough floatplane course should cover the following procedures and techniques:

- **Preflight inspection.** While the basic preflight inspection techniques are the same for both landplanes and floatplanes, floatplanes have additional systems that must be checked and specialized equipment that must be on board to ensure the safety of each flight.
- **Boarding and starting.** As soon as a floatplane is untied from the dock, it's at the mercy of the wind and the current. It's important that you learn the quickest way to get in and get going so your plane won't drift into trouble.
- **Low-speed taxiing.** Directional control is by means of the water rudders, and you will begin to develop the judgment necessary to maneuver your plane in tight quarters around docks and boats.
- **Engine run-up and systems checks.** These procedures are basically the same for both landplanes and floatplanes, but since you'll be moving while you do them, you'll have to learn to keep an eye on where you're going.

- **Takeoff.** You'll learn to control a floatplane during the three phases of a takeoff run: the displacement phase, the plowing, or "hump" phase, and the planing phase. The planing phase is also known as being "on the step."
- **Airwork.** You'll get used to your floatplane's slower climbing and cruise speeds, and you'll learn that you need to pay a little more attention to your turn coordination when you're flying a floatplane.
- **Landing.** There are techniques for determining wind direction, judging water conditions, and choosing a landing site, which you'll learn as you practice landings.
- **The step-taxi.** The step-taxi is an efficient way to cover distance quickly while on the water, but it takes practice to develop the correct "feel" for this maneuver.
- **The step-turn.** You'll learn how to do this odd-feeling maneuver, when to do it, and when *not* to do it.
- **Sailing.** This is how you'll dock or beach your floatplane when the water rudders aren't powerful enough to overcome the plane's weathercocking tendency in a strong wind. You'll learn to use the air rudder, ailerons, flaps, engine, and even the cabin doors to control your direction and speed as you drift backwards toward the dock or beach.
- **Docking.** It takes practice to be able to judge the best approach to a dock, and you'll learn the specific techniques for stopping a floatplane alongside a dock and mooring it securely.
- **Rough-water takeoffs and landings.** Rough water can subject your floatplane to a pounding severe enough to overstress or break the float system components. You'll learn to get your plane off the water as

soon as possible during takeoff and how to make the touchdown and runout as gentle as possible when you land.
- **Glassy-water landings.** Landing on glassy water is one of the most dangerous situations you'll face as a floatplane pilot. The problem is not the water's effect on your airplane, but its effect on your ability to judge altitude. There are specific procedures for making safe glassy-water landings, and your instructor should make sure you get plenty of opportunities to practice them.

LEARNING TO FLY: Wheels or floats?

There's nothing that says a person has to learn to fly in a landplane, and each year people receive their private pilot certificates in floatplanes. I've had several friends who were interested in learning to fly ask me which I thought made the better primary trainer, a wheelplane or a floatplane. Unfortunately, there's no easy answer, and each class of airplane has its advantages and disadvantages. Let's examine the advantages first.

Landplanes are more numerous and are generally less expensive to rent than floatplanes. Ground handling is easy to master in a landplane, and as a student, you won't have to contend with currents, winds, tides, boat wakes, and docking techniques. Probably one of the biggest advantages of learning to fly in a landplane is that you will become proficient with the radio. Most airports of any size require you to communicate with ground control and the tower, and often with approach and departure control as well. Some airports even want you to contact clearance delivery before each flight. Talking on and listening to the radio will soon become second nature to you, and you'll also learn to scan constantly for other aircraft—a good habit to get into regardless of the type of airplane you might be flying.

If you learn to fly at a busy airport, you'll also get used to being around many different sizes and shapes of aircraft, all of which are traveling at different speeds. I learned to fly at Honolulu International Airport, and many times I would find myself landing wingtip-to-wingtip with a Boeing 747 that was touching down on the parallel runway. I'll never forget how important I felt when one busy day the tower controller barked out, "United heavy, follow the Cessna 150 to the ramp." All I could see in the 150's little rearview mirror was a huge nosewheel strut.

As you become used to flying in the congested airspace around a busy airport, you'll be able to concentrate on flying safely, and you won't let all the traffic flying in your vicinity intimidate you into making a mistake.

Learning to fly in a floatplane has its advantages, too. The fact that you *do* have to contend with currents, winds, tides, boat wakes, and docking techniques makes learning to fly all that much more interesting and challenging. You also won't spend a lot of your valuable flight time waiting in line to take off or chasing vectors around the sky as the tower controller lands the six planes that are in front of you. In fact, one of the best things about learning to fly in a floatplane is the absence of control from the ground. You'll learn to think for yourself, and the success and safety of each flight will depend primarily on your good judgment. This is why floatplane pilots tend to be more self-sufficient than their landplane counterparts.

The flying characteristics of landplanes and floatplanes are very similar, so there's no real advantage of one over the other as far as your airwork will be concerned. They both turn, climb, descend, cruise, and stall for the same reasons and with the same flight controls. As noted previously, an airplane on floats doesn't have the climb and cruise performance enjoyed by the same plane on wheels, but this won't make much difference to a student pilot.

The decision as to whether or not you should receive your primary training in a floatplane is re-ally dependent upon what you hope to get out of the flying experience. If you're primarily interested in visiting cities and towns a state or two away, or you want to make use of the air traffic control system and fly really long distances on instruments, or you have a burning desire to get into aerobatics, you're better off receiving your initial flight instruction in a landplane. You can always add a seaplane rating to your pilot certificate later.

If, on the other hand, your idea of flying is to head for a remote lake for a weekend of fishing surrounded by spectacular, unspoiled scenery, or perhaps to spend a day digging for clams on a distant, deserted beach, you should think about using a floatplane for your primary instruction.

THE INSURANCE PROBLEM

There is another difference between landplanes and floatplanes you should be aware of—insurance. Let's say you receive your private certificate at a land-based flight school. After filling out and signing a form that says that you understand and will comply with the school's insurance requirements, you are free to rent their airplanes for your own use, be it a short, local flight or a three-day cross-country trip. Any damage that might occur to the airplane will be covered, less the deductible amount you're responsible for, by the flight school's insurance policy. The insurance on an airplane itself is called *hull insurance*, and a hull insurance policy for a landplane is fairly reasonable in cost. Because the flight school can afford to insure its aircraft, it is willing to let you rent them for an extended period of time and take them on cross-country flights.

Unfortunately, this is not the case with floatplanes. Most flight schools carry *liability insurance*, which covers the occupants of their planes, but hull insurance is incredibly expensive, and many operators simply can't afford it. Consequently, their floatplanes are uninsured, which means they—the owners—have to pay the cost of repairing any damage, regardless of why it occurred. So while a floatplane flight school will teach you to fly, or give you the instruction necessary to obtain a seaplane rating, most of them will not rent you a floatplane for your own use after you graduate because of the risk involved. The few flight schools that do rent out their floatplanes generally have restrictions on where you can take their planes and the length of time you can keep them. You may also have to sign an agreement stating that for the time you are renting one of their floatplanes, you will be responsible for it. In other words, you break it, you pay for it.

Each flight school handles the insurance problem differently. The *Water Flying Annual*, published by the Seaplane Pilots Association, lists every seaplane flight school in the United States and Canada and indicates which schools have solo rates on their planes. A copy of the *Water Flying Annual* can be obtained directly from the Seaplane Pilots Association at 421 Aviation Way, Frederick, Maryland 21701.

According to the insurance companies, the reason for the extremely high hull insurance rates on floatplanes is simple. If a landplane is damaged, it doesn't go anywhere, and unless it's completely wrecked, it can generally be repaired. A floatplane, on the other hand, can become a total loss as a result of what is actually very minor damage, or at least that's what the insurance companies claim. They've decided that a damaged floatplane usually *sinks*, adding salvage and water-damage costs to the total cost of repairing the original damage, however slight it might have been. Floatplane accident statistics do not necessarily support the insurance companies' claim, but insurance rates remain high nevertheless, and the debate between floatplane operators and insurance companies continues.

CHOOSING A FLIGHT SCHOOL

The ideal flight school should be big enough to offer all the facilities and services you'll need and small enough to give you the personal attention you should have (Fig. 5-1). Of the two, the latter is

Fig. 5-1. *Instructor and charter pilot Neal Ratti explains the purpose of the stabilizing fin on a Beaver to a new student.*

more important. There's nothing more valuable than good, personalized flight instruction, and this can often make up for a lack of fancy facilities.

It's also important that the flight instruction staff, even if it's only one person, actually has the time to give instruction. Many floatplane schools also do charter work, and there's nothing more frustrating than arriving at the lake only to be told that the airplane you were going to use is off on another assignment, or that your instructor had to make a last-minute charter flight.

I ran into this a lot while I was working toward my seaplane rating, but I was lucky in that the owner of the flight school, who was also my instructor, would often let me go with him on those spur-of-the-moment charters. He would even let me fly after he dropped off his paying passengers, enabling me to add several hours of free flying time to my logbook. So there *can* be advantages to having a lesson canceled in favor of a charter flight, but most of the time it's just a frustrating inconvenience. Make sure your instructor will be able to give you the kind of attention you should have and will be paying for.

Take the time to wander around and look over the flight school's airplanes. The age of the airplanes is not as important as their condition. I would rather fly an immaculate 1946 Taylorcraft than a run-down, abused, 1983 Cessna 172. Are the interiors of the airplanes in good shape? Are the exteriors kept clean and waxed? Are the aileron, flap, elevator, and rudder hinges well greased? This is very important on a floatplane, especially if it's operated on salt water. Check for surface corrosion, which looks like bubbles in the paint, especially on the tail surfaces. The presence of a lot of corrosion indicates poor maintenance. Do the floats, attachment hardware, and water rudder cables look like they're in good shape? I realize that, at this point, you might not be very familiar with floatplane hardware, but a frayed cable is a frayed cable! The condition of the airplanes and the facility in general will tell you a great deal about the quality of the instruction you're likely to receive at that school.

Fine, you say, but how do I go about finding a flight school that offers floatplane instruction? Again, the *Water Flying Annual* is your best bet. The flight school directory includes the types of floatplanes used at each school, the hourly rates, and the average length of time required to obtain a seaplane rating at each facility. The schools are listed by state, so it's a simple matter to find the facility nearest you.

DOCKS VS. RAMPS

Some flight schools operate their floatplanes from docks, and some operate from ramps. Which is better?

Ramps are certainly easier to operate from because the floatplane is simply run up onto the ramp nose-first—also because the maneuver is done under power, which means that wind direction and strength are rarely crucial factors. Prior to departure, the floatplane is pushed into the water, turned around, and pulled tail-first back up onto the ramp. The pilot can then take all the time

he or she wants getting in, adjusting the seat, and starting the engine. There's no need to hurry because the plane will not leave the ramp until power is applied.

Operating a floatplane from a dock, on the other hand, requires considerably more skill on the part of the pilot. The moment it's untied, the airplane is at the mercy of the winds and currents. In a good breeze, things can get pretty lively while you clamber in and get the engine started (Fig. 5-2). When you return, you're often faced with the challenge of trying to slip the plane into the last open spot on the dock, which is inevitably sandwiched between two other floatplanes.

Fig. 5-2. *Departing a dock crowded with floatplanes can be tricky. Fortunately, the wind was light the day this picture was taken at Kenmore Air's facility at the north end of Seattle's Lake Washington.*

Don't be intimidated, though. Personally, I think a dock makes the best learning environment. If you plan to do any cross-country floatplane flying after you get your rating, you'll find that docks are far more common than ramps. Many of the most interesting places to go in a floatplane have only boat facilities, so the more docking practice you can get, the better. If, however, the floatplane school in your area uses a ramp, don't despair. Just make sure the course of instruction includes plenty of docking experience using boat docks in the area for practice.

FLOATPLANE TRAINERS

Another question commonly asked is: "What's the best kind of floatplane to learn in?" I'm afraid there's no easy answer because just about anything from an ultralight to a de Havilland Twin Otter can be mounted on floats. The final decision is usually based on economics, but there are some other factors to consider as well.

Many people consider the Piper J-3 Cub and the venerable Cessna 150 to be the best primary trainers ever made. Both airplanes can be mounted on floats, but there are a couple of reasons why I don't think either one of them makes as good a trainer on water as it does on land. Both airplanes are underpowered when fitted with floats, and the floats themselves are rather small. The combination of small floats and low horsepower make both of these airplanes unsuitable for use in anything other than relatively calm water.

I don't mean to imply that the Cub and the 150 don't make good floatplanes. They do, but considering their limitations, I don't believe they are suited for dual instruction. In fact, two good-sized adults and a load of fuel could easily exceed either plane's gross weight.

Floatplanes need more horsepower than their wheeled counterparts to overcome the additional weight and drag of the floats and to pull the floatplane free of the water's suction and onto the step. The most popular floatplane trainers are the Cessna 172, especially the newer models with the 160-horsepower engine, and the Piper PA-18 Super Cub, which has a 150-horsepower engine (Fig. 5-3). The 150-horsepower Citabria is also used for instruction. Both the Super Cub and the Citabria, with their high horsepower-to-weight ratios and good load-carrying capabilities, are also used as working floatplanes by commercial operators. In fact, the Super Cub might well qualify as the most popular all-around bush plane in northern Canada and Alaska.

The Cessna 172, on the other hand, has some definite limitations as a floatplane. As a landplane, the 172 is a nice, economical, four-place airplane, with a useful load of 993 pounds.

Fig. 5-3. *The Piper PA-18 Super Cub is one of the most popular floatplane trainers around.* EDO Corp.

The floatplane version of the 172 has a useful load of only 634 pounds, 359 pounds less than the landplane. Three of the FAA's theoretical, 170-pound adults weigh a total of 510 pounds, leaving 124 pounds of useful load for fuel, or about 20 gallons. That's assuming the three people aren't taking anything heavier than a wallet apiece, of course. Any baggage carried will reduce the fuel load even more.

Four 170-pound passengers weigh a total of 680 pounds, or 46 pounds more than the floatplane's useful load, so the only time you'll ever get four adults into a float-equipped 172 is while it's sitting on the showroom floor. With only two people on board and just enough fuel for a lesson plus some reserve, however, the 172 makes a nice, economical floatplane trainer with adequate performance, and the floats are big enough to allow the student to safely get some rough water experience.

In my opinion, the 230-horsepower Cessna 180, or its 300-horsepower look-alike, the Cessna 185, are the ideal floatplane trainers. They are probably the most widely used commercial floatplanes, and their powerful engines, constant-speed propellers, and large floats enable them to take on all kinds of wind and water conditions. Unfortunately, they are fairly expensive to rent, especially when you add in the cost of an instructor.

Of course, if money is no object, and you really want to go first class, you could get your seaplane rating in a de Havilland Beaver. With its 450-horsepower Pratt & Whitney R-985 radial, eight-place cabin, and 22-foot-long floats, you'd be getting your rating in one of the best floatplanes ever made. In reality, though, the flight school in your area will probably use a Cessna 172, a Piper Super Cub, or a Citabria for flight instruction, any one of which makes an excellent trainer that's also a lot of fun to fly.

FLOATPLANE FLIGHT INSTRUCTORS DEFINED

There is really no difference between a good landplane instructor and a good floatplane instructor. The basic elements are the same.

A good instructor should have a thorough knowledge of what he or she is trying to teach and a way of passing that knowledge on to you that is both understandable and interesting. A good instructor should be genuinely interested in teaching and not just trying to "build hours" toward that hoped-for airline job.

A good instructor knows just when to take over the controls; too soon or too often, and the student's confidence can be seriously eroded; too late, and an accident might be the result. It's a fine line and probably one of the hardest decisions an instructor has to make. Patience is important too because something that is almost second nature to an instructor might be frustratingly difficult for a student to master.

There's no way an instructor, however dedicated, is going to prepare you for every situation you might encounter. The floatplane environment encompasses a lot of variables. Every takeoff, every landing, and every docking will be different, even if you take off, land, and dock at the same places every day. Wind and water conditions are constantly changing, and the dock that's empty today might be crowded tomorrow. Add to this the need to be constantly alert for boat wakes, currents, floating debris, and other surprises, and you can see how complex the world of float flying can get. The best your instructor can do is see that you

thoroughly understand the basics so that you can safely begin adding to your floatplane skills through your own experience (Fig. 5-4).

Fig. 5-4. *Neal Ratti explains the cold-start procedure for the Pratt & Whitney R-985 radial engine used on the de Havilland Beaver. His student will need to pump the engine primer at least five or six strokes before she can hit the start switch.*

Earlier, I mentioned that many of the same companies that offer floatplane instruction also specialize in air taxi work and that you should make sure your instruction won't suffer because of it. There is a definite advantage, however, to having a working charter pilot for an instructor. Charter pilots run into just about every situation imaginable, and they often will pass techniques and "tricks of the trade" on to their students, along with examples of things not to do. When a high-time charter pilot tells you about the time he sat for six hours on a mudflat in a Beaver full of irate passengers because the tide went out faster than he did, you'll probably make a mental note to always carry a current tide chart with you and use it.

You can't put a price on experience. I learned many of the techniques described in this book from a bunch of air taxi pilots who fly de Havilland Beavers, turbine Otters, and Cessna 180s along the coasts of Washington, British Columbia, and Alaska, fighting fog, rain, snow, and 10-foot tides. Occasionally they have a nice day. If you hang around people like this long enough, you're bound to pick up some valuable information, so pay attention if your instructor starts telling you about the time he flew a creaking, old, overloaded Norseman into a high mountain lake that was so small, the only way he could take off again was to . . . and so on. His story might get you out of a tight spot someday.

6

Launching the floatplane

BEFORE WE DO ANYTHING with a floatplane, we have to put it in the water. Most floatplane operators sleep a lot better at night if their planes are pulled out of the water when they aren't being used. For one thing, all floats other than brand new ones seem to leak a little, and if a plane is left in the water for any length of time, the floats could conceivably accumulate enough water to pull the airplane under. Wakes from passing boats can slam floats against docks, and a plane's constant motion could possibly chafe through its mooring lines. High winds can be a threat if the wings aren't tied down, and heavy snowfalls have been known to sink unattended floatplanes.

OUT OF THE WATER

As you will see in later chapters, there are techniques for preventing all of these disasters if you find yourself forced to leave your airplane on the water, but the best safeguard is to get the plane out of the water completely. There are basically two ways to do so. The first and easiest is to run it up on a wooden ramp after each flight, using just enough power to pull the floats clear of the water before the plane comes to a stop. This is the method used most often by private floatplane owners who keep their planes on their own property and by the smaller commercial operators whose waterfront space is limited (Fig. 6-1). Although simple, there is a proper procedure for ramping a floatplane, which is examined in detail in chapter 13.

Fig. 6-1. *The owner of this Piper Tri-Pacer is able to keep his plane at home, thanks to this backyard ramp.*

The second form of dry storage is a little more complicated and is used primarily by large commercial operators. The floatplane is positioned over a submerged platform, usually a railcar or elevator. The platform lifts the plane out of the water, and a modified forklift is used to pick up the plane and move it to a tiedown area. Most operators prefer to rest the floats on a couple of boards instead of setting the plane directly on the pavement. The wings can then be tied down to rings set in the pavement, concrete-filled oil drums, or some other form of heavy weights.

A variation of the forklift method involves the use of a small dolly that fits under the airplane's floats. An empty dolly is fastened to the elevator and goes down with it. The floatplane is positioned over the submerged dolly, and when the elevator is raised, the dolly comes up under the floats. The elevator stops level with the dock or parking area, the dolly is unfastened, and the plane is wheeled by hand to a parking place. The procedure is reversed when it's time to put the plane back in the water.

INTO THE WATER

If the floatplane you're going to fly is still in its tie-down position, you'll have to get someone on the line crew to put it in the water for you. Driving a forklift with an expensive floatplane balanced on the forks is a real art and not something you should undertake yourself. The specially designed forks are very long and are surfaced with wood, carpet, or rubber to avoid marring the airplane. In addition to the usual lifting and tilting movements common to all forklifts, some of them have been modified so the width between the forks can be adjusted from the cab. The forklift is positioned facing the nose of the plane and driven forward until the forks are under both spreader bars between the floats. The operator then adjusts the width of the forks so they will contact the spreader bars as close to the floats as possible. If the forks are set too close to the center of the spreader bars, the bars could be bent when the plane is lifted.

The driver then gently brings the forks up under the spreader bars and lifts the airplane. In a crowded parking area, the plane will have to be lifted quite high so its wings will clear the tails of the airplanes around it. It's quite a sight to see a big de Havilland Beaver perched 10 feet in the air, rocking and swaying on its trip to the railcar (Fig. 6-2).

Fig. 6-2. *A Beaver on its way to the railcar. The forklift has been equipped with special forks that can be adjusted from the cab to exactly match the width between the floats. The forks are surfaced with wood so they will not mar the undersides of the spreader bars.*

Once the floatplane is set on the railcar or elevator, the operator will lower it into the water until the plane is floating on its own, at which point it can be pulled down the dock and tied up. The line crew might have more planes to put in the water after yours, so if you are the one responsible for mooring your plane to the dock after it's been put in the water, make sure you leave enough space for the other floatplanes as they come off the lift.

If your floatplane is on a ramp, the launching procedure is somewhat different. Actually, you're not so much launching it as turning it around so you can pull it back up the ramp tail-first. The next chapter will cover the proper preflight inspection procedures for a floatplane, but because it's easier to preflight a ramped floatplane before it's turned around, we'll assume you've already performed your inspection. Make sure the water rudders are retracted (up) before sliding the floatplane backwards down the ramp. If they're down, they could dig into the wood and suffer severe damage.

The floats will slide easier on the wooden ramp if it's wet, so throw a couple of bucketfuls of water under and behind the floats to soak down the boards. Before you untie the plane and get ready to push it backwards into the water, fasten one end of a long line to the stern cleat on one of the floats, and hold on to the other end. Once the plane is in the water, this line is the only way you're going to get it back, so hang on to it.

Although you wouldn't think so, there is a trick to pushing a floatplane backwards down a ramp. Don't lift up on the bows of the floats as you push. If you do, all the weight of the plane will be put on the rear edges of the float steps, and they'll dig into the wood, making it very difficult to slide the plane backwards. Many floats have little rounded keel extensions designed to protect the sharp trailing edges of the steps, but these extensions will dig into the wood, too, if you lift up on the floats. The idea is to push straight back, which keeps the weight of the plane distributed along the length of the forebody keel of each float. True, there is more float surface in contact with the ramp, and theoretically there should be more friction, but the weight at any given spot along the keel is less, and the plane slides easier. Once the plane starts to slide, make sure you give it enough of a push so it will drift well clear of the ramp.

When the plane is floating free, you need to turn it around and pull it back up on the ramp tail-first so you can get in and start the engine. The reason you couldn't do so before is obvious: With the plane pointed up the ramp, you could get in, but you couldn't go anywhere.

Now you can see the reason why the line you are hopefully still hanging onto is fastened to a stern cleat. When you pull on it, the floatplane will turn around (Fig. 6-3). If you had fastened the line to one of the bow cleats, the plane would come back to the ramp nose-first, and you'd be back where you started.

You don't need to pull the floatplane very far up the ramp this time. In fact, most of each float will remain doing just that: floating. All you want to do is keep the plane from sliding forward into the water before you're ready to go. As you pull the plane in toward you, the tail will extend back over the ramp. To securely "park" the floatplane after the rear of the floats have contacted the

Fig. 6-3. *Before pushing this Beaver backwards off the ramp, Neal attached a long line to one of the stern cleats. With the plane now floating free, he is using this line to turn the plane around prior to tailing it back up onto the ramp. Note the water rudders in their retracted position.*

ramp, position yourself in front of and facing the leading edge of the horizontal stabilizer. Put your hands under the stabilizer close to where it joins the fuselage and preferably under one of the spars or stiffeners. Lift up and back to raise the rear of the floats and set them farther up the ramp. Again, make sure the water rudders are up before you do this step. Depending on the angle of the ramp and the weight of the floatplane, you might have to repeat this lifting maneuver a couple of times before the plane is securely resting on the wood. Now you and your instructor or passengers can get in, and you can begin going through your prestart checklist (Fig. 6-4).

A word of caution about ramps: They get wet a lot and they're usually slippery, especially at the water's edge. This can be a real advantage when you're driving a floatplane up the ramp or sliding it off, but when you're working around the plane, be very careful of your footing. Once you start to slide, it's hard to stop. The ramp I learned on was so slick and mossy, a student who slid into the water one day was unable to pull herself back up until someone threw her a line. Ducks and geese are particularly fond of seaplane ramps because the ramps make it easier

Fig. 6-4. *The Beaver has been turned around and is tailed up onto the ramp, ready for loading.*

for them to get in and out of the water, too, and the droppings they leave in gratitude don't do much to improve the situation.

Those of you operating from ramps have already done your preflight inspections, but the rest of you are still standing on the dock next to your airplanes, waiting, so let's take a look at what goes into a proper and thorough preflight inspection of a typical floatplane.

7

The preflight inspection

ONE OF THE BEST WAYS to guarantee a safe and enjoyable flight in any airplane is to perform a thorough preflight inspection. It's better to be on the ground when you discover a problem than to be in the air. A proper preflight inspection is an absolute necessity when you're flying a floatplane. Everything is riding, literally, on your floats, and you must make certain that they are watertight and that their attachment hardware is strong and secure. Although the preflight checks of the fuel, oil, pitot-static, and flight control systems are essentially identical to those you would perform on a landplane, there are a couple of things to keep in mind when you're checking these items on a floatplane.

First of all, try not to fall in the water. I've seen at least one person step off a dock in an attempt to get a closer look at the outboard aileron hinge. Unless you're preflighting a ramped floatplane, the water is never more than a couple of steps away. As noted in the previous chapter, ramps have their little problems, too, so be careful.

If you get lucky and the floatplane you're about to fly hasn't been put in the water yet, you might be able to talk the line crew into letting you perform your preflight inspection before they launch the plane. Now you can give the plane a good going over without the worry of stepping off the dock or slipping on the ramp. For now, however, I'll assume the airplane is already in the water and securely moored alongside one of the flight school's docks.

There are probably as many different ways to perform a preflight inspection as there are pilots, but the order in which things are inspected is not nearly as important as the fact that they *are* inspected. There is an advantage to developing a routine, however, because it will keep you from overlooking something. Your instructor will undoubtedly have a favorite way to perform the preflight and, in time, you'll come up with your own system. In the meantime, let me describe how I was taught to do it as a way of introducing you to the items you will need to inspect.

THE COCKPIT

The first thing you should do when you open the door to the cockpit is reach across and open the other door. In order to inspect the other side of the airplane, you're going to have to turn it around, and there's nothing more annoying than turning the airplane around only to find the other door locked.

Remove the control locks and make sure the magnetos are off. Next, turn on the master switch to check the amount of fuel in the tanks. Some airplanes, such as the Beaver, have a separate switch for the engine instruments, so don't forget to turn that on, as well. While the master switch is still on, lower the flaps if they are electric. If the flaps are manual, as in the Cessna 180/185 series of airplanes, or manual/hydraulic, like those in the Beaver, turn off the master switch, and lower the flaps with the appropriate lever. Make sure the water rudders are down, and lower them if they're not. Finally, get the bilge pump out of the cabin and set it on the dock.

On some radial-engined airplanes, like the Beaver, the oil filler pipe, with its cap and dipstick, protrudes through the firewall and into the cabin. While you're up in the cockpit, check the oil level, and make sure you put the oil cap back on securely. After you start the engine, the pressure in the tank will increase, and if the cap is not fastened tightly, it will blow off, covering the front seat occupants with hot engine oil.

THE PROPELLER

I like to preflight each side of a floatplane in two stages: first the airframe and engine, then the float system. Starting at the front, check the prop spinner, and make sure it's fastened securely. Next, carefully inspect the propeller for erosion (Fig. 7-1). The effect of spray on a metal propeller is almost like sand blasting, and if the tiny pits are not dressed out, they will deepen until the metal actually begins to split. If this is allowed to continue, the propeller will not only become less efficient, but a crack could develop that could weaken the blade and lead to eventual failure.

Incidentally, raindrops can also erode propellers, and some pilots reduce engine rpm if they have to fly through rain for any length of time. Unfortunately, floatplane propellers are subjected to the greatest amount of spray while they are turning at maximum rpm during takeoff, and be-

Fig. 7-1. *Checking the propeller for spray erosion.*

cause the water drops found in spray generally are much larger than raindrops, propeller erosion is virtually unavoidable.

The pitting that results can be dressed out by honing the leading edge of the prop with a smooth steel bar to even out the rough surface without removing any metal. If the initial dimpling of the propeller is allowed to develop into deeper pits, the leading edge will have to be filed smooth, a process which *does* remove metal. Care must be taken to file each blade equally. If one blade has more metal removed than any other blades, the propeller could become slightly unbalanced and begin to vibrate.

As you're pulling the propeller through to check the blades, it's a good idea to turn it in the same direction it turns when it's running. One of the country's best engine mechanics told me it's easier on the valve cams if the engine is always turned in the same direction. Be very careful when you do this. If there's a fault in the ignition switch, the magnetos could be "hot," and the engine could fire as you pull it through. Stand well behind the propeller as you're pulling on it. You'll eliminate the possibility of an accident completely if you make it a practice to assume the engine will kick over whenever you touch the prop, so take the appropriate steps to keep yourself and your passengers well clear of the line of fire.

If you're flying an ultralight or kitplane on floats, be aware that water erodes the leading edges of wooden propellers extremely fast. In fact, a wooden propeller could lose a noticeable amount of efficiency after only one or two exposures to spray. Several manufacturers of ultralight and kitplane propellers have come up with solutions to the erosion problem, so if you've attached floats to your plane or are thinking of doing so, you would do well to consider replacing the standard wooden propeller with a prop specifically designed to resist spray erosion.

One manufacturer inlays a "steel composite" leading edge into its scimitar-shaped wooden propellers, and several others build the entire propeller out of composite materials. In each case, the problem of spray erosion is dramatically reduced. Many kitplanes use metal propellers, and they should be checked in the same manner as the props used on the larger floatplanes.

THE ENGINE

While you're up front checking the prop, take a look at the engine, too. If you're preflighting an airplane with a closely cowled, horizontally opposed engine, you won't be able to see very much of it, but what you're looking for are signs of corrosion or rust that could indicate poor maintenance and possible engine problems. It's not uncommon to see a little bit of surface rust, especially on the cooling fins, but be careful if the engine is heavily encrusted with rust or corrosion.

You should be able to see the spark-plug wires going to the first cylinder in each bank, so make sure they appear to be in good condition. Insulation that's cracked or split is a good indication of a worn-out wiring harness and possible ignition problems.

On larger floatplanes such as the Beaver, make sure the oil cooler and carburetor air scoops are unobstructed. If the airplane has cowl flaps, check the operating linkages for signs of damage or wear. Wiggle the exhaust stack or stacks back and forth. If they're loose, they should be checked over by a mechanic. You don't need carbon monoxide leaking into the cabin during your flight.

If the floatplane you're preflighting has a radial engine, it's easy to get a good look at its general condition because most of it's sitting right there in front of you. The magnetos, fuel pump, carburetor, oil tanks, and other engine accessories are all mounted on the rear of the engine, however, so you won't be able to get a look at them unless you remove the cowls completely, which is a time-consuming and tedious process. Radial cowls come off easily enough, but they're a real pain to put back on, and they never seem to fit right.

There is an additional preflight duty to be performed on a radial if it hasn't been run for some time, and this is to drain any accumulated oil out of the lower cylinders. Any oil left in the engine after shutdown will eventually drain down into the lower cylinders and collect there. Given time, some of it will work its way past the piston rings and into the combustion chambers. If this oil isn't removed, a hydraulic lock could occur when the engine is turned over by the starter, and the resulting pressures could send the offending cylinder heads to the bottom of the lake. To remove any oil that might have accumulated in the lower combustion chambers, remove one spark plug from each of the lower cylinders, and turn the engine over by hand. If there is any oil present, it will drain out the spark plug hole.

If the oil dipstick is on the side of the engine closest to the dock, check the oil level. If it's on the other side, you'll have to wait until you turn the floatplane around to check it. If the airplane is equipped with a fuel sump drain, this is a good time to make sure the fuel in the line is uncontaminated. If possible, try to catch the fuel in a container of some sort so you don't dump raw fuel into the water. You can throw it out later on the dock where it will evaporate, or if the fuel is clean and you're really budget-conscious, you can put it back into the tank.

THE FUEL SYSTEM

If your floatplane has fuel tanks in the wings, climb up on the fueling steps and visually check the fuel level. While you're up there, check for any damage to the wings. Be on the lookout for dents and dings in the leading edge that might have been caused by scraping or hitting the tall pilings found in many boat harbors. Obviously, you'll have to wait until you turn the airplane around before checking the fuel tank on the other side.

Not all floatplanes carry their fuel in the wings. De Havilland Beavers and Otters, for example, have their fuel tanks in the belly, and the fuel caps and filler necks are located behind a hinged panel aft of the pilot's door. Because of the plumbing layout, it's impossible to visually check the amount of fuel in the tanks, so you'll have to trust the gauges in the cockpit. All you can do during your preflight inspection is make sure the filler caps are fastened securely.

Next, drain some fuel from the tank, or tanks, into the sample cup, and make sure it's free of dirt, rust, and water. This step is especially important if the plane has been fueled with gas from drums or 5-gallon cans. The marine environment is not all that clean, and even large fuel storage tanks and transfer pipes can become contaminated with water and rust, particularly if they are near salt water. Determining the cleanliness of your fuel is a particularly important step if your floatplane has a fuel-injected engine. A tiny piece of dirt or rust can cause a very big problem if it manages to plug an injector.

THE PITOT-STATIC SYSTEM

Check the pitot tube for blockage and make sure it hasn't been damaged or loosened by striking a piling or other obstruction. Remember also to check the static port. This often overlooked item is very important, because if it should become plugged with wax or dirt, all your pressure instruments will read erroneously. Static port locations vary, and you might have to refer to the owner's manual to find the exact location of the port on your particular airplane. Incidentally, don't be alarmed if the airspeed indicator jerks erratically when you fly through a rainstorm. The jerks are caused by rainwater momentarily blocking the static port.

THE CONTROL SURFACES

Check the flap tracks and extending mechanism. They should be well-greased, and the adjustment and lock nuts on the control rod should be tight. The ailerons, if you can reach them, should move freely without binding. Some floatplanes, such as the Cessna 172, have spring-loaded interconnects between the ailerons and the rudder, so you might feel some resistance as you move the ailerons, but there should be no obvious binding. The aileron control rod should be free of any longitudinal play, and the adjustment and lock nuts should be tight. If you can see the aileron hinges, make sure the cotter pins that keep the hinge pins from falling out are in place and that the hinges themselves are thoroughly greased. Finally, check the trailing edge of the wing for damage. Careless pilots sometimes run the wing backwards into an object while they're sailing or turning the plane around.

As long as you're checking control surfaces, walk back and take a look at the horizontal tail. (If you're preflighting an Otter, you'll need a 12-foot stepladder for this part.) The elevator should travel between full up and full down without binding. Make sure the trim tab is working properly. As with the ailerons, the elevator and trim tab hinge points should be well greased.

The horizontal tail is often completely enveloped in spray during takeoffs and landings, and it's not just the outside skin that gets soaked. The water will find its way to the inner surfaces as well, and if the plane is operated on salt water, severe corrosion could be the result. To combat this corrosion, the floatplane must be thoroughly hosed off with fresh water after the last flight of the day, with particular attention given to the tail. If a floatplane has been poorly maintained, corrosion might begin to pit the outer surfaces of the horizontal and vertical tails, and the paint will start to blister and flake off. Usually, however, corrosion forms where it's difficult to see—in the nooks and crannies around the spars, stringers, and other structural members of the airplane. One place to check for corrosion is in the gap between the stabilizer and the elevator. Depending on the construction of the airplane, you might be able to see some of the inner structure and check it for evidence of corrosion.

Don't feel you have to include a magnifying glass in your flight bag, though. Most floatplanes used for flight instruction get a lot of attention, and any potentially serious corrosion is usually discovered and eliminated long before it becomes a problem. The main thing to look for is corrosion evidence on the outer skin surfaces, as it might be warning you of a much more dangerous situation inside the plane.

The warmer and more humid the climate, the faster corrosion will develop and spread, so if you're flying in Florida, you'll need to be more wary of corrosion than if you are flying in Canada or Alaska.

THE FLOAT SYSTEM

After you've finished checking the first side of the airframe, go back to the nose, where you will now begin to inspect the hardware that makes it all possible: the float system. As we learned earlier, the float system is made up of the floats themselves, the spreader bars, float struts, bracing wires, and water rudders with their steering and retraction cables, brackets, and pulleys. Each component should be inspected carefully before flight because the safety of the airplane is dependent upon their integrity.

Pump out the floats

Starting at the bow of the float, check each compartment for water using the bilge pump, which should be kept in the floatplane at all times. If the float is equipped with built-in bilge pump down-tubes, operate the pump in the manner described in chapter 3. The recessed opening at the top of each down-tube is kept plugged with a soft rubber ball. The ball keeps spray, rain, and waves that break over the deck from running down the tubes into the float compartments. To prevent the rubber balls from being lost overboard, they are fastened to the float decks with short lengths of string. A word of caution: The balls do not float, and if the string is broken, it's all too easy to pop a ball out of its tube only to watch it bounce overboard and sink out of sight. Pull them out carefully, and make sure they are securely tied to the float before laying them down on the deck.

If the floats on the airplane you're flying don't have built-in bilge pump down-tubes, you'll have to remove an inspection cover from the top of each compartment and insert the pump directly into the float to remove any accumulated water. If the airplane doesn't have a long enough bilge pump on board, the access hatches in the floats are large enough to permit you to scoop out the water with a small bucket, or to swab it out with a sponge (Fig. 7-2).

Water in the floats

Floats always seem to have a little water in them, so don't worry if the pump brings up a cup or two of water out of each compartment. Water can enter a float several ways. It can leak in around the rubber balls plugging the down-tubes (the balls don't always fit perfectly). It also can seep in around the access-hatch covers in the float deck. Another source of water is the condensation of moist air on the cold metal inside the float. And finally, water can enter through float seams that have worked open.

Even under ideal conditions, floats receive quite a pounding as they skim over the water at

Fig. 7-2. *Some floats don't have built-in bilge pump-down tubes, so you'll have to check for water by removing the access hatches in the float deck.*

speeds of up to 50 and 60 knots, and eventually some of the seams in aluminum floats will begin to work open. This situation is not as bad as it sounds, for while a little water might begin to seep in through an unsealed seam, the strength of the riveted seam is not at all compromised. It just isn't quite as watertight as it used to be. This is more of a problem on older floats that used a zinc chromate putty as a seam sealer. The putty has no adhesive properties, unlike the sealing compounds used on the floats built today, which bond to the aluminum and do a much better job keeping the seams watertight despite the pounding and flexing of the floats.

Because a floatplane travels fastest while riding on the step, that part of the float is subjected to the greatest pounding, and the seams will generally begin to leak there first. Floatplanes that are used for training spend much of their time taking off, landing, and step-taxiing, so don't be surprised if you discover a fair amount of water in the float compartment directly above the step. If you do pump a lot of water out of one of the float compartments, you don't necessarily have to cancel the flight, but the fact that one of the compart-

ments contained a lot of water should be reported to the flight school. The school might already be aware of the problem, but because resealing a float is an expensive and time-consuming process, they might be trying to make it through the season before pulling the plane out of service for repairs. There's nothing wrong with this; just make sure you remember to pump out the floats before each flight.

The rear float compartment is also susceptible to water accumulation. The movement of the water rudders tends to put pressure on the seams around the stern of each float, and they could eventually open up slightly, allowing water to seep in. Leaving the water rudders down accidentally during a takeoff or while step-taxiing can also cause the float seams to work open. The floatplane's rapid forward motion through the water will cause the rudders to bang violently against their stops, stressing the rear bulkhead seams.

Why is it so important that all the water be removed from the floats? For one thing, any water trapped in the floats will reduce their buoyancy, and as the compartments fill up, the floatplane will ride lower and lower in the water. While the regulations state that floats must continue to support the airplane with any two compartments flooded per float, a badly leaking float could eventually fill completely and drag the plane under.

Water weighs approximately seven pounds per gallon. Any water trapped in the floats is weight the airplane is being asked to carry, and the plane's useful load will be reduced accordingly. If you neglect to pump out the floats, you obviously won't know how much water—and weight—is in them. If you then load your airplane with passengers, baggage, and fuel, you can see how the plane's gross weight could be exceeded without your knowing it. Almost every hangar flying session includes at least one story about someone plowing madly around a lake unable to take off because the airplane's floats were full of water. These stories all end in one of two ways. The pilot either returns to the dock and sheepishly pumps out the water, or the plane ends up on the rocks or in the trees at the end of the lake. Neither situation is desirable, so pump out the floats before you cast off.

While the image of a waterlogged floatplane frantically dashing back and forth as it tries to take off is rather comical, there is another more dangerous condition that can be brought about by a flooded float compartment. If water has accumulated in any of the rear compartments, its weight could conceivably move the airplane's center of gravity aft of its certified envelope. This condition would be most likely to occur in floatplanes with long, spacious cabins such as the Cessna 206 and the de Havilland Beaver and Otter. These planes are often loaded to the extreme aft limit of their center of gravity envelopes to begin with, and any extra weight back in the tails of the floats could create a serious out-of-balance condition. Because the heavily loaded airplane will be riding low in the water anyway, the pilot might not notice that the tails of the floats are a little lower than they should be. Too often, a center-of-gravity problem does not become apparent until the airplane is airborne, at which time it might be too late. Make sure you check *all* the float compartments for water, not just the ones that are easily accessible.

THE ATTACHMENT HARDWARE

As you pump your way aft along the float, check the spreader bars and float struts as you come to them. You're primarily looking for cracks in the fittings that attach these components to the floats and the airframe. If you spot a crack, report it immediately. It might turn out to be just a scratch or crack in the paint, but don't let that stop you from reporting anything that looks suspicious. Most floatplane operators would rather send a mechanic out to investigate a paint scratch than send a salvage boat out to recover a capsized airplane.

If the floatplane you're flying is equipped with brace wires, check their attachment fittings too, and make sure the wires themselves are tight. A loose brace wire will allow the float system to flex and vibrate, possibly causing one or more of the strut or spreader bar attachment fittings to fail.

Make sure all the attachment bolts and lock nuts are tight and in place and that none of them are badly rusted. Most float struts are fitted with boarding steps up to the cabin, and they should be checked for cracks, too.

You might notice that many of the floatplane's fittings are covered with a kind of yellow or brown varnish. This is *paralketone*, and it's applied as a liquid over exposed parts to prevent rust and corrosion. When it dries, it forms a protective barrier to keep water from contacting the metal. Moving parts such as the rudder cable pulleys and pulley bracket hinges, are usually coated with grease.

THE WATER RUDDERS

As we saw earlier, the water rudders are operated by cables that are either attached to the floatplane's air rudder or directly to the rudder pedals in the cockpit. A separate set of cables retracts the rudders. The steering and retraction cables are guided around corners by brackets and pulleys attached to the exterior of the floats and airframe, and it's important that these pulleys rotate smoothly. As you work your way down the float, check the pulleys for freedom of movement, and make sure their mounting brackets are securely fastened to the float, strut, or airframe.

Inspect the cables, too. Look for signs of wear near the pulleys, and check the cable ends for fraying. The crimp fittings used to fasten the cables together should show no signs of slipping.

After you've pumped out the last compartment, inspect the water rudder itself. Make sure the steering cables are securely attached to the steering bar at the top of the rudder post, and that the retraction cable is firmly fastened to the rudder. Pull the water rudder up and check for damage. The rudder should hinge up and down smoothly, and the blade should not be bent or cracked.

It's important to check for weeds or branches that might be caught in the water rudders. I once rented a floatplane that had just been taxied through a weed bed on its way back to the dock. Although I checked all the cables, I didn't bother to pull up and inspect the rudders themselves, so I never saw the long streamers of water milfoil hooked on each blade. As I taxied away from the dock, I pushed down on the right rudder pedal to begin a turn toward the main part of the lake. Nothing happened. I had the pedal all the way down, but the plane kept plowing straight ahead. I opened the door and looked back at the water rudder on my side of the airplane. Even though I was pushing the pedal clear to the floor, the rudder was pointing straight back. I frantically seesawed the pedals back and forth, but the water rudder wouldn't budge. Finally, I saw the long streamers of weeds trailing behind the airplane. They were just under the surface, and their weight was holding the spring-loaded water rudders centered. The only thing I could do was shut off the engine, walk back to the tail of each float in turn, and remove the weeds. Fortunately, there was no wind, so I was in no danger of drifting into anything expensive. The only casualties were my shoes, which got soaked as the tail of first one float and then the other was forced underwater by my 200-plus pounds as I removed the weeds.

This situation could have been much more serious had it occurred in a crowded harbor where the inability to steer might have resulted in a collision with a boat, a dock, or another seaplane. Remember, a floatplane has no brakes, so all your defensive driving must be done with the water rudders.

As long as we're on the subject of weeds, you might be wondering what to do if you pick up weeds or branches with the water rudders after you leave the dock. Raising and lowering the rudders several times in quick succession will often knock the debris clear. If this doesn't work, and if you have plenty of room, add power until your floatplane is on the step. The increased speed through the water might tear the weeds loose. Remember to raise the water rudders before you do this, however, so they won't be damaged. If all else fails,

you can always shut down the engine, climb out onto the floats, and manually remove the debris from the water rudders. This procedure works every time, but you'll probably get your feet wet.

TURNING THE PLANE AROUND

After you've finished preflighting one side of the floatplane, you'll have to turn it around to inspect the other side. It might not be practical, or possible, to turn a large floatplane like a de Havilland Beaver or Otter around, so you'll have to climb through the cabin to the outboard float. You can't get a good look at the wing and tail assemblies from there, but at least you can pump out the float and check its attachment hardware, water rudder, and related cables. If you're flying a smaller floatplane, however, get in the habit of turning it around to ensure a thorough preflight inspection.

Before you untie the plane, determine the direction and strength of the wind. The plane will drift a little with the wind as it's turning, and you want to make sure the wings and tail will clear any pilings, boats, or other floatplanes that might be nearby.

After making sure the plane will clear any obstacles, untie the lines and push the nose of the plane out from the dock. Always push the nose out, as this will bring the tail back over the dock and give you something to hold onto as the plane turns (Fig. 7-3). Also, as the tail swings over the dock, you'll get a chance to inspect the rudder and vertical fin—items you couldn't get close to before. Don't let the water rudders hit the dock as the plane turns. If they get caught between the tires or in the planking, they could be bent, or the steering mechanism could be damaged.

As the plane continues to turn, walk forward, take hold of the wingtip grabline as it comes in over the dock, and pull the plane in sideways toward the dock. When the float is against the dock, fasten the mooring lines on the float struts to the dock cleats and begin your inspection of this side of the airplane.

Fig. 7-3. *The proper way to turn a floatplane around at the dock: Always push the nose out and turn the plane by its tail. This will give you better control of the plane, especially if there's a wind blowing.*

If the floatplane you're flying doesn't have grab lines hanging from the wingtips, or if it's windy, you might want to tie a long line to one of the float cleats and hold on to it, just to make sure the airplane doesn't get away from you. The important thing is to hold on to some part of the airplane at all times. There's nothing more embarrassing than watching your floatplane drift gently out into the middle of the harbor while you helplessly jump up and down on the dock and wave your arms. The plane will not come back when you do this, so it's best not to let it get away from you in the first place.

One of the dumbest things I've done so far with a floatplane is to try to turn one around at a dock by pushing the tail out instead of the nose. The Cessna 172 I was preflighting was tied up between a Beaver and another Cessna, and I barely had enough room to turn my plane around. All three planes were moored with their tails to the 10-knot wind that was blowing off the lake, and I was afraid that in the time it took me to turn my plane around, it would be blown forward into the floatplane in front of me. After pondering the situation (not long enough, as it turned out), I came up

with this great scheme of fastening a line to the bow cleat of the outboard float, untying the plane, and pushing the tail out from the dock. In theory, the wind would push the tail of the plane around as I pulled on the line attached to the outboard float, and the plane would pivot neatly around without drifting anywhere. It was a good theory, but it didn't work.

Oh, the plane pivoted around all right, but between my pulling on the rope, and the 10-knot wind pushing on the tail, the plane spun around at an alarming rate of speed. On top of that, it still drifted downwind, and only blind luck kept the downwind wingtip of my plane from slamming into the tail of the plane in front. Unfortunately, after letting my wingtip escape unscathed, blind luck went home, and the tails of the two airplanes collided. Only the quick action of a nearby instructor kept the situation from getting totally out of hand, and thanks to his intervention, no damage was done to either floatplane.

I include this little episode because I learned two important things from it. First, never turn a floatplane around at a dock by pushing the tail out, especially if the tail is pointing into the wind. Even if there had been no floatplane tied up in front of me, my plane would have pivoted into the dock with considerable force, possibly damaging the floats or their attachment hardware.

Second, I learned (again) that things can get out of control very fast, and the importance of thinking through your actions and their consequences cannot be overemphasized. If I had thought through this situation a little more thoroughly, I would have realized that the thing to do was to first give myself more room at the dock by untying the floatplane in front of me and moving it forward (there was plenty of room in front of it), and then get someone to assist me while I turned my plane around using the correct method. At least I was smart enough not to try to depart the dock by myself that day, but instead got someone to hold the tail of my plane while I climbed aboard and started the engine.

SPECIAL EQUIPMENT

Mooring lines, paddles, bumpers, anchors, life jackets, and life rafts—this sounds more like a checklist for the family boat than for an airplane, but all this equipment can come in handy on a floatplane, and some of it should be carried at all times.

Every floatplane should have at least two long lines on board, and preferably more. The lines should be at least 50 feet long, and it's helpful if one end of each line is spliced into an eye, or loop. If you plan to do any cross-country flying, chances are you'll run into some pretty strange docking situations, and what had seemed like too much line can easily become just barely enough. The lines can be carried in the baggage compartment, but keep one up near the pilot's seat where you can grab it in a hurry. The preflight inspection is a good time to make sure the lines are coiled neatly and are free of tangles.

Shortly after I received my seaplane rating, I misjudged my taxi speed and stopped a floatplane too far from the dock. An instructor happened to be nearby, and he offered to pull me in if I would throw him a line. Because I was slowly drifting toward another airplane, I thought this was an excellent idea, so I grabbed the line I had remembered to place on the floor behind my seat. Unfortunately, I hadn't remembered to coil it neatly, and when you're in a hurry, things tend to get snarled up even more. By the time I had untangled enough line to throw to the instructor, I was five feet from the other plane. Everything worked out fine in the end, but I learned a valuable lesson. Always check the lines before each flight.

Make sure there is a paddle on board the floatplane. This is your emergency engine, and while it isn't much use if the wind is blowing, it can be invaluable on a calm day if you have to inch the plane into that last open spot on the dock or slowly and carefully approach a rocky beach. In the unlikely event you have an engine failure, the paddle might be your only way to get the plane to shore.

If your floatplane doesn't have a paddle mounted on one of the floats, it will have to be carried inside the cabin, but don't put it in the baggage compartment. You might need it in a hurry sometime, and you don't want to have to climb over a couple of seats and wrestle it out from under all the other stuff that's back there. If you're flying a Cessna 172, a good place to keep the paddle is on the cabin floor with the handle between the front seats and the blade under the rear seat. It's easy to reach, and it doesn't obstruct the seat tracks or inconvenience the backseat passenger. In a later chapter, we'll look at what I've found to be the best way to maneuver a floatplane with a paddle, but for right now, just make sure there's one in the plane, and that it's positioned where you can reach it in a hurry if necessary.

Not all docks have tires or rubber strips around them, and it's a good idea to carry bumpers for those times you have to tie up to a bare wood, metal, or concrete dock. Two bumpers are generally sufficient, and while the heavy-duty, air-filled, rubber boat bumpers are best, they take up a lot of room in the plane. One alternative is to make some bumpers using an old automobile tire (Fig. 7-4). Cut some pieces of rubber two feet long and the width of the tread out of the tire. Punch a hole in one end of each piece, tie on some lengths of lightweight line, and you have a handy set of bumpers that won't take up much room in the baggage compartment.

Fig. 7-4. *An easy-to-make bumper using a section of automobile tire and a short length of line. It's light, and several of them can be nested together and kept in the baggage compartment, where they won't take up much room.*

Unlike mooring lines, paddles, and bumpers, anchors are an option. Some pilots like them; some pilots don't. If you want to land on a lake and fish from the airplane, an anchor will keep you from drifting away from your selected spot. If a mooring buoy isn't available, you can anchor your floatplane off a beach in tidal waters so you won't get left high and dry when the tide goes out.

The main disadvantage of an anchor is that in order for it to be effective, it has to be heavy. Many pilots don't like the idea of having a sharp, heavy piece of iron on board that could tear loose and fly around the cabin in heavy turbulence or during a forced landing. The anchor, together with its long line, also takes up space, and in a smaller floatplane, this could be a problem. If you do decide to carry an anchor, remember to include it in your weight and balance calculations. Don't rely on an anchor for overnight moorage except in an emergency. Unlike the large, heavy anchors used to position mooring buoys, floatplane anchors must be small enough to fit in the plane, and lightweight enough to be pulled up by hand. These relatively small anchors can begin to drag if the current or wind is strong, and your floatplane will be damaged or destroyed if it ends up on the rocks.

While anchors are optional, life vests are not, and *the plane should be equipped with enough vests for everyone on board*. Make sure the vests are in good condition, and that the CO-2 bottles used to inflate them are still sealed and charged.

In the northern United States, Canada, and Alaska, the temperature of the water becomes the greatest danger if a floatplane capsizes or sinks. The survival time of the human body is measured in minutes in these frigid northern waters, and some pilots in the region now carry the same survival suits used by commercial fishermen. Although bulky and quite expensive, these suits offer the only protection against hypothermia in the event a person is forced into the water. Many of them are equipped with strobe lights for night use, and some even come with a built-in emergency locator transmitter (ELT).

Another survival item found in some floatplanes is an inflatable raft. The raft should be big enough to hold all the people that can be carried in the plane. In other words, a four-place plane should have a four-person raft, a six-place plane should have a six-person raft, and so on. Like the survival suits, rafts are fairly expensive, but if you plan on flying over large bodies of water in unpopulated areas, it could prove to be a good investment.

It is extremely unlikely that your floatplane trainer will be equipped with survival suits or a raft, but it should definitely have life vests in pouches attached to the seats. Make sure they are there.

After you've completed the preflight inspection, turn the bilge-pump upside down to drain the water out of it, and put it back in the plane. It's time to cast off from the dock and head for open water.

8
Starting out

DEPARTING A DOCK in a powerboat is pretty easy. You simply start the engine, untie the mooring lines, push the boat away from the dock, turn the wheel hard over, shift from neutral to forward, and leave. Getting a floatplane underway is a little more difficult. For one thing, you'll begin to move forward as soon as you start the engine. Unless you're flying a fancy turboprop with a feathering and reversing propeller, you won't have the luxury of a neutral or reverse gear.

On top of that, a boat can make much sharper turns than a floatplane. A boat's rudder is usually placed behind the propeller (or propellers) so the propwash provides a turning force as soon as the helm is put over, even if the boat is standing still. This is why a powerful ski boat, for example, can be "kicked" around, or pivoted, almost within its own length from a dead stop. The water rudders on a floatplane, on the other hand, don't work unless the plane is already moving forward, and at low-power settings the propwash is too weak and the air rudder is too small to provide much pivoting action. If enough power is applied to make the air rudder effective, the floatplane will begin to move through the water so fast that the turn will be very wide.

Boats and floatplanes do have one steering trait in common, however, because of the aft location of their rudders. Let's say you want to make a turn to the left. If you're driving a boat, you turn the wheel left; if you're piloting a floatplane, you push down on the left rudder pedal. In both cases, the rudders are pivoted to the left. Boats and floats do not turn to the left because their bows are pulled to the left, however, but because their sterns are pushed to the right; therefore, if your right side is up against a dock, the application of left rudder will not turn the front of a boat, or a floatplane, away from the dock, but will instead push its rear end into it. Rather than pulling away from the dock, you will merely slide down it.

What all this means to you as a floatplane pilot is that even with the rudder pedal pushed clear to the floor, your plane will tend to move forward down the dock when the engine is started rather than turn away from it. This isn't a problem if you're at the end of the dock, since you will quickly move into open water (Fig. 8-1), but if you are behind another floatplane, or if a piling or some other obstruction is up ahead, you won't be able to turn away to avoid it. So how can you get your floatplane out from between two other float-

Fig. 8-1. *This is one of the easiest departure situations you can find. The pilot of this Cessna 172 simply has to untie the plane, step onto the left float, and shove off.*

planes or away from those pilings that are supporting the dock?

THE 90-DEGREE DEPARTURE

Most floatplane pilots turn their planes out 90 degrees from the dock before getting in and starting the engine. The advantage of doing this is that as soon as the engine fires, the floatplane will begin to move away from the dock, and the risks of tangling with other floatplanes or boats moored nearby are minimized.

The procedure is quite simple. After completing your preflight inspection, load your passengers or cargo and prepare the engine for starting. Remember, as soon as you untie the airplane and let go of it, it will be free to drift with the current or wind, so you want to minimize the time required to climb in and start the engine. Before you untie your plane, reach into the cockpit and move the mixture control to full rich, and, if necessary, prime the engine. If you're flying a floatplane with a radial engine, build up the fuel pressure with the wobble pump if that's part of the starting procedure. If the airplane has a key start, make sure the key is in the ignition, but leave the magnetos off. Some pilots like to turn the master switch on before untying the plane. If your floatplane has cowl flaps, make sure they are open, and

if the wing flaps are still down from your preflight inspection, raise them. This last item is very important.

Before you untie the plane, take a moment to determine the best path to follow to open water. Once you start, you're committed, so check for any floatplane or boat traffic that might get in the way, and make sure you'll be able to clear any pilings, docks, or other obstacles in the area.

When you're satisfied the course is clear, untie the plane and push the nose away from the dock. Grab the tail as it swings around toward you and back the floats up to the edge of the dock, taking care not to damage the water rudders. Step onto the tail of the left float, walk quickly forward to the pilot's door, get in, and start the engine (Fig. 8-2). If you're flying a two-place, tandem floatplane such as a Citabria or a Super Cub, you'll obviously step onto the right float because the pilot's door is on that side.

Fig. 8-2. *Once you've turned your floatplane out from the dock, you've got to get aboard quickly and start the engine before you drift into something that could damage your plane.*

Now you see why it's so important to raise the flaps before you board the airplane. When the flaps are extended, their trailing edges hang quite low, and in your haste to move forward, hop in, and start the engine, you might not notice them. At best, you will suffer a painful blow if you run into a flap, and the shock of slamming full tilt into the sharp trailing edge could even pitch you overboard.

One other word of caution: If you're heavy, as I am, and you're flying a small floatplane like a Cessna 172 or a Super Cub, the stern of the float will probably submerge as you step onto it. The challenge here is to step forward on the float before the water has a chance to wash over the stern and soak your shoes. I make it about 50 percent of the time.

In my experience, the hardest plane to board when it's turned out from the dock is the Cessna 180. Its floats extend back almost to the tail, and when it's backed straight up to the dock, there isn't any room to get around in front of the stabilizer and step onto the float. If you turn a Cessna 180 out from the dock at an angle, it's easier to squeeze past the leading edge of the stabilizer and jump onto the float.

STARTING OUT FROM A RAMP

If your floatplane is tailed up on a ramp, getting underway is easy. After you've loaded your passengers or cargo, climb in yourself and get ready to start the engine. There's no hurry because the floatplane won't go anywhere until the engine fires and pulls it off the ramp. Once you're in the water, however, there's no backing up, so make sure you know where you're going before you hit the start switch. Take a moment to check for traffic and obstacles, and pick the safest path to open water.

If you've tailed the floatplane up on the ramp yourself, the floats will be just barely out of the water, and the plane will slide off the ramp the moment the engine fires. If for some reason the floatplane is sitting solidly on the ramp and clear of the water, you'll need to use a fair amount of power to start it moving forward. The airplane will slide easier if there is some form of lubrication between the floats and the ramp, so before you get in and start the engine, wet the ramp down thoroughly with water.

As soon as the floatplane leaves the ramp, lower the water rudders. Some pilots like to lower the rudders before they start the engine. Their rea-soning is that the rudders will drop into position as soon as the floats clear the ramp, making one less thing for the pilot to worry about if things get busy. I'm sure this works most of the time, but the water rudders could be damaged if they catch on a board or if they hit the edge of the ramp as the plane settles into the water. It's better to play it safe and leave them up until the plane has cleared the ramp.

WHEN THE WIND BLOWS

So far, we've been assuming that your flight is taking place on a nice, calm, no-wind day. I've heard that such days exist but that they go into hiding whenever they see someone preparing to launch a floatplane. While this statement doesn't sound very scientific, it certainly seems to be based on fact, and the chances are good that there will be at least some wind on the day that you decide to go up.

Wind is the floatplane pilot's greatest concern. It affects every aspect of float flying, and it's often the determining factor when you're trying to decide whether to fly or not. As far as the wind is concerned, a floatplane is just a big weather vane, and it will always point its nose into the wind. A weather vane, however, remains in one place, rotating around the top of its stationary pole. Not so with a floatplane, which is free to drift wherever the wind wishes to take it.

To do battle with the evil forces arrayed against them by the wind, floatplane pilots have mooring lines, water rudders, an air rudder, an engine, and a propeller. As we've already seen, however, the water rudders are ineffective until the floatplane is moving forward, and the air rudder isn't worth much until the floatplane is moving fast. Between the time the mooring lines are released and the engine is started, the wind is in command.

Although there's nothing you can do about the wind, you at least have the advantage of knowing what it will do to your floatplane, and you can plan your moves accordingly. For instance, you know your plane will start to pivot into the wind as soon as you let go of it, so make sure the wings and tail will swing clear of any nearby obstacles. You also know the airplane will drift with the wind as you're scrambling aboard, so give yourself some extra time by moving the plane upwind as far as possible from any obstacles on the dock or tied to the dock.

There is, however, no getting around the fact that no matter how weak or strong the wind is, your floatplane will begin to drift—generally the wrong way—as soon as you let go of it and start to climb on board. In the time it takes you to get on, get in, and get going, the airplane could be blown into a boat, a piling, or another floatplane, or pivoted so you'll taxi forward into something expensive as soon as you start the engine.

This all sounds very intimidating, but there is an easy solution. If you get someone to hold the tail of your plane after you turn it out, your problems will go away. With someone on the dock holding the tail, the plane can't drift or start pivoting into the wind the moment you step aboard. It's not an admission of incompetence to ask someone to hold the tail for you on a windy day while you get aboard and start up. On the contrary, it's a sign of an experienced, conscientious floatplane pilot. It makes no sense to run the risk of damaging one or more expensive floatplanes by trying to prove you can beat the wind. Eventually, you'll lose, and the consequences are irreversible.

Large floatplanes such as the de Havilland Beaver and Otter are easily shoved around by the wind thanks to their large vertical surfaces, and on blustery days they can quickly become too much for one person to handle. In fact, the massive Otter is almost too much for one person on a calm day, let alone a windy one, so it would be advisable to have several people on the dock to help keep the monster under control. Regardless of your floatplane's size, though, make it a practice to get someone to hold the tail for you when the wind kicks up. It's good insurance.

If the wind is quite strong and your floatplane is on the downwind, or lee, side of the dock, it might be easier to get in and simply let the wind push you out into open water before starting the engine, instead of fighting the plane's weathercocking tendency at the dock. If you do decide to drift, or sail, away from the dock, remember that your nose will point into the wind and back toward the dock, so don't start the engine until there's enough distance between you and the dock to allow you to safely turn away from it.

This is actually your first introduction to the fine art of sailing, and a later chapter will be devoted specifically to these techniques. There is, however, one rule you need to know now. Whenever you drift a floatplane backwards, the water rudders should be up. When the rudders are up, the floatplane is free to point directly into the wind, and it will travel backwards in a straight line. Once you're well clear of the dock, you can start the engine, lower the water rudders, and turn toward the takeoff area.

9
Taxiing the floatplane

ON THE WATER, floatplanes have three forward speeds. The slowest gear is called the *displacement taxi*, second gear is the nose-high *plowing taxi*, and high gear is called the *step-taxi*. Since the steering on a floatplane is somewhat vague and the brakes nonexistent, it's important that the plane's speed be kept well under control when maneuvering on the water. For this reason, you'll spend most of your time on the water taxiing in the displacement mode. You'll use the displacement taxi when you approach or depart a dock, ramp, or beach, when you maneuver through a crowded harbor, and when you have to taxi across rough water. In the displacement mode, the floatplane is being supported solely by the flotation properties of the floats, and all steering is done with the water rudders.

THE DISPLACEMENT TAXI

As a general rule, a floatplane's maximum displacement taxi speed is one at which there is only a slight increase in nose-up pitch over the plane's at-rest attitude on the water (Fig. 9-1). Most floatplanes seem to reach their maximum displacement speed at an engine speed of approximately 1,000 rpm, but most of the time you will be taxiing with the engine turning over only slightly

Fig. 9-1. *The displacement taxi. Note the lowered water rudders and up-elevator.*

faster than idle rpm. At this speed, the propeller won't pick up any spray, and the engine won't overheat.

When you're entering or leaving a dock or ramp area or maneuvering carefully in a crowded harbor, you'll want your plane to move at the slowest speed possible. The slower the propeller turns, the slower you will taxi, so many floatplanes have their idle rpm adjusted until their engines are just barely ticking over. In fact, if the engine in your plane starts easily and runs smoothly, but has a tendency to die when the throttle is pulled all the way back, it probably means the idle speed is set too low and needs to be adjusted by a mechanic. Another technique you can use to slow the engine down while taxiing is to switch off one magneto and pull the carburetor heat on. This will reduce the engine's rpm, but if you operate too long in this configuration, you could foul the spark plugs.

STEERING

In calm or light wind conditions, the floatplane will be quite responsive to the water rudders, and you'll easily be able to turn to crosswind or downwind headings. You might notice that the plane turns to the left faster than it turns to the right. This is due to P-factor. It's the same force that requires you to hold right rudder in any single-engine airplane when you take off, climb, or fly in a nose-high attitude while carrying power. The fancy engineering term for it is *asymmetrical disk loading*, and it means that the propeller blades going down generate more thrust than the ones going up. You can give yourself an interesting demonstration of this force on a no-wind day by pulling up the water rudders while the engine is at idle. With no rudders to help maintain directional control, the floatplane will start turning to the left, pulled around by the P-factor, and it will keep on turning until you either run out of gas or lower the water rudders again.

If there is any breeze at all, the plane will weathercock, or point its nose into the wind, when you pull the water rudders up because the force of the wind moving past the tail will be greater than the left-turning P-factor from the propeller. That P-factor is always there, however, so don't forget about it. It will come in handy later when you are trying to make turns in stronger winds.

As mentioned previously, most water rudders are spring loaded. In other words, stiff springs are inserted into the steering cable system. These springs might be attached between the steering cables and the rudder bar in the cockpit, the steering bar on top of each rudder post, or the rudder bar in the air rudder assembly in the tail. The springs are there to protect the water rudders from damage if they strike an obstacle. The springs are also responsible for the somewhat "mushy" feeling you'll experience when you're maneuvering on the water.

In fact, there might even be a time when the floatplane will refuse to turn, even though you have the rudder pedal clear to the floor. While debris might be the culprit, there are times when movement of the rudders is prevented by water pressure alone. If you're taxiing in a crosswind or at right angles to the waves, your plane might be forced slightly sideways through the water, and the resulting side pressure might be enough to hold the rudders centered against their springs. You are most likely to encounter this problem in small floatplanes such as the Cessna 172, which doesn't have much rudder travel to begin with.

The solution is to relax the pressure on the rudder pedals, pull up the water rudders, apply and hold full left or right rudder, and lower the rudders again. The water rudders on most floatplanes respond to pedal inputs in both the raised and lowered positions, so by pulling them up, you can turn them in the desired direction free of the water's influence. They should stay that way when you lower them again, and the floatplane will begin to turn in the direction you want to go.

The larger the floatplane, the more positive the steering. A de Havilland Beaver is much more responsive on the water than a Cessna 172 because, compared to the Cessna, the Beaver has huge water rudders, very stiff steering-cable springs, and a lot of travel in the rudder system. The Cessna, on the other hand, has relatively small water rudders, the rudder springs are easily overridden, and the amount of rudder travel is quite limited.

It's a good idea to keep "testing" the water rudders as you taxi. By making slight turns from side to side to check your plane's steering response, you'll know what to expect if you have to make a sudden turn to avoid an obstacle or maneuver through a crowded harbor on your way to or from the dock. By knowing in advance how your plane will respond, you can plan ahead, and your first indication that you can't make a sharp enough turn to the dock won't be the sound of your wingtip slamming into another airplane.

KEEP THE FLOAT TIPS UP

It's important that the control wheel or stick be held full back while taxiing at slow speeds. The propwash, together with whatever headwind is present, will push the tail down and raise the nose. This slightly nose-high attitude is desirable for several reasons.

First of all, raising the nose gets the propeller that much farther above the water and any spray that might be kicked up by the floats. This is especially important if the water is choppy because the floats will throw up a fair amount of spray as they butt their way through the waves. Raising the nose will also submerge more of the water rudders, and the floatplane will handle better.

Finally, keeping the nose up will prevent the bows of the floats from digging into the water. This is extremely important because, if the float tips should submerge, the forward speed of the airplane could drive them even deeper, causing the propeller to strike the water. Besides damaging the propeller, the sudden load could conceivably overstress the engine mounts, to say nothing of its effect on the engine's internal components.

There is another danger, as well. The floatplane might veer off to one side when the bows of the floats are driven beneath the surface, and if this causes a wingtip to contact the water, the plane will probably capsize.

The best way to avoid these expensive problems is to remember to keep the float tips up by holding full back pressure on the control column whenever you are taxiing in the displacement mode. The only exception to this rule is if you are taxiing downwind in a stiff breeze. You still want to keep the nose up, but since the wind is now coming from astern, you should hold the elevator in the full down position by moving the control column all the way forward. The wind will strike the trailing edge of the elevator and push down on the tail, thus raising the float tips.

USE THE AILERONS PROPERLY

It's very important that you use your floatplane's ailerons properly while taxiing. While you're on the water, the ailerons will help you keep the wind from getting under, and lifting, the upwind wing. If the upwind wing should start to lift, the downwind float will be forced deep into the water, and the added drag could cause the plane to capsize, especially if the downwind wingtip contacts the surface.

The proper aileron procedures are the same for both floatplanes and landplanes (Fig. 9-2). On any heading from directly upwind to directly crosswind, the yoke or stick should be held into the wind. In other words, the upwind aileron should be up, and the downwind aileron should be down. On any heading from crosswind to downwind, the yoke or stick should be held away from the wind. The upwind aileron will now be down, so the wind striking it from the rear will push the wing down, and the downwind aileron will be up. The ailerons should be neutral when taxiing either directly upwind or downwind. Always use the ailerons properly, even if the wind is light. If you aren't prepared, a sudden gust could ruin your whole day.

If you aren't sure which way the wind is blowing, there is an easy way to find out. Once you are well clear of the dock and any nearby obstructions, pull the power back to idle and raise the water rudders. If there is any breeze at all, your floatplane will weathercock into it.

THE WEATHERCOCKING TENDENCY

As we have seen, taxiing a floatplane in light- or no-wind conditions is not much different than taxiing a landplane. The water rudders are more than sufficient to overcome whatever weathercocking tendency exists, and turns can be made to any point of the compass without difficulty. The picture changes, however, when the wind starts picking up.

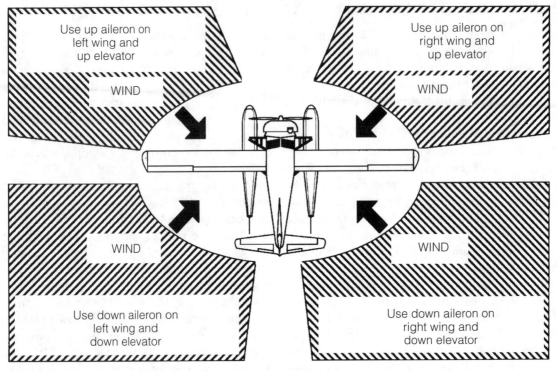

Fig. 9-2. *The proper aileron and elevator positions for taxiing in the wind.*

As the wind gets stronger, so will the weathercocking tendency, and it will get harder and harder to turn the plane to a crosswind or downwind heading. Eventually, the application of full left or right rudder will only swing the nose a few degrees off the wind before the weathercocking force stops the turn in its tracks. This isn't a problem if your destination lies directly upwind, but what if you need to taxi in a crosswind or downwind direction?

In order to understand how to taxi a floatplane across or down the wind, you should first understand why the plane is so determined to weathercock into it.

Every airplane has a vertical axis about which it pivots, or yaws, appropriately called the yaw axis. Most airplanes are designed with quite a bit more vertical surface behind the yaw axis than in front of it. This additional surface behind the yaw axis is the vertical tail. Like the feathers on

an arrow, the tail keeps the airplane headed in the direction it's pointed, and prevents it from slewing around all over the sky making everyone sick.

When a floatplane is taxied across the water in its normal displacement attitude, a crosswind will strike all parts of the airplane with equal force, but because there's more vertical surface to "catch" the wind behind the plane's yaw axis than ahead of it, the plane will swing its nose, or *weathercock*, into the wind. The stronger the wind, the faster the plane will pivot.

We don't have any control over the factors that are responsible for the weathercocking tendency, but we do have some control over the factors that tend to amplify this tendency. By using the flight controls and the engine, we can reduce these amplifying factors, and make it possible to make crosswind and downwind turns that would otherwise be impossible.

When viewed from the side, the deepest part of a float is forward of the step. Aft of the step, the float tapers up to a very shallow stern. Somewhere along the length of the float there is a point at which any sideways, or lateral, force will move the float sideways through the water. This point is called the *center of resistance to lateral motion*. If you push sideways on the float anywhere forward or aft of this point, the float will pivot in the direction you push, rather than move straight sideways. Because a float has a deep forward section and a relatively shallow after section, the center of resistance to lateral motion is not located exactly halfway down the length of the float, but is somewhere forward of the step. It's important to note that when a floatplane weathercocks, it pivots around the centers of resistance to lateral motion, not the yaw axis.

Now things start getting a little complicated (not that they weren't already). There is a point on the top of a float where, if a downward force, or weight, is applied, the float will settle deeper into the water, but will maintain the same level attitude, or fore-and-aft trim. This point is called the *center of buoyancy*. For a bunch of exotic mathematical reasons, a float's center of buoyancy is aft of its center of resistance to lateral motion.

A floatplane is joined to its floats by the float struts, which, in effect, connect the airplane's center of gravity, or weight, to the floats' center of buoyancy to ensure that the plane will float on the water in the correct attitude. Since the center of buoyancy is located aft of the center of resistance to lateral motion, the wind's sideways force on the airframe is transmitted to the floats behind their pivot points, amplifying the weathercocking tendency and causing the floatplane to swing around into the wind even faster (Fig. 9-3).

Perhaps the easiest way to visualize this weathercocking business is to think of the floatplane's silhouette as a huge weather vane. Instead of mounting our weather vane at what would be the airplane's normal yaw axis, however, we have moved the mounting point even farther forward, to the float's center of resistance to lateral motion. With that much more of the weather vane's body aft of the pivot point, it's that much easier for the wind to swing it into a streamlined position.

As the wind gets stronger, so will the weathercocking tendency, until eventually the water rudders will no longer be able to overpower the wind. At this point, it will become impossible to turn out of the wind unless some means of reducing the weathercocking tendency is found. Fortunately, there is such a means.

THE PLOWING TURN

When the floatplane is in its normal displacement attitude on the water, the shallow keel area aft of its center of resistance to lateral motion makes it easy for the tail to skid sideways and weathercock. If enough power is added to make the floatplane lift its nose and drive the rear of the floats deeply into the water, the floatplane's centers of buoyancy and resistance to lateral motion will move aft, and there will be less wetted keel area ahead of these two points than behind them (Fig. 9-4). With the pivot point of the plane moved so far aft, the plane can now even weathercock downwind, but in any case, turns to crosswind or downwind headings will be much easier to make.

This nose-high, partial-power turn is called a *plowing turn*, so named because the floatplane is mushing, or plowing, through the water. It should only be used to turn the plane downwind in windy conditions. To put your floatplane into a plowing attitude, add power and hold the yoke or stick all the way back. The force of the propwash striking the elevator will drive the sterns of the floats down and raise the bows out of the water. The added power will also make your floatplane taxi faster, and as the water "piles up" in front of the floats, the increased hydrodynamic pressure will force the bows of the floats even higher. Besides moving your floatplane's pivot point farther aft, this nose-high attitude has another advantage. As the sterns of the floats are driven down into the water,

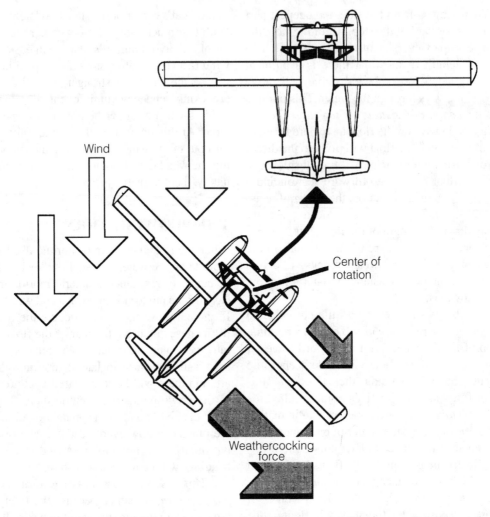

Fig. 9-3. *The weathercocking tendency. The plane will pivot around its center of rotation and point into the wind. The water rudders will help counter this tendency, but when the wind reaches a certain velocity, even the water rudders will be unable to keep the plane from pivoting into the wind.*

the water rudders will become more effective and exert even more turning force on the plane.

In addition to driving the tail down, the blast of air from the propeller will also make the air rudder more effective, which will also help you turn downwind. And don't forget the P-factor mentioned earlier. Take advantage of your airplane's left-turning tendency, and make your plowing turns in that direction whenever possible. Having the P-factor working for you might make the difference between completing a downwind turn and getting "stuck" part way through it.

If the wind is strong enough, the weathercocking force might stop even a plowing turn shortly after you begin it. To avoid this problem, start your turn to the left by initially turning to the

Tel: (207) 342-4040
Fax: (207) 342-4090

1376 Waterville Rd.
Waldo, ME 04915

www.thompsonsoil.com
info@thompsonsoil.com

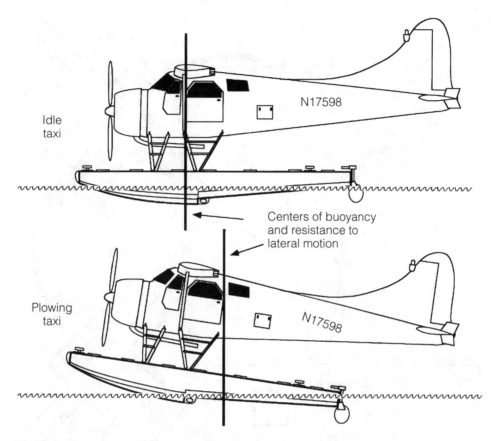

Fig. 9-4. *The centers of buoyancy and resistance to lateral motion will shift aft when the floatplane is taken from an idle attitude to a nose-high, plowing attitude.*

right while remaining in the displacement attitude. As soon as the plane is turned to the right, apply full left rudder. Aided by its weathercocking tendency, the airplane will begin a rapid swing to the left. As it passes through its original upwind heading, apply just enough power to raise the nose and shift the centers of buoyancy and resistance to lateral motion aft. Continue to hold full left rudder until the plane approaches the downwind heading. Stop the turn when you are headed directly downwind, pull the power back to idle, and resume taxiing in the displacement attitude (Fig . 9-5).

Seen from above, your turn will look like a giant question mark. By first turning the floatplane to the right, you will take advantage of the wind's weathercocking force to accelerate the plane into the left turn, and this added momentum will help swing the plane through to the downwind heading.

TAXIING DOWNWIND

Once the turn to a downwind heading has been made, the power should be reduced to idle, and the floatplane taxied downwind in the displacement attitude. Great care must be exercised while taxiing downwind, however, because if the plane should begin to turn even slightly off course, the wind will catch the side of the plane, and it will weathercock around with considerable force. Be alert for the first signs of weathercocking, and correct them immediately with the water rudders.

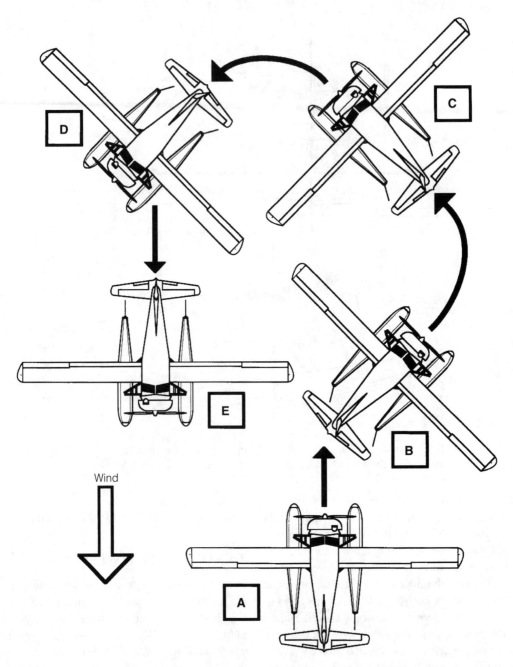

Fig. 9-5. *Turning the plane with a strong wind. Start facing into the wind (A), turn as far to the right as the wind will let you (B), apply full left rudder and the plane will swing to the left (C). As it passes through its original upwind heading, apply power to shift the centers of buoyancy and resistance to lateral motion aft. Continue to hold the plowing attitude as the plane turns downwind (D). Stop the turn and return to idle power when you are heading directly downwind (E).*

If the plane should begin to weathercock and using the opposite rudder doesn't stop it, you have to make a quick decision. You can either raise the water rudders and let the plane swing around into the wind, or you can try to force the plane back to its downwind heading. The course of action you take depends primarily on the strength of the wind and the handling and stability characteristics of your floatplane.

Generally, the safest thing to do is pull the water rudders up and let the floatplane pivot around into the wind. Raising the water rudders reduces the floats' resistance to weathercocking, and your plane will be less likely to capsize if the wind is strong. Once turned around and headed safely into the wind, you can decide whether you want to chance another downwind turn or sail the floatplane backwards (see chapter 15).

Your alternative course of action is to stop the plane from weathercocking and return it to its downwind heading. As soon as the plane begins to weathercock, apply power, opposite rudder, and full up-elevator. These actions will raise the nose to the plowing attitude, and the sudden blast of air from the propeller will bring the air rudder to life, making it easier to turn the plane back to the downwind heading.

Don't try this method if the wind is strong, however, because if it doesn't work and the plane continues to weathercock, the plane might capsize as it swings around into the wind. Floatplanes are least stable when they are in a plowing attitude, and when this instability is combined with the high inertial forces generated as the plane weathercocks around under power, the plane will lean toward the outside of the turn. The wind can now get under that upwind wing and lift it, and the plane might be on its back before you even realize what's happening.

If the wind is moderately strong, the problem of weathercocking can be reduced by keeping the floatplane in the plowing attitude as you taxi downwind. With the centers of buoyancy and resistance to lateral motion moved aft, the plane

will be much easier to control. As noted earlier, it might even weathercock downwind. Be careful, however, because there are probably limitations to the length of time you can maintain a plowing attitude.

First of all, the engine might overheat. Because you're developing power, the engine will be generating a lot of heat, but because you aren't moving very fast, the flow of air over the cylinders might not be sufficient to cool them properly. Keep a close eye on the oil and cylinder head temperature gauges if you decide to keep the airplane plowing through the water for any length of time, and be prepared to reduce the power to idle and swing around into the wind if the engine gets too hot. Radial-engined floatplanes such as the Beaver are especially prone to overheating while plowing. The big radials develop a lot of heat, and at slow taxi speeds, the flow of cooling air over the cylinders is rather poor.

In addition, your forward visibility might be restricted by the floatplane's nose-high attitude while plowing, and it might be difficult to see and avoid other boat or floatplane traffic in the area. If the distance you have to cover is relatively short, however, and if the wind is strong, it might be a good idea to keep the plane in a plowing attitude during the entire downwind taxi.

JUDGING THE WIND SPEED

If the wind is light and you are taxiing downwind faster than the wind itself is moving, hold the yoke or stick all the way back to keep the float tips up. If the wind is moving faster than you are, hold the yoke or stick all the way forward. As we saw previously, the wind will strike the down elevator from the rear, pushing the tail down and raising the float tips. How can you tell, though, if the wind is moving faster than you are?

Most floatplanes have grablines hanging down from the wingtips or the upper ends of the wing struts. Besides coming in handy while maneuvering the airplane around a dock, the grablines make nifty wind speed indicators. If you're taxiing downwind and the lines are streaming aft, you're moving faster than the wind. As long as you keep moving, there will be no tendency for the plane to weathercock around if you should deviate from your downwind heading.

If the grablines are hanging straight down, you are moving the same speed as the wind. Although there will be some tendency for the plane to weathercock when you turn away from your direct downwind heading, this tendency will be easily overpowered by the water rudders.

If, however, the lines are streaming out ahead of the wing, beware, for the wind is moving faster than you are. You'd better get that yoke forward and be extra careful, because things could get real exciting, real fast. Any deviation from a direct downwind heading will immediately cause the plane to weathercock, and you'd better be prepared to deal with it one way or another.

BOATS AND BOAT WAKES

As a floatplane pilot, you might be the master of your environment while you are airborne, but as soon as you touch the water, you become a member of a minority group. The people in charge of the water are the people with boats, and you're going to have to learn to get along with them. Boats can move much faster than you can unless you're on the step, and they're much more maneuverable. They also have a habit of appearing out of nowhere. Keep a sharp eye peeled for boat traffic, and practice defensive driving by trying to anticipate what the boats will do.

Actually, the problem you'll have with boats will not be with the boats themselves, but with their wakes. Most floatplanes cannot operate safely in very rough water, and that's exactly what a boat wake is: rough water. As we shall see, boat wakes pose the greatest threat to floatplanes that are taking off, landing, or taxiing on the step, but wakes can create problems for planes taxiing in the displacement mode, too.

Boats have the same three forward speeds through the water as floatplanes, and the size of the wake depends on what speed the boat is going at the time. Boats moving slowly leave very little water disturbance behind them. Sailboats under sail fall into this category, and their wakes are almost negligible.

At the other end of the speed scale, powerboats that are planing across the water don't generate large wakes, either. The reason is that, like a floatplane on the step, only a small portion of the boat's hull is actually touching—and disturbing—the water.

The problem lies with boats that are being driven fast through the water, but not fast enough to plane. The result is a bow-high plowing attitude that moves a lot of water and creates a large wake. The swells pushed up by a boat traveling at this speed can be several feet high and are a real threat to floatplanes.

As a rule, boat wakes of any kind should always be crossed at the slowest speed possible, as it's often hard to tell just how big the swells are until you're right on top of them. If an approaching boat wake looks like a big one, it's best to cross it at a 45-degree angle.

This choice is a compromise between taking the waves head on, which could pitch the airplane up and down violently enough to cause the propeller to strike the water, and taking them from the side, which could set up a rocking motion that could drive a wingtip beneath the surface. Remember, with its high center of gravity, narrow "wheelbase," and long, momentum-generating wings, your floatplane is a somewhat "tippy" machine.

Be particularly careful not to take a large boat wake from the side while you are taxiing in a crosswind. The wind would very much like to get under your upwind wing and flip you over, and the side-to-side rocking motion induced by the boat wake might give the wind its chance.

It's important that you understand the proper procedures for dealing with boat wakes, because you should always try to pass behind a boat that's crossing your path. Many skippers get nervous at the thought of being on a collision course with a whirling propeller, so an early indication that you intend to pass behind them is usually appreciated. There's no way of knowing which way a power boat or sailboat is going to turn, or if it's going to suddenly accelerate, but it's a pretty safe bet that it isn't going to instantly reverse its course or start backing up.

The past few years, however, have seen the growing popularity of a pair of boats that have given new meaning to the word unpredictable. One of them is the sailboard, or Windsurfer, and if they are popular in your area, be very wary of them. They are extremely fast and maneuverable and can reverse directions and accelerate almost instantaneously. On top of this, the person sailing the boat stands up behind the sail, which greatly restricts the visibility to leeward. He or she might not even see you coming.

The worst thing about sailboards is that they tip over a lot, and you never know when, or where, they're going to do it. Just when you think you have the darn thing's course figured out, and have turned your floatplane to pass behind it, the person sailing it spins it around, crosses directly in front of your nose, and falls over.

To make matters worse, when a sailboard is down, it's almost impossible to see. The owner is in the water with it, the board itself is only a few inches thick, and the mast and sail are hinged to lie flat on the surface. If you're concentrating on the other boat traffic in the area, a downed Windsurfer is easy to overlook. The first indication you will probably have of its presence is when the owner scrambles back onto it, yanks the mast and sail up out of the water, and accelerates out in front of you, only to fall over again.

The other source of waterborne frustration is the jetski. While a jetski doesn't disappear from view when the driver falls off, the watercraft is every bit as maneuverable as a Windsurfer. Even worse, the driver might not hear you coming thanks to the ever-present snarl of the jetski engine. Jetski drivers tend to be young, and the loud engines and fast acceleration tend to impart a feeling of invincibility. It's a bad combination. I've had jetski drivers try to outrun my floatplane at the start of a takeoff and then cut across in front of me just to prove they could do it. If you see this sort of thing developing, you're better off pulling the power and waiting for the person to go away than to run the risk of an accident. Even if the jetski driver is totally at fault, the specter of a floatplane plowing into the driver's unprotected body brings on the kind of publicity the floatplane community just doesn't need.

RIGHT-OF-WAY RULES: Water operations

Let's say you're taxiing your floatplane toward the takeoff area, and a boat approaches you from the left. At your present speeds and headings, your courses will intersect, and a collision might result. Obviously, one of you must give way to the other, but who has the right of way?

The answer is found in Part 91, Section 69, of the *Federal Aviation Regulations* (FARs), entitled Right-of-Way Rules: Water Operations. The rules in this section are as follows:

(a) **General.** Each person operating an aircraft on the water shall, insofar as possible, keep clear of all vessels and avoid impeding their navigation, and shall give way to any vessel or other aircraft that is given the right of way by any rule of this section.

(b) **Crossing.** When aircraft, or an aircraft and a vessel, are on crossing courses, the aircraft or vessel to the other's right has the right of way.

(c) **Approaching head-on.** When aircraft, or an aircraft and a vessel, are approaching head-on or nearly so, each shall alter its course to the right to keep well clear.

(d) **Overtaking.** Each aircraft or vessel that is being overtaken has the right of way, and the one overtaking shall alter course to keep well clear.

(e) Special circumstances. When aircraft, or an aircraft and a vessel, approach so as to involve risk of collision, each aircraft or vessel shall proceed with careful regard to existing circumstances, including the limitations of the respective craft.

So the answer to our right-of-way question lies in paragraph (b) of FAR 91.69. If a boat approaches you from your left, you have the right of way because you are to the boat's right.

These rules apply to all aircraft that are operating on the so-called inland waters of the United States, which include the country's lakes, rivers, harbors, and anything else lying within the boundary line dividing the inland waters from the international waters, or high seas. Seaplane operations conducted on the high seas outside these boundary lines fall under the jurisdiction of the United States Coast Guard, while seaplane operations conducted on the inland waters are under the jurisdiction of the FAA.

10
The takeoff

IT'S VERY DIFFICULT to paint white lines on the surface of the water, let alone expect them to stay there, so it's going to be up to you to determine the location of your "runway," or takeoff lane. There are a few seaplane facilities—Lake Hood in Anchorage, Alaska, for example—that have permanent takeoff and landing lanes marked with buoys, but for the most part, it will be up to you to select the best and safest place to take off.

This is one of the advantages you, as a floatplane pilot, have over your wheel-bound friends, because you can almost always take off into the wind. Sometimes it seems the approved method of designing an airport is to first determine the direction of the prevailing winds in the area, and then lay out the runways at precise 90-degree angles to this direction, but floatplane pilots are not limited by these unsuccessful attempts to second-guess the weather. Even on those occasions when the shoreline or other obstructions make it impossible to take off directly into the wind, you will almost always be able to take off in a direction that will at least reduce the crosswind component.

DETERMINE THE WIND DIRECTION

By the time you have left the dock or ramp and are taxiing out into open water, you should already have a pretty good idea of the wind direction. Sometimes, however, the shape of a lake, bay, or harbor might be such that the wind direction near the shore is different than the wind direction out in open water. Trees, buildings, or surrounding hills can all conspire to alter the prevailing wind, so it's a good idea to double-check the wind's speed and direction as you taxi out. Fortunately, there will be lots of clues to help you out.

We've already talked about using the floatplane itself to determine the wind direction by raising the water rudders and letting the plane weathercock into the wind, but there are other indicators all around you. Trees along the shoreline will bend or sway with the wind, as will tall reeds and marsh grass. If anyone on shore is burning trash, the smoke will be an excellent wind indicator.

The water itself is probably the best wind direction indicator, once you learn to "read" it. The friction of the wind passing over the water's surface creates waves, and the direction and size of these waves indicate the direction and strength of the wind. When the wind reaches 7 to 10 knots, the surface will be pushed up into wavelets that will begin to break, making it fairly easy to determine from which way the wind is coming. It's important to remember that as the wave crests move and break with the wind, they will leave a trail of foam stretching back upwind. While this seems very logical when you think about it, for some reason it can become very confusing when seen from an airplane, and it's easy to be fooled into thinking that the wind is actually going in the opposite direction.

If the wind is less than 8 knots, it's a little harder to determine its direction by looking at the water. Wavelets will still be formed, but they won't break, and it might be difficult to pick them out from the other ripples and waves left over from boat wakes and the passage of other seaplanes. A very light wind will generate ripples with the appearance of scales with their rounded edges pointing downwind, but it takes a practiced eye to pick them out.

This is one time when it's nice to have boats around, because they can be very helpful in determining the wind direction. Boats, barges, or ships that are moored to a single buoy will always point into the wind unless there is a very strong current running, in which case they will line up with the moving water. Both power boats and sailboats often have flags or streamers flying from them, and while these don't help you much if a boat is underway, they are as good as windsocks if the boat is stationary.

Sailboats, both moored and under sail, make wonderful wind indicators. All of them have some form of onboard indicators ranging from simple *telltales* (lengths of light string tied to the mast stays) to sophisticated masthead direction indicators. Observing a sailboat under sail is also a good way to determine the wind direction if you know how to interpret the position of the sails.

Sailboats cannot sail, or *point*, directly into the wind. Depending on the design of the boat, the best they can do is generally about 30 to 45 degrees off the wind, and to be able to do even this, the sails must be tightly sheeted in, or positioned nearly along the centerline of the hull. The boat will also lean, or heel, in the direction the wind is blowing.

When a sailboat is *reaching*, or sailing across the wind, the sails are let out farther than when the boat is pointing. The boom will no longer be close to the centerline of the boat, but will be let out some distance to leeward, and the sails will have a definite curve, or belly.

When a sailboat is *running*, or sailing downwind, the sails will be let out all the way, and the boom might be let out almost at right angles to the boat. If you should see a sailboat with the mainsail set out to one side and the jib set out to the other, you can be sure that the boat is heading directly downwind. This configuration is known in sailing jargon as running "wing and wing."

Another excellent, and beautiful, indicator that a sailboat is heading downwind is if it is flying a spinnaker, the huge and often colorful triangular sail that is set forward of the mast in place of the jib. It is generally used only when the boat is running, but there are exceptions. Spinnakers can be used from dead downwind to reaching across the wind, but the giveaway is the position of the sail. If it is evenly across the front of the boat, and the boat is upright, the boat is very close to a downwind heading. If the spinnaker is sheeted around to one side of the boat, and the boat is moving fast with a lot of heel, it is heading across the wind.

In summary, if you see a sailboat with its sails nearly flat, and the boom pulled tightly in toward the centerline of the boat, it is heading as close into the wind as it can get. By mentally adding another 30 or 40 degrees to windward of its heading, you will get a rough but usable indication of the wind's direction. If you see a sailboat with some curve, or belly, in its sails, and the boom is let out to leeward, it is sailing across the wind, so you can get an idea of the wind direction by adding 90 degrees to windward of the boat's heading. Finally, if you see a sailboat standing nearly erect with its sails let way out or flying a spinnaker, it's heading downwind, and you should take off or land in the opposite direction.

You might think I've spent a lot of effort to explain something relatively insignificant, but believe me, sailboats can come in handy, especially when you are landing. At certain speeds, the wind forms streaks, or lines, on the surface of the water which are very obvious from higher altitudes. While these streaks precisely indicate the direction of the wind across the water, it's often very difficult to tell the upwind end of the streak from the downwind end.

On one particular flight, wind streaks were the only indication I could find of the wind's direction. There wasn't any smoke, and I was too high to see which way the trees were bending. I decided that the wind was coming from the south, so I flew my approach and lined up with the wind streaks on final, heading south. As I approached the water, I thought I was going awfully fast, but because I was convinced I was landing into the wind, I didn't do anything about it.

Then I saw the sailboat. It was off to my right, and heading toward me at about a 45-degree angle. The sails were sheeted in tight, and it was heeling away from me. I'd done enough crewing on racing sailboats to recognize immediately that it was pointing as close into the wind as possible, and that the wind was coming from behind me, not ahead of me. It was a simple matter to add power, go around, and land down the wind streaks in the opposite direction, this time into the wind. Although in this case a downwind landing probably would not have gotten me into trouble, the presence of the sailboat enabled me to make a safe landing into the wind, and the risk of touching down at too high a speed was eliminated.

CHOOSE YOUR TAKEOFF LANE

Once you've determined the wind direction, you can select the best place to put your "runway."

Obviously, you'd like to be able to take off directly into the wind, and most of the time you probably can. There are, however, several things to consider first:

- Make sure there's enough water in front of you to take off from (Fig. 10-1). I realize this is pretty elementary, but judging by the number of floatplanes that run out of room and end up in the bushes each year, it's a rule that bears repeating. Don't stop measuring at the far shore, either. It doesn't do much good to lift safely off the lake only to hit the trees growing around it.
- Don't overlook the fact that your best route out of the area might not be straight ahead. If the water surface is long enough to take off from, but you don't think you can climb at a steep enough angle to clear the trees directly ahead of you, check the landscape on either side of your planned departure route. There might be an area where the trees are not so high, or a river might create a break in the forest altogether. If the obstacle in front of you is a hill or mountainside, there might be a valley off to one side you can fly through as you climb out. There's nothing wrong with making a gentle turn after takeoff to avoid an obstacle, but make sure you know exactly what you're going to do before you start your takeoff run. The time to begin looking for an escape route is not while you're approaching a row of trees at 80 knots.
- Make sure there won't be any boats or boat wakes crossing your path as you take off. The wakes from boats that are some distance away can end up in your takeoff lane, so check out all the boat traffic in the area, not just the boats that are immediately in front of you. You still have to go through your engine runup and pretakeoff checklists, so don't despair if someone is plowing across your chosen

takeoff lane in a 60-foot cruiser. By the time you're ready to go, the boat and its wake should be gone.

Of more concern would be the 60-foot cruiser that is still some distance away because it, or its wake, will probably arrive just as you get ready to take off. If you see this situation developing, you can do one of three things. You can expedite your run-up and takeoff checks as much as possible and try to get away before the monster arrives, you can pick another takeoff lane, or you can simply taxi around a while longer until the cruiser and its wake have come and gone. If you are operating from a crowded lake or harbor, this can get extremely frustrating when one boat leaves only to be replaced by another. Fortunately, this situation doesn't happen very often.

- Make sure the takeoff lane you have chosen is free of obstructions. Things like pilings, docks, rafts, and buoys are easy enough to see, but underwater obstructions like mud banks, gravel or sandbars, rocks, and floating logs can be impossible to spot from a floatplane on the surface. If you arrived at this location by plane, you will have spotted any obstructions from the air before landing, but if you are new to the area, you'll have to rely on your instructor, other seaplane pilots, or local boaters to point out the places where hidden obstructions are lurking just beneath the surface.

Floating logs and stumps, called *deadheads*, are a real problem, especially in the logging areas of the Pacific Northwest. As they get waterlogged, they float lower and lower in the water, until they are just about impossible to see from a plane on the surface. Add to this the fact that deadheads don't stay in one place, but drift around with the currents, and you

have a real threat to both seaplane pilots and boaters. Be very wary of any small branches you see sticking out of the water, for while they might be nothing more than small branches, they also could be attached to a 2,000-pound, float-puncturing log. Steer clear of any seagulls that appear to be standing or walking on the water, too. Seagulls can float, but they can't walk on water. If they're standing up, they have to be standing on something, and if it's big enough for a seagull to land and walk around on, it's probably big enough to put a good-sized hole in the bottom of one of your floats.

Fig. 10-1. *Make sure you can safely clear any obstacles that might be in front of you when you take off. This picture was taken with a telephoto lens, and the houses and apartments are actually a mile or so away from the departing Beaver. Soon after liftoff, the pilot turned to the left and flew down the lake while gaining altitude as a noise abatement procedure.*

THE PRETAKEOFF CHECKLIST

Both landplane and floatplane pilots are required to perform engine runups and to check off items on a pretakeoff checklist prior to flight. The only difference is that the floatplane pilot must perform these operations while his or her airplane is moving. This procedure isn't nearly as tricky as it might sound, but there are a few basic rules to follow:

- First of all, watch where you're going. When you were taxiing away from the seaplane base, all your attention was focused outside, but during the engine runup and pretakeoff checks, you're going to be concentrating on things inside the cockpit. It's important that you keep glancing outside as you work through the checklists so you don't run into anything.
- Whenever possible, perform the engine runup into the wind, especially if the wind is strong. You will be adding quite a bit of power during the magneto, propeller, and carburetor heat checks, and the plane will move from a level displacement attitude to a nose-high plowing attitude. Recall that your plane is somewhat unstable in this attitude, and in a strong crosswind, the right combination of waves and gusts could put your floatplane on its back.
- Finally, keep the control wheel or stick all the way back during the engine runup. This action will help protect the propeller from spray by holding the nose of the floatplane up. For the same reason, keep the actual runup time as brief as possible. Perform your engine checks quickly (but don't skip any of them), and return the engine to idle as soon as possible to minimize the time the propeller is exposed to spray.

The actual engine, instrument, and control system checks will vary among planes and should be done in the order printed in the airplane's operating manual, with one exception. If you're flying a high-wing floatplane, don't lower the flaps to their takeoff setting at this time, even if the checklist calls for it. When the flaps are down, your visibility might be blocked aft of the wing. You won't be able to tell if you're being overtaken by a boat or another seaplane, or if you will collide with one if you start to turn. The visibility restriction varies among planes, depending on the design and amount of flap used for takeoff. It's not much of a problem in a Cessna 172, which uses only 10 degrees of flap during takeoff, but if you're flying a Cessna 185 or a de Havilland Beaver, a large portion of the landscape behind you will be hidden when the flaps are lowered to their takeoff settings. Keep the flaps up until you are ready to begin your takeoff run.

After you've performed the normal engine checks as spelled out in the manual, it's a good idea to add one more item I've never seen included in any of the factory manuals. Pull the throttle all the way back and check the minimum idle rpm. As mentioned in chapter 9, many floatplanes have their minimum idle rpm set as low as possible, so the plane will taxi as slow as possible. You want to make sure the engine will continue to run when it's throttled all the way back. It might not when it's cold, but by the time you've taxied out to the takeoff area and run up the engine, it should be warm enough to continue to run at its minimum idle setting. If the engine dies when the throttle is pulled all the way back, report this fact to the flight school or the airplane's mechanic as soon as possible so the idle can be adjusted. You don't need to have the engine die on you just as you're trying to maneuver through a crowded harbor on a windy day.

After you've performed the engine runup and run through all the items on the pretakeoff checklist, it's time to get airborne—well, almost. If the wind conditions will safely permit it, clear the area first by making a 360-degree turn. This will give you a chance to look for any new boat traffic that might have snuck up while you were busy doing your pretakeoff checks and also to make sure there are no other floatplanes coming in to land on the same piece of water from which you're about to take off.

After you have completed your inspection of the surrounding sky and water, make sure your takeoff lane is still free of traffic and boat wakes. If it isn't, you can either wait for a while or shift your planned takeoff path left or right to smoother or less cluttered water.

When you're lined up on the takeoff lane you've selected, lower the flaps to the recommended takeoff setting. Before you start your takeoff run, however, take a moment to let other pilots who might be in the area know your intentions.

Some seaplane facilities have an assigned unicom frequency you can use, and at those that do not, broadcast your takeoff and departure intentions on the multicom frequency of 122.9 MHz.

THE TAKEOFF

A takeoff can be divided into four distinct phases. Their names might vary slightly, but for the purposes of this book, I will refer to them as the displacement, hump, planing, and rotation phases.

The displacement phase

Just before you apply takeoff power, raise the water rudders. This will prevent them from banging up and down and damaging both themselves and the floats.

Next, hold the yoke or stick all the way back and smoothly apply takeoff power. This will be full power in most modern floatplanes, but be careful if you're flying an airplane equipped with a mechanical supercharger. The Pratt & Whitney R-985 radial engine used on the de Havilland Beaver has a supercharger that can maintain sealevel manifold pressure up to 5,000 feet. Because it is not equipped with a waste gate to dump excess supercharger pressure, it's possible to overboost the engine at lower altitudes if the throttle is simply pushed all the way up, so keep an eye on the manifold pressure gauge as you advance the throttle.

This first phase of the takeoff is called the *displacement phase* because full power will at first simply force the floats bodily through the water. Spray will be a problem because the plane will be moving relatively slowly while the floats are bulldozing water ahead of them. If the control wheel

or stick is held all the way back, the blast of air striking the elevator will push the tail down, and as the nose comes up, the propeller will be lifted clear of some of the damaging spray.

As the plane's speed through the water increases, the bows of the floats will begin to rise. This is because the weight of the floatplane is starting to be supported by the pressure of the water against the bottom of the floats, rather than the flotation qualities of the floats alone. This water, or *hydrodynamic*, pressure is created by the floatplane itself as it accelerates through the water.

The reason full up-elevator should be applied at the beginning of the takeoff run is simply to help get the propeller out of the spray as soon as possible. Raising the nose this way also prevents the bows of the floats from digging into any waves that might be present. Even if the elevator is kept in its neutral position, the increasing hydrodynamic pressure will force the bows of the floats to eventually rise.

The hump phase

The noseup phase of the takeoff is called the *hump phase* because the floatplane appears to be climbing up a hump, or hill, of water in front of it (Fig. 10-2). As the plane accelerates, its nose will lift higher and higher as the hydrodynamic pressure gets stronger and the center of hydrodynamic sup-

Fig. 10-2. *The hump phase of the takeoff run. The extreme nose-high attitude can restrict forward visibility, so make sure your takeoff lane is clear before adding power.*

port moves farther aft. When the center of hydro-dynamic support reaches the portion of each float's bottom that is just ahead of the step, the floatplane will drop its nose to an almost level flight attitude and skim across the water. At this point, the plane's weight will be supported completely by the hydrodynamic pressure on the bottom of the floats. This, the third phase of the takeoff, is called the planing phase, but let's not get ahead of ourselves.

The floatplane's left-turning tendency, caused primarily by P-factor, will be strongest during the nose-high hump phase of the takeoff run, but you can't counteract it using the water rudders because they've been retracted. The only other directional control available to you is the airplane's air rudder, but it isn't very effective unless there's a rapid slipstream of air moving past it. Since the floatplane is still moving relatively slowly while it's in the hump phase, you might have to push the right rudder pedal clear to the floor in order to counter the plane's desire to swing to the left, and in some floatplanes, even full right rudder won't keep the plane heading straight (Fig. 10-3). The blast of air over the tail resulting from the engine going to takeoff power will help bring the rudder to life, but don't be surprised if the plane swings a little to the left as it raises its nose.

Fig. 10-3. *This picture was taken moments after the pilot applied full takeoff power. Note the right rudder to counteract the P-factor and the up-elevator to help raise the propeller out of the spray.*

The only time this swing to the left could really be a problem is when you are taking off from waters that are crowded with boats or other obstacles, or from a narrow channel. If you are flying a floatplane that always swings a little to the left at the beginning of a takeoff run, despite your best efforts on the rudder pedals, you can anticipate it by aiming the plane a little to the right of your intended takeoff path. By the time the inevitable left turn has brought your plane around to a heading in line with your chosen takeoff lane, you will be moving fast enough for the air rudder to be fully effective, and you'll have excellent directional control throughout the remainder of the takeoff run.

Probably the most dramatic example of the effect P-factor can have on a floatplane is the experience the British had with their series of Supermarine racing floatplanes. Their engines were so powerful, and their two-bladed, fixed-pitch propellers were so immense, the planes had to be aimed at right angles to the wind before the pilot could begin his takeoff run. By the time the plane was going fast enough for its air rudder to be fully effective, the P-factor from that giant prop had pulled the plane through a full 90-degree arc to the left.

The other problem you'll encounter as the plane "climbs the hump" is the reduction of your forward visibility. The nose gets quite high during the hump phase, and your forward visibility might even be blocked completely. For this reason, it's very important that you know what's in front of you before you apply takeoff power. Once the airplane drops over into the planing attitude, your visibility will be restored, but for a few moments you'll be vulnerable to boats wandering into your path, especially from the right, or to obstacles you failed to notice earlier. Even if you do see them, you won't have the maneuverability to avoid them, so before you advance the throttle, make sure your takeoff lane is, and will remain, clear.

As soon as the floatplane has reached its maximum nose-high attitude, ease the yoke or stick forward to its neutral position. The idea is to get the floatplane on the step as soon as possible, and if you continue to hold up-elevator, you will only succeed in delaying the moment when the plane pitches forward onto the step and begins to accelerate to flying speed. The nose of your floatplane should never stop moving until it has settled into the proper planing attitude. As you apply takeoff power, help the nose up with the elevator, but as soon as you sense the plane has reached its maximum hump angle, help the nose ease down into the planing attitude.

The planing phase

As the floatplane's forward speed increases, so will the hydrodynamic pressure under the floats, until finally the entire weight of the airplane will be supported by the pressure of the water against the float bottoms. At this point, the floatplane will pitch forward to a nearly level attitude, and begin to skim, or *plane*, across the surface of the water (Fig. 10-4). This is appropriately called the planing phase, and the floatplane is referred to as being "on the step."

When the floatplane is in the proper planing attitude, only a small portion of the float bottoms just ahead of the steps will be touching the water. The forward and after sections of each float will

Fig. 10-4. *The planing phase of the takeoff run. The plane is being supported only by the hydrodynamic pressure on the float bottoms just ahead of the step. As the plane accelerates, its weight will be transferred to the lift generated by the wings until finally the aerodynamic lift will equal the weight of the plane, and it will become airborne.*

ride above the surface, minimizing the wetted surface of each float, and thus minimizing the hydrodynamic drag on the floats. With the water's drag almost gone, the plane can quickly accelerate to rotation speed.

It is very important that you maintain the proper planing attitude once your floatplane is on the step. Any deviation from this attitude will result in additional drag that will extend the takeoff run. If the nose is held too low, the forebodies of the floats will begin to *rub*, or drag on the water, and if the nose is held too high, the tails of the floats will start to dig into the water.

The most common error is to hold the nose too high. If the nose is held too low, the rubbing of the forward keels will be quite obvious, and the plane will slow down and pitch forward almost as though the pilot were applying brakes. On the other hand, if the nose is too high, causing the tails of the floats to drag, the only indication that something is wrong will be the extended length of the takeoff run. Since an excessive nose-up attitude might look and feel correct to an inexperienced floatplane pilot, this fault is much harder to detect because its effects are less obvious than the effects of holding the nose too low.

The only way to learn to recognize the proper planing attitude is to practice it with an instructor. Eventually, you'll be able to "sense" when the floatplane is properly on the step, but for now, concentrate on consistently establishing the proper attitude by reference to the nose as it appears in relationship to the horizon or shoreline ahead of you.

New floatplane pilots are often surprised by the roughness of the takeoff run, even on what appears to be smooth water. Water becomes a relatively unyielding substance when slammed into at speeds exceeding 10 or 20 knots, and the rotation speed of your floatplane will be at least twice that fast. Even small waves can send quite a jolt through the airframe, and the noise can be rather unnerving to the uninitiated. You can relax, however, for despite what your ears and the seat of your pants might be telling you, a floatplane is more than a match for its environment. The floats and their supporting hardware are extremely strong, and, when properly maintained, they will stand up to tremendous punishment.

Directional control

It's not uncommon to see a floatplane threading its way gracefully through a busy harbor as it makes its takeoff run because once the plane is on the step, its air rudder will become quite effective. It's easy to make turns to avoid boats or other obstacles that appear in your path, and if you should suddenly become aware of a log or some other floating debris in the water ahead of you, it's a simple matter to steer around it. Keep your turns as gentle as possible, though, because a sharp turn creates a lot of drag and will slow you down.

Helping your plane over the hump

Normally, a floatplane will make the transition from the hump phase to the planing phase on its own, but if you're carrying an extremely heavy load, you might need to "assist" your plane over the hump and onto the step. If, after reaching its maximum nose-up angle, your plane doesn't seem to want to pitch over into a planing attitude, first determine that the engine is developing its maximum takeoff power. If it is and the plane still doesn't want to get onto the step, make sure you aren't keeping it from doing so by holding back pressure on the stick or yoke. If excess back pressure isn't the problem, take a quick glance at the trim wheel to make sure you haven't inadvertently left it in a nose-up setting. If the trim is set properly, you aren't holding the nose up yourself with the elevator, and the engine is developing full power, your only recourse is to try and "help" your plane over the hump and onto the step.

By applying forward pressure on the stick or control wheel, you might be able to pitch the plane over into a planing attitude. If the floatplane still refuses to get on the step, try gently rocking the plane back and forth with the elevator. The theory

here is that the plane will eventually rock forward onto the step, where it can be held with the elevator until it picks up enough speed to stay there on its own. Be careful if you decide to try this, however, because you don't want to set up an oscillation that could lead to the plane's porpoising out of control.

PORPOISING

Porpoising in a floatplane can be likened to bouncing down a runway while trying to do a wheel landing in a taildragger. In both cases, it is a cyclic oscillation that can be aggravated easily by the pilot's attempts to stop it. Modern float design has considerably reduced the likelihood of porpoising, but it's still possible, so you should know what it is and how to stop it.

Porpoising is generally a result of carrying the nose too low during the planing phase of the takeoff run. Instead of riding a few inches above the water, the forebodies of the floats are forced into it, and as a result, they push up a "wall" of water ahead of them. As this wall of water becomes bigger, the bows of the floats will finally ride up and over it, pitching the nose of the floatplane into the air. As the floats pass over the crest of the wave they have created, the plane will pitch back down again, and the floats will dig in even deeper, pushing up an even larger wall of water. This, in turn, will pitch the nose of the airplane even higher into the air, and so on. If these oscillations are allowed to continue, the floatplane will eventually be pitched so high that when it comes back down it will bury the bows of the floats in the water and probably flip over.

Porpoising can also be initiated by carrying the nose too high while the plane is on the step. If the plane is being forced into an unnaturally nose-high attitude, it might suddenly pitch forward, driving the forward part of the floats down into the water, and the porpoising cycle will begin.

Rough water can induce porpoising, especially if the plane is heavy or if a downwind takeoff requirement keeps the plane on the water longer and at a higher rate of speed than is normal. Avoid crossing boat wakes or large waves and swells while the floatplane is on the step, for they can easily start the porpoising cycle, as well.

If your plane should start to porpoise, stopping the oscillation is simply a matter of adding elevator back pressure at the right time. The trick is to add the back pressure just as the nose reaches its highest point. As the plane settles back down on the water in a nose-high attitude, ease off on the back pressure to return to the proper planing attitude. Proper timing is crucial because if you add the back pressure too late, you will only succeed in accelerating the plane into its next oscillation.

If your plane is not under control within about three oscillations, pull the power back to idle, apply full up-elevator, and let the floatplane come to a stop. This is a better alternative than trying to continue, which will probably result in damaging the airplane. Once you are safely back in the displacement attitude, you can begin the takeoff run again.

THE USE OF FLAPS DURING TAKEOFF

There are several theories about the use of flaps during takeoffs. Some pilots never like to use them, while others use them all the time. Each point of view has some merit.

The biggest objection to the use of flaps during takeoff is that the extra drag induced by the flaps will lengthen the takeoff run. If flaps are not used, the floatplane will accelerate faster and will go over the hump to the planing attitude and reach liftoff speed in the shortest time possible. Pilots who elect not to use the wing flaps during takeoff claim that their airplanes' increased acceleration might make the difference between a successful takeoff and an ignominious invasion of the woods along the shore of a lake that's just a bit too small on a day that's just a bit too hot.

On the other hand, proponents of flaps claim their airplanes can be taken off the water sooner,

thus shortening the takeoff run and reducing the time their planes are subjected to the water's pounding. Let's briefly review the reasons flaps are put on an airplane to begin with, and perhaps this will help you decide whether you want to be proflap or antiflap. Of course, if the operating manual of your airplane *requires* a specific flap setting be used during takeoff, you have no choice.

A fully loaded de Havilland Beaver floatplane weighs 5,090 pounds, so to support it in flight, its wing needs to develop 5,090 pounds of lift. It makes no difference whether the Beaver is flying fast or slow, the wing still needs to develop 5,090 pounds of lift. Because both speed and angle of attack generate lift, the faster the Beaver flies, the less angle of attack is required to create the necessary 5,090 pounds of lift. Conversely, as the plane slows down, the only way to maintain the required lift is to increase the wing's angle of attack.

As every pilot knows, there is a limit to the amount a wing's angle of attack can be increased. When this limit is reached, the air will cease to flow smoothly around the wing and will instead separate from the upper surface, causing the wing to lose its lift and stall. By using flaps to change the shape of the wing, the speed at which air separation occurs can also be changed. In other words, the use of flaps on a wing enables it to have a lower stall speed. Extending the flaps on a Beaver allows the wing to fly at a speed that would have resulted in an immediate stall had the wing flaps been left up. A lower stall speed means a lower flying speed. This means that an airplane with extended flaps can take off at a lower airspeed than the same airplane with its flaps retracted. Score one for the proflap pilots.

On the other hand, the generation of lift also generates drag, and as the flaps are extended, the extra lift they generate increases the total amount of induced drag on the airplane. This is not much of a problem for a landplane, but remember, a floatplane is already fighting an incredible amount of hydrodynamic drag as it struggles to first get on the step and then accelerate to flying speed. Even a small amount of additional drag, regardless of the source, can make a big difference in the length of the takeoff run. Score one for the antiflap pilots.

"Okay," you say, "you've succeeded in proving that both sides are right. That doesn't help me much. What should I do with the flaps when I take off?"

The answer is one of judgment and compromise. In most cases—and I emphasize the word *most*—the best procedure is to use flap, but not a lot of flap. Generally, the first half of an airplane's total flap extension yields a lot of lift for a relatively small amount of drag. The second half of the flaps' total extension doesn't add much lift, but that second half generates a tremendous amount of drag. In other words, half-flap lowers the stall speed, and full-flap lets you come down like a rock. The latter comes in handy during landings, but it can really mess up a takeoff. If your floatplane is equipped with flaps (some of them aren't, which solves your problem), don't use more than half-flaps when you take off. For example, the recommended flap setting for a Cessna 172 is 10 degrees, while 20 degrees is the recommended setting for a Cessna 180, 185, or 206.

The recommended flap setting for takeoff will be listed in your airplane's flight manual, and unless special circumstances dictate otherwise, you should make it a practice to use this setting for each takeoff. Some floatplanes, such as the de Havilland Beaver, require that flaps be used for all takeoffs, and in fact, the Beaver won't even lift off the water unless the flaps are deployed.

While the amount of flap recommended for takeoff will not generate much drag, it will generate some, and if your floatplane is heavily loaded, or if the amount of room available for the takeoff run is limited, you can use a slightly modified flap procedure. Instead of lowering the flaps to their takeoff setting before you apply takeoff power, which is the procedure called for in most flight manuals, leave the flaps up until you are over the hump and on the step. As soon as you are positively on the step and accelerating, lower the flaps to the recommended takeoff setting. By leaving

the flaps retracted until you are on the step, you will minimize drag during the crucial transition from the hump phase to the planing phase while still retaining the benefit of a lower liftoff speed.

The only disadvantage to this procedure is that you will be performing a task inside the cockpit at a time when all your attention should be directed outside. If you are flying a floatplane with manual flaps, such as a Cessna 180, a Cessna 185, or a Maule, this isn't much of a problem because the flap lever can be positioned by feel alone. Floatplanes with electric flaps require a bit more attention because the flap position should be verified by looking at the flap indicator or out at the wing flaps themselves. It's also important to learn to apply the flaps with one hand, while not disturbing the proper planing attitude that is being held with the other hand.

The use of flaps during takeoff can shorten the takeoff run and reduce the time that the floatplane is subjected to the water's pounding. The success of some future takeoff might well depend on your ability to properly use the flaps, so make sure you thoroughly understand their use, and then practice what you've learned.

ROTATION AND LIFTOFF

Once a floatplane is on the step, it will accelerate rapidly to *rotation*, or *liftoff*, speed. If the plane has been trimmed for a climb, it might fly itself off the water, but generally you will have to initiate the rotation yourself by applying back pressure to the stick or yoke. Try to take the floatplane off the water as soon as it has reached flying speed; remaining on the step any longer than necessary only subjects the plane to a needless pounding. As the plane leaves the water, you will feel a slight acceleration as the floats shake off the last vestiges of hydrodynamic drag (Fig. 10-5).

If you are taking off from smooth, glassy water, it might take a sharp tug on the control wheel to pull the floats free of the water's suction. Water that is ruffled with wind ripples or small waves is

Fig. 10-5. *You will feel a slight acceleration when the floats break free of the water. The standard reciprocating engine in this Cessna 206 has been replaced with a turboprop by Soloy Corporation, Inc., located in Olympia, Washington, and the resulting performance increase is impressive. This particular plane is mounted on Wipline amphibious floats.* Soloy Corporation

much easier to take off from because the irregular surface introduces air under the floats in the form of small cavities and bubbles. The air dissipates the water's suction, and the plane will lift easily off the water.

Be careful not to rotate the floatplane too much. The tails of the floats could drag in the water and slow the plane down considerably. In fact, the airplane could easily be dragged back to a speed less than its liftoff speed, causing it to stall back on to the water and extending the length of your takeoff run.

Since you will be flying the floatplane off the water at its minimum controllable airspeed, lower the nose slightly after liftoff and build up some airspeed before retracting the flaps, but don't lower the nose so much that you fly back onto the water. Wait until you have established a positive rate of climb before raising the flaps and reducing the power to the proper climb setting.

DOWNWIND TAKEOFFS

Sometimes it's more convenient to take off downwind as opposed to making a long, slow taxi to the far end of the lake or the other side of the harbor just so you can take off into the wind. If the wind is light, a downwind takeoff is a perfectly accept-

able procedure, but if the wind begins to get up around 9 knots, you'd better think twice before taking off with it chasing your tail.

If you take off into the wind, your airspeed will be equal to the sum of your ground speed and the speed of the wind. For example, if you're planing across the water at 45 knots into a wind blowing at 10 knots, your airspeed will be 55 knots. As the wind's velocity increases, the planing speed (ground speed) required to attain rotation speed will decrease. This, of course, is the advantage of taking off into the wind. You will spend less time on the water, and your planing speed at liftoff will be reduced. This in turn will reduce the amount of pounding inflicted on your airplane.

If you take off downwind, your airspeed will be equal to your speed across the water *minus* the velocity of the wind. To use the same example as before, if you are planing across the water at 45 knots with a 10-knot tailwind, your airspeed will be 35 knots. In order to attain an airspeed of 55 knots, you will have to plane across the water at 65 knots, subjecting your airplane to a severe pounding for a relatively long period of time.

The only thing that determines whether or not your floatplane will get up on the step is its speed *through the water*; airspeed is not a factor. If the tailwind were strong enough, you could conceivably skim along on the step with no airspeed whatsoever. This, then, is the danger of a downwind takeoff in a medium or strong wind. You will go faster and faster across the water, and the pounding will get worse and worse, but the airspeed indicator will appear to be broken. You'll begin to wonder if you're even going to reach rotation speed. The hammer blows on the bottoms of the floats will be transmitted directly to your spine, and the instrument panel will be vibrating so violently it will just be a blur. The banging, squeaking, creaking, and groaning emanating from the plane will convince you it is moments from disintegration—which it might very well be if the water is rough enough. If you try to pull the plane off prematurely, you'll only succeed in digging in the sterns of the floats, which will slow you down and prolong your agonizing takeoff run even more. It's not a pleasant experience.

Before you decide to make a downwind takeoff, consider the strength of the wind, the roughness of the water, and the length of the available takeoff area. If the wind is light and the water is relatively smooth, a downwind takeoff will be perfectly safe if there is enough room for the takeoff run. If the wind is strong and the water is rough, a downwind takeoff will subject your plane to a severe pounding, the result of which might be a badly damaged or even capsized floatplane. In these conditions, the convenience of a downwind takeoff is not worth the risk, so take the time to taxi slowly downwind far enough to permit a safe takeoff back into the wind.

NOISE ABATEMENT

It has become very fashionable to live on or near a body of water. Homes that can claim even a glimpse of a distant lake are in constant demand and command substantial prices. As the number of waterfront houses, apartments, and condominiums increases, so does the number of noise complaints. Unfortunately, seaplanes seem to draw the greatest fire, and it's a sure bet that as people move into an area used regularly by seaplanes, somebody will begin to complain about the noise. The newcomers don't care that seaplanes might have been coexisting with the long-time residents for years; they want all seaplane activities banned immediately.

Seaplanes are noisy by their very nature. As we saw in chapter 3, they require the maximum available horsepower from their engines in order to get off the water, and since horsepower is a function of rpm, long, flat-pitch propellers are used to allow the engine to spool up to its redline speed. The noise you hear as a seaplane takes off is not the sound of the engine, but the howl of that long, flat prop as the tips of its propeller approach the speed of sound. It is this piercing snarl that waterfront residents find so objectionable. Fortu-

nately, there are a couple of things you can do to reduce the noise, or at least its duration, and improve community relations.

As soon as you are safely off the water and have established a positive rate of climb, pull the power back to a lower setting. For example, the engine in a Cessna 172 floatplane will spool up to 2,700 rpm on takeoff if the airplane is fitted with a seaplane propeller. (By comparison, the same engine will only turn up to 2,300 to 2,420 rpm on takeoff when the standard propeller is installed.) At 2,700 rpm, the seaplane prop is quite noisy, but if the power is pulled back to 2,500 rpm as soon as the plane is off the water, the noise will be reduced considerably. Obviously, the safety of you and your airplane is the first consideration, and if there are obstacles ahead, no power reduction should be made until they are cleared. If the takeoff area is unobstructed, however, a 200-rpm reduction in engine speed can go a long way toward improving relations between the seaplane community and the local residents.

Takeoff noise also can be reduced by a modification to the floatplane itself. If the airplane is normally fitted with a two-bladed propeller, replacing it with a three-bladed prop will make a big difference in the amount of noise generated at full power settings. The individual blades of a three-bladed propeller are shorter than the blades on a two-bladed propeller. When the engine is turning over at its maximum rpm, the blade tips of a three-bladed propeller will be moving slower than the tips of a two-bladed propeller turning at the same rpm, and the propeller noise will be reduced. Not all airplanes can be fitted with three-bladed propellers, but some of the more popular planes, such as the Cessna 180, 185, and 206, as well as the de Havilland Beaver, can be converted.

Kenmore Air Harbor, in Kenmore, Washington, operates a fleet of Beavers, Otters, and Cessna 180s from the north end of Seattle's Lake Washington. The area is ringed with private homes and condominiums, but after the company installed three-bladed propellers on all its Beavers and 180s, complaints about the airplanes' noise dropped off dramatically. In addition, the Kenmore Air Harbor pilots practice noise abatement procedures by reducing power immediately after takeoff and climbing to at least 1,000 feet above ground level over the lake before leaving the area, instead of crossing the shoreline at low altitude under climb power. These are good procedures for all seaplane pilots to follow, for if we do everything we can to reduce the noise of our airplanes, our relationships with the communities in our areas will be vastly improved.

TAKEOFF EMERGENCIES

Most engine failures seem to occur during the first power change after takeoff. Landplane pilots who experience engine problems shortly after liftoff are often faced with the prospect of "landing" amid buildings, trees, fields, or whatever else happens to be beyond the airport fence. As a floatplane pilot, you are a lot better off. Unless the takeoff area is very restricted, the procedure after experiencing an engine failure during, or right after, liftoff is simply to land straight ahead. Because you are not restricted to a narrow ribbon of concrete, you can turn to the left or right to avoid any boats or obstacles that might lie directly in front of you. Whenever possible, pick a takeoff lane that is clear of any obstacles for some distance beyond your intended liftoff point, just in case you need the extra space. If you are approaching the shore and have gained enough altitude, it might be possible to execute a sharp left or right turn and land on the water parallel to the shoreline.

The important thing is to keep your head and continue to fly the airplane. If the engine loses power immediately after takeoff, don't bother to look for the problem, but concentrate instead on getting your plane safely back onto the water. If you experience engine trouble after you have gained a few hundred feet of altitude, you can quickly check obvious items like the mixture control, fuel selector, fuel boost pump, mag switches, and carburetor heat, but don't become so engrossed in finding the problem that you neglect to fly the airplane or prepare for your imminent landing.

Some floatplanes, like the de Havilland Beaver, will lose airspeed rapidly if power is lost right after takeoff or during a climb. It's important to keep the airspeed up by immediately lowering the nose when the engine failure occurs. If you don't, the airplane will either stall or sink back to the surface with insufficient airspeed to initiate a landing flare. In either case, it will slam into the water with tremendous force.

Personally, I always assume that the engine of my airplane will quit at the worst possible moment, right after takeoff. By mentally preparing myself for this occurrence, I like to think that my reaction will be quicker if I actually experience an engine failure. This attitude paid off a number of years ago when the engine in the Cessna 180 I was flying began to lose power right after takeoff from a remote lake deep in Canada's Coast Range. We had gained enough altitude to enable a turn back to the lake followed by a safe landing, but I was grateful that my first instinct was to do what was necessary to ensure a survivable landing rather than panic or become frantically engrossed in determining the cause of the problem.

11
Flying the floatplane

ONCE YOUR FLOATPLANE is airborne, you won't notice much difference between it and the landplanes you're used to flying. In fact, the most noticeable difference will probably be the sight of that big float suspended beneath you when you look out the window. The floats certainly look as though they should have a tremendous impact on the flying characteristics of the airplane, but in reality they don't. Some airplanes even benefit from the addition of floats. For example, wheel-equipped de Havilland Beavers, Otters, and Helio Couriers tend to move around a lot in turbulent air, thanks to their huge, high-lift wings. All these planes gain a more stable and solid feel when they are mounted on floats.

If the floatplane you are flying is the same make and model as the plane you used to fly on wheels, you will find that both airplanes have virtually the same response to roll and pitch inputs. Some floatplanes, such as the Cessna 172, have spring and cable interconnects between the aileron and rudder control cables, and the amount of rudder you are used to applying during a turn might now prove to be too much. The interconnects are installed to help the plane meet directional stability requirements, a subject we will look at in detail in a moment.

The next thing you might notice is that all those lines that are attached to the wingtips, the float struts, and possibly even the wing struts are behaving quite nicely. The grablines hanging from the wings will be streaming aft against the bottom of the wing, and the mooring lines on the floats will just lie quietly on top of the float decks (Fig. 11-1). Assuming the lines have been cut to the correct length, nothing will be flapping in the wind or beating against the airplane.

FLOATPLANES CLIMB SLOWER

Right about the time you decide there really isn't any difference between floatplanes and landplanes in flight, you'll realize you aren't climbing as fast as you're used to. This is one of the penalties of attaching floats to an airplane. If you used to fly a Cessna Turbo-206 on wheels, don't fall into the trap of thinking that a float-equipped T-206 will climb just as fast. This kind of reasoning could get you into real trouble on the day you have to take off from a small lake and clear the inevitable trees along the shore. Using the Turbo-206 as an example, the wheeled version has a sea-level rate of climb of 1,010 feet per minute on

Fig. 11-1. *If they have been cut to the proper length, the wingtip grablines will stream back under the wing without flapping around or beating on the bottom of the wing.*

a standard day at a gross weight of 3,600 pounds. On the same day, at the same gross weight, the float-equipped T-206 has a sea-level rate of climb of only 835 feet per minute, a difference of 175 feet per minute.

Some planes are less affected than others. The popular Beaver, which has a maximum rate of climb at sea level of 730 feet per minute as a land-plane, climbs at 650 feet per minute when floats are installed, or a loss of only 80 feet per minute. Regardless of the kind of floatplane you're flying, make sure you know its rate of climb, for someday this knowledge might keep you out of the trees (Fig. 11-2).

FLOATPLANES CRUISE SLOWER

Once you reach your cruising altitude and level off, you will experience the next big difference between floatplanes and landplanes. Floatplanes are just plain slow. There's no way to hide the drag of those big floats and their associated struts, brackets, pulleys, and cables, and the parasite drag they generate takes a toll on the airplane's cruising speed. Given the appearance of all that hardware dangling into the slipstream beneath the plane, the speed penalty really isn't as great as you might think, but it's a penalty just the same, and it's

Fig. 11-2. *A Cessna 180 climbing out after takeoff. This particular plane has been fitted with a larger engine and a three-bladed propeller.*

something you'll have to take into consideration when planning a cross-country flight.

For example, a wheel-equipped Cessna 172 normally cruises at 116 knots at 75 percent power at an altitude of 4,000 feet. The same power setting will drag a float-equipped 172 through the air at only 95 knots, which is 21 knots slower. Down at sea level, a wheel-equipped de Havilland Beaver will thump along at 108 knots when the power is set for economy cruise, but the addition of floats to the airplane will lower the cruising speed to 96 knots. Meanwhile, up at 20,000 feet, pilots who like to wear oxygen masks can zip along at 167 knots in a Cessna Turbo-206 that's developing 80 percent power, and they will be cruising 20 knots faster than anyone who happens to be up at the same altitude in a T-206 floatplane.

The stalling characteristics of a floatplane are virtually identical to those of a landplane. Some floatplanes, such as the Cessna 172 and 206, actually have a lower stall speed than their wheeled counterparts because of the aerodynamic characteristics of the floats, but in each case, the difference is only 2 or 3 knots. On the other hand, a de Havilland Beaver always stalls at 39 knots, regardless of the type of undercarriage installed: wheels, floats, or skis.

THE DIRECTIONAL INSTABILITY PROBLEM

Rate of climb and cruise speeds are not the only things affected when a landplane is converted to a floatplane. The addition of floats has an adverse effect on a plane's directional stability, and many airplanes require stability augmentation systems, usually in the form of additional tail surfaces, to restore directional stability after the floats have been installed (Fig. 11-3).

As seen in chapter 9, the purpose of the vertical tail is to keep the airplane directionally stable by putting more vertical surface behind the airplane's yaw axis than in front of it. If a gust of wind or an uncoordinated turn causes the plane to yaw, skid, or slip to one side or the other, the tail presents more resistance to the air than the front of the plane. If the flight controls are returned to their neutral positions, the plane will straighten out.

Fig. 11-3. *The ventral stability fin on a Cessna 206.*

If you look at a floatplane from the side, however, you will see that more of each float projects forward of the airplane's yaw axis than aft of it, thus adding a large amount of vertical surface to the front of the floatplane. The effect is a little like putting feathers on the front of an arrow as well as on the back. As long as the air is smooth, and the floatplane is kept perfectly coordinated, it will obediently follow its nose. If rough air or poor coordination of the flight controls causes the floatplane to yaw, this delicate balance will be upset.

If the plane should yaw, the relative wind, or wind caused by the airplane's movement through the air, will begin to strike the side of the plane instead of its nose. Normally, the force of the relative wind striking the tail will straighten the plane out, but if the plane is on floats, the relative wind striking the sides of the floats out in front of the plane's vertical axis might almost, or even completely, cancel the stability effect of the tail (Fig. 11-4). In other words, while the tail is trying to straighten the plane out, the forward portion of the floats will be trying to slew the plane sideways into a skid. At best, the floatplane will be very reluctant to stop skidding, and at worst, it might actually start to chase its tail.

This is not a very pleasant way to fly, so the airframe manufacturers came up with a simple

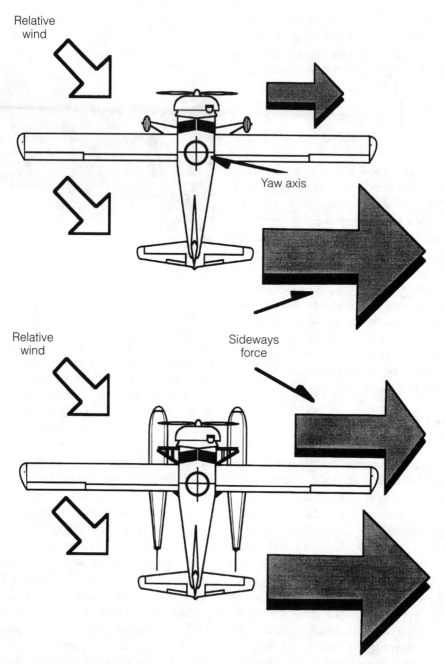

Fig. 11-4. *Forces affecting the stability of a floatplane in flight. The landplane has comparatively little vertical surface in front of its yaw axis, so it will straighten itself out in the event of a skip, skid, or yaw. A floatplane, on the other hand, can have almost as much vertical surface ahead of the yaw axis as behind it, and it will not be as quick to come out of a yawing situation. The solution is to add more vertical surface behind the yaw axis.*

method of restoring directional stability when their planes are put on floats. By adding more vertical surface area behind the yaw axis of their floatplanes, the destabilizing effect of the floats is overpowered, and the airplane will once again straighten itself out.

This additional surface is almost always in the form of one or more fins mounted on the empennage. Cessna 150, 172XP, and 206 floatplanes use a single ventral fin installed beneath the tail. Float-equipped de Havilland Beavers and Otters, Twin Beeches, Maules, and some Pipers also use a single ventral fin (Fig. 11-5). Another popular method is to install a small vertical fin at each end of the horizontal stabilizer. Stabilizer fins are used on float-equipped de Havilland Twin Otters, Cessna 195s, and de Havilland Beavers as modified by Kenmore Air Harbor in Kenmore, Washington (Fig. 11-6). Another form of stabilizer fin is the "shark" fin, which mounts on top of the horizontal stabilizer (Fig. 11-7). One of the advantages of mounting a pair of fins on the stabilizer is that, unlike a ventral fin, they don't hang down lower than the tail of the airplane. This makes them less susceptible to damage from docks or shoreline logs and brush.

However—and this is an important however—any additional surface installed on any airplane, be it a Piper Cub or a Boeing 777, will generate additional drag, which means the airplane will fly slower or use more fuel to fly the same speed. Over a period of time, this additional drag can make a significant contribution to the operating cost of the airplane, so the size of a floatplane's stabilizing fin,

Fig. 11-6. *Twin stabilizer fins on a Cessna 195 floatplane.*

Fig. 11-7. *A pair of so-called "shark fins" mounted on a de Havilland Beaver.*

or fins, is kept to a minimum. What this means to you as a floatplane pilot is that although your floatplane is directionally stable according to the certification standards set forth by the FAA, in reality it might be flying on the ragged edge of instability.

Why all the fuss over this directional stability business in the first place? As long as the plane doesn't actually start chasing its tail, what difference does it make if the plane won't come out of a slipping or skidding condition on its own? After all, that's what the rudder is for, isn't it?

Well, yes, and if every pilot flew in a perfectly coordinated fashion all the time, we wouldn't have to worry about the directional instability of floatplanes. Unfortunately, we don't always fly with the

Fig. 11-5. *A de Havilland Otter in Vancouver Harbor, British Columbia. Note the ventral fin under the tail.*

ball dead center, so floatplane stability is a big concern to float and airframe manufacturers, as well as the FAA. One reason why the Cessna 172 floatplane has a spring-and-cable interconnect between the ailerons and the rudder is to help keep the plane coordinated as it rolls into and out of turns, even if the pilot is lax in the use of the rudder.

The problem is that even with their stability augmentation systems installed (ventral or stabilizer fins, oversized dorsal fins, etc.), many floatplanes can easily begin to skid in a turn —especially a steep turn—if the pilot doesn't pay attention to his or her coordination. This is because the stabilizing fins are kept as small as possible to minimize drag. When an airplane skids in a turn, the inside wing slows down in relation to the outside wing. If the skid occurs when the airspeed is low—during a steep turn while climbing out after takeoff, for example— the inside wing could slow down enough to stall. When it stalls, the plane will fall out of the turn to the inside and begin to spin.

In fact, this is exactly what happens when you intentionally practice spins at altitude. You first reduce your airspeed until your plane is just about to stall. Then you induce a skid by applying full left or right rudder. The inside wing stalls first, and the plane drops into a spin.

The destabilizing effect of the floats replaces the application of right or left rudder to start a floatplane skidding, but the end result is the same. Because you're only likely to be making steep turns at low airspeeds right after takeoff or during a landing approach, you probably won't have enough altitude to recover from a skid-induced stall.

The easiest way to avoid a skid/stall situation is to keep the bank angles shallow, the airspeed up, and the ball in the center. On those occasions when you absolutely must crank in a steep turn at minimum airspeed to avoid an obstacle, keep an extra-sharp eye on that ball!

Some landplanes, such as most Cessna 180s and 185s and the Helio Courier, do not require any additional vertical surface at all when floats are installed because their tails are already quite large. Floats have the same effect on these planes as on any other, however, and the pilot should always pay close attention to his or her turn coordination, especially at low airspeeds.

The de Havilland Beaver, considered by many pilots and commercial operators to be the ultimate bush plane, has acquired a reputation for being an easy plane in which to have a skid/stall accident. The story behind this reputation is an interesting one. When the plane was first certified for floats, de Havilland installed a large ventral fin under the tail as part of the float kit. Some pilots complained this made the plane hard to land in a crosswind, so the manufacturer, with the approval of the Canadian Department of Transport, made the ventral fin an option. Shortly after operators began flying the Beaver without the auxiliary fin, it began to acquire its then-deserved reputation as being prone to skid/stall accidents. Kenmore Air Harbor, a company that probably has had more experience with the de Havilland Beaver than de Havilland, flew its Beavers without auxiliary fins on the strength of the factory's advisory, which made the fin an option in Canada. The Kenmore pilots, however, found the plane to be quite directionally unstable when it was flown without the ventral fin.

Shortly after the ventral fin was made optional, the Beaver was certified for larger floats, and this time there was no question about the installation of an auxiliary fin. The fin was required when the Beaver was installed on the larger floats, and that was that. Kenmore Air Harbor received a supplemental type certificate (STC) for two small fins that mounted on the ends of the horizontal stabilizer in place of de Havilland's single ventral fin, but no matter which type of fin was installed, the Beaver became a well-behaved airplane once again.

Auxiliary fins became mandatory in the United States on all float-equipped Beavers, but they were still optional on Canadian-registered

Beavers equipped with the original small floats. Reports of the big de Havillands skidding into a stall continued to trickle in until 1983, when the Canadian Department of Transport amended its rules, and required auxiliary fins on all float-equipped Beavers of Canadian registry, regardless of the size and type of floats used.

If you get a chance to pilot a float-equipped Beaver, jump at it, for the airplane is an absolute delight to fly. Don't let its smooth controls and excellent handling lull you into sloppy turn coordination, though, because that skid/stall tendency is still there, waiting for the day you crank in a steep turn as you struggle for altitude after takeoff or twist in through the trees on final. A Beaver will take a lot of abuse, but if you persist in ignoring the ball, that skid will eventually reach around and bite you.

12
The landing

I FIRST BECAME INTRIGUED by floatplanes during a trip to Alaska, when I spent the better part of a day watching the floatplanes come and go from Anchorage's Lake Hood seaplane base. A fellow who looked like a bush pilot was doing something to the engine of a Cessna 206 at the dock in front of me, and after a while I worked up the nerve to engage him in a conversation about floatplanes. When I asked him if it was difficult to learn to fly one, he thought for a minute, and then asked, "You ever flown a nosewheel airplane? Floatplanes land just like nosewheel airplanes. If you want to fly a floatplane, see if you can find yourself a nosewheel plane to practice in first."

I found his answer an amusing commentary on the nature of Alaskan aviation, because while I had never flown anything but "nosewheel planes," he talked of tricycle-geared airplanes as though they were a species of exotic bird, to be glimpsed only once or twice in a lifetime. He was correct, however, in his observation that a nosewheel airplane closely duplicates the landing attitude of a floatplane. If you're used to flying a landplane with tricycle landing gear, you will feel very much at home while making a normal landing in a floatplane. (We'll save rough-water, crosswind, and glassy-water landings for subsequent chapters.)

DETERMINE THE WIND DIRECTION

The first thing you need to do when you arrive over your intended landing site is to determine the wind direction. Actually, it's a good idea to practice figuring out the direction of the surface wind in your immediate vicinity during your entire flight. It will sharpen your wind-reading skills, and it's one way to relieve the monotony that sometimes sets in during long cross-country trips. In the event of an emergency, knowing the wind direction in advance will save you a few precious seconds, and might even make the difference between a successful landing and an out-of-control arrival.

Some of the methods of determining wind direction discussed in chapter 10 will also work when you are surveying a landing area from the air. Blowing smoke or dust, the set of the sails on nearby sailboats, and windstreaks on the water are all excellent wind-direction indicators that are visible from higher altitudes. Windstreaks appear as long, straight, narrow streaks of smooth water on an otherwise ruffled surface. They will be parallel to the direction of the unseen wind. Windstreaks are as good as windsocks for showing the exact path of the wind, but it can sometimes be difficult to tell the upwind end of a windstreak from the downwind end, especially if the wind is not quite strong enough to begin forming whitecaps. If this is the case, you will have to look for other clues to help you determine the direction.

WATER

A shoreline always rises higher than the water it touches. In wooded country, the trees might tower 50 to 100 feet over the water lapping the beach at their feet, while in the desert, the top of a sandy bank might be only inches above the surface of the lake it surrounds. In either case, though, the shoreline is always higher than the water. This obvious geological fact sets the stage for one of the best indicators of wind direction a floatplane pilot can have.

Waves are generated by the friction of the wind passing across the surface. The stronger the wind, the greater the friction, and the larger the waves will become. Conversely, if the wind is weak, or if it is somehow kept from contacting the surface of the water at all, the waves generated will be small or nonexistent.

When the wind reaches the edge of a body of water, it does not immediately drop down and begin to stir up waves on the surface. Instead, it sails off the edge of the shoreline and contacts the surface of the water some distance from shore. This distance is determined by the height of the shoreline. If the shoreline is composed of a dense forest of tall trees, the trees will form a windbreak, and the wind won't hit the surface of the water until it has traveled quite a ways from shore. If the shoreline is composed of grass, low bushes, or scattered trees, the wind will be able to start sweeping the surface of the water almost immediately after clearing the bank. In either case, however, there will be a band of smooth water extending out from the upwind shore (Fig. 12-1).

The strength of the wind also helps determine how far out from the upwind shore the band of smooth water will extend. As we have seen, waves are formed by the friction of the wind on the surface of the water, but the waves do not form instantly. It takes a while for the wind to overcome the surface tension of the water and begin to pile it up into waves that it can then push along. Until the point where the waves begin to form, the water will remain smooth. A light wind will have to "rub" on the surface for a long time before it can begin to form waves, so the band of smooth water will extend quite a ways out from the upwind shore. A strong wind, on the other hand, will begin to hump the water into waves almost immediately, so the band of calm water will be quite narrow.

Even in a light breeze, the area of smooth water extending downwind from the upwind shoreline will be quite obvious from your aerial vantage point, and the distance this smooth water extends out from shore before becoming textured with ripples or waves will give you valuable information about the wind's direction and its strength.

INSPECT YOUR DESTINATION

Before you begin to pick the location of your landing lane, take a moment to overfly your intended docking or beaching site. Once you're on the water, the low perspective often makes it very difficult to judge which docks are open or just how much room there is between the two planes that are already tied up. It also will be practically impossible to figure out the position of that gravel bar someone told you was just off the entrance to the channel.

From the air, the layout of the docks, the amount of space between the moored floatplanes, and the whereabouts of that elusive gravel bar will become immediately obvious. Armed with this information and what you know of the wind's direction and strength, you can decide to which dock you want to go and figure out the best way to approach it. By doing this planning in the air, you avoid the potentially dangerous situation created by entering a crowded boat harbor or seaplane base unprepared, only to find that the dock that looked like it had enough room for you is full. By the time you are close enough to realize that you

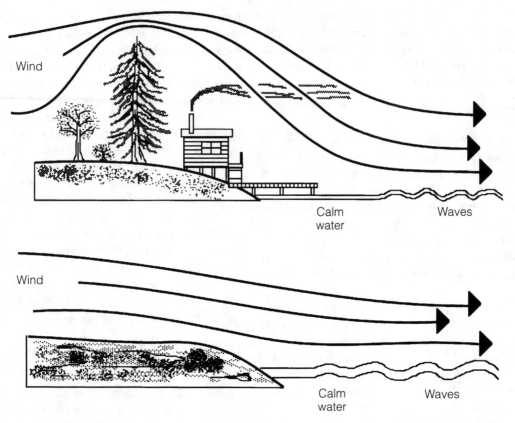

Fig. 12-1. *The effect of the shoreline's profile on the wind. Regardless of the height of the shoreline, there will always be a band of smoother water extending out from the upwind shore that will be readily visible from the air.*

will have to tie up elsewhere, you might be in too close to maneuver clear of the boats and planes that are already there.

If your destination is a beach or a lake shore, definitely check it out from the air before you land and taxi in. An aerial survey is the only way to spot deadheads, rocks, or reefs that might be lurking just beneath the surface, waiting to tear bottoms out of your floats as you approach the shore. Again, by knowing the direction and strength of the wind, you can determine the best approach to the beach and then make sure that the approach is clear of underwater obstacles by inspecting the area from the air.

Don't be in a hurry to land. The second safest place for a floatplane to be is in the air. (The *safest* place is in a hangar.) Once you're on the water, you're dealing with a machine that has no brakes, no reverse, and is often at the mercy of the wind, so the more preplanning you can do while you're safely airborne, the fewer surprises you'll get after you touch down.

CHOOSE YOUR LANDING SITE

Once you have determined where you're going to dock or beach your plane, it's time to lay out your "runway." Naturally, you want to land into the wind if possible, and one of the nice things about flying a floatplane is that you can almost always do so. It also would be nice to avoid a long taxi back to shore by coming to a stop in the vicinity of your destination. You want to make sure that your landing lane is clear of floating and underwater obstacles, too.

Determine the water conditions

A floatplane always should be landed in the smoothest water available at the slowest speed possible. Your goal is to minimize the amount of pounding to which your airplane is subjected. Different water conditions require different landing techniques. Absolutely flat water, or *glassy water*, is potentially very dangerous—not to the floatplane, but to you, because you will find it very difficult, if not impossible, to judge your height off the water. (A special technique for glassy-water landings is covered in chapter 14.) Water conditions considered ideal for floatplane operations are created by wind velocities of 7 to 10 knots. These velocities will create a surface covered with large wavelets whose crests are just on the verge of breaking. There might even be a few small, scattered whitecaps.

If the surface of the water is covered with whitecaps, it means the wind is blowing in excess of 13 knots, and unless you are experienced at making rough-water landings, you should start looking for another, more protected place to land, especially if you're flying a relatively small floatplane like a Super Cub or a Cessna 172. Rough-water takeoffs and landings are covered in chapter 14, but keep in mind that rough water will always subject a floatplane to quite a pounding, no matter how good the pilot's rough-water technique might be.

Make sure there are no boat wakes crossing your intended landing area. They are just as dangerous to a landing floatplane as they are to one that is taking off. Remember, too, that boats some distance away can generate swells that might end

up running across your landing lane. One positive note is that boat wakes are much easier to detect from altitude than they are when you're sitting on the water getting ready for takeoff. If there is a boat wake crossing the area to which you want to land, it's a simple matter to circle while you wait for the wake to dissipate or travel beyond your chosen landing lane.

Boats are responsible for another surface condition that can really fool an unsuspecting floatplane pilot. I know because one day I was one of those unsuspecting pilots who was fooled. Behind the city of Seattle, Washington, is a large lake named, appropriately enough, Lake Washington. There are many marinas on this 19-mile-long lake, and most of the homes that ring the shoreline also have boats tied up in front of them. The lake is popular with water skiers and sailboats, but the real problem is caused by the many big power cruisers that call the lake home. The lake is connected to the salt water of Puget Sound by a set of locks. On any given Saturday during the summer, an armada of cruisers heads for the locks and a weekend on the Sound. On Sunday, the armada comes back.

The deep wakes generated by these boats start bouncing back and forth across the lake in all directions, and as the day progresses, the result is a lumpy, confused lake surface that, to the uninitiated, looks fairly smooth from the air. Because there are no whitecaps, the pilot's tendency is to think that the conditions are ideal for landing. They aren't, and if the pilot should actually land, he or she will find—as I did—that the water is extremely rough and quite dangerous to small floatplanes. So beware of lakes that have a lot of boat traffic on them; the water is probably a lot rougher than it looks.

Make sure there aren't any swells running through your chosen landing lane. I have already discussed the swells caused by boats, but the parallel swells found in large bodies of open water are generally caused by earlier winds or distant storms. Taking off or landing in water that contains swells is very dangerous and should be avoided except in an emergency.

Swells are sometimes difficult to see from an airplane, and even if you can see them, it's hard to tell how large they are. A good way to tell if there are any swells present in the water below you is to look at the waves breaking on shore. Long, straight lines of waves breaking in a constant rhythm indicate the presence of swells. The bigger the waves, the bigger the swells.

While landing in swells should be left for emergencies only, there *is* a proper technique for it, which is described in chapter 14. For now, I will assume that the water you're going to land on falls in the "ideal" category and that you will also be able to land directly into the wind.

Inspect the area for obstacles

After you have determined the location of your landing lane, make one or more passes over the area to make sure there are no obstacles that could interfere with your landing. Your inspection passes should be made at pattern altitude or lower, and if you still have some doubt that the area is clear, don't be afraid to bring the plane right down to the surface and overfly your landing site at 50 feet. You want to make sure that the water is not only free of floating logs, branches, and other debris, but that it's deep enough for you to land in it.

If you're landing in tidal waters, look carefully for the little buoys people use to mark the locations of their crab, shrimp, and lobster pots. They can be difficult to see, and they can do a lot of damage to one of your floats or your prop if you hit one. During the shrimping season, some areas of Puget Sound become so clustered with buoys that it becomes almost impossible to find a long enough stretch of clear water in which to land.

Many of the lakes from which floatplanes operate are created by flood control or hydroelectric dams, and the water level can change overnight. If the water level is high, be extra-alert for logs, stumps, and other debris that might have been picked up off the bank by the rising water. Remember that anything floating on the surface will be blown downwind. If you are landing on the downwind side of a lake, take a little extra time to check for floating debris. Be especially careful if the water is muddy because anything from a submerged log to a rocky reef can be hidden just beneath the surface.

Extremely clear water presents a problem, too, because it can be difficult to judge its depth from the air. If you can see the bottom, pick an area that you think is deep enough, and then give yourself a safety margin by landing even farther out than that.

The water is not the only place to look for obstacles that might interfere with your landing. Power and phone lines are even more of a problem to floatplane pilots than they are to landplane pilots. The lines themselves are almost impossible to see from the air, so look for the poles that hold them up. If you see any poles, it's a sure bet that they are supporting one or more lines, and it only takes one to ruin your day. Be especially careful if you are landing between an island and the mainland, between two islands, or on a river. If the distances are not too great, the residents might have strung aerial power and phone lines out to the islands, and farmers might suspend a power line across a river to run pumps or other equipment on the other side. These lines are almost never indicated on sectional or WAC charts, and they rarely have any warning markers hanging from them. The only way to find them is by a careful examination of the area as you fly over it.

While they are much more obvious, check for any bridges that might obstruct your landing path. Bridges often carry power lines across them, and there might be gas or water lines suspended nearby, as well. While a nearby bridge might not pose any problem to your landing pattern and final approach, remember that you might have to go around, and an obstacle that posed no threat to your landing plans could suddenly become a very real threat in the event of a go-around.

This situation brings up another point. Make sure that the body of water on which you intend to land is big enough for you to take off from later. Floatplanes come to a stop very rapidly, but their takeoff runs are longer than a landplane's, so it would be easy to land somewhere with plenty of room to spare only to find it impossible to take off again. A float-equipped Cessna 172, for example, requires only 590 feet to come to a stop after touchdown, but it will cover 1,400 feet before it lifts off the water on takeoff, a difference of 810 feet. The powerful Turbo-206 floatplane will come to a stop in 845 feet, but requires 1,810 feet to take off, a difference of 965 feet. It's interesting to note that the takeoff roll of the same airplane on wheels is only 835 feet.

Of the floatplanes I am familiar with, the de Havilland Beaver is once again the champion, with a takeoff distance over a 50-foot obstacle of 1,610 feet, which is only 100 feet more than the landing distance over the same obstacle. If you're going to be flying into small lakes, it's pretty hard to beat a Beaver.

THE NORMAL LANDING

As stated previously in this chapter, the main objective when landing a floatplane is to touch down on the water at the slowest possible speed. This is the same objective you have when landing a landplane. Also like a landplane, there are two ways to land a floatplane: power-on and power-off. Because it's difficult for pilots new to float flying to accurately judge their height above the water, the power-on method is the most recommended because it gives the pilot more control over the sink rate and landing attitude of the airplane.

The power-on landing

As mentioned at the beginning of this chapter, landing a floatplane is very similar to landing a tricycle-geared landplane. Certainly the approach is the same, with the plane flown through downwind, base, and final-approach legs. Remember to verify the position of the water rudders as you run through your prelanding checklist. The rudders must remain retracted during a landing. If they are down, they will kick up violently as soon as the floats contact the water with a good chance of damaging the blades or the steering mechanism.

Unless the wind is very gusty, you should use the maximum landing flap setting for your particular airplane to ensure that your touchdown is made at the minimum possible airspeed. Every pilot develops his or her own preferred procedure for flying an approach, but the important thing is that you keep the airspeed under control throughout the approach and arrive at the touchdown point with the correct flap setting for landing. I like to put in the first increment of flaps on downwind and the second increment right after turning base. I save the final flap increment until I'm established on final approach and can judge my glide path to my intended touchdown point. If I'm a little too high, I can get the rest of the flaps on right away; if I'm a little too low, I can wait awhile before pumping them down. This is a pretty standard procedure and was taught by most of the instructors I've had over the years, but there are other procedures that work just as well. The important thing is to fly your approaches as accurately and consistently as possible.

Don't get hypnotized into watching the water directly in front of you on final. Doing so will severely impair your ability to judge the proper time to begin your landing flare. Instead, watch the shoreline out ahead of you or use your peripheral vision to judge your altitude by watching the shoreline next to you. Any boats in the vicinity will make it even easier to judge your height above the water.

The surface of the water can fool you into thinking that you're drifting sideways, when in reality you aren't. When the wind shifts, it might take some time before the waves on the water reflect this change, and it's possible to land into the wind, but diagonally across the waves. If you become fixated on the waves directly in front of you,

you might start to think you're landing in a crosswind. If you roll in some compensation for this nonexistent crosswind, you'll get a big surprise when you touch down. If you *are* landing in a crosswind, only your position relative to the shoreline ahead of you can be relied upon to indicate your true rate of drift.

The actual flare and touchdown are a little like doing a soft field landing in a wheelplane. As you flare, bring in just enough power to hold the floatplane in the correct attitude for touchdown (Fig. 12-2). Ideally, you want the plane to touch down on the steps of the floats, with the nose a little higher than it is during the planing phase of the takeoff. In fact, it's okay if the plane touches down on both the step and the afterbody of each float at the same time. The important thing is to keep the nose up so the bows of the floats won't dig into the waves. The correct touchdown attitude is not unlike that of a tricycle-geared airplane, which touches down on its main wheels while the nosewheel is held off the runway.

Fig. 12-3. *A perfect landing. The bows of the floats are high enough to prevent them from digging in, but not so high as to cause the sterns of the floats to strike the water and pitch the plane forward.*

Fig. 12-2. *Moments before touchdown. The floats are being held slightly nose-high, and contact will be made just ahead of the step.*

After you've established the proper touchdown attitude and are holding the floatplane just off the water, decrease the power slightly and allow the plane to settle smoothly onto the surface (Fig. 12-3).

My first floatplane instructor, Lana Kurtzer, had been flying seaplanes since 1928, and he'd developed a unique way of teaching power-on landings. After I had flared the floatplane to the correct touchdown attitude, he would have me add power until the plane was slow-flying a few feet above the surface of the water. My job was to hold the airplane in a constant attitude. If I had to make any altitude adjustments, I was to make them with power only. If a gust of wind ballooned us upward, I reduced power. If we started to sink towards the surface, I added power. Once I had the plane firmly stabilized a few feet off the water in the correct touchdown attitude, Mr. Kurtzer would then have me reduce the power by a hundred rpm or so and count to six without changing the airplane's attitude. I'm not sure if he wanted me to count to six because that's how long it took the plane to settle onto the water, or if it was simply to give me something to do so I wouldn't get impatient and try to force the plane down, but whatever the reason, the resulting touchdowns were the smoothest I've ever experienced. This method uses up more water than other power-on procedures, but if you have the space and plan your approaches accordingly, the touchdowns are real passenger-pleasers. It's also a very effective way of teaching a new pilot to recognize the proper touchdown attitude.

This technique of holding the plane just above the water can come in handy if you're landing in a busy harbor with lots of active boat traffic. Up at pattern altitude it sometimes can be difficult to determine the best touchdown spot because the boat wakes will have changed so much by the time you get there. It might be better to fly an approach that gets you down close to the water well in advance of your landing area, and then drag the plane in with power in the touchdown attitude. You can skim safely along over the boat wakes and choppy water until you approach a smooth spot. Reduce the power just before reaching the smoother water, and the plane will settle down right where you want it.

There's no place for indecision in this approach. If you keep skimming the water hoping to find an even better spot than the one you just flew over, you'll very likely run out of space altogether and hit something solid, unless you have the presence of mind to go around before you get into trouble. This kind of approach simply helps you pick the best water to land in within your preselected touchdown area.

Some floatplanes, such as a heavily loaded Beaver or Cessna 206, have a tendency to sink right through a landing flare, and if you don't anticipate and prevent this with a little burst of power, the plane could arrive on the water with a resounding whack—a touchdown that definitely will *not* please the passengers.

As soon as the floats touch the water, close the throttle. This is important because, unless you intend to step-taxi, any further application of power will only prolong the landing runout.

When the floats touch the water, they will be subjected to a lot of drag, and the plane will tend to pitch forward. The severity of this sudden pitch-over will depend largely on the speed you're traveling when you touch down. The faster you're going, the greater will be the water's drag, and the more the plane will want to pitch over—another reason why it's important to touch down at the slowest speed possible. If your floatplane is traveling fast enough, it's conceivable that contact with the water could nose it over far enough to en-

able the float bows to dig in. The end result would probably be a graceful forward somersault as your plane trips over its float bows and pitches onto its back.

Be prepared to bring in a little back pressure when your plane touches down to counter this tendency to pitch forward, but don't get carried away and suck the yoke or stick back into your stomach. Too much back pressure too early can rock the plane back onto the tails of the floats, which will cause the float bottoms to smack into the waves instead of cutting through them. Maintain the same slightly nose-high attitude during the first part of the landing runout that you established for the touchdown itself, and only apply enough back pressure to offset the plane's tendency to pitch forward.

If the water is smooth, its suction will contribute greatly to the drag on the floats, and the tendency of the floatplane to pitch forward will be magnified. You might have to apply quite a bit of back pressure to overcome the nose-over force experienced right after touchdown on smooth water. On the other hand, if the water is choppy or covered with waves, the nose-over tendency might be very slight because the air introduced under the floats by the irregular water surface will reduce the water's friction against the float bottoms. In fact, if the water is choppy, it's sometimes advisable to gradually apply forward pressure during the planing phase of the landing runout to take advantage of the wave-cutting ability of the float keels and give the plane and its occupants a smoother ride. This procedure takes practice, however, because you don't want to push the float bows down to the point where they are in danger of digging in.

When a floatplane lands, it goes through the same phases it did during takeoff, only in reverse order. After touchdown, the plane will run along on the step for a short distance. As the airplane's speed decreases, so will the hydrodynamic pressure that is supporting it, and the floats will settle deeper into the water. Soon, the plane will fall off the step completely and come back down over the hump to the displacement phase. As the floatplane slows down and begins to come back over the hump, the yoke or stick should be brought all the way back to help keep the nose up and the propeller clear of the spray that will be thrown out as the plane settles back into a displacement attitude (Fig. 12-4). When the landing runout is completed and the plane has slowed to an idle taxi speed, lower the water rudders and head for the dock, ramp, or beach that is your destination.

Fig. 12-4. *This Beaver has just landed, and it's coming back down over the hump to the displacement attitude.*

The power-off landing

Power-off landings are different from power-on landings only in the fact that no power is used to ease the plane onto the surface of the water. Instead, the throttle is closed before or during the flare, and the plane is landed in a full stall. The advantages of the power-off, full-stall landing are that it uses much less space than a power-on landing, and the touchdown is made at the slowest airspeed of which the airplane is capable. The disadvantage of this type of landing is that it is often difficult for an inexperienced floatplane pilot to accurately judge his or her height above the water. The common tendency is to flare the airplane too soon, and it might run out of flying speed while it is still some distance above the surface. If power isn't added immediately, the plane will drop hard onto the water, possibly bending a float strut or breaking a spreader bar fitting in the process. A hard landing

can easily become a sinking, which does amazing things to your insurance rates.

The landing runout after a power-off, full-stall landing will be identical to the runout after a power-on landing only shorter, thanks to the floatplane's lower touchdown speed.

WIND GUSTS AND JUMPING FISH

One of the advantages floatplane pilots have over landplane pilots is the ability to see and correct for wind gusts during landings.

While landplane pilots can only react to gusts after their airplanes have flown into them, floatplane pilots can see the gusts coming and take corrective action before the gusts reach their planes.

Wind gusts appear as darker patches on the surface of the water. It's important to remember that the leading edge of a gust will be slightly in advance of the dark patch on the surface, so don't wait until you are right on top of the patch before making your power adjustment. An airplane will tend to balloon upwards when it's hit by a gust, and then sink back down as the gust passes. If you are landing on a body of water where dark patches of ruffled water are announcing the presence of gusts, reduce power just as one of these gusts approaches, and then put the power back in again as the gust passes by. Your objective is to cancel out the ballooning and sinking effects the gusts have on your airplane. The ability to see and correct for wind gusts is especially helpful as you are flaring your airplane for landing because, by adjusting the power, you can reduce the risk of being ballooned back into the air in a nose-high attitude with no airspeed.

Landing with full flaps in gusty conditions increases the risk of getting ballooned back up, so if the wind is gusty, you might want to land using something less than the maximum flap setting for your particular airplane. In a Cessna 180, for example, you might want to use only two notches of flap, or 20 degrees, instead of the usual four notches, or 40 degrees. If you're flying a Beaver, pumping the flaps to a point midway between the

"Takeoff" and "Climb" settings, instead of all the way down to the "Landing" setting, will reduce the ballooning tendency of the airplane.

There is one other hazard to waterborne floatplanes that none of us can do a thing about: fish. You would think that the only time fish would present a problem is when we're having terrible luck catching them, but in some parts of the country, fish have been known to do some rather severe damage to floatplanes. Certain species of large fish like to jump out of the water occasionally, and if one of them should choose to become airborne at the same time you are, your floatplane could end up spending some time in the shop.

In the Pacific Northwest, the salmon return in the autumn to the rivers they left several years earlier. When they first enter fresh water, many of them leap high into the air and fall back with a resounding smack. One theory is that they are trying to knock off any parasites that might have been picked up during their stay in salt water, but whatever the reason, the sight of a 40-pound Chinook salmon launching itself three or four feet out of the water is impressive. It's unlikely that one of these fish would come up under a taxiing floatplane that was moving slowly, but if one were to jump into the propeller of your floatplane as you were taking off or landing, the damage to the prop—and possibly other parts of the floatplane as well— could be substantial.

Another fish that is notorious for jumping high out of the water is the paddlefish, found in many lakes of the south-central United States.

Sometimes called the spoonbill catfish, these primitive fish can grow to a length of five to six feet and weigh up to 100 pounds. I've read of one case where a large paddlefish jumped up in the path of an approaching seaplane, splintered the propeller, and cracked the windshield. The pilot was startled, to say the least.

You really can't do anything to avoid hitting an aerobatic fish because you have no way of knowing when one is going to launch out of the water in front of you, but fortunately collisions between fish and floatplanes are relatively rare.

NO TWO LANDINGS ARE THE SAME

At the beginning of this book, I said that one of the best things about flying a floatplane is the fact that you are on your own, and that the success of your flight depends solely on the decisions you make as a pilot. To me, the landing is the most challenging and rewarding aspect of flying floats because each landing requires a different set of decisions based on a different set of observations.

No two landings are ever the same, even if they are made in the same place. Wind and water conditions are constantly changing, to say nothing of the varied and unpredictable surface traffic with which you might have to contend. There is no such thing as a routine water landing, but the sense of satisfaction you'll experience each time you plan and execute a smooth, safe, and accurate touchdown is difficult to match in any other type of flying.

13
After the flight

UNLESS YOU'RE LANDING AN amphibian at an airport, your ultimate destination will be either a ramp, a dock, a buoy, an anchor line, or the shoreline itself. It's said that most accidents occur in the home, and I think this statement applies to floatplanes as well. More floatplanes are dinged, dented, bent, scraped, scratched, holed, or sunk at their moorings than anywhere else. No matter where you plan to secure your floatplane, there are some basic procedures to follow. As long as you follow these procedures, plan for the unexpected, and think through the consequences of each action, the odds that you will damage a floatplane will be slim indeed.

RAMPING

Ramping a floatplane is pretty easy. You simply hit the ramp head-on, slide up it, and stop. Because you carry power all the way to the ramp, the wind won't affect your plane as much as it will when you coast up to a dock with the engine cut. As easy as it seems, however, there is a right way and a wrong way to ramp a floatplane.

First, make sure there is enough room for your plane on the ramp. This seems like a fairly obvious thing to do, but you'd be surprised at the number of pilots who taxi in only to discover—sometimes too late—that the ramp is full, or that the airplane won't fit between the other planes already there. If you've checked out the area from the air prior to landing, you should already know what kind of space is available on the ramp.

As you taxi in, maneuver your floatplane so that you will be able to approach the ramp head-on. Make sure no one is standing on the section of the ramp you intend to use and that there are no mooring lines from adjacent floatplanes stretching across your path. Approach the ramp at minimum speed, but when you are about 15 to 20 feet out, bring the yoke or stick all the way back and apply enough power to raise the bows of the floats (Fig. 13-1). As the bows of the floats come up, they will bulldoze a wall of water ahead of them onto the ramp. The wall of water accomplishes three things. First, it helps the floats ride up onto the ramp. Second, it cushions the impact of the float keels against the boards, and third, by lubricating the surface of the ramp, the water helps the plane slide up the ramp to the point where it's no longer in danger of sliding back down again.

The crucial thing here is the timing. If you apply the power too late, or if you don't put enough in, your plane might barely get its floats onto the

Fig. 13-1. *Ramping a Beaver. Note the use of full up-elevator. The small tubes sticking out of the sides of the float just forward of the step are attach points for beaching gear.*

ramp before it comes to a stop. If it doesn't slide back into the water right away, the movement caused by your getting out might be enough to start the plane slipping backward. This is a potentially dangerous situation, because if your plane does slide back into the water, it immediately will be at the mercy of the wind. If the wind should turn the airplane at an angle to the ramp, restarting the engine could get you into even worse trouble if there are ramped floatplanes on either side of you. The only thing you can do in this case is to get out the paddle and fend yourself off as best you can until you drift or paddle out far enough to restart the engine and try again.

Kurtzer Flying Service, where I received my float rating, had a long, floating, double-sided ramp. The planes were pulled up nose-to-nose down the length of this ramp, with only about five feet separating the spinner of one plane from the spinner of the plane facing it. It was nerve-wracking enough to deliberately taxi in toward the nose of another very expensive floatplane, but it was far worse to slide up the ramp, propeller whirling, headed for what seemed like an imminent collision. Because of this, I tended to be very timid about putting in enough power to get the airplane properly up on the ramp. As we would cling pre-

cariously to the edge of the ramp, Mr. Kurtzer would gingerly ease himself out of the plane and onto the slippery boards so he could fasten a dock line to the bow cleat on one of the floats. Sometimes I slid off the ramp before he could get a line on the float, and I'd have to scramble out and catch the line he'd throw before I drifted into the plane next to me. Mr. Kurtzer was a firm believer in letting his students know when they had screwed up, and while I eventually learned to ramp the plane properly, I'll never know if it was through practice, or simply because I couldn't face the verbal consequences of yet another humiliating backward slide off the ramp. I never did get used to sliding up to within a few feet of another floatplane, however.

The other thing you can do if you hit a ramp too lightly is power yourself up, but bear in mind that without that wave of water preceding you up the ramp, it will take a lot of power to slide the floats up the dry boards. Make sure that the top of the ramp is free of obstacles because the floats might wait until you're practically at full power before suddenly becoming unstuck, and the plane could surge forward quite a distance before you got it under control again.

Adding power too early as you approach the ramp is just as bad as adding it too late. If you put the power in too soon, the plane will have time to overcome the water's resistance, and it will begin to accelerate before it reaches the ramp. Depending on your speed and the angle of the ramp, you might strike the ramp too hard, slide up the boards too far, or both.

If you've added power at the right time, don't chicken out and pull it off just as you get to the ramp. If you do, the plane will pitch forward as it decelerates, and instead of sliding smoothly up the ramp, the float bows will strike the boards quite hard as they nose down. Keep the power on and the yoke back until you are far enough up the ramp to be in no danger of sliding back again (Fig. 13-2).

Be very careful if the ramp is covered with ice. Your float keels will become a pair of giant ice

Fig. 13-2. *Properly tied down on the ramp. The plane was powered up far enough to prevent it from sliding back into the water, after which lines were attached to keep it securely in place.*

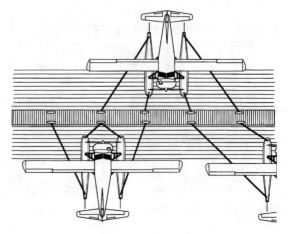

Fig. 13-3. *One of the best ways to secure a floatplane to a ramp. Be careful when putting a plane onto a double-sided ramp like this. You don't want to add so much power that you slide up over the top and into the floatplane in front of you!*

skates, and if you use too much power, you'll slide right up over the top. On the other hand, you'll be more likely to slide back into the water if you don't get the plane firmly onto the icy boards, so the whole operation becomes a real judgment call. Once you get the plane on the ramp, watch your step on the ramp, for the icy boards will be delighted to send you sliding, arms flailing, into the equally icy water below.

When the floatplane is firmly on the ramp, shut down the engine and secure the plane to the dock with at least two lines. Every floatplane pilot has his or her own favorite way of securing a floatplane, so I will describe the method we used on Kurtzer's double-sided ramp by way of an example. We'd run a line from the bow cleat on each float to a single, large cleat set in the top of the ramp directly in front of the plane. We then ran a long line from the stern cleat on each float to ramp cleats set 15 or 20 feet on each side of the center cleat. In the event of a strong wind, the bow lines would hold the nose of the airplane down, and the stern lines would keep the plane from pivoting on the ramp (Fig. 13-3).

Incidentally, the ramping procedure described here should only be used on wood-decked ramps. Do not try to power a floatplane onto a concrete boat ramp. The concrete is quite rough, and you will severely abrade the keels of your floats. If you should have to put your plane on a boat ramp for some reason, treat the concrete ramp as if it were a beach, and use the beaching procedures described later in this chapter.

DOCKING

Other than an elevator or railcar ride to dry storage, ramps are the most ideal way to secure a floatplane, but they are only found at facilities that cater specifically to floatplanes. These facilities are relatively few and far between, so most of the time you will be tying your plane to a dock. Docks come in all shapes and sizes, ranging from sturdy, floating platforms lined with tires to protect your floats from damage, to a couple of boards nailed to a log sticking out from shore. There are only two absolute requirements for a floatplane dock. First, it has to be low enough to clear the floatplane's wing, wing strut, and horizontal stabilizer. Second, if the dock is in tidal waters, it must be of the floating variety. While lakes are not subjected to tides, their water levels can fluctuate, either through man's manipulation or from seasonal run-off and evaporation. As a result, most freshwater boat and seaplane facilities use floating docks as well.

Most docks are equipped with mooring cleats or some other means of securing the lines from your plane, but you might have to get creative when figuring out how to tie your plane to one of the more primitive wilderness docks you might encounter. If you are going to an area where you're not sure of the docking facilities, carry plenty of extra line in the plane with you. You might end up having to pass lines completely around a dock, or even around trees on shore to safely secure the plane.

If you're flying in a logging region, you might have occasion to tie up to a floating log raft. These actually make pretty good docks because they are usually bound together with stout cables to which you can fasten your mooring lines (Fig. 13-4).

Fig. 13-4. *Log booms (bottom left) make sturdy docks, and the cables that bind them together provide good places to fasten your mooring lines.*

Unless your destination is a seaplane facility or a harbor that has docks specifically designed and reserved for seaplanes, you will most likely have to tie up to a dock that was built for boats. Examine the dock carefully as you approach it. Things like pilings, light poles, railings, and equipment lockers don't get in the way of a boat, but they can play havoc with your attempts to dock a floatplane.

Pilings are the worst offenders. One of the most popular methods of keeping a floating dock from floating away is to secure it to piles the size of telephone poles driven deep into the bottom of the harbor. Loosely fitting metal rings are placed around each pile and attached to the dock. This keeps the dock from drifting off, while still allowing it to ride up and down with the tide. Pilings usually stick up a good 10 or 15 feet above the water and can be even higher in areas of extreme tides. While they present no problem for boats, they can make it impossible for a floatplane to approach what would otherwise be a perfect dock.

Consciously remind yourself that you have wings as you taxi in. It's easy to forget them as you concentrate on maneuvering into that last open spot on the dock. I forgot my wings once, and I almost put one of them into a building because I was so busy doing such a terrific and skillful job of docking the fuselage. Only the quick action of a pilot already on the dock kept the plane out of the repair shop.

Like landings, every docking is different, and one of the things that keeps float flying from becoming routine is the challenge of figuring out the best way to get your plane to the dock. There is not enough room in this book—or any book, for that matter—to illustrate every docking situation you could possibly encounter. Instead, we'll look at docking procedures and techniques in general and see how they apply to a few basic docking situations. Armed with this knowledge, together with plenty of good training and practice with an instructor, you should be able to solve just about every docking problem that presents itself.

First, never let yourself be rushed into making a move before you are ready. Remember, you have no brakes and no reverse. It's very important to carefully check out a dock from the air before you land and taxi up to it. Ask yourself the following questions:

- Is the dock low enough for a floatplane?
- Is there sufficient room for me to approach the dock and stop? (You will need at least

two or three floatplane lengths of open space at, or in front of, the dock before you can safely approach it, come alongside, and stop.)

- Can I taxi to the dock without hitting any pilings or other obstructions?
- Will my wings clear the boats that are moored nearby or tied to the dock? (Don't forget, even a low-profile, open fishing boat can have a tall radio or loran antenna on it. It might not damage your plane if you should hit it, but you might end up having to buy the boat owner a new antenna.)
- Will my inside wing be able to extend over the dock without hitting anything?
- Once I'm tied up, will other boats or aircraft be able to get past my outside wing?
- Finally, if I have enough room to get to the dock, will I have enough room to depart from it later on? (You'd be amazed at the number of pilots who don't ask this question until it's too late.)

If the answer to each of these questions is "Yes," then you've found a good dock to tie up to. There are still questions to be answered about the direction and strength of the wind, plus the possible danger from boat wakes, swells, and other details, but at least you'll know you can physically get your plane alongside the dock.

Make it a practice to remove your seat belt and open the door as you taxi in after landing, and have your front-seat passenger do the same. If it's windy, or if the dock is crowded, things could start getting hectic, and one of you might have to jump out onto a float in a hurry. The time to start fumbling with a door latch or discover that your seat belt is still fastened is not as you are coasting inexorably toward the floatplane in front of you. As you get closer to the dock, slide your seat far enough back so you won't have to struggle to get out the door. How far you have to slide the seat depends on your airplane and your size. I'm six-foot

three inches tall with a gross weight of a bit too much over 200 pounds, and if I'm flying a Cessna 180, I have to slide the seat all the way back before I can get comfortably out the door. I've found that by sitting on the forward edge of the seat and holding on to the V-brace above the instrument panel, I can still reach and operate the rudder pedals. I don't have to move the seat back in a Beaver because I have to put it there to begin with so I can fly the plane. The challenge in a Beaver is not the seat, but the size of the cockpit doors. It was certainly considerate of de Havilland to include them in the design, but I sure wish they'd made them a little larger. (Forget flying skill and experience; the real mark of a good bush pilot is his or her ability to gracefully exit the front door of a Beaver!) The point is that every floatplane—and every pilot—is different. The important thing is that you be able to get out onto the float in a hurry if you have to.

Docking on a calm day

Docking a floatplane when there is no wind to contend with is relatively easy. If there are no other planes or boats in the way, you can come straight in parallel to the dock (Fig. 13-5). If the end of the dock is occupied, you'll have to approach at an angle just ahead of the moored floatplane or boat, turning parallel to the dock at the

Fig. 13-5. *Approaching a dock in Seattle's Lake Union. Pilot Neal Ratti has shut down the engine and has opened his door in preparation to stepping onto the dock and stopping the plane.*

last moment. The reason you need two or three floatplane lengths of open space at a dock will become apparent the first time you do this (Fig. 13-6). While you're still three or four plane lengths from the dock, shut off the engine and coast the rest of the way in. Remember to turn off the mag and master switches as soon as the engine stops turning over. You don't want anybody, including yourself, to get a nasty surprise if he or she happens to pull on the prop for some reason.

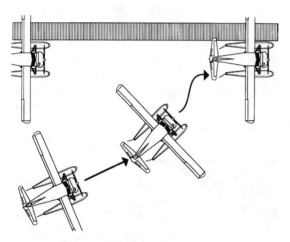

Fig. 13-6. *It takes more room than you might think to bring a floatplane alongside a dock and get it stopped, especially if there are other planes already there.*

If you've timed everything correctly, you'll drift to a stop just as you come alongside the dock, and all you'll have to do is step out and secure the plane. One of the trickiest things about learning to dock a floatplane is judging the right moment to shut off the engine—too soon, and you'll drift to a stop before you get to the dock; too late, and you'll be going too fast when you get there. If you stop too soon, and there's no wind, you can either throw a line to someone standing on the dock or get out your trusty paddle. Don't restart the engine to carry you those last few yards to the dock. Aircraft engines don't quit the instant you pull the mixture control back to idle cutoff, and in the time it would take for the engine to shut down again,

you could be carried quite a distance—assuming you didn't fetch up against a piling or somebody's yacht first.

Most of the time, you'll arrive at the dock carrying some degree of forward speed, and since the plane doesn't have any brakes of its own, you'll have to hop out and stop the plane yourself. You would think this would be a fairly self-explanatory procedure, but there's even a right and a wrong way to do this. The logical thing to do would be to jump onto the dock, grab the wing strut, and pull back on it to stop the plane. This is the wrong way. When you pull back on the strut, your hands become a pivot point around which the airplane will start to rotate. Because the plane will probably be a foot or two away from the dock when you jump off, the bow of the inboard float will pivot into the dock. If it pivots into something unyielding, the float could be damaged.

The right way is to step onto the float deck and pick up one of the permanent mooring lines that are attached to the float struts. Then you can jump onto the dock. Using the mooring line and a firm grip on the wing strut, pull the plane in against the side of the dock while walking forward with it. When the side of the inboard float is firmly against the dock, pull back slightly; this, plus the friction of the float against the dock, will bring the plane to a quick stop (Fig. 13-7). Obviously, you don't want to pull the floats up against a dock that does not have tires or some other type of cushioning material on it. If you encounter a dock that has metal or concrete sides, you'll have to stop the plane while holding it away from the dock, but the principle is still the same. Walk along with the plane while slowing it to a stop, and don't let the bow of the inboard float pivot into the dock.

If there are people on or near the dock that you are approaching, someone will probably come over to catch your wing and help you stop. This is great if that person knows the correct procedure, but unfortunately, few people other than floatplane pilots understand the danger of trying to stop a floatplane by pulling back on its wing strut. It might be better

Fig. 13-7. *The right way to stop a floatplane at a dock. Neal is holding onto the strut and one of the mooring lines as he slows the plane down, but he is not allowing the bow of the inboard float to pivot in and strike the dock.*

to wave the helpers off and stop the plane yourself rather than risk having your floats damaged.

Docking a floatplane always seems to generate a sense of urgency, especially if you're relatively inexperienced. You want to get out and get the plane stopped as quickly as possible. It's certainly faster to hop onto the dock and simply grab the wing strut, but try to get into the habit of picking up the mooring line first, before you step to the dock. You can get a better grip on a line than you can on a sometimes-slippery wing strut, and the line will actually give you better control of the plane. Its attachment point on the float deck is a lot closer to the centerline of the airplane than a handhold out at the middle of the wing strut, so the tendency of the plane to pivot into the dock will be considerably reduced. Also, if the plane is moving a bit too fast because of a current, or because you waited too long to kill the engine, you can snub the line around a cleat to bring the plane to a quick stop. It's better to spend an extra two or three seconds picking up a line than to be dragged down the dock by a heavy floatplane, your heels skidding across the boards as you pull awkwardly on the wing strut, desperately trying to stop your plane before you hear that quiet crunch that usually precedes a whopping repair bill.

Mooring lines and bumpers

If the dock you're using can accommodate several floatplanes, walk your plane as far forward as you can before cleating off the mooring lines. This will make it easier for the next pilot to get in behind you and will make maximum use of the available dock space.

The best way to tie off, or belay, a mooring line to a cleat is shown in Fig. 13-8. Notice that the last turn is tucked under itself. This is called "jamming" the line, and it's frowned upon in sailboat circles, where sheets and halyards sometimes have to be uncleated in a hurry; however, the same tenacious qualities that make this method so unpopular with sailboaters are a benefit to floatplane pilots. A line secured to a cleat in this manner will not work loose, and your plane will be right where you left it when you return.

Fig. 13-8. *The best way to cleat a line. The line was brought in from the bottom of the picture, fastened to the cleat, and the free end coiled out of frame to the right.*

Use at least two lines to secure your plane to the dock. If it's going to be tied up for some time, it's a good idea to use a pair of spring lines in addition to the bow and stern lines. A spring line runs diagonally from one end of the float to a point on the dock opposite the other end of the float. The spring line on the bow will keep the plane from moving forward, while the spring line attached to the tail of the float will prevent the plane from moving backward. By holding the plane firmly in position, the spring lines keep the inboard float from rubbing back and forth against the dock.

If the dock has tires lining its sides, you won't have to worry about protecting your floats, but if the dock has bare wood, metal, or concrete sides, you'll have to use bumpers of some sort to keep the floats from scraping themselves raw. If you don't have room in the plane for a set of the popular air-filled bumpers used by boaters, you can make some effective bumpers using sections of old automobile tires. A description of these inexpensive bumpers can be found in chapter 7.

The importance of bumpers cannot be overstressed. If a float is allowed to bang repeatedly into the unyielding side of a dock, it won't be long before dents begin to appear or seams begin to open up. If the float starts rubbing on an exposed nailhead or a metal dock fitting, there's a good chance a hole could be worn completely through the aluminum or fiberglass skin. Those of us who operate in salt water have to be especially careful, for even a tire-lined dock can become encrusted with barnacles. When you combine those razor-sharp shells with the wave action normally encountered in a marine environment, you can see how a float could be holed in short order if it isn't protected by a pair of substantial bumpers.

Some docks can accommodate floatplanes on both sides. Which side you choose depends on a couple of factors. The wakes from passing boats can start a plane banging into the dock, so if there is a lot of boat traffic in the area, try to put the dock between you and the swells. If the wind is strong and gusty, you might want to secure the plane to the downwind side of the dock. As explained in the next section, there are definite disadvantages to approaching a dock on its downwind side, but once the plane is tied up, being in the lee of the dock can make life a lot easier on your plane. The wind will hold the floats away from the dock, and the dock itself will provide some protection from the waves.

Another advantage of being secured to the lee side of a dock is that the upwind wing can be tied down. I know of one case where a floatplane that was tied to the windward side of a dock was flipped upside down by a heavy gust of wind that hit the plane just as the upwind wing was being pitched up by the heavy wave action. As the plane went over, the mooring lines tore the cleats right out of the dock. If the plane had been tied to the lee side of the dock (which wasn't possible in this case), the upwind wing could have been secured to the dock, and the accident prevented.

However, if putting the plane on the downwind side of the dock will also expose it to the swells created by heavy boat traffic, choose the lesser of two evils, and tie up on the side away from the boat wakes.

Docking in the wind

Docking in calm conditions can be challenging enough, but your judgment and skill will really be put to the test when the wind kicks up. Not only will the ever-present weathercocking force be lurking about, waiting to swing your plane in the wrong direction, but as you slow down after shutting off the engine, your water rudders will become less and less effective. Don't despair, however, for there are some very slick ways of using the wind to help you dock that, when properly executed, will leave you feeling like a real pro.

The ideal way to approach a dock is on an upwind heading on the upwind side of the dock (Fig. 13-9). The wind will help you in two ways. First, it will help slow you down as you coast up to the dock after shutting down the engine. Second, it will push you into the dock and hold you against it. If you shut off the engine a little too soon, and your momentum doesn't carry you quite up to the dock, it's not a big crisis, because the wind is going to push you over to it anyway.

If you approach on the downwind side of a dock and stop short, the wind will immediately start to push you *away* from the dock, and possi-

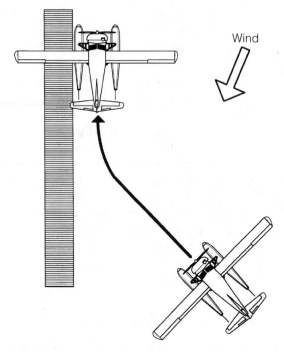

Wind

Fig. 13-9. *The ideal way to approach a dock in the wind.*

the wind doesn't read books like this one, the day will come when you will have no other choice but to approach a dock on a downwind or crosswind heading. If the dock is long, and there are no other floatplanes immediately in front of you, you might be able to get away with a normal docking procedure, but bear in mind your plane will be moving down the dock at a pretty good clip, and it will require extra space to bring it to a halt.

A better technique is shown in Fig. 13-10. Make your downwind approach some distance from the dock. When you are a short distance downwind of your intended parking place on the dock, start a turn toward it, and pull up the water rudders. With the water rudders retracted, the wind coming from astern will weathercock your floatplane around very quickly. As the airplane swings into an upwind heading, lower the water rudders and proceed with what has now become a normal upwind docking. Again, try to perform this maneuver on the upwind side of the dock so that the wind will push you into the dock instead of drifting you away.

The two most common errors pilots make when executing this maneuver are taxiing too close to the dock on the downwind leg to safely make the upwind turn and starting the turn too early, which might cause the plane to overshoot the intended arrival spot on the dock. This isn't a problem if the dock ahead of the plane is clear, but it will be a big problem if there's a tied-down floatplane up ahead.

Different planes react differently to the retraction of the water rudders during a turn to an upwind heading. Cessna 172s, Piper Super Cubs, and even Cessna 180s use floats with relatively shallow afterbodies. If the water rudders are pulled up during an upwind turn, the weathercocking force against the tail will "skid" the shallow-draft float sterns sideways through the water, and the turn rate will accelerate. The turn rate can be slowed at any time by putting the water rudders back down. The afterbodies of the floats used on de Havilland Beavers and Otters have relatively

bly into something expensive. Unless you can scramble out onto the float and throw a line to someone on the dock, all you can do is wait until you've drifted out far enough to be able to restart the engine and try again.

Whenever possible, avoid approaching a dock on a downwind or crosswind heading. For one thing, you might have to taxi faster to keep the water rudders effective. This, plus the fact that the wind might also be pushing you from behind, will cause you to coast up to the dock at a much higher rate of speed, and it might be difficult to get the plane stopped. This is especially dangerous if there is another floatplane tied to the dock up ahead of you, as you run the risk of colliding with it before you can get out and drag your own plane to a stop.

It's easy to say, "Never approach a dock on a downwind or a crosswind heading," but because

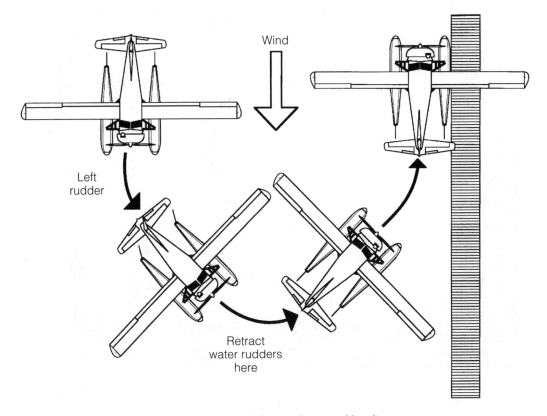

Wind

Left
rudder

Retract
water rudders
here

Fig. 13-10. *The safest way to approach a dock from a downwind heading.*

deep drafts, which tend to resist sideways skidding forces. Pulling up the water rudders on a Beaver during an upwind turn won't have much effect on the turn rate, but there's nothing wrong with doing it.

Another variation of a downwind docking is shown in Fig. 13-11. In this case, the dock is lying perpendicular to the wind. Approach the dock at the minimum possible speed, but be very careful not to let the wind get around to one side of you and weathercock the plane. Shut down the engine when you are two or three plane lengths out and start a turn to parallel the dock, pulling up the water rudders as you do so. If you have judged everything correctly, the plane will arrive at the dock at the same time it has pivoted around parallel to the dock's edge.

While the downwind approach illustrated in Fig. 13-11 was required because of obstructions at either end of the dock, the same procedure can be used in a situation where the dock itself is unobstructed, but the normal approach to it would require you to taxi across the wind. In order to maintain directional control while taxiing crosswind, you might have to taxi faster than you normally would, and you might even have to put the plane in a plowing attitude. In either case, you will arrive at the dock going much too fast. A safer alternative is shown in Fig. 13-12.

Docking a floatplane when there is a current running is not unlike docking when the wind is blowing. The same general rules apply, except there won't be a weathercocking force to deal with, unless, of course, the wind is also blowing. In fact, if

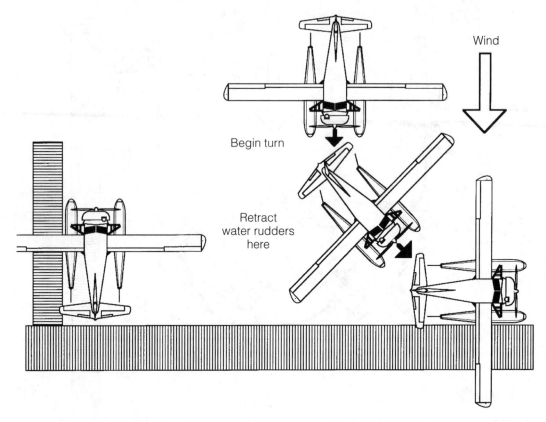

Fig. 13-11. *One technique for approaching a crosswind dock from a downwind heading.*

the current is strong—in a fairly swift river, for example—you might be moved along fast enough to create a relative wind that will cause you to weathercock downstream. Because a current can be moving at a fairly good clip, it's best to always head into it when approaching a dock. On a river or in a strong tide, you might find that it takes more than idle power just to stay in one place. If you were to attempt to approach a dock while heading downstream, you might not be able to stop. By taxiing into the current, you can control your forward speed quite precisely with the engine. It's even possible to move a floatplane sideways while remaining opposite the same place on the shore. We'll look at river operations in more detail in chapter 16, but the general rule is to always head into the current when approaching a dock.

You might have noticed that some of the illustrations in this chapter show the pilot's side of the floatplane next to the dock, while in others, the dock is against the passenger's side. Wind, current, and available mooring space, not convenience, will determine which side of the plane will end up against the dock, so you won't always be able to put it next to your door. If you're by yourself, and it looks like the dock is going to end up on the passenger's side of the airplane, all you have to do is slide over into the passenger seat and taxi the plane from there. Of course, this solution assumes that your plane has dual controls, and that there is a door on the passenger's side of the cabin. Floatplanes such as the Cessna 172, 180, and 185 are very easy to dock from the passenger's side, as is the de Havilland Beaver. All of these planes

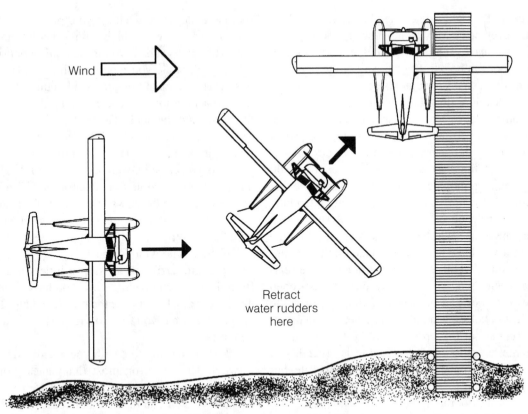

Wind

Retract
water rudders
here

Fig. 13-12. *It's better to approach this dock on a downwind heading than to approach it straight in on a crosswind heading.*

have front doors on both sides of the cabin, and while few Beavers are equipped with dual yokes, its single yoke is the throw-over type.

A Cessna 206, on the other hand, has a front door only on the pilot's side of the airplane. The plane does have nice, big double doors on the right side of the plane, but they are for the rear-seat passengers or freight. To use the rear doors, the pilot has to climb over the backs of the front seats. If the plane is full of freight, this could be a very difficult, if not impossible, task. Some 206 operators stretch a length of aircraft cable between the bow cleats on the floats. Then, if the pilot has to put a dock on the right side of the plane, he or she can climb out on the left float after shutting down the engine, walk forward, and cross to the right float via the cable, hold-

ing onto the propeller for balance. From there, the pilot can step to the dock and stop the plane. Obviously, this will take more time than simply stepping out of the pilot's seat to the float and then to the dock, so pilots planning to use the cable method will have to make sure there's sufficient space at the dock for the plane to continue coasting while they cross from the outside to the inside float. One more thing: If you ever decide to "walk the cable" in a 206, make sure you turn off the master and magneto switches before you get out of your seat. The last thing you want to do is inadvertently hand-prop the engine back to life when you're balancing in front of it on a wire!

For pilots who don't feel like scrambling over seats or walking a wire every time they have to dock on the right side of the plane, Wipaire, Inc., has developed a nifty front passenger door for the 206 that makes it as easy to dock as a 180 or 185. The door can be retrofitted to any of the later versions of Cessna's popular six-seater.

Docking a floatplane on the passenger's side becomes a lot easier if you actually have a passenger sitting over there. After explaining the proper way to stop the plane, you can have your passenger step to the dock and bring the plane to a halt. As you're removing your seat belt and opening your door while you're taxiing in after landing, have your front seat passenger do the same. That way, he or she will be ready to step out onto the float if you have to dock the plane on the passenger's side. If you're flying a 206 and have rear-seat passengers, you can have one of them open the rear door and prepare to climb out onto the right float. As a general safety rule, instruct your passenger not to step out onto the float until the engine has stopped. If the timing is crucial, you might have to make an exception to this rule, but if you do, don't allow your passenger to walk forward of the door until the prop has stopped.

Remember, when you kill the engine, turn the mag and master switches off, too. They're easy to forget if you're coasting into what might be a tricky docking situation, but as you, your passenger, or a helper on the dock scramble to get the plane stopped and some mooring lines attached, it's quite conceivable that someone could grab hold of the propeller. If the mags are still hot, you could have a real disaster on your hands.

Docking nose-first

All the docking techniques we've examined so far have assumed that you are going to moor your floatplane with one of its floats parallel to the side of the dock. While this is certainly the most recommended method, there can be times when you won't be able to approach a dock in the normal manner. For example, your aerial survey prior to landing might reveal that, although there is enough

room at a particular dock for your plane, the dock itself is surrounded by high pilings that will interfere with your wings if you try to come alongside. In cases like this, you might be able to approach nose-first. The main thing to avoid in this situation is approaching too fast and ramming the bows of the floats into the dock. The trick is to shut down the engine soon enough so that by the time you reach the dock, you are just barely moving forward. As you coast in, walk to the bow of the float and prepare to become a shock absorber. Your objective is to keep the bows of the floats from striking the dock, and any technique you can come up with that accomplishes this is a good one.

If there is no wind to speak of, one way to ensure a gentle arrival is to stop a little ways out from the dock and paddle in. If you have time to get it out, you also can use the paddle to help slow the plane down if you find you're coasting in a little too fast.

Take a mooring line with you when you walk forward. The floats on most floatplanes project out ahead of the nose, so once you step to the dock, there won't be much to hold onto other than the bows of the floats themselves. Believe me, it's a lot easier to keep a floatplane from drifting away by holding onto a line attached to a bow cleat than it is to kneel on the dock and hold onto the cleat itself. You'll probably have to use one of the coiled lines from inside the plane; the mooring lines permanently fastened to the float struts rarely are long enough to reach all the way forward over the floats to the dock.

Pilots who operate out of crowded boat harbors frequently have to approach docks head-on. Many of these pilots fasten permanent mooring lines to the bow cleats of their airplanes' floats. The lines are cut long enough to reach back almost to the water rudders. To avoid the danger of these lines being picked up by the propeller, they should be fastened to the rear cleat or tied to the forward float struts with pieces of lightweight string. The procedure with a setup like this is to head nose-first for the dock, shut off the engine, step out onto the float, uncleat the aft end of the line or break it free of its string tie, walk forward, stop the plane, and then step to the dock with a mooring line long enough to reach any cleat in the vicinity.

Nosing a floatplane up to a dock can be very tricky if the wind is blowing from any direction other than straight ahead. In order to avoid damaging the floats, it's imperative that you approach the dock at the slowest possible speed; however, your directional control over your airplane will decrease as its forward speed decreases, and a crosswind could begin to weathercock your plane away from the dock before you get close enough to jump onto it. The very fact that you have to approach the dock nose-first means it's probably crowded or obstructed in some way, so the chances are good that the wind will quickly push you into something unyielding. You'd be better off looking for another place to dock the plane, even if it isn't as convenient.

Once you are nosed up against the dock, you might be able to pivot your plane and secure it alongside the dock in the normal manner. If pilings or other obstructions prevent you from doing this, you'll have to leave the plane as it is. Pull the plane forward so the bows of the floats are against the dock, protecting them with bumpers, if necessary, and run a line from the bow cleat of each float to the dock. If possible, secure the sterns of the floats using the same method you would use if you were on a ramp—run a line from each stern cleat diagonally out to a cleat on the dock. This will keep the tail of the plane from swinging back and forth.

If you have to depart the dock from a nose-in position, simply cast off all the lines, step onto the bow of the float on the pilot's side of the plane, and shove the plane backward. If there isn't any wind to help you drift back, you might have to get out the paddle, but whatever you do, don't start the engine until you're far enough away from the dock to be able to turn away from it when you fire up. And be careful if there's a crosswind. Figure out what the airplane is going to do before you cast those lines off.

If you think the plane will be blown into a boat, piling, or other obstruction as soon as you shove off, you'll have to come up with some other way of departing the dock. One alternative might be to attach some long lines to the upwind float and have helpers on the dock use them to hold you away from the obstructions as you drift or paddle backward. When you're safely clear of the obstructions, your dockside helpers can simply toss their ends of the lines in the water and you can haul them in. Of course, if you're lucky enough to be flying a turbine equipped with a beta prop, all you have to do is put it in reverse and back out.

Docking a large floatplane

You probably will earn your seaplane rating in a relatively light floatplane such as a Cessna 172, a Citabria, or a Piper Super Cub. These planes will coast to a stop fairly quickly once their engines are shut off, as their low mass doesn't generate much inertia. Consequently, on windy days you might have to carry power right up to the dock to avoid stopping short and being blown back before you can get out and secure the plane. Eventually, you will develop the ability to judge just the right moment to cut the engine, based on the wind and current conditions, and what you know to be the deceleration rate of your airplane.

When you make the transition to a larger, heavier floatplane, don't fall into the trap (as I have done on occasion) of driving the larger plane as close in to the dock as you would the smaller one before cutting the engine. If you do, you'll be in for a surprise. A Beaver, for example, will coast much farther than a Cessna 172 thanks to the Beaver's tremendous mass. At best, you'll have a hard time bringing the plane to a stop, and if it just isn't your day, you could end up shortening the overall length of the floatplane in front of you. When you start flying a larger plane, anticipate the fact that it will need more room to stop, and be prepared to pull the mixture back to idle cutoff sooner than you're accustomed to. It won't be long before you're used to the new plane's characteristics.

The other thing you need to be aware of when you start flying larger floatplanes is the fact that since they present much more vertical surface to the wind, they will be blown around with much greater force than the smaller planes you're used to. Manhandling a Beaver at a dock on a windy day can be a real experience, especially if you're by yourself, and a huge floatplane like the de Havilland Otter requires a full dock crew to keep it under control when the wind kicks up. On the other hand, the de Havilland Twin Otter is a surprisingly easy plane to dock, thanks to its twin turboprops and reversible-pitch propellers. By manipulating the throttles and propeller controls, Twin Otter pilots can maneuver up to docks that a conventional, single-engined floatplane half the Twin Otter's size couldn't approach at all (Fig. 13-13).

Fig. 13-13. *Docking a Twin Otter in the crowded harbor at Vancouver, British Columbia. The pilot will come up to the dock nose first, stop by putting both propellers in reverse, and then pivot the plane by reversing the right propeller while pulling forward with the left one. This neat maneuver will put the plane alongside the dock, facing out, ready for its next scheduled departure.*

Docking in the snow

In most parts of the country, winter means snow, and a heavy snowfall can severely damage an airplane. The problem is the snow's weight, which can collapse hangar roofs and overstress skin panels, spars, and struts on planes parked outside. The only solution is to keep brushing the snow off the wings and tail before its weight can become dangerous.

In many areas, the arrival of fall signals the end of the floatplane season, but in the Pacific Northwest and southeast Alaska, the floatplane season continues year-round. While the saltwater harbors, bays, and fjords don't freeze up in these areas, late fall, winter, and early spring still bring snow, and with it comes a special threat to floatplanes.

If you visit a seaplane facility or boat harbor that doesn't have a ramp or some other means of removing your plane from the water, you will have no choice but to leave your plane at a dock overnight. Regardless of the time of year, it's a good idea to check the airplane every few hours in this situation just to make sure the airplane isn't in any danger from a leaking float or a chaffing mooring line. If the forecast is predicting snow, however, you'll have to take special precautions.

If the snow is wet and heavy, it can sink an unattended floatplane in a very short period of time. As the snow builds up on the horizontal stabilizer, its weight will gradually force the sterns of the floats underwater. The rear float compartments will begin to flood as water leaks in around the access hatch covers and the rubber balls that plug the bilge-pump down tubes. This will add even more weight to the rear of the plane, and the floats will sink even deeper. Soon, the next compartment forward will begin to fill, which will force the floats deeper still. A friend of mine once described the results of this liquid "domino" effect on a Super Cub he had seen in southeast Alaska. Where a few hours before, the plane had been bobbing high and dry at its moorings, the only thing showing above the water in the morning was the prop spinner. The only sure way to prevent this from happening is to stay with the airplane, sweeping the snow off the wings and tail surfaces before it can accumulate.

But what can you do if, for some reason, you can't stay with your airplane? There *is* something you can do to prevent the snow from submerging the floats of your plane, but first you have to get your plane into a boat slip between two floating docks. Moor your plane in the slip so it can't move forward or backward. It's very important that the plane not be able to move, so use spring lines to hold the floatplane in position, and even tie the wings down if you think it will help. After the plane is securely positioned in the slip, take a heavy line at least half an inch in diameter and fasten it to a dock cleat next to the tail of one of the floats. Run the line under the tails of both floats, forward of the water rudders, and to a cleat on the opposite dock (Fig. 13-14). Pull the line as tight as you can, and run it back under the floats again to the other side. Repeat this two or three times and tie off the line. If you have someone stand on the bow of one of the floats, this will raise the tail of the airplane and allow you to pull the line even tighter. Now if it starts to snow, the floats will sit on the line instead of sinking beneath the surface.

This technique should not be used as an excuse for leaving your floatplane unattended, but if you absolutely must be away from the plane for awhile, it can make the difference between continuing your flight in the morning and searching for a salvage crew.

MOORING TO A BUOY

If you mess about in floatplanes long enough, you will someday find yourself circling over your destination while you look in vain for an open spot at a dock. You might even find yourself looking for a dock, period. Or perhaps your destination is a beach—a beach that turns out to be covered with large, float-puncturing rocks. In cases like these, your only option will be to moor, or anchor the plane offshore.

Many harbors, resorts, and marinas have permanent mooring buoys you can use if there's no other alternative. The greatest challenge will be figuring out how you're going to get from the plane to shore and back again; the actual mooring procedure is quite simple.

First, you'll need a mooring bridle of some sort. This is simply a V-shaped harness made out of rope or cable. Each arm of the V should end in an eye splice just large enough to fit over the bow cleats on the floats, while a large snap hook should be fastened to the point of the V. If you don't have

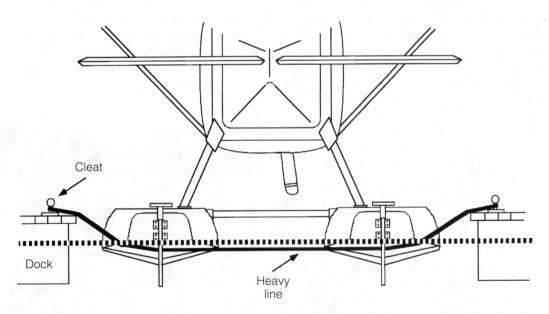

Fig. 13-14. *Here's a handy technique for keeping a floatplane from sinking when the weight of accumulated snow threatens to drive the sterns of the floats underwater.*

a ready-made bridle, you can fashion a reasonable facsimile using the lines you're carrying in the plane.

Since a mooring buoy is generally located some distance from shore, you will almost always be able to head directly into the wind or current while approaching it. Treat a buoy the same as you would a dock, and come up alongside it. Don't let the buoy get in between the floats. For one thing, it will be difficult to get hold of when it's bobbing around among the spreader bars, brace wires, and rudder cables under the plane. Also, you might have to carry power all the way up to the buoy if your bucking a strong headwind or current, and if the buoy passes between the floats, it could be struck by the propeller.

When you're a couple of plane lengths away from the buoy, shut down the engine and climb out on the float. You can always reach back through the door and work the rudder pedals by hand if you have to make some last-minute adjustments to your heading. If it's windy, you can leave the engine running and operate its controls from the float, too. Grab the buoy as you come up beside it (this is when a collapsible boat hook can come in handy) and fasten the center of your mooring bridle to the ring on top of the buoy. If the engine is still running, shut it down, and turn off the mag and master switches. Then walk forward and fasten one of the two legs of the bridle to the bow cleat of the float you're standing on. Toss the other half of the bridle across to the opposite float, or tie it to one of the propeller blades. The important thing is to make sure you can reach the other half of the bridle from the other float. Climb back through the cabin and secure the second leg of the bridle to the bow cleat on the second float.

The bridle will keep your floatplane centered on the buoy while allowing the plane to pivot into the wind or current. Always remember to raise the water rudders after you've made fast to a buoy. This will enable the plane to pivot quickly in the event of a sudden wind shift and reduce the chances of a capsizing.

Some pilots prefer to use a yoke around the propeller in place of a mooring bridle between the floats (Fig. 13-15). They put a loop of line around each blade close to the hub and join the two loops together beneath the propeller. They then run a single line from the junction of the two loops to the mooring buoy. This method seems to be most popular with the pilots of small, lightweight float-planes with high-lift wings, such as the Super Cub and the Citabria. One advantage of this system is that the nose will be held down if the wind starts blowing hard, and the plane will be less likely to lift off the water. It's also the most convenient way to moor a floatplane that only has a door on one side. Unless you're an accomplished calf roper, or are extremely adept with a boat hook, it can be very difficult to slip the other half of a mooring bridle over the bow cleat on the float you can't get to—to say nothing of getting it off again. I would not recommend that a propeller yoke be used on a floatplane equipped with a variable-pitch or constant-speed propeller. The constant tugging on the propeller blades could conceivably damage the pitch-changing mechanism in the propeller hub.

To depart the buoy later, simply reverse the procedure you used when you arrived. Release the bridle from the float on the passenger's side of the plane, climb back through the cabin, and walk to the bow of the float on the pilot's side.

Fig. 13-15. *A Citabria moored with a line fastened to the propeller. Note the water rudder in the retracted position.* EDO Corp.

Release the other half of the bridle, and walk the buoy back alongside the float to the pilot's door. Unfasten the bridle from the buoy, put it and yourself into the airplane, and start the engine. If the buoy is back beside the plane, it will be clear of the propeller when the engine starts and you begin to taxi forward.

On a windy day, you can release the plane from the buoy right away. You'll immediately begin to drift backward, and by the time you've removed the bridle from the floats and stowed it, you should be able to start the engine and turn away from the buoy with no danger of hitting it. Make sure, however, that you won't be blown backward into a boat or up on shore while you're removing the bridle and getting ready to start the engine.

If you *are* in danger of drifting backward into something, first release the bridle from the floats and walk the buoy back alongside the pilot's door as described earlier. After temporarily securing the bridle to one of the float struts to keep the plane from drifting back, fasten one end of a mooring line to the base of a float strut and pass its free end through the ring on the buoy. You might be able to use one of the plane's permanent mooring lines for this. Take up all the slack in the line and tie off the free end near the top of the strut, where you can reach it from the pilot's seat. Then remove the mooring bridle from the buoy and the strut and stow it in the plane. When you're ready to go, climb into the cockpit, unfasten the mooring line from the top of the strut, and hold on to it as you prepare to start the engine. This will keep you alongside the buoy until the engine starts. As the plane begins to move forward, allow your end of the line to be pulled through the ring on the buoy. The other end of the line will remain tied to the base of the float strut, and you can retrieve it when you've taxied well clear of the danger behind you. If it's a relatively short line, you can even leave it tied to the strut until you get home; it will lie quietly on top of the float deck during the flight.

Obviously, this whole mooring business becomes much simpler if you have a passenger on board. He or she can get out on the float and pick up the buoy when you arrive and release it when you depart, allowing you to concentrate on maneuvering the airplane. Remember, don't let your passenger walk forward of the door unless the propeller is stopped and the mag and master switches are off.

If a stiff breeze has made the water choppy and you think your passenger might have trouble picking up the buoy, this little trick might make it easier for him or her: Kill the engine as soon as you're alongside the buoy and make a sharp turn into it. As the plane stops and begins to drift backward, the buoy will be pinned against the side of the downwind float, and your passenger will have more time to get a line or bridle fastened to its ring.

It's important that your plane be able to swing a full 360 degrees around the buoy without hitting anything. Currents change and winds shift, and in the course of an hour, your plane can easily pass through every point of the compass. Murphy, or one of his friends, came up with a law that states, "Whatever can go wrong, will," so your plane will invariably swing in the direction that offers the best chance of a collision with something else.

Unfortunately, things can go wrong no matter how many precautions you take. Several years ago, the pilot of a beautiful new float-equipped Cessna 185 moored the plane to a buoy in a resort harbor in Washington's San Juan Islands. Later in the day, a large yacht arrived and anchored nearby. The captain of the yacht set the stage for the ensuing accident by putting out a stern anchor in addition to the usual bow anchor. The two anchors held the yacht in a fixed position, while the floatplane was free to pivot around its buoy. The tide turned, and the plane slowly swung around to aim in the opposite direction. Its wing rode up over the unyielding yacht until the plane was pinned against the side of the hull by the current. As one wing slid up onto the yacht, the other one dipped into the water. The force of the current drove the outside wing down until it hit the bottom of the shallow harbor. The pressure of the strong tidal current pressed down on the waterlogged wing until suddenly the outer four feet of the wing gave way and bent up. While this was the only serious structural damage to the plane, the owner faced an astronomical repair bill. The engine and cockpit had been immersed in the salt water, and everything, including the instruments, had to be disassembled, cleaned, and reassembled or replaced completely.

I include this depressing account to make a point: Never go off and leave a floatplane for any length of time unless it's completely out of the water in dry storage or securely tied down on a ramp. No matter how many disasters you anticipate and guard against, there will always be one you didn't think of. Neptune and his freshwater friends have been doing strange things to boats for thousands of years, and there's no reason why floatplanes should be exempted from their warped sense of humor. The owner of the 185 had no idea that someone would show up and park a steel island next to her carefully moored plane, but perhaps if a little closer eye had been kept on the situation developing out in the harbor, the accident could have been avoided. We'll never know, but it's something to think about.

ANCHORING

Permanent mooring buoys are generally confined to developed harbors, marinas, and waterfront resorts. If, after you earn your seaplane rating, you decide to visit one of the many remote areas the floatplane makes accessible, you'll have to use an anchor if you want to moor your plane offshore. There are several strong disadvantages to anchoring a floatplane, however, and you should be aware of them before you try it.

First of all, any anchor is worthless if it won't hold your plane, so you'll need one that's big enough to hold in the worst conditions you think you'll encounter. This anchor will not be light, so don't forget to allow for it in your weight and balance calculations. You'll also have to find some-

place to put it, and its sharp edges and awkward shape won't make this an easy task.

There's more to anchoring a plane than simply tying a line to an anchor and tossing it overboard, followed by a hopeful desire that it catch on something. In order for an anchor to work, it has to lie on its side so its flukes will dig into the bottom. If you let out just enough line for the anchor to reach the bottom, the pressure from the plane as it's pushed backward by the wind or current will keep the anchor from falling over and digging in, and it will simply drag across the bottom.

The correct nautical term for anchor line is *rode*, and the recommended length of rode to properly anchor a boat is five times the depth of the water under the keel. You should adhere to this practice when anchoring a floatplane, too, which means if you're going to anchor in 20 feet of water, you'll need at least 100 feet of rode, which you'll obviously have to stow onboard somewhere. Nylon makes the best rode, by the way, as its elasticity helps absorb shock if the wind, waves, or current start bouncing your plane around.

It's a good idea to have several feet of heavy chain at the bottom end of the rode, as this prevents the line from chafing if the bottom is rocky. The chain also works like a shock absorber, enabling the anchor to hold better, but when you're not using it, it's just more dead weight the plane has to carry around.

After dropping the anchor, don't simply fasten the free end of the rode to the bow cleat on one of the floats. This will keep the plane from pointing directly into the wind, and it could capsize in a strong breeze. Instead, you should secure the rode to the floats with the same kind of bridle you would use if you were mooring the plane to a buoy. In fact, it's a good idea to attach a small buoy (one more thing to carry) to the free end of the rode, and secure your plane to the buoy with the mooring bridle. If you decide to make short flights away from your anchorage during the day, you can leave your anchor in place, and the buoy will make it easy to find when you return. Approach and pick up this buoy using the same procedures described earlier.

You should consider anchoring your plane only as a last resort. Besides the inconvenience of having to haul around a lot of heavy, awkward equipment, there is always the danger of dragging the anchor. Permanent mooring buoys are usually kept in position by things like 55-gallon drums filled with concrete or old truck bodies. An anchor small enough to be carried in a floatplane is pretty puny by comparison and won't have anywhere near the holding power of a mooring buoy's anchor. If the current or wind is strong, the movement of your plane could work your anchor free, in which case the plane would start to drift, dragging its little anchor along behind it. Once an anchor starts to drag, it generally keeps dragging, and your floatplane could very well end up on the rocks. Because of the danger of dragging the anchor, it's vitally important that you stay with or near your anchored floatplane until you can move it to the safety of a ramp, dock, or beach.

HIGH WINDS AND MOORING DON'T MIX

If strong winds are forecast, do not plan to anchor your plane or moor it to a buoy, no matter how well that buoy is anchored to the bottom. Even though your plane will be free to pivot into the wind, it's just a matter of time before the combination of strong, gusty winds and large waves will flip it over.

There is one method of mooring a floatplane so it will weather most storms, but you can't carry the necessary equipment around with you in the baggage compartment. It involves taking two 55-gallon drums and filling them with just enough concrete so each one will float with its top just barely breaking the surface of the water. Each barrel is sealed, and a large ring is welded to its top. When in use, one barrel is positioned under each wing of the moored floatplane, and a nylon line is

run between the ring in the top of each barrel and the tiedown ring set in the wing above it. As long as the wind and water remain calm, the wings won't have to support the weight of the floating barrels, but in the event of a storm, the barrels will act as tiedowns and prevent the plane from lifting off the water or rocking violently from side to side. Nylon line works the best in this case because it stretches and absorbs shocks. An even better arrangement incorporates the strong, rubber shock absorbers that boaters use in their mooring lines.

Since the barrels are not anchored to the bottom, the plane is still free to pivot into the wind, although not as quickly. This system will effectively guard against a capsizing, but if heavy rain, large waves, or the weight of accumulated snow on the wings and tail surfaces cause the floats to fill up with water, the plane will not be prevented from sinking. The only way to completely eliminate the threat of sinking is to put your plane in dry storage, on a ramp, or on the beach.

BEACHING

When you start to explore new territory in a floatplane, it won't be long before you'll want to put the plane on a beach. Clam digging, oyster gathering, fishing, picnicking, camping, or just sitting in front of a spectacular view are all activities made more enjoyable by a floatplane because it makes possible an escape from the ground-bound crowds. Since it's unlikely that your favorite clam beach is equipped with either a seaplane ramp or a convenient, tire-lined dock, you'll have to learn to secure your plane to the shore itself.

Aerial surveillance

The first step in beaching your plane takes place in the air. Overfly the shoreline several times if necessary, and carefully check it over. Does it appear to be covered with rocks? If so, you might have to anchor offshore or bypass it completely, rather than risk damaging your floats. Is the water offshore free of obstructions? Be especially alert for pilings that have been cut or broken off below the surface. If you're landing on a lake or a man-made reservoir, check carefully for deadheads and the jagged remains of tree trunks covered by a rising water level.

Will your taxi toward shore take you over, or near, large underwater boulders or ledges? They're easy to spot from the air, but impossible to see once you're on the water, and a sharp rock or jagged ledge can easily rip the bottom out of one of your floats.

Is the water offshore deep enough, or is there a chance you might run aground before you even reach the beach? It can be very difficult to accurately judge the depth of either murky or exceptionally clear water. Murky water obscures the bottom, while clear water might make the bottom appear closer than it really is. Many of the lakes in Canada and Alaska are so clear that on a bright, sunny day, rocks on the bottom in 50 feet of water appear to be just inches beneath the surface. Marine charts contain valuable information about water depths, and many topographical charts include the configuration of lake bottoms as well as land contours. It's a good idea to carry the appropriate marine and topographical charts in your plane, along with the traditional sectional and WAC charts.

Once your plane is on the beach, will you be able to secure it to anything to keep it from being blown or washed off? If your destination is the wooded shoreline of a lake, there will be plenty of trees, logs, and stumps for you to run lines to, but if the beach is wide, or the shoreline barren, it can take a lot of line—and some creative thinking on your part—to keep the plane where you want it.

Which way is the wind blowing? You'll need this information anyway to determine your landing direction, but it will also tell you in advance the safest way to approach the shore.

If you're landing in tidal waters, there is one more thing you need to know before committing your airplane to the beach: Is the tide coming in or going out? Although it's often easy to visually determine if the tide is high or low, the only accurate way to tell which way it's going is with a current, published tide table, and you should keep one with your marine and aeronautical charts. If you put your plane on the beach at high tide and leave it there, you'd better not want to leave in a hurry because you're not going to go anywhere for the next 12 hours. Conversely, if you beach your plane at low tide, you'd better *not* go anywhere, because if you do, your plane might not be there when you get back.

Beaching the plane

The most important rule to follow when approaching the shore is to do it slowly. Even nice sandy beaches are very abrasive to float bottoms and should be approached with caution. If the wind is on-shore (blowing from the water toward the shore), beaching is easy. If you're sure the bottom is free of obstructions or rocks, taxi in until you're three or four plane lengths from shore, start a turn away from it, and shut down the engine. Raise the water rudders as you turn, and the wind will weathercock your plane around until its tail is facing the beach. The wind will then begin to push it slowly backward, so it's important that you leave the water rudders up to avoid damaging them when the sterns of the floats touch shore. When the plane runs aground, all you and your passengers have to do is walk to the rear of the floats and step onto the beach. If you're lucky, you might not even get your feet wet.

If the wind is off-shore (blowing from the shore toward the water), the beaching technique is different. Nose the plane gently up to the beach at a 45-degree angle. This will allow you to quickly turn away if you find that the bottom is too rocky, or if you see that you're in danger of running aground too far from shore. You want to contact the beach at the slowest speed possible, so don't wait too long before shutting down the engine. Remember to raise the water rudders before you run aground. It's an easy thing to forget because you'll be busy watching the bottom for rocks and trying to pick the best place to bring the plane ashore, but it's important that the rudders come up before they hit—and possibly dig into—the bottom. A good way to remember to raise them is to hold the retraction handle in your hand as you coast in. Then you won't have to fumble around on the floor looking for the handle, and the fact that you're holding on to it should remind you to raise the rudders when you reach shallow water.

If you know the beach is free of sharp rocks, wait until the inshore float contacts the beach before getting out and walking forward. If you walk to the front of the float before you reach the shore, your weight will force the bow of the float a little deeper, and it will run aground farther out from dry land. Depending on the slope of the bottom, the difference might be only a few inches or it might be several feet, but it might be enough to keep the water from running over the tops of your boots when you step off the float.

Before you walk to the front of the float and step—or splash—onto the beach, secure one of your long mooring lines to the stern cleat of the inshore float and pay out the line as you walk forward and go ashore. When you've stepped off the float, give the plane a good shove away from the beach and into deeper water, paying out the line as it goes. When the plane is out far enough to be in no danger of running aground as it turns, pull its tail back in toward you with the line until the sterns of the floats slide up on shore.

Now you can see why it's so important that the water rudders be retracted; if they are still down as you pull the plane in backward, they will dig into the bottom and become jammed against their stops. The rudder mechanism is not designed to take this kind of punishment, and the chances are good that the blades will be bent. The pivot and retraction system could even be broken, which would really be a disaster. If, as you're turning the plane around, you notice that the rudders are still down, you have no choice but to wade out and retract them before

pulling the plane ashore. It's far cheaper to dry out your clothes than it is to repair a set of bent or broken water rudders.

Many of the lakes we visit in southeast Alaska have shallow, muddy bottoms that stop our plane several yards from shore. By approaching the beach at a shallow angle, I'm assured of hanging the inshore wingtip over dry land when the plane grounds out (Fig. 13-16). Instead of attaching a line to the rear of the inboard float, one of us can step off the bow (hip boots are strongly recommended for this maneuver) and turn the plane nose-out by walking the wing forward with the wingtip grabline. Pulling on the wingtip gives us a lot of leverage to pivot the floats in the sticky ooze of the bottom, and as the tail of the Beaver swings in over the shore, it's an easy matter to get under it and back the plane in as close to the beach as possible.

Fig 13-16. *Approaching the muddy shore of this lake at an angle will put the wingtip over firmer ground when the plane comes to a stop. A person on shore can then use the wingtip grabline to pivot the plane into a position where it can be tailed in as close to dry land as possible.*

Obscure or rocky bottoms

If you are unsure of the bottom near the beach, or if it's rocky, stop your plane before you get into shallow water and look the situation over carefully. If there isn't any wind, you might want to paddle the plane slowly to shore; be ready to back-paddle or fend the plane off if it looks like the floats are in danger of being damaged. If muddy or murky water obscures the bottom, the only thing you can do is jump overboard and slowly pull your plane toward shore, feeling carefully for rocks and other float-damaging objects. (It's a good idea to keep a change of clothes in the plane for occasions like this.)

If the wind is blowing, or if the water is choppy, you might be better off abandoning the beaching attempt altogether. The plane will be very difficult to handle, and you'll run the risk of its being blown out of your control into a rocky area, or pounded against the bottom. A better decision would be to go in search of a calmer area to beach the plane. You can try the first spot again when the wind and water conditions are better.

Always beach a floatplane tail-first

Regardless of the method you use to approach the beach, your plane should always be pulled up on shore tail-first. For one thing, you'll have to point the nose toward the water anyway when you leave, so you might as well do it now; however, the main reason for pulling the sterns of the floats onto the beach is that the afterbodies of the floats draw much less water than the forebodies, and you'll be able to pull the plane farther up on shore. With the floats resting solidly on the beach, your plane will be in much less danger of drifting away if the wind starts whipping up the waves.

The procedure for sliding the sterns of the floats onto a beach is identical to the procedure for tailing a floatplane onto a ramp. Position yourself in front of the horizontal stabilizer, facing the shore, and lift up on the stabilizer while pushing the plane backward. Remember to place your hands under the stabilizer spar to avoid denting the aluminum skin or puncturing the fabric. Obviously, you'll be able to get a lightweight floatplane like a Super Cub or a Citabria farther up on the beach than a Cessna 206, and you might not be able to get a big plane like a Beaver out of the water at all, although the floats will be resting firmly on the bottom (Fig. 13-17). The important thing is

Fig. 13-17. *Although this Beaver looks like it's still floating, the sterns of its floats are firmly on the bottom. The lines attached to the wings, floats, and tail will hold the airplane in position against the shore, but they will not hold the plane down if a high wind should decide to flip it over.*

that the plane be sitting solidly on the ground, even if the ground happens to be underwater.

Make sure the floats won't be damaged as you pull the plane up on shore. It's obvious what sharp rocks can do to the floats, but even smooth gravel can be damaging if waves cause the plane to rock back and forth. If the beach is rocky, you can help protect your floats by resting them on branches or poles cut from nearby trees, and I know of at least one pilot who carries thick rubber mats for the same purpose.

When you've slid your plane as far up on shore as you can, make sure its weight isn't resting on the water rudders. Even though they're retracted, they could be touching the beach, especially if the slope is steep. I've occasionally had to dig a little relief trench under each water rudder so the weight of the plane wouldn't bend them over.

Securing the plane

The last step in beaching a floatplane is making sure it will stay on the beach. If you've beached your plane while the tide is ebbing, you've got nothing to worry about for awhile, but if you're on a lake, a reservoir, or a river, you'll need to get some lines ashore.

If you're going to be flying and beaching your plane in unfamiliar territory, you should carry at least 300 feet of good, strong line, and if you can fit more in with your luggage, do so. Beaches have a way of making what you thought was far too much line seem like not enough. You might have to run lines across a lot of sand or gravel before you reach something solid enough to hold your plane.

If you're going to be on the beach for only a short time, a single line that is run from the tail tiedown ring to a nearby tree, log, or boulder will suffice, but if you plan on remaining for several days, or if it looks as if the wind and waves are going to kick up, get several lines on the plane. In addition to the line on the tail, run a line from each wing back to the beach. Finally, lines run out at an angle from the bow or stern cleats will help keep the plane from pivoting if the wind or waves should strike the plane at an angle.

The one thing you generally can't do on a beach is tie the wings down. Running lines back to trees or logs along the shore will hold the plane firmly in position, but they will do little to keep the plane from being flipped over if the wind really gets nasty. On a lake with a wooded shoreline, you might be able to beach the plane beside a fallen tree or a submerged log that you can use as a tiedown. If you can determine from which direction the heaviest gusts will come, try to put the log on that side of the plane, so it will hold down the upwind wing.

If you're on a broad beach, or on the shore of a lake out in the barrens, you'll probably be out of luck when it comes to tiedowns for the wings; however, if you feel there's a real danger of your plane being flipped by high winds, there is one thing you can do. Fill the floats with water. Actually, you shouldn't have to fill the entire float. Remember, a float that displaces 3,000 pounds of water will hold about 3,000 pounds of water. Both floats half-filled with water will weigh more than your empty airplane. Filling the floats is a time-consuming process, and you need the right equipment to do it: a bucket and a large funnel. Bear in mind that your floats are not designed to contain this much weight inside them. Make sure they are

sitting on a bottom that will support them evenly; you don't want to snap a keel over a branch or a ledge of rock.

Remember to pump the water out as soon as the danger has passed. This, too will take a long time. It's a good idea to carry a bilge pump with the longest possible tube. You don't have to bend down awkwardly to use it, but there's another advantage. Filling the floats with water can cause the bows of your floats to sink below the surface, but if you have a long-tubed bilge pump, you will still be able to pump out the forward compartments. This assumes, of course, that your pump seals up tight in the bilge tube openings and that the seals around the inspection plates are watertight.

Flooding the floats is a last resort, but it works. Do it only if your plane is sitting firmly on a beach or a ramp. Never fill the floats of a moored or docked floatplane. All you're doing is helping Mother Nature sink the plane. Adding weight to the floats of a moored plane won't add much to its stability. As long as it's light enough to float, it's light enough to be flipped over.

If you're tailed into a sandy beach and there's nothing around that's solid enough to tie the plane to at all, you can steal a page from the four-wheel-drive enthusiasts' book and make your own tiedown. All you need is a shovel. Find a large piece of driftwood or the largest rock you can move yourself. (If nothing else is available, you can even use the paddle from your plane.) Pick a spot on the beach behind your plane and dig a deep hole. Fasten the tiedown lines from your floatplane to your improvised anchor, place the anchor in the hole, and bury it. This makes a great tiedown, although it takes a while to construct. Off-road drivers use this technique to provide a solid anchor for a winch line in the event they get stuck out of reach of a tree or a boulder.

If you've beached your plane in tidal water and only want to stay on shore for an hour or two, you won't have any choice but to move the plane every 15 minutes or so. If the water is very calm, and the tide is coming in, you can run a line to a log or tree and just let the plane float off the beach. It won't go very far, and when it's time to leave, you can use the line to retrieve it. If the wind or passing boats are stirring up swells, however, keep the plane solidly tailed onto the beach so it won't be bumped or ground against the shore by the waves.

If the tide is rising, you'll have to keep moving the plane farther up the beach to keep it from floating free, and if the tide is ebbing, you'll have to keep pushing the plane farther out so you won't get stranded. The best method of dealing with the tides is to do a little preplanning. If, for example, you want to spend four hours on the beach digging for clams, get a tide table for your area, and plan to arrive at the beach two hours before low tide. Put your plane on the beach, where it promptly will be stranded, and don't worry about it again for four hours, when the rising tide will float it free again. Make sure you put a line on the plane, however, because if you're late getting back to it, you don't want to find that it's left without you!

DRY STORAGE

The safest way to secure your floatplane after your flight is to take it out of the water completely. This requires some expensive equipment, to say nothing of a lot of tiedown space, so dry storage is limited to the larger, established seaplane bases (Fig. 13-18). Your plane will be removed from the water on an elevator or a railcar and will be taken to its tiedown spot by a specially equipped forklift. Seaplane bases not equipped with elevators or railcars might pick your plane directly off the ramp with the forklift, or they might position a special dolly under the spreader bars. Hydraulic lifters on the dolly will raise the plane a few inches off the ground, and a tug or a tractor will pull your plane to the tiedown area. Several seaplane bases in the Pacific northwest have made unique floatplane transporters by welding a hydraulic dolly arrangement to the front half of a front-wheel-drive Oldsmobile Toronado or four-

Fig. 13-18. *Welcome to Beaver Row at Kenmore Air Harbor. Kenmore Air operates an average of 10 piston Beavers during the peak summer charter season, and is famous for its modifications to the big workhorses. Note the rubber-protected cylinders of cement used as tiedowns.*

wheel-drive pickup. The resulting rig looks pretty bizarre, to say the least, but it works quite well (Fig. 13-19).

Some floatplane bases use what is, in effect, a portable ramp. A large wood-decked trailer is shoved into the water by a pickup truck. You drive

Fig. 13-19. *Homemade floatplane transport at work in Ketchikan, Alaska. The rigid transporter frame fits between the floats and is supported (out of the picture to the right) by four closely spaced wheels and tires. A pair of hydraulic arms mounted on top of the frame come up under the spreader bars to lift the plane off the ground.*

your plane onto the trailer just as though it were a ramp, although you won't need to power yourself on since the trailer will be slightly under water. Instead of shutting down, however, you'll probably be instructed to help the truck back up the ramp by throttling up to half power (Fig. 13-20). This will also prevent your plane from rocking over backward as the trailer is pulled up the ramp. Once the rig has reached level ground, your plane might be left on the trailer and tied down, or it might be removed by a forklift or transporter and placed on the ground.

Fig 13-20. *Retrieving a Vazar Dash-3 Otter in Ketchikan. Advancing the power to half throttle keeps the plane from tipping backwards and makes it easier for the pickup driver to pull the plane up the ramp. The process will be reversed when it's time to put the plane back in the water.*

If the tiedown area is paved, ask the ground crew to set your plane on a couple of boards, rather than directly on the pavement. The boards will protect the float keels from abrasion as the plane is set down or picked up. Just make sure the boards don't have any nails in them. The parking area also should be equipped with tiedown rings. They might be set directly into the pavement, in the top of large concrete weights, or welded to the top of cement-filled drums. Tie down the wings and tail of your plane just as you would a landplane. If no tiedowns are available, you can make some by lashing a couple of water- or fuel-filled 55-gallon drums together and placing a pair under each wing and the tail. Your tiedown lines can be looped around the barrels and back up to the plane's tiedown rings. Barrels aren't as good as bona fide tiedown rings, but they're better than nothing. As a last resort, you can partially fill the floats with water if high winds are expected.

This has been a long chapter, but I haven't even begun to describe all the docking, ramping, and beaching situations you'll encounter when you begin to explore new territory in your floatplane. Each one will be a challenge, but as long as you take the time to thoroughly check out each situation, weigh the alternatives, and exercise good judgment, the experiences will be rewarding ones. You'll never stop learning, and every challenge successfully met will prepare you for the next one. Above all, don't get cocky. Right about the time you think you've mastered every possible docking situation, you'll hear that dull crunch of collapsing aluminum.

It's okay to approach a new docking situation with trepidation. Stay humble, and stay alert, and your chances of bending an airplane will be pretty remote. The payoff comes when you stand on the dock of a bustling coastal village, your airplane securely moored behind you, and watch the eagles fish in the harbor, or walk the silent shore of an arctic lake, or share the company of friends in a snug, northwoods cabin listening to the mournful cry of a loon echo off the moonlit water. The challenges and rewards of float flying never cease.

14
Advanced techniques

THE PROBLEM with instructional books like this one is that in order to clearly describe specific techniques and procedures, it is necessary to assume that the conditions are ideal for performing these techniques and procedures. Ski books assume you're on the perfect slope in perfect snow; auto repair books assume you've got every known tool and a large, uncluttered garage; home improvement books assume your house was built to some standard (which never seems to be the one to which your house was built); and so far, this book has assumed the wind is light, the water is slightly ruffled, and the takeoff and landing lanes are right next to the dock. In reality, conditions are usually a little different. Sometimes they're a lot different.

Your first lesson probably will be conducted under relatively "ideal" wind and water conditions. Mr. Kurtzer postponed my first lesson three times until the wind finally stopped whipping the lake into whitecaps, so don't be surprised or disappointed if you have to wait a day or two for your first logbook entry under "Single-engine, Sea." Your first lesson is not the time to be learning rough-water techniques. As your training progresses, you'll soon learn to cope with rough water, glassy water, strong winds, crosswinds, short lakes, and long taxi distances.

The floatplane's world is an ever-changing one, and you rarely will encounter the elusive "ideal" conditions. Think how boring it would become though, if every takeoff, every landing, and every docking or beaching were the same. In the next few chapters, we will look at some of the techniques designed to cope with the reality of float flying.

THE STEP-TAXI

So far, the only method we've examined for moving a floatplane from Point A to Point B on the water is the displacement, or idle, taxi. On windy days or when the water is rough, this is the safest way to taxi a floatplane, but there's no getting around the fact that it's slow. Landplane pilots don't have to worry about kicking up propeller-eroding spray, so they can taxi faster if they have long distances to cover. Not so the floatplane pilot, who not only has to worry about throwing up too much spray, but also has to keep the engine temperatures down. Both landplanes and floatplanes will taxi faster if you add power, but where the landplane's engine only has to overcome a slight increase in rolling resistance and aerodynamic drag, the floatplane's engine must work to overcome the tremendous increase in hydrodynamic drag created by accelerating the plane forward. The result is that the engines in most float-planes will begin to overheat if a faster displacement or plowing taxi speed is maintained for any length of time.

On the other hand, it's frustrating to land a safe distance out from shore only to face a long, slow taxi to the dock. If you're renting the floatplane, a long taxi in can easily add another tenth of an hour or more to your bill. Fortunately, there's a faster way to travel across the water, and while you can't always take advantage of it, the times when you can will be worth it in terms of both time and money. Besides, it's a lot of fun. It's called a step-taxi.

A *step-taxi* is simply a takeoff run that never accelerates to liftoff speed. Its advantage over a normal displacement taxi is obvious. Instead of slogging through the water at 4 knots, you skim along over it at upwards of 30 knots (Fig. 14-1). Since the air rudder is very effective at this speed, the plane is quite maneuverable, so it's easy to follow a channel, thread your way through boat traffic, or avoid obstacles.

You initiate a step-taxi in the same manner as you would a takeoff run. After retracting the water rudders, hold the stick or yoke all the way back and apply full power. As in a normal takeoff, you'll probably have to add some right rudder to counteract the P-factor. When the floatplane reaches its maximum nose-up attitude in the hump phase, relax the back pressure and allow the plane to pitch

Fig. 14-1. *Step-taxiing a Cessna 206. This is an efficient way to cover long distances on the water.* EDO Corp.

forward over the hump into a planing attitude. The floats will begin to skim along over the surface of the water, supported by hydrodynamic pressure.

This time, however, you don't want the airplane to take off. You want to remain on the surface, skimming along like a ski boat, covering as much distance as in as short a time as possible. You also want to subject the plane to as little pounding as possible, so the trick is to find and maintain the slowest speed that will still create enough hydrodynamic pressure to support the floats.

As soon as your floatplane is solidly on the step, start reducing the power. The plane will immediately stop accelerating and, as you continue to pull the throttle back, it will begin to slow down. You'll be surprised at how little power it takes to keep the plane on the step. If you reduce the power too much, of course, the plane will start to fall off the step, which is inefficient and might cause the engine to begin overheating. If you do begin to fall off the step, go back to full power to get the plane back on to the step as quickly as possible, and start the power reduction procedure again. You will soon discover the minimum power setting that will keep the plane on the step, and next time, the process won't take so long.

At this speed, the air rudder is quite effective, and it's easy to make slight directional changes to avoid obstacles. Remember to hold the correct planing attitude at all times. In this respect, a step-taxi is identical to a takeoff run. If the nose is held too low, the forebodies of the floats will begin to rub, and if the nose is held too high, the sterns of the floats will dig in to the water. Also as in a take-off run, the plane is susceptible to porpoising if you don't maintain the correct attitude.

If you're going to step-taxi across the wind, remember to position the ailerons properly to keep the upwind wing from lifting. If you're on a heading between crosswind and directly upwind, hold the aileron up on the upwind wing. If you're on a downwind heading, the aileron position is not as crucial because you should be traveling faster than the wind. If you're not traveling faster than the wind, you shouldn't be taxiing on the step in the first place because the strong wind and rough water conditions will either pound your plane to pieces or flip it over when you try to stop.

Pay careful attention to the water ahead of you as you're skimming along. Floating logs and other debris are hard to spot when you're on the water, and at this speed a floating log or deadhead could punch a hole in one of your floats that would put your plane on the bottom in short order. Don't step-taxi into shallow water or even water that you suspect might be shallow. If you should unexpectedly touch bottom while on the step, the sudden drag on the floats will probably pitch your plane over onto its back before you can take any corrective action with the elevator. Be very alert for boat wakes and swells. Remember, a boat does not have to be in your immediate vicinity to generate a wake that could cause you serious problems. If you see that you're going to cross some swells, stop the step-taxi immediately. Swells, whatever the cause, should only be crossed in the displacement mode with the engine at idle.

To stop a step-taxi, simply pull the power back to idle. Since the plane is barely on the step to begin with, it will immediately come back over the hump and settle into the displacement attitude. As soon as the plane has slowed down, lower the water rudders and taxi to your destination.

The step-taxi is most commonly used to quickly cover the distance between a landing area and a ramp, dock, or beach. To initiate a step-taxi after landing, add power as soon as the floats touch down, but be careful not to add so much power that the airplane takes off again. It's important that you add this power immediately, because if you hesitate a moment or two, the plane will have already started to fall off the step. If you do delay a moment or two, you'll have to apply extra power to pull yourself back up firmly onto the step before reducing the throttle to maintain a minimum step-taxi speed.

Some floatplanes step-taxi better with flaps than others, but it isn't a good idea to taxi with full flaps. The drag will be considerable, and it might take more power than you really need to stay on the step. If you've landed with full flaps, retract them at least partially after you've initiated the step-taxi. Every type of floatplane will be different, and you'll just have to experiment to find which flap setting works best on the particular airplane you're flying. A Cessna 172, for example, will step-taxi quite nicely with the flaps retracted, but a de Havilland Beaver has to have the flaps partially deployed.

Don't step-taxi too close in to your destination. Allow yourself plenty of room to come to a stop after you pull the power back to idle. Whatever respect you might have garnered by executing a perfect landing followed by a flawless transition to a smooth step-taxi will most likely be lost if you end the performance by slamming into the dock in a shower of spray, splinters, and float struts.

THE STEP-TURN

We've seen how the air rudder can be used to make gentle turns while the plane is on the step. It's also possible to make sharp turns, or step-turns, using the air rudder. The procedure is a little more involved, and there are times when a step-turn can be downright dangerous.

You must contend with two forces when you initiate a step-turn. One is the additional drag on the floats, and the other is the capsizing tendency caused by the centrifugal force generated by the turn itself.

Float drag

When you start a step-turn by applying rudder in the direction of the turn, the floats will no longer skim straight ahead but will start to slide sideways across the water. The keel and chines of the float will resist this slide and force the plane to move forward in the direction of the turn (Fig. 14-2). The act of resisting the sideways slide increases the hydrodynamic drag on the floats, so in addition to turning, the airplane also will slow down. Then

Fig. 14-2. *Neal Ratti demonstrating a step-turn to the right. Note the increased amount of spray thrown out by the left, or outside, float.*

there's the action of the centrifugal force generated by the turn, which forces the outside float deeper into the water, increasing the drag, and slowing the plane even more. Since it's barely going fast enough to stay on the step to begin with, any further reduction of speed will cause the plane to drop back off the step into the plowing attitude.

The only way to counter this decrease in speed during the turn is to add power. The sharper the turn, the more power you'll have to add. It's important that you add the power as you begin the turn. If you wait until the turn is established, it will be too late because your plane already will have started to fall off the step. To get back onto the step while the airplane is turning will require a lot of extra power, possibly even full power. It might be better to stop the turn, get back onto the step while taxiing straight ahead, and then resume the turn.

In an airborne turn, the ailerons are used to establish the desired bank angle and then returned to neutral for the duration of the turn. A step-turn is more like driving a car. You'll have to *hold rudder pressure* throughout the turn to oppose the tendency of the float keels to travel in a straight line. To stop the turn, return the rudder to its neutral position and reduce the power back to the original setting.

A step-turn will feel very strange, to say the least, because unlike a boat, the plane will not lean into the turn. It either will maintain a wings-level attitude throughout the turn, or, if the turn is sharp,

lean to the outside of the turn. Only your seat belts will keep you and your passengers in your seats as centrifugal force tries to mash you either into the side of the cabin or the person next to you.

Centrifugal force and the wind

As the plane turns, centrifugal force will try to upset the plane toward the outside of the turn. The only thing resisting this upsetting tendency is the outside float. The tighter the turn, the greater the centrifugal force, and as the centrifugal force increases, the outside float will be forced deeper and deeper into the water. Eventually, the plane will be leaning so far over that the outside wingtip will contact the water, and the plane will flip or cartwheel.

One way to partially counter this capsizing tendency is to hold the wings level with the ailerons. By holding full aileron in the direction of the turn, the outside wing will be held up while the inside wing is pushed down. Initially, you'll have to rely on your instructor to tell you when your turns are getting too tight, but as you practice them, you'll acquire a feel for when you're getting too close to the limit. Factors that determine how tight your airplane can turn are the width of the floats, the distance between the floats, the wingspan of the airplane, the size and effectiveness of the ailerons, and the vertical distance between the floats and the fuselage. A floatplane that sits low over a pair of wide floats set far apart will be able to make tighter step-turns than a floatplane perched high above a pair of narrow floats set close together, all other factors being equal.

It's usually easier to make a step-turn to the left than it is to make one to the right. For one thing, you'll have a better view of where you're going. Of course, if you're flying a tandem-place floatplane like a Super Cub or a Citabria, you'll have an excellent view no matter which way you turn. The P-factor also will make it easier to turn the plane to the left because a turn in that direction will not require as much rudder deflection as a turn to the right.

In calm air, you can make step-turns in any direction you like. The only way you can get into trouble is if you try to make your turns too tight or if you taxi into swells or rough water. It's another story when the wind starts to blow. You're okay if you turn from an upwind heading to a downwind heading, but if you try to turn from a downwind heading to an upwind heading, watch out! The chances are good that you'll flip the airplane.

Let's say you're step-taxiing directly into the wind and need to make a 90-degree turn to the left into the bay toward your dock. As you begin the turn and add power, the centrifugal force generated by the turn will cause the plane to lean to the right, to the outside of the turn. This time, however, the centrifugal force will be offset somewhat by the wind, which will strike the right side of the plane and try to lift the outside wing. As a result, the floatplane will tend to remain on an even keel (Fig. 14-3).

Now let's look at the other side of the coin. Your floatplane is beached on the upwind side of a small lake, and you've decided that the wind is too strong to risk a downwind takeoff. Rather than endure a long, slow, idle taxi to the downwind end of the lake, you decide to save time and zip down on the step. There's nothing wrong with this, but as you approach the other end of the lake, you decide to save even more time by doing a 180-degree step-turn to the left. Not only will this head you back into the wind, but because you're already on the step, you'll be that much farther along in your takeoff run. You begin the turn, and a short time later—as you wade ashore and look back at your capsized plane drifting gently in the breeze—you wonder what went wrong.

What went wrong is this: As you began the left turn, the centrifugal force caused the plane to lean to the right, toward the outside of the turn. This time, however, instead of being opposed by the force of the wind, the centrifugal force was *assisted* by the wind, which pushed against the left side of the plane and lifted the inside wing (Fig. 14-4). The two forces combined were more than

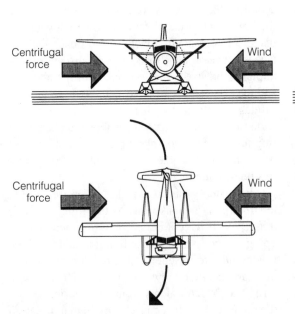

Fig. 14-3. *The forces at work during a step-turn from an upwind to a downwind heading.*

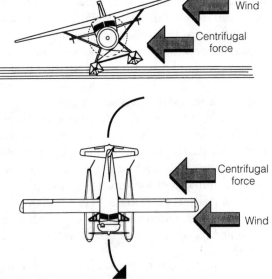

Fig. 14-4. *The forces at work during a step-turn from a downwind to an upwind heading.*

the outside float could resist, and it was pushed deep into the water. The lean to the right was made even more severe as the wind got underneath the inside wing and lifted it higher still. When the opposite wingtip struck the water, over you went.

The only thing you can do to try to save yourself is apply full opposite rudder if your plane starts to capsize while in a step-turn. If you're lucky, this action will accomplish two things. First, the centrifugal force generated by sharply turning the plane in the opposite direction will cancel out some of the forces that are trying to capsize you. Second, this new turn will take some of the pressure off the outside float, which has now become the inside float. The buoyancy of this float will bring it back up to the surface, thus righting the plane. Bear in mind that this maneuver is not something you should count on to save you, because if the plane has tipped over too far, nothing you can do will keep the plane from capsizing or cartwheeling.

As a general rule, never make a step-turn out of a downwind heading unless the wind is very light, and even then, keep the turn as wide as possible to minimize the centrifugal force. If at any time during the turn you feel the plane is in danger of capsizing, begin a turn in the opposite direction. When the plane is back on an even keel, stop the turn and pull the power back to idle. Once you're safely back in the displacement attitude, you can figure out what to do next.

Before you start a step-turn, make sure you'll have enough room to finish it. It's very dangerous to pull the power off while the floatplane is still turning. A floatplane is laterally unstable as it comes back over the hump, and if the plane is still in a turn, the centrifugal force might capsize it as it slows down and falls off the step. If you start a step-turn and then begin to wonder if you have enough room to complete it, straighten the plane out immediately, and pull off the power. It's better to sedately finish the turn at idle speed than to risk slamming into the shore or capsizing the floatplane when you realize, too late, that you're not going to make it.

If there's a good breeze blowing, don't forget the weathercocking tendency. It could cause you problems if you turn to a crosswind heading and then stop the step-taxi. As we've seen, you're vulnerable as you drop off the step and back over the hump, and a strong breeze could weathercock your plane around with enough force to cause it to capsize. It might be better to make another step-turn to a direct downwind heading before stopping the plane.

If the wind is strong enough to generate a noticeable weathercocking effect on your plane during a step-turn, the water will probably be rough enough that you shouldn't be maneuvering on the step in the first place. A step-turn is a real seat-of-the-pants maneuver. You're going to be too busy to sense and analyze all the subtle effects the wind will have on the plane during the turn. Just stick to the basics: If you're heading into the wind a step-turn is okay; if you're heading downwind in anything other than a gentle breeze, it's not.

GLASSY WATER

Nothing is more beautiful than a remote wilderness lake on a calm day. The mirrorlike surface reflects the surrounding mountains, broken only by the concentric circles of ripples spreading slowly from the spot where a feeding trout has chanced upon an unlucky bug. The lake is after bigger prey than the occasional errant insect, however. It's waiting for you, or any other unsuspecting or careless floatplane pilot who attempts to land on its glassy surface.

Flat, or glassy, water is probably the single most dangerous water condition a floatplane pilot can face (Fig. 14-5). Ironically, the danger is not to the plane itself, but to you, its pilot. With no waves to lend definition to the surface, it becomes almost impossible to judge your height above the water. The general tendency is to believe you are higher than you actually are; most glassy-water accidents result from pilots flying their planes headlong into the water. Glassy water also can af-

Fig. 14-5. A classic example of glassy water. How high are we off the lake? Ten feet? Fifty feet? Actually, our plane is sitting on the lake, but you can see how easy it would be to think you were higher.

fect your perception during takeoff, and pilots have been known to lift off a mirror-smooth surface only to fly right back into it again, all the while thinking they were climbing out.

If you obtain a seaplane rating and begin to fly floats on a regular basis, it's a sure bet that you will encounter glassy water. Every good seaplane course, therefore, puts a great deal of emphasis on the special techniques developed to deal with it.

Glassy-water landings

There are two methods of landing a floatplane on glassy water, and neither one of them uses the water as a reference. The first method, and the most commonly used, sets up a controlled descent that ends with your plane contacting the water in a landing attitude at a minimum sink rate. Your job is to maintain the proper landing attitude and keep the rate of descent constant. Since there is no way you will be able to judge the moment of contact, you won't even try it.

The second method depends on a pattern of visual objects on the water that will enable you to judge your height off the surface. These objects can be anything from the ripples created by throwing stones out of the plane to several life jackets dropped on the surface. In some cases, you might be able to use the shoreline as a reference. The important thing to remember is that the objects will be the focus of your attention, not the surface of the water.

The constant-attitude/constant-descent rate method

If you arrive over your destination and find the surface of the water is glass-smooth, you have at least one thing going for you. There is obviously no wind, so you can land in any direction you wish. A glassy-water landing covers a lot more distance than a normal landing, so make sure you'll have enough room to make the long, slow descent that's required.

When you have mapped out your landing lane, fly a normal approach until you're about 200 feet above the surface of the water. Both your instruments and the surrounding terrain will make it fairly easy to tell when you still have several hundred feet of air beneath your float keels. When you are approximately 200 feet up, transition your plane to a slow-flight attitude by reducing the power and raising the nose. The nose should be raised just slightly higher than the normal landing attitude to ensure that the bows of the floats will be in no danger of digging in when the plane touches down. Don't raise the nose too far because that could also make the floats dig in if their tails strike the water with enough force to pitch the plane forward.

Your airspeed is not as important as establishing and holding the correct attitude. How much flap you use depends on the characteristics of the particular floatplane you are flying. Obviously, the slower you touch down, the better, but some planes cannot maintain the proper nose-up attitude when the flaps are fully extended. If your plane is one of these, you will have to use less flap and settle for a slightly higher airspeed in order to maintain that all-important landing attitude.

Once you've established the proper touchdown attitude, don't vary it. Use the throttle to adjust your sink rate until you are descending at a rate of 150 (or less) feet per minute. Now comes the challenging part. You have to accurately maintain this attitude and sink rate until the plane contacts the surface of the water. Your instruments will be the greatest aid to keeping the descent rate constant, but the only way to maintain the proper attitude is to look at the horizon or shoreline ahead of you. Don't allow yourself to become fixated on either the horizon or your instruments, however, and correct immediately any variations in your attitude or descent rate. *Do not, under any circumstances, try to anticipate the moment of touchdown.*

When your plane approaches to within a few feet of the water, there might be a subtle change in the feel of the controls as the plane enters ground effect, but don't relax your concentration just because you sense you're within moments of touchdown. Continue to maintain the proper attitude and descent rate until the floats actually contact the surface. The touchdown will be harder than normal because you won't be flaring the plane smoothly onto the surface.

As soon as the floats touch the water, pull the power back to idle. Your forward speed will be higher than your normal touchdown speed, and you don't want to get bounced back into the air. If you should happen to touch down very hard and get bounced high into the air, you'll be better off if you immediately apply full power and go around for another try rather than attempt to feather the plane gently back onto a surface you might not be able to distinguish.

Be prepared to pull the yoke or stick back the moment the floats contact the surface. With no waves or wavelets to introduce bubbles and pockets of air underneath the floats, the glassy water will exert a lot of drag on the floats; this drag will combine with your higher-than-normal touchdown speed and tend to pitch the plane forward. It's important that you counteract this nose-over tendency as soon as it starts because it could conceivably be strong enough to dig in the float tips and pitch your plane over onto its back. Don't jump the gun and pull the yoke back too soon,

though, or you could bounce back into the air. Wait until you feel the plane begin to pitch forward before applying up-elevator. You'll soon learn the proper timing after a little practice.

The visual method

The landing procedure just described is for textbook glassy-water conditions in which there are no visual aids to help you judge your height above the water. It's the procedure you would use if you had to land away from shore on a large lake or bay that has only a distant or indistinct horizon. While you might find yourself in this situation occasionally, most of the time you will have some degree of visual assistance while making your landing.

The main problem with the standard glassy-water landing technique is the amount of room you need to do it. A small lake can have the same confusing, glassy conditions as a large lake, but there might not be room enough to make a slow, power-on letdown from 200 feet. Fortunately, many visual aids are available to help you get your plane safely on the water in these situations.

The most obvious visual aid is the shoreline. Since the lack of wind means you can land in any direction you like, landing close to and parallel with the shoreline will make it much easier to judge your height above the water. Plan to land close to shore, but far enough out to be in no danger of hitting any underwater obstructions like fallen trees, rocks, or pilings. It still will be almost impossible to judge the proper moment to flare the airplane, but the "horizon" beside you in the form of the shoreline will allow you to fly a normal approach down almost to the water. Then when you are 30 or 40 feet above the surface—an altitude you can easily judge by referencing the nearby shoreline—pitch the nose up to the proper touchdown attitude and add power to slow your descent rate to 150 or less feet per minute. Fly the last part of the approach in the same manner you would the textbook method described previously in this chapter. Maintain the proper attitude and descent rate until you touch down, reduce the power to idle, and pull back on the yoke or stick as necessary to counter the nose-over tendency.

By using the shoreline as a reference, you can fly a normal or even steep approach path down to within a few feet of the water before transitioning to the proper glassy-water landing attitude and descent rate, and you will not need anywhere near the amount of room it would take to fly a glassy-water approach from 200 feet up.

If you use a shoreline as a reference, make sure you look at the actual shoreline and not at its reflection. Don't be tempted to judge your height from what seems to be the bottom just below the surface. If the water is very clear and the lighting conditions are just right, a bottom that might appear to be just a few feet beneath the surface might actually be 10, 20, or even 30 feet down. If you use it to judge the right moment to flare the plane, you'll be in for quite a shock when you suddenly slam into the surface and water you didn't even know was there starts pouring into the cockpit.

Another optical illusion that can really mess up an otherwise perfectly executed glassy-water landing is the reflection of clouds in the mirrorlike surface of the water. Since the clouds are far away, their reflections will keep pace with you, and it will appear that you are standing still or hovering over the water. You might feel that you are about to stall, and your natural reaction will be to add power, lower the nose, or do something, anything, that will get your airplane moving forward again. Don't do it! Trust your instruments, look at the shoreline ahead of or beside you, maintain your attitude and descent rate, and ignore the reflections in the water. They're just part of the plot to get you to donate your plane to the Homeless Fish Society.

There might be times when the shoreline will be unusable as a reference. In certain parts of northern Canada, thousands of little lakes dot the flat, featureless landscape, while overhead, the sky is an unending pewter sheet. Gray water blends into gray shorelines, and height and distance judgments are almost impossible to make.

At times like these, floatplane pilots must create their own visual landing aids.

Water covered with ripples or waves has definition because your eyes have something on which to focus, and your depth perception enables you to accurately judge your height above the surface. The problem with glassy water is that it has no definition. Your sense of depth perception is worthless if your eyes have nothing to look at. The trick, then, is to put something on the surface of the water to give your sense of depth perception something with which to work.

Anything that floats or makes ripples on the surface will suffice, but try to exercise good judgment when selecting the items to be thrown into the water. Large, heavy tools generate excellent ripples when they hit the surface, but this practice can get expensive. Some pilots who routinely fly to glassy water lakes carry large, flat rocks in the cockpit that can be thrown out to create ripples, and others say they fire rifle or pistol shots into the surface for the same reason. The ripples created by small-arms fire are not very large, however, and they don't last very long, so I suspect the pilots who claim to use this method do so more to preserve their bush-pilot image than to actually create something that will help them land the plane. (They probably got the idea from the pilots of large flying boats during World War II who roughed up glassy surfaces by firing bursts from their forward .50-caliber machine guns into the water ahead of the plane.)

The best visual aids are those that remain floating on the water. Some pilots carry branches that act as runway markers when thrown out in quick succession as the plane overflies the water. Others advocate tossing out several crumpled-up maps. (If you decide to try this, make sure you throw out maps you won't need any more. And don't litter; make every effort to safely pluck the maps out of the water for proper disposal.) Probably the best things to throw into the water are life jackets, now called *personal flotation devices* (PFDs). The foam-filled life jackets will float high on the surface of the water, and a row of two or three of them spaced some distance apart will provide an excellent means of judging your altitude. (Make sure that you still have enough PFDs onboard for all occupants in an emergency.) After you've landed, you can taxi back and pick them up.

Even with visual aids on the water to help you, fly your final approach very carefully. Although the objects you've tossed out of your plane will certainly make it easier for you to determine your height above the water, make it a practice to transition to a nose-up touchdown attitude while you know you are still a safe distance above the surface. If you should happen to be a little off in your altitude estimation and touch down sooner than you anticipated, you might land hard, but at least your float tips will be up.

Glassy-water takeoffs

Glassy water also can be a problem during takeoff. As mentioned earlier, the slick, smooth surface will exert quite a bit of drag on the floats, and it might be difficult to get the floatplane on the step, especially if it's heavily loaded. Without the lubricating effects of the bubbles and pockets of air carried under the floats by ripples and waves, the plane will feel sluggish and will accelerate slowly. A simple way to ruffle up the surface of the water is to taxi around on it for awhile. Put the plane in a plowing attitude, and taxi around in circles over the area you've chosen for your takeoff lane and then return to your starting position and begin the takeoff run before the ripples and waves disappear.

If there is someone nearby with a boat, you can ask him or her to run down your takeoff lane ahead of you. When they are safely out of the way, make your takeoff run over the water they've stirred up, but be careful. You don't want to cross any swells that are too big for you or your plane to handle. The best thing to do is to follow exactly the same path the boat took. That way, your floats

will be running over the water churned up by the boat's propeller and transom, while the swells that make up the wake will be moving away on either side of you. If the boat is a small, outboard-powered skiff, it can run around at random through your takeoff area; its wake will not be large enough to cause you any problems.

A few pilots have experienced vertigo after taking off from glassy water, especially if the surrounding terrain is flat and featureless and the sky is hazy or overcast. The water and the sky are the same color, the horizon is indistinct, and suddenly it's not only impossible to tell how high you are, but you're not even sure if you're still climbing. While this phenomenon is most often experienced by skiplane pilots taking off from white snow into a white sky (a condition appropriately known as *whiteout*) it can happen to floatplane pilots, too. The only remedy is to use and trust your instruments. Keep the wings level and maintain a positive rate of climb at a constant airspeed. Until you're high enough to positively identify a shoreline, the horizon, or some other geographic feature, don't trust what you think you see out the window. You could be flying right back into the water and have no idea you're doing so.

THE ONE-FLOAT TAKEOFF

If you're taking off in glassy water and your plane is reluctant to accelerate to liftoff speed, or if you're concerned the lake might not be quite long enough for your heavily loaded floatplane, one technique you can use might help you accelerate a little faster. Once your plane is on the step, roll it to one side with the ailerons and lift one of the floats out of the water (Fig. 14-6). The theory is that this action will reduce the hydrodynamic drag by almost half, and your plane will be able to accelerate to liftoff speed faster.

One school of thought claims the additional load transferred to the other float increases the hydrodynamic drag on the one float to the amount previously shared equally by both floats. In other

Fig. 14-6. *Neal Ratti demonstrating a drag-reducing one-float takeoff. Great care must be taken to keep the low wing from contacting the water. Many pilots feel this technique does little to reduce the takeoff run, while greatly increasing the chance of an accident.*

words, the total amount of hydrodynamic drag remains the same, and you don't really gain anything. The pilots I know enjoy doing the maneuver, but they're evenly split as to whether or not it actually accomplishes anything.

It might take full aileron to pull the float out of the water, but once the wing starts coming up, it will come up fast. Be ready to immediately ease off a bit on the ailerons to stop the roll as soon as the float is clear of the surface. It's a tricky maneuver that requires a sensitive touch on the controls. If you overdo it, you can easily dip a wing tip into the water, and we all know what that leads to. On the other hand, you don't want to let the float fall back onto the water because that will slow you down again. Most pilots find it more natural to lift the right float, but if you're taking off in a crosswind, make sure you lift the downwind float out of the water and tilt the airplane into the wind. If you lift the upwind float, the wind will be able to get under the upwind wing and capsize your plane.

Do not attempt a one-float takeoff until you've had some instruction from someone who knows how to do it properly. It's a real balancing act that will take some practice before you're able to do it with confidence, and it's nice to have a competent instructor in the other seat to keep you from getting into trouble.

ROUGH WATER

In some ways, rough water is easier to deal with than glassy water. For one thing, you can see it. Rough water is dangerous, however, because of the potential damage it can do to your floatplane. Your takeoff and landing speeds remain unchanged, but suddenly your runway has become a series of unyielding crests and troughs. As you slam from wave to wave, the punishment inflicted on the struts, spreader bars, brace wires, and even the floats themselves can be tremendous. There is only one foolproof technique for turning rough water into smooth: Sit on the shore until the waves subside. The good thing about this technique is that it's infallible; it works every time. The bad thing about it is that you might have to sit on the shore for several days while you wait for the smooth water to appear. Since this is not always practical, techniques have been developed by which you can at least minimize the stress and strain put on your floatplane by rough water, allowing you to take off and land with relative safety.

Notice I said "relative safety." There is always an element of risk when operating in rough water. An undetected crack in a float mount, the one wave that's bigger than all the rest, the sudden gust of wind that pitches your airplane up at exactly the wrong moment: Any one of these things can bring your flight to a quick and soggy end. There is no substitute for common sense and good judgment when operating in rough-water conditions. The only person qualified to decide whether or not you or your plane can cope with a rough-water situation is you; don't let your passengers or anyone else make that decision for you. If the water looks too rough for you to handle, it probably is, and the best decision you can make at that point is to sit on the beach until things calm down a bit.

Rough water is generally the result of one of three things: boats, currents, or wind. The technique for dealing with the rough water caused by boats is fairly simple. You either wait for the boats to go away, or you taxi your plane to a spot where their wakes will not interfere with your takeoff run. If you have no other choice but to take off through water stirred up by boats, use the same rough-water techniques subsequently described in this chapter.

The second rough-water generator is the current. When two or more strong currents collide or merge, the result is often a very rough and confused water surface. This condition is most often encountered in rivers or tidal waters where there is a considerable difference between high and low tide. The coastal waters of Washington's Puget Sound, British Columbia, and southeast Alaska contain countless bays and channels, and the tide range can be as much as 22 feet. The tremendous volume of water pouring through these narrow channels can create extremely hazardous water conditions that would instantly destroy any floatplane foolish enough to attempt a landing (Fig. 14-7).

Fig. 14-7. *The Skookumchuck Rapids at the entrance to Sechelt Inlet in British Columbia. Violent tidal currents like this are common in the coastal waters of British Columbia and Alaska; a floatplane landing anywhere near here would stand a good chance of being swept out of control and slammed into the rocky shoreline, or flipped.*

The wind and the waves

You can thank the wind for most of the rough-water conditions you will encounter. Almost everyone has heard the expression, "a Force Nine gale." Force Nine is one of the wind classifications on the Beaufort Scale of Wind Forces. The entire scale and the way it relates to land and water conditions is found in Fig. 14-8. The information contained in this chart can be very helpful. Aviation weather reports do not include wave heights, and the information contained in marine forecasts is aimed primarily at boat operators. Water conditions that would merely bounce a boat around a bit could do serious damage to your floatplane. Aviation and marine weather reports and forecasts do include wind velocities, however, and by relating the reported or forecast surface winds to the water conditions generally associated with these wind velocities, you will be able to make a fairly educated guess as to what sort of water surface you will encounter when you arrive at your destination.

When a breeze starts blowing across a body of calm water, the surface tension of the water will resist distortion until the breeze reaches a velocity of about 2 knots. At this point, the friction between the moving air and the surface of the water will cause the water to be humped up into little ripples. If the wind velocity increases to approximately 3½ knots, the ripples will be pushed up into wavelets. The size and distance between these wavelets will continue to grow as the wind velocity increases. Until the wind reaches a speed of about 10½ knots, the waves will remain smooth in appearance. When this velocity is exceeded, the waves will begin to form crests. A bubbly froth will begin to appear on the wave crests, and the wind will blow long streaks of this froth straight downwind. Unlike the wind streaks that are sometimes formed at slower wind velocities, these streaks will be whitish in appearance.

White wind streaks are a good indication that the water is starting to move into the "rough" category, especially if you are flying one of the smaller floatplanes. As the wind velocity begins to

BEAUFORT SCALE and MAP SYMBOL		TERMS	VELOCITY (Knots)	ESTIMATING VELOCITIES ON LAND
0	o	Calm	Below 1	Smoke rises vertically.
1		Light air	1–2	Smoke drifts, wind vanes unmoved.
2		Light breeze	3–6	Wind felt on face; leaves rustle; ordinary vane moves by wind.
3		Gentle breeze	7–11	Leaves and small twigs in constant motion; wind extends light flag.
4		Moderate breeze	12–16	Dust and loose paper raised; small branches are moved.
5		Fresh breeze	17–21	Small twigs in leaf begin to sway; crested wavelets form in inland water.
6		Strong breeze	22–27	Large branches in motion; whistling heard in telephone wires; umbrellas used with difficulty.
7		Moderate gale	28–33	Whole trees in motion; inconvenience felt in walking against the wind.
8		Fresh gale	34–40	Twigs broken off trees; progress generally impeded.
9		Strong gale	41–47	Slight structural damage occurs.
10		Whole gale	48–54	Trees uprooted;
11			55–65	considerable structural damage occurs.
12		Hurricane	66+	

Fig. 14-8. *The Beaufort scale of wind forces.*

ESTIMATING WIND VELOCITIES ON WATER	REMARKS
Surface like a mirror.	Review your glassy water technique before flying under these conditions.
Ripples with the appearance of scales are formed, but without foam crests.	
Small wavelets; still short but more pronounced; crests have a glassy appearance but do not break.	
Large wavelets; crests begin to break. Foam has glassy appearance. Perhaps some scattered whitecaps.	Ideal water flying conditions in protected water.
Small waves, becoming longer; fairly frequent whitecaps.	Might be too rough for small floatplanes.
Moderate waves; taking a more pronounced long form; many whitecaps are formed. Chance of some spray.	This is considered rough water for seaplanes and small amphibians, especially in open water.
Large waves begin to form; white foam crests are more extensive everywhere. Probably some spray.	
Sea heaps up and white foam from breaking waves begins to be blown in streaks along the direction of the wind.	This type of water condition is for emergency only in small aircraft in inland waters and for expert pilots of large flying boats in the open sea.
Moderately high waves of greater length; edges of crests break into spindrift. The foam is blown in well-marked streaks along the direction of the wind.	
High waves; dense streaks of foam along the direction of the wind. Sea begins to roll. Spray might affect visibility.	Landplane takeoffs and landings should be made with caution.

Very high waves with long, overhanging crests. The resulting foam, in great patches, is blown in dense white streaks along the direction of the wind. On the whole, the surface of the sea takes on a white appearance. The rolling of the sea becomes heavy and shocklike. Visibility is affected.

exceed 11½ knots, the wave crests will begin to break, and whitecaps will begin to appear. This is just about the limit for small floatplanes like Super Cubs, Citabrias, and Cessna 172s. Once the wind reaches 16 or 17 knots, the surface of the water will be covered with whitecaps, and the pilots of larger floatplanes like Cessna 180s, 185s, and 206s should start thinking seriously about waiting for another day.

Only the pilots of Beavers, Otters, Twin Otters, and other very large floatplanes should consider taking off or landing on water that's being whipped up by winds in excess of 18 knots, and even then, their planes will have to endure quite a beating. The only reason they can get away with it is that the structural components of their floatplanes are relatively large and strong.

Another factor that helps determine the size of the waves is the distance the wind has been traveling over the water. The nautical term for this distance is *fetch*. If the wind velocity is less than 8½ knots, the waves it generates will not grow beyond a certain size, no matter how long the fetch. Once the wind exceeds 8½ knots, the waves will grow in proportion to the fetch. The surface near the downwind shore of a lake or a bay might be far rougher than the surface near the upwind shore, even though the wind velocity is identical in both places. As a general rule, large, open bodies of water will become too rough for floatplane operations when the wind exceeds 8½ knots, because the long fetch will permit the formation of large waves or swells. In smaller lakes of less than 3 miles in length, floatplanes can sometimes be taken off or landed in winds of 20 or even 30 knots because the relatively short fetch will not allow the formation of extremely large waves or swells.

Another problem encountered in rough water is spray. Even at the slowest possible taxi speed, your floats will fall off the crests of the waves into the troughs with quite a splash, and it's virtually impossible to keep the propeller clear of the spray. If you're facing a long taxi in rough water, visibility might even become a problem as the propeller

picks up spray and throws it into the windshield. I was once practicing rough-water takeoffs and landings with an instructor in a Cessna 180 that had been equipped with a 270-horsepower engine (the standard engine is rated at 230 horsepower) and a three-bladed propeller. The water was extremely rough and getting rougher, but the high-horsepower C-180 seemed to be holding its own, especially on takeoff. It was a valuable experience, but when the prop started throwing solid sheets of water into the windshield, we both decided it was time to call it quits. If you have to fly in rough-water conditions, make sure you check the propeller frequently for spray erosion. If you're operating in salt water, it's especially important that you thoroughly wash down all parts of the plane with fresh water after each flight.

How can you tell if the water is too rough for your floatplane? Fortunately, rough water, and the wind that accompanies it, tends to be rather intimidating to inexperienced floatplane pilots, and the sight and sound of the wind and waves generally sends them in search of an experienced pilot for advice. The seaplane base where I fly does not allow students or renters to fly the company's Cessna 172s if the wind exceeds 13 knots, and other schools have similar policies.

The Beaufort velocity chart in Fig. 14-8 provides some general guidelines for determining water conditions, but the best way to develop an eye for the waves is to go out to your local seaplane base on a windy day and do some serious hanging around. Listen to the exaggerations the pilots are telling each other about their rough-water experiences. They're always entertaining, and there is usually enough truth in what they're saying for you to learn something. When they say the water is too rough for such-and-such a type of floatplane, they probably know what they're talking about. Try to memorize what the water looks like, and compare the planes that *are* flying with the plane that you fly. If the only things moving are de Havilland Beavers and you fly a Citabria, you'll know what to do the next time you see the same kind of waves. You'll stay inside and drink coffee with the other sensible pilots who are telling each other about the times they landed J-3 Cubs on lakes whipped into waterspouts by 90-knot winds.

The larger your floatplane, the rougher the water it can handle, but that's only part of the picture. *You* have to handle the rough water, too, and if you don't feel you're up to it, don't try.

The rough-water takeoff

Your main objective when taking off in rough water is to accelerate your plane to liftoff speed while subjecting it to the least amount of pounding possible. Always use the recommended amount of flap during a rough-water takeoff. Unless your plane is very heavily loaded, you'll come up onto the step fairly quickly, and you won't gain anything by waiting to deploy the flaps until you're in a planing attitude. If the waves are large enough to cause the nose of your plane to pitch up and down, wait until the plane is starting to pitch up before adding takeoff power. If you put the power in as the nose is descending, you might drive the floats into the next wave.

Once the plane is on the step, carry the nose slightly higher than you would during a normal takeoff. A higher pitch angle will reduce your chances of digging a float tip into a wave. Don't carry the nose too high, however, because you'll only succeed in extending the takeoff run.

Most inexperienced floatplane pilots are guilty of carrying the nose too high because they're afraid of "hooking" a float tip in a wave. I certainly was. As my rented Cessna 172 bounced from crest to crest, my mind would project a slow-motion image of the plane digging in its floats and pitching onto its back, and I'd haul back on the yoke a little more. In doing so, I accomplished two things, both of them bad. First, by increasing the angle of attack, I increased the drag and prolonged the plane-pounding takeoff run. Second, by raising the float tips too high, I made the pounding even worse by slamming the float bottoms flat against the front of the oncoming waves. I was, in effect, stalling from wave to wave. I have since learned to hold a less radical nose-up attitude.

By carrying the nose only slightly higher than normal, your plane will accelerate faster, and the floats will cut through the wave tops instead of slamming into them. If a wave happens to bounce the nose up too high, you might find it necessary to relax the back pressure a bit or even apply a little forward pressure to bring it back down again.

As soon as your floatplane has reached flying speed, pull it off the water. You can pull it off at its minimum stall speed or even a little slower if you remain in ground effect while you accelerate to a safe climbout speed, but don't pull it off so soon that you risk setting back onto the water in that nose-high, float-pounding attitude I just described. The plane might even be bounced into the air by the waves before you can pull it off, but in either case, you'll be flying on the ragged edge of a stall. Lower the nose slightly (but don't fly back into the water) and build up some airspeed before you initiate your climbout.

If your plane is equipped with manual flaps, there is a neat trick you can do that will help you get off the water a little sooner. If you're flying a Cessna 180, for example, you will normally begin your takeoff run with 20 degrees of flap, which means the flap handle will be pulled up two notches from the floor. Shortly before the plane reaches its minimum liftoff speed, rapidly extend the flaps another 5 to 10 degrees by giving a sharp upward tug on the handle, while at the same time pulling back slightly on the yoke. The sudden application of flap and up-elevator will balloon the plane off the rough water and into the air. Now comes the hard part.

The plane isn't quite ready to fly yet, and you'll need a sensitive touch on the yoke and the flap handle to keep it staggering along in ground effect while the airspeed builds up. The extra flap adds a lot of drag, and the trick is to bleed it back to 20 degrees as quickly as possible without letting the plane settle back onto the waves. You'll also have to lower the nose back to the proper takeoff attitude almost as quickly as you pulled it up to prevent the plane from stalling. If your plane has electric flaps, you can move the flap selector down as the plane approaches liftoff speed, but the ballooning effect won't be as great because the flaps move rather slowly.

This technique will not work in all floatplanes, and in some, it might be downright dangerous. The application of additional flap might produce so much drag that after the initial ballooning effect, the plane might simply stall and drop back onto the water with enough force to break something. Don't attempt this technique until you're sure it's safe to do in your airplane, and get some instruction from an experienced pilot before you try it on your own.

The first time you make a takeoff in even moderately rough water, you will be amazed at the pounding inflicted on the plane. The noise is terrific because everything that can possibly vibrate, rattle, or squeak, does. The instrument panel jiggles around in front of you, the engine cowl shakes, and you'll swear the plane is moments from destruction. You'll soon discover that floatplanes are tougher than they look and feel, and they'll absorb a lot of punishment before giving up. Every pounding, rough-water takeoff and landing, however, contributes a little more to wear, tear, and fatigue, so give your plane the smoothest ride you can.

Avoid downwind takeoffs in rough water. The very fact that the water is rough will mean that the wind is strong, and you'll have to slam along over the water for a long time until you reach flying speed. If your plane's liftoff speed is 55 knots and the wind is blowing at 15 knots, you'll have to accelerate to 70 knots before you can pull it free of the pounding waves, and the punishment inflicted might be more than the float and airframe components can take. If you take off into the wind, you'll have to accelerate to a water speed of only 40 knots, and your airplane will thank you for it.

Rough-water landings

Your goal when landing in rough water is the same as it is when taking off; subject the plane to as little pounding and stress as possible. Land in the smoothest water you can find. When you arrive over your destination, try to estimate the size of the waves as you make your aerial check of the area. When you think you know how high the waves are, double your estimation. Waves have a way of looking half their size when you're flying around over them at pattern altitude. If the water near your destination looks too rough, you might be able to find a nearby cove or bay that is more sheltered from the wind and waves. If your destination lies on the downwind shore of a lake, it might be prudent to land in the lee of the upwind shore and wait until the waves subside before moving the plane to the other side. Regardless of where you land, always land into the wind if the water is rough. If you land across the wind, the rolling and pitching of the airplane will make it easy for the wind to get under the upwind wing and capsize the plane.

While you want to contact the water at the slowest speed practical, do not make a full-stall landing. Doing so will put the airplane in a nose-high attitude, and the bottoms of the floats will smash into the crests of the oncoming waves. Instead, carry a bit of power throughout the approach and contact the water in a relatively flat attitude. Although your touchdown speed will be slightly higher than your speed in a full-stall landing, the floats will cut through the waves rather than slam into them, and the landing will be easier on the airplane. Don't let the nose get too low, however. Digging the float tips into a wave while landing is just as dangerous as doing it while taking off.

Keep a sharp eye out for gusts. The winds that bring about rough water are often gusty, and your plane might be ballooned up or dropped down just as you're trying to ease it onto the waves. Gusts appear as dark patches on the water, but remember that the actual gust will slightly precede its "shadow."

If the water conditions are varied, or if you're having a problem finding a smooth touchdown spot amid a lot of boat wakes, you can skim along a few feet above the surface using power to keep the airspeed slightly above the stall. As you approach a good touchdown spot, pull the power off, and the plane will settle onto the surface almost immediately.

Ideally, rough water landings should be made with full flaps, but there might be times when this setting is not appropriate. If the wind is gusty and your floatplane has large, effective flaps, a lesser setting might keep you from being ballooned back into the air just as you're about to touch down. Some floatplanes, such as the de Havilland Beaver, come down like a rock with full flaps (even the Beaver's flight manual cautions against using full flaps except in an emergency), and partial flaps will yield a better landing attitude in rough water. Again, an instructor or a pilot experienced in rough-water flying will be your best source of information regarding the ideal flap settings for your particular floatplane.

Be prepared to bring in full power and go around if you get tossed back into the air by a large wave. It's better to go around than to attempt to rescue the landing and end up contacting the water in a nose-high, full-stall attitude. Also be prepared to put in the power and leave if you find that the water just looks too rough when you get down close to it. Don't get desperate to land the plane—as long as there is fuel in the tanks, it's a lot safer in the air than it is in the rough water. If you feel the water at your destination is too rough for you or your floatplane to handle, look for another place to land. It's better to land somewhere inconvenient and wait for conditions to improve than risk losing your floatplane and possibly injuring yourself or your passengers.

Once you've decided to land and your plane has contacted the water, chop the power immediately. You'll only prolong the beating your plane is about to receive by keeping the power in and attempting to "smooth out the bumps." I've tried this once or twice, and believe me, it doesn't work. You'll just have to sit there and take your lumps. As long as you're running along on the step, you'll be

able to control the pitch angle, and you can keep the attitude flat so the floats will cut through the waves. (Remember, though, to keep the float tips high enough so they won't dig in.) Once the plane begins to settle off the step, however, there's not much you can do, and as the nose comes up, the ride will get pretty rough. If anything is going to break, this is probably the time it's going to do it.

Things will calm down a bit once the plane is back in a displacement attitude, but you'll still have to contend with the wind and spray. You might not be able to turn out of the wind, so if your destination lies behind you, you'll have to sail the plane backward to the dock. Before we examine the fine art of handling a floatplane in the wind, however, there is one other water condition you should be aware of, although you will never encounter it if you're lucky.

SWELLS

Swells are no fun at all. *Webster's New World Dictionary* defines a swell as a large wave that moves without breaking, but the definition doesn't go on to say what swells can do to a floatplane. Boat wakes are a form of swell, and if you ever have the misfortune to hit one while taking off or landing, you'll probably be amazed at the effect those seemingly innocent little lumps of water can have on your plane. The wake from a 16-foot boat can flip a floatplane, and the intersecting wakes from continuous boat traffic can make it impossible to land in a busy harbor.

Most floatplane accidents do not occur upon the first impact with the water. Usually, the plane is pitched or tipped into an attitude from which the pilot cannot immediately recover. Successive contacts with the water only worsen the situation, and eventually a structural member will break or a float or wingtip will dig in deep enough to capsize the plane.

If you should hit a boat wake, the two things to remember are keep the bows of the floats from digging in and keep the wings level. As in a rough-water takeoff, the wake will probably pitch your nose up, and you'll have to relax the back pressure or apply momentary forward pressure to get it back to the proper attitude. If you're running along on the step when you approach the wake, the addition of full power might enable you to take off before you reach it, or you might be able to jerk the plane out of the water long enough to stagger over the wake before settling back down again. If you settle back into the water before you've cleared the swells, however, you're liable to slam into the top of one at a high angle of attack, and you'll be worse off than you were before. Also, don't forget there are two halves to a boat wake. You don't want to successfully clear one set of swells only to run into the swells coming off the other side of the boat.

Generally, your best course of action is to pull the power off as soon as you see that you're going to run into a wake. If you're already in the swells, you'll get a pretty rough ride as you fall off the step and come back through the hump, but it might be safer than trying to power through the wake or yanking the plane off the water before it's ready to fly.

Boat wakes can almost always be seen and avoided. Far more dangerous are the big swells found in large bodies of water or harbors and bays exposed to the sea. Most of the time these swells are obvious from the air, but sometimes they're not visible until you approach the surface. Everything from the color of the sky to the angle of the light can affect their appearance, and you might get all the way to the end of your final approach, only to find the water covered with widely spaced swells. These swells are the remains of large waves that have been whipped up by the wind some distance away. While the wind might die, the energy stored in the waves will keep them moving for a long time, and they will gradually run together and form the rhythmic patterns of swells so familiar to boaters who venture into open water. It might take a long time for swells to dissipate; the huge swells that are responsible for the excellent surfing conditions along the north shore of Oahu in the Hawaiian Islands begin life as waves whipped up by violent storms in the Gulf of Alaska, thousands of miles away.

There is really no safe way to land a floatplane on water that is covered with swells. Only the experienced pilots of large flying boats can hope to operate in and out of swells with any degree of success, and even the large flying boats will be subjected to a considerable pounding. With their strong hulls and low centers of gravity, flying boats can cope with much rougher water than can floatplanes. The Japanese Shin-Meiwa PS-1, a large, four-engined, amphibious flying boat that first flew in 1967, is designed to operate in winds of up to 25 knots and seas up to 13 feet high—conditions that would make short work of even the largest floatplane.

While you should never deliberately set out to take off or land in swell-covered water, an inflight emergency might leave you no other choice but to land in whatever water lies below you. If that water happens to be covered with swells, you'll just have to do the best you can. Fortunately, there are a few basic guidelines that will increase your chances of making a successful landing, or at least one in which no one is injured.

First, try to determine the distance between the swells. This distance, or wavelength, is measured from the top of one swell to the top of the next one. If the swells are close together, half the length of your floats or less, your plane will always be supported by at least two swells, and the touchdown will be relatively smooth. This isn't to say that your plane won't come apart when it starts to slow down, but the initial touchdown and runout will be tolerable.

If the wavelength is between one and two times the length of your floats, your plane will only be supported by one swell at a time, and you will pitch in and out of the troughs between the swells. This is a very dangerous situation because if your plane should touch down on a crest and immediately pitch forward into a trough, the floats will dig into the face of the next swell, and you'll be flipped onto your back while traveling at a fairly high rate of speed.

If the distance between the swells is four or more times the length of your floats, you can, wind permitting, land parallel to them, which will considerably lessen the chances of damaging the plane.

Because the swells were probably generated some distance away by winds that have long since dissipated, you'll often find that the swells and the local surface winds are coming from two different directions. Sometimes the local winds will be generating their own wave pattern, which will be superimposed over the swell pattern. Things can get very confusing, but whenever possible, land parallel to the swells. To land into them is to risk slamming into the front of an oncoming swell, sort of a monster version of making a full-stall landing into the crest of a wave.

The only time you should consider landing into the swells is if the wind is blowing very hard in the same direction as the swells are moving, making a crosswind landing parallel to the swells difficult, if not impossible. If possible, try to touch down on the back of a swell or in the trough between two swells. If the wind velocity appears to be less than 10 knots, however, land parallel to the swells. The more you can head into the wind, the better, but your first consideration should be to touch down parallel to the swells.

The only guideline for taking off in water covered with large swells, or a combination of swells and other wave patterns, is to head as closely into the wind as possible without heading directly into any of the prevailing wave and swell patterns. As a general rule, however, floatplanes should never be operated on any body of water when swells are present. By the way, the procedures for landing a floatplane in water covered with swells are the same you should use if you ever have to ditch a landplane under the same conditions.

15
Floatplanes versus the wind

JUST ABOUT EVERYTHING you do in a floatplane is affected by the wind. It affects the water conditions, your steering, your takeoff and landing directions, your cruise, your taxiing, and your docking. The wind even affects you by its absence—when you have to make a glassy water landing, for example. Much of your floatplane instruction will be spent in learning how to cope with the whims of the wind, and the more you fly, the more you'll realize that the wind's supply of tricks is infinite.

CROSSWIND TAKEOFFS AND LANDINGS

One of the advantages floatplanes enjoy over landplanes is their ability to almost always take off and land into the wind; however, there will be times when boat traffic, obstructions in the water, or the narrow width of a channel will dictate your takeoff or landing lane, regardless of the wind direction. The lake where I fly is sometimes subjected to strong northwest winds during the summer. The seaplane base is at the north end of the lake, which gives us floatplane pilots three options. We can taxi a mile or so down the lake and take off into the

wind, but this takes forever. We can take off downwind, but this subjects the plane and our passengers to a pretty severe pounding. Our third option is to taxi out in front of the base and take off diagonally across the lake. Because we're not going directly downwind, our takeoff runs are shorter, but we have to have our crosswind takeoff technique down pat in order to pull this off safely.

The crosswind takeoff and landing procedures in a floatplane aren't that much different from the ones you're used to using in a landplane. Because of the yielding nature of the water's surface, though, it's very important not to let the wind begin to lift the floatplane's upwind wing, for this will begin to bury the downwind float. If corrective measures aren't taken immediately, the plane could capsize. Another difference will be the fact that your landing surface will be moving. This makes it very difficult, if not impossible, to judge your drift by looking at the water. The texture and movement of even the smallest ripples and wavelets might make it appear that you're moving sideways faster than you actually are, or maybe even in the wrong direction. The only way you can get an accurate picture of your drift is by referencing a point on shore in front of you.

The crosswind takeoff

If the wind is light to moderate, the takeoff run is made using the same procedure you would use if you were flying a landplane. Hold full aileron into the wind to keep the upwind wing from lifting, and then gradually bleed off the aileron as the speed increases.

Because the consequences of having the upwind wing lift out of control are irreversible, it's best to play it safe and hold some aileron into the wind all the way through the takeoff run. It's even a good practice to lift off the water with the upwind wing lowered slightly, holding the bank angle until you're well clear of the water and have established a positive rate of climb. Then, if the plane should settle back onto the water after a premature liftoff, the upwind wing will still be in a position to resist being lifted by the wind. Make sure, however, that when you pull the plane off the water, you don't let the upwind wing drop low enough to contact the surface.

When you line the plane up prior to starting your takeoff run, the water rudders will keep you heading across the wind. As soon as you pull the rudders up, however, the plane will begin to weathercock into the wind, and in the short time it takes you to secure the water-rudder handle to its bracket, you could be pivoted away from your takeoff lane. The solution is to turn to a heading downwind of your takeoff heading before raising the water rudders. By the time you've gotten the retraction handle secured to its bracket—a process that seems to take forever when you're in a hurry—the wind will have pivoted you into alignment with your takeoff lane, and you can put in the power and go.

Be prepared to put in a lot of downwind rudder at the start of the takeoff run to resist the wind's weathercocking force and keep the plane following a straight path. You'll have to hold even more downwind rudder if the wind is coming from the left because you'll be opposing both the weathercocking effect and the P-factor.

There have been times when beginning a takeoff diagonally across Lake Washington that I've been unable to keep the plane from veering sharply into the wind despite shoving the downwind rudder pedal clear to the floor. Continuing the takeoff would have sent us plowing into the nearby marina long before the air rudder had enough authority to turn me back toward the open water of the lake. The solution in a situation like this is to begin the takeoff run with the water rudders down. This will give you the steering authority you need to keep the plane headed in the proper direction. As you come up onto the step and the air rudder begins to work, pull the water rudders up before they start banging around enough to inflict damage on themselves or the floats.

Depending on the configuration of your plane and its floats, a strong crosswind could conceivably try to weathercock your plane *downwind* as you come up into the hump phase of the takeoff. The principle is the same as the one that lets you make a plowing turn to a downwind heading.

The important thing to remember regardless of which way the wind tries to veer your plane is to pull the power off and stop the moment you sense things aren't going according to plan. It's far better to idle around and think about the situation for a few minutes than to continue on the theory that you can power your way out of trouble. I know of several beautiful floatplanes that ended up sunk or on the rocks because their pilots thought they could bull their way through a crosswind takeoff that was getting out of hand.

The threat of the upwind wing lifting is always present during a crosswind takeoff in a strong wind, particularly at the beginning of the takeoff run. If you have enough room, the best procedure is start your takeoff directly into the wind. Once you're on the step and accelerating, your ailerons will be more effective, and you can turn to the required crosswind heading. The important thing is to keep that upwind wing from lifting. Your plane is most vulnerable during the hump phase, so if you can accomplish the transition from displacement to planing while heading directly into the wind and waves, your chances of capsizing will be greatly diminished.

If the upwind wing should start to lift during a crosswind takeoff and additional aileron doesn't immediately bring it back down again, pull the power back to idle and let the plane weathercock into the wind. Any attempt to continue the takeoff will probably result in burying the downwind float, which will, in turn, capsize the plane. If you let things get so far out of hand that the downwind float actually does become buried, pull off the power and turn the plane downwind as hard as you can. This will lower the forward speed of the downwind float and relieve some of the pressure that's forcing it down. There is no guarantee that this procedure will save the plane, so it's best not to let the situation progress to the point where you have to hope that it does.

In severe crosswind conditions, you might be able to get the plane on the step while heading into the wind only to find that you can't hold the crosswind heading when you try to turn toward it. This is the one situation when it's permissible to lower the water rudders during the takeoff run. They'll help you hold the plane on course, but they'll probably take a beating in the process. Don't forget to raise them as soon as you're going fast enough for the air rudder to give you the control you need.

If the wind is so strong that you need to use the water rudders to hold a takeoff heading across it, you'd better be in a pretty hefty floatplane. Any wind this strong will have whipped up some very rough water, and your plane will probably be subjected to a terrific pounding before you get it airborne. This technique is for de Havilland Beaver and Otter drivers; a Cessna 172 shouldn't even be in the water on a day like this.

The crosswind landing

Landing a floatplane in a crosswind is no different from landing a landplane under the same condi-

tions. By holding the upwind wing low and applying opposite rudder, you can slip the plane sideways into the wind. Properly done, the upwind slip will cancel your downwind drift, and you will track straight down the runway or, in this case, your chosen landing lane on the water. The touchdown will occur on the low (upwind) float, and you should continue to hold the aileron into the wind as you decelerate to keep the wind from lifting the upwind wing. As you slow down, the plane might begin to weathercock, so you'll have to counter this tendency with the rudder. As in a crosswind takeoff, your plane will be at its most vulnerable as it comes off the step and back over the hump, so be prepared to apply full aileron into the wind to keep the plane on an even keel.

As you begin your final approach, it will be difficult to judge your rate of downwind drift by looking at the water. The waves will be moving at an angle across your path, and it can even appear that you are drifting upwind instead of downwind. Since your goal is to touch down without any sideways drift at all, it's necessary that you be able to see your true rate of drift so you can correct for it. The only reliable way to do this is to use a point on land as a reference. As you begin your final approach, pick a house, a dock, a tree, or any prominent object on shore, and fly toward it. (If you use a boat, make sure it's anchored. Flying an approach using a moving boat as a reference could be an interesting experience.) Like the centerline on a runway, the fixed object ahead of you will immediately show you if you're drifting downwind and whether or not you're using the proper amount of correction to stop the drift.

As you get closer to the water, it will be harder to ignore the false information you might be getting from the waves, but if you continue to judge your crosswind correction using the fixed reference you've chosen, you'll make a nice, smooth touchdown on the upwind float without that sickening, sideways lurch that makes the passengers grab for the armrests.

SAILING

As we have seen, turning a taxiing floatplane from an upwind to a downwind heading can be difficult—or even dangerous—on a windy day. If the wind is above a certain velocity, it might be impossible to turn the floatplane at all, thanks to the weathercocking effect. If your destination lies directly upwind of your landing site, it's a simple matter to land and continue taxiing straight ahead. But what can you do if your destination lies downwind of your landing site or somewhere off your left or right wing? You'll have to resort to one of the most interesting and challenging floatplane techniques there is: sailing.

Sailing a floatplane is an art. Put simply, sailing is the technique of making a floatplane go in a direction the wind doesn't want it to go. It's one of the few times you'll be able to foil the wind and make it work for you instead of against you. By manipulating your plane's control surfaces and engine, you can sail the plane diagonally backward to the left or right, or even straight sideways. By combining the different sailing techniques, you can make your floatplane go just about anywhere you want it to, even if the wind is so strong that you can only turn a few degrees to the left or right.

The techniques for sailing a floatplane are based on two principles, which I call the keel effect and the deflection effect. If the force of the wind is not opposed by thrust from the engine, the plane will be pushed backward through the water. The wind's effect will be slight, other than to produce the drift, so the plane will tend to head in the direction the floats are aimed. In other words, if there was some way to point the tail to the left or right of a dead-downwind heading, the float hulls and keels would resist the wind's attempt to continue pushing the plane straight downwind, and the plane would drift (sail) backward to the left or right. This is the *keel effect*.

The *deflection effect* is used to move the floatplane sideways. If the plane is held in position with the engine, the hulls of the floats will not be moving through the water, so they will have little steering effect on the airplane. If the plane could then be turned a few degrees to the left or right, the wind would strike only one side of the fuselage. With more pressure on one side than on the other, the plane would be pushed, or deflected, sideways. Most of the time, you will use a combination of both of these methods to reach your destination. (Practicing with an experienced instructor onboard would be very wise.)

The primary controls used in sailing are the air rudder, the ailerons, the engine, the flaps, and the doors. With all the flight controls in their neutral positions, the floatplane will point directly into the wind and drift straight back. To sail backward to the left, raise the water rudders, apply full right rudder, and hold full left aileron. Right rudder will push the tail to the left. Holding the stick or yoke all the way to the left will lower the right aileron and raise the left one. Since the down (right) aileron will present more surface to the wind than the up (left) aileron, it will help the rudder swing the tail of the airplane to the left. It's important to raise the water rudders when sailing backward because if they are left down, they will oppose the air rudder. As the wind swings the tail to the left, the plane will begin to move in that direction (Fig. 15-1).

You can also control your sailing speed. Lowering the flaps will present more surface to the wind, and you will be blown backward at a faster rate. If you're still not satisfied, you can hold the cabin doors open to add even more wind-catching surface. (If you're sailing to the left, holding open only the right-hand door might help swing the tail to the left even farther.) Be careful if the winds are strong, however. The sterns of your floats will become the bows when you start sailing backward, but the sterns don't have as much flotation as the bows and forebodies. If you start drifting backward too fast, you might drive the sterns of the floats deep into the water, and the wind could get under the wing and fuselage and flip the plane over its tail

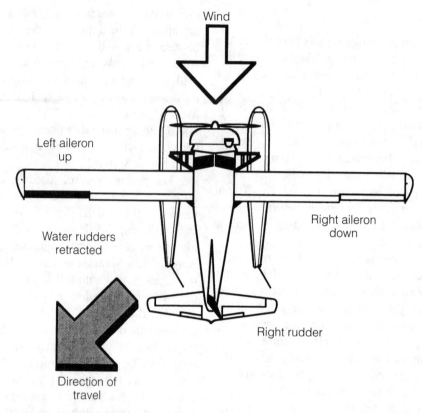

Wind

Left aileron
up

Right aileron
down

Water rudders
retracted

Right rudder

Direction of
travel

Fig. 15-1. *These are the proper positions to hold the controls to sail a floatplane backwards to the left.*

and onto its back. Hold the yoke or stick all the way forward when you're sailing backward. This will help hold up the tail and the sterns of the floats.

If you're sailing backward to a dock, you can use the engine to stop your backward drift when you get there. When you're sailing with the engine shut down, always keep it ready to start; you might need it in a hurry if you suddenly have to stop or pull forward. Some of the larger floatplanes, such as the de Havilland Otter, should never be sailed backward unless the engine is running. Because the Otter presents so much surface to the wind, it will drift backward very quickly, but the afterbodies of its floats have very little flotation compared to the size and mass of the airplane. Without any braking action from the engine, the sterns of the floats will easily be driven under, and the wind

will get under the huge wing and drive the tail into the water or even put the plane on its back.

You can use two methods to reach a dock that is directly off your wing. The first method is to sail backward in the direction of your destination for awhile and then taxi straight forward, followed by another angled drift and other taxi forward (Fig. 15-2). Repeat this pattern until you reach your destination. The second method is to sail the plane sideways using the deflection effect. Using the engine to hold your position, apply rudder in the direction you want to go. The water rudders should be down because they'll help the air rudder turn the plane. As you maintain your position opposite your destination, the wind will start to push you over toward it.

I've been asked about the advisability of using the water rudders when trying to sail directly

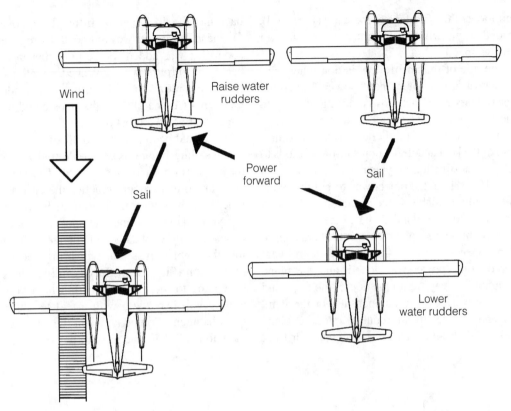

Fig. 15-2. *Using a combination of sailing and taxiing to zigzag toward a destination off your wing. If the water is extremely rough, or the wind very strong, you might only be able to taxi straight ahead, and it will take more repetitions of this pattern to reach the dock than are shown in this illustration.*

sideways. The concern was that the lowered rudders would act like a pair of sailboat keels and actually impede the sideways movement of the plane. In fact, they do impede the sideways movement of the plane, but in a beneficial manner.

Let's assume you want to sail your floatplane to a point directly off your right wing. You've already started your engine, and you're using it to counteract the wind's tendency to push you backward. The next step is to push down on the right-rudder pedal. The right-deflected air rudder will catch the wind and some of the propwash and will push the tail of your plane to the left. The wind against the left side of the fuselage will then begin to push your whole plane through the water to the right; this is the deflection effect.

This maneuver will work with the water rudders retracted. It will work faster, however, if you lower the water rudders before starting your sideways sail. To understand why, take a look at the location of the water rudders. They're way back there at the float sterns, far behind the pivot point of the airplane. The lowered rudders will indeed resist being moved sideways through the water, but because of their extreme aft location, the resulting drag will pivot the floats, not slow them down. In the case of a sideways sail to the right, the drag from the lowered water rudders will pivot the plane slightly to the right, which is exactly what you are already trying to do with the air rudder. The lowered water rudders will give you a few more degrees of turn, which will expose a little bit more of the fuselage to the wind (Fig. 15-3). The end result will be a slight increase in your sideways speed.

The rule of thumb I follow is that when sailing backward, with or without power, I keep the water rudders up. When power sailing directly to the left or right, I put the rudders down.

Occasionally you might have to use a combination of the keel and deflection sailing methods to reach your destination. A typical example is shown in Fig. 15-4. Here, the object was to put the plane into the only available space at the dock during a storm with 20-knot winds. The plane was sailed backward into the seaplane base until it was opposite the open spot. Then the water rudders were lowered, some power was added, and the plane was sailed sideways up to the dock. The flaps and the engine were used to compensate for the wind gusts and to keep from running into the plane ahead; the flaps and engine also prevented drifting

back into the dock behind. If the plane moved too far ahead, the power was momentarily reduced and some flap was added. If the plane began to drift back, the throttle was advanced slightly, or the flaps were retracted. This particular episode took place in a Cessna 180, so the flaps could be lowered or retracted almost instantly.

It would be impossible to illustrate all the different sailing situations you could find yourself in; they're as unlimited as the wind. The best thing you can do is learn and practice the basics. Then, whenever the opportunity presents itself, try sailing your plane to a specific spot on a dock or a beach. It's slow, but it's a challenge to figure out just the right moves that will bring you to your destination (Fig. 15-5). Successfully sailing your floatplane to the exact spot for which you were aiming will leave you with a real feeling of accomplishment. Someday, when the wind is really whistling, all that practice will pay off.

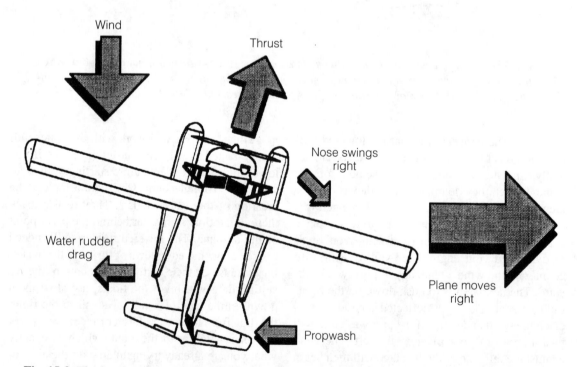

Fig. 15-3. *The forces acting on a floatplane while sailing sideways. The maneuver will work with the water rudders retracted, but lowering them will help pivot the nose a little farther in the direction you want to go.*

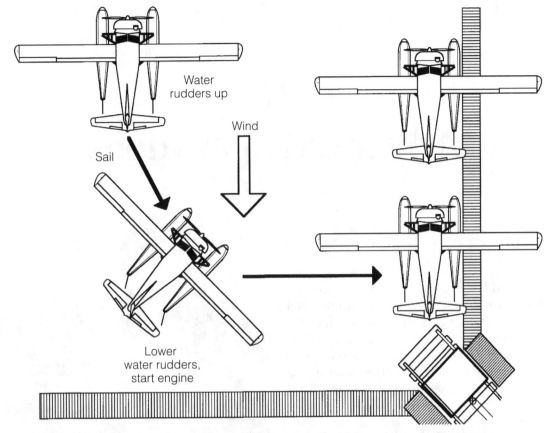

Water
rudders up

Wind

Sail

Lower
water rudders,
start engine

Fig. 15-4. *The combination of two sailing techniques to reach a tight spot on a dock.*

Fig. 15-5. *Sailing a Beaver backwards to the right. The water rudders are retracted, and Neal is applying full left rudder. It's important to retract the water rudders because they will oppose the air rudder when the plane is moving backwards through the water. Note also that the left aileron is down and the right one is up.*

16
Advanced operations

THE MAIN REASON for the floatplane's continuing popularity is its versatility. From a busy downtown dock to a remote wilderness lake, a floatplane gives its pilot an almost limitless range of destinations. The purpose of a floatplane trip is often recreation, but that great fishing or camping spot might be a little difficult to get to unless the pilot is experienced in the advanced techniques used to land a floatplane on a river or a small mountain lake. This chapter will introduce you to some of these techniques, but you should never attempt any of them on your own until you get some dual instruction from a pilot well-experienced in these procedures. Rivers and mountain lakes have claimed a lot of floatplanes, and you don't want yours to be next. If you have a competent instructor in the other seat the first few times you practice these techniques, it will relieve a lot of your self-imposed pressure and anxiety, and the experience will be an enjoyable one.

RIVERS

River landings and takeoffs can be made safely if you follow a few basic guidelines. Give the section of river you want to land on a thorough going over from the air (Fig. 16-1). Your inspection passes

Fig. 16-1. *Inspecting a river from the air prior to landing. This is the Snohomish River in Washington state.*

should be made at an altitude low enough to enable you to see any obstacles that might be in, or across, the river, and you should continue making inspection passes until you're sure the area is clear.

First, make sure the river itself is safe to land on. Determine the location of any shallow areas, sand or gravel bars, and submerged rocks or logs. These hazards will be easy to spot if the water is clear, but if the river is muddy, it will be almost impossible to tell what lies beneath the surface. Look for disturbances on the water. Ripples or waves that remain in one place are indications of underwater obstacles. Be wary of patches on the surface that are slicker in appearance than the surrounding water. They often mark the locations of underwater ledges or boulders.

Irregularities in the banks of the river will produce their own currents and back eddies. If you land or taxi into one of these eddies, it might take control of your plane and spin it into the bank.

Never land in white water. It's shallow and full of rocks and will tear the bottoms out of your floats the instant you touch down.

Check for floating debris in the water. Be especially careful if the water is muddy; this usually indicates that the river is receiving a lot of runoff from recent rainstorms. As the water rises, it will float downed trees and branches off the banks, any one of which could do serious damage to your floats. Take the time to check the river upstream from your intended landing site for floating debris. By the time you're on final approach, that big tree that was up around the bend could be drifting right through the middle of your landing site.

Check carefully for wires or cables strung across the river. The problem is not so much from big, high-tension power lines; they are usually marked on the map, and the wires themselves are often marked with orange balls. The danger is from smaller lines that might have been strung across the river by local residents. Farmers will often suspend a power line across a river to an outbuilding, pump, or irrigation system on the other side, and it's a sure bet it won't be on any of your maps. These single lines are almost impossible to see from the air, so rather than look for the wires themselves, look for the poles that support them. The poles are easier to see in the foliage that lines most river banks, and once you've spotted them, you can start looking for the actual wires. Try to get a good view of the river with the sun behind you. The light will make any wires strung across the water more visible.

Check the banks for fishermen, too. While their lines can't really damage your plane, you won't help our public image much by cutting or stripping all the line off their reels or, worse yet,

jerking their fishing rods out of their hands and into the river.

Make sure you'll be able to take off again before you commit yourself to a landing. Remember, you'll need a lot less room to land than you will to take off. A bridge that won't interfere with your landing might obstruct your takeoff run. Make sure the river itself will permit you to take off again. You don't want to land only to find that your takeoff run will carry you into a shallow or rocky stretch of water.

The landing

It's just as important to determine the wind direction and strength when preparing for a river landing as it is when preparing to land on a lake or in a harbor. Unless obstacles prevent it, try to land into a strong wind, regardless of the direction of the current. In very light or no-wind conditions, landing downstream, with the current, will give you the slowest touchdown speed since you and the current will both be moving in the same direction. If your plane normally touches down at an airspeed of 50 knots and the river is moving along at 10 knots, your actual touchdown speed will be 40 knots. An upstream landing made under the same conditions would result in a touchdown speed of 60 knots. The ideal landing would be one that is made into the wind and with the current, but these will be rare because rivers seem to generate their own winds that blow in the same direction as the current.

It's important to keep the actual touchdown speed as slow as possible because of the nature of the water. The surface of most rivers is very smooth, almost glassy in appearance, and a great deal of drag will be exerted on the floats when you touch down. Just as in a glassy-water landing, this drag will tend to pitch the floatplane forward, and you'll have to counter this tendency by pulling back on the stick or yoke. The faster you touch down, the greater will be the tendency to nose over. Eventually you'll reach a touchdown speed that will cause the plane to pitch forward in spite of your holding full up-elevator. The bows of the floats will dig in, and the plane will very likely end up on its back. For this reason, it can be very dangerous to make a downwind landing in an upstream direction, against the current, because your normal touchdown speed will be increased by both the speed of the wind and the speed of the current. The result could easily be a wrecked floatplane.

As long as the current is moving faster than a breeze blowing in the same direction, land downstream whenever possible. Once the velocity of the wind exceeds the velocity of the current, however, land upstream into the wind.

These rules are fine as general guidelines, but they should never overrule common sense. Landing downstream will minimize your touchdown speed, but it also will move you along at a very high rate of speed after you're off the step. Given the floatplane's relatively slow steering response, you might not be able to maneuver around obstacles or even bends in the river as you hurtle along. Landing upstream means you'll touch down at a faster speed, but you'll have the advantage of coming to a quick stop with excellent directional control the moment you're off the step.

Take the time to analyze the situation before you commit yourself to landing in one direction or the other. If the river is wide with no obstructions, a downstream landing might be the best idea, especially if the current is swift. On a narrow river, or where sandbars, fallen trees, or bends in the river present navigational hazards, you're probably better off landing upstream to maximize your ability to maneuver.

Whether you are landing upstream or down, always make your landing in line with the current (Fig. 16-2). Landing across the current, even slightly, will have the same effect as landing in a crab on a runway, and your plane will veer sideways. If the current is strong enough or your angle across the river great enough, your plane could tip up on one float, and if a wingtip contacts the surface, you'll shortly find yourself wading ashore.

Fig. 16-2. *When landing on, or taking off from, a river, always land parallel to the current.*

The banks of most rivers have trees lining their banks, and in a crosswind, they can create downdrafts and turbulence right over the water. Always be prepared to add full power and go around for another try if things start getting too bumpy when you drop below the tops of the trees. It's best to make a power-on approach and fly a few feet off the surface, carrying just enough power to keep the plane in the air. (Allow an extra margin of speed if the air is turbulent.) As you approach your touchdown spot, chop the power and let the plane settle onto the river, adding back pressure to counter the nose-over tendency. Although the water will most likely be glassy, the proximity of the banks on either side will give you a good idea of your height above the water.

One of the hardest things to get used to is the sight of trees whizzing past your wingtips. The photographs for this section were taken on the Snohomish River in Washington State, and it's obvious from Fig. 16-2 that there is more than enough room on this stretch of river for the Beaver to maneuver. I got an entirely different view from the cockpit, however, and during the inspection passes and the first couple of landings, I was convinced that I was going to finish the day flying the only clipped-wing Beaver in existence.

If, after you touch down, the plane suddenly feels like it's caught in molasses, you're thrown against your seatbelt, and the nose starts to pitch down, put in full power immediately and try to jerk the plane back into the air. You've touched bottom, and if you don't succeed in getting the plane out of the water, it will probably go over onto its nose. Running aground when the float-plane is in displacement is no real problem unless the bottom is covered with rocks, but if the floats should touch bottom while the plane is on the step, the sudden drag will pitch the plane forward almost uncontrollably. This problem will be most likely to occur when the river is muddy and the bottom is obscured from view. If you are unable to locate the shallow areas, you probably shouldn't attempt a landing at all, unless you're very familiar with the river and know the exact locations of the deep water channels.

Once you're off the step, lower the water rudders. If you're facing upstream, you can hold your plane motionless with power, or allow it to drift backward by pulling the throttle to idle. By partially deflecting the water rudders and adding some power, you can move your plane sideways across the river to a dock or some other spot on the bank.

Turning a floatplane around on a river is an interesting visual experience. As the plane begins to turn away from its upstream heading, it will begin to accelerate downstream, and the bank of the river in front of you will appear to be going by faster and faster. You will be heading downstream at a much higher speed than you're used to going, but your actual taxi speed through the water will be the same as it always is. As you turn from a downstream to an upstream heading, you will appear to slow down and stop as you swing around into the current.

When maneuvering a floatplane on a river, remember that the deepest water is almost always against the outside bank in a bend. That's usually where the strongest current is, too. If the wind is strong, you'll have to contend with the weather-cocking force as well as with the current, so it's vitally important that you carefully plan out your actions well in advance. Always approach a dock while heading upstream. If you approach on a downstream heading, you'll probably be going too fast to stop, and if you should hit something in

the process, your excessive forward speed could cause considerable damage.

Things could get tricky if a strong wind blowing against the current makes it difficult for you to control your upstream taxi. One solution might be to turn downstream into the wind, shut down the engine, lower the flaps, open the doors, and hope the wind will push you upstream as fast as the river is pushing you downstream. Then you could sail the plane sideways up to the dock. Maybe. In any event, you can see the importance of preplanning when maneuvering on rivers.

If you're dropping people off, and there's no convenient dock anywhere in sight, you'll have to work the plane in as close to the bank as possible. Keep an eye on your wingtip. You don't want to get it tangled up in the brush or trees lining the bank. Watch the bottom as you approach shallow water. Unless the current is very slow, the bottoms of most rivers are made up of rocks or gravel. The bottoms of slow rivers are usually covered with silt and mud. If the bottom looks too rough for your floats, your passengers will have to jump out and wade ashore. Since you'll have to keep the engine running to hold your position, make sure they jump off the back of the floats and wade straight away from the airplane. Under no circumstances let them walk forward. The same thing goes for picking people up. Instruct them to wade toward the airplane from the rear and climb on the aft portion of the floats.

If you're going to beach the plane, try to pick an area where the current is relatively weak. If possible, position the plane upstream and let it float back onto the bank, using the engine to control the speed of your backward drift. Don't forget to raise the water rudders before you reach shallow water. Most rivers have gently sloping bottoms, so you'll probably run aground before you reach the bank. Be prepared to shut off the engine and jump out into the water to pull the plane securely onto shore. After you beach your plane, make sure the current won't keep rocking it back and forth. If the bottom is covered with small rocks or gravel, the constant motion could seriously abrade the bottoms of the floats or even wear a hole through the skin. Use the same tiedown method you use on a lake: Run one line straight back from the tail plus a line diagonally out from each wingtip (one straight line and two diagonal tiedown lines).

The takeoff

If there isn't any wind blowing down the river, a downstream takeoff is better because you'll start off with whatever airspeed the current is giving you for free. Don't be alarmed by what looks like an excessively high ground speed during your takeoff run. Remember, the bank will be rushing past your wingtips at a higher rate of speed than your floats will be planing over the water. As far as your airplane is concerned, everything will be normal.

The ideal takeoff, like the ideal landing, would be made downstream into the wind. If the wind is blowing downstream faster than the current, take off upstream into the wind. Never take off upstream with a tailwind, however, unless downstream obstructions force you to. Not only will your speed over the water be excessively high, but you'll end up traveling quite a distance before you attain flying speed. You will very likely run way past the section of river you so carefully scouted earlier, and you might encounter shallow water, rocks, or even a bridge before you can get airborne.

If you make an upstream takeoff into the wind, your plane will appear to be standing still when you put in full power and begin to come up over the hump. Again, this is an optical illusion, and your floats will actually be moving through the water at their normal speed. Once you're on the step, lifting one float out of the water might help you accelerate faster and get off the water sooner. There's nothing wrong with taking off or landing in a curve to follow the course of the river. The important thing is to keep the plane lined up with the current. If you have to make some turns

after takeoff to stay over the river until you can clear the trees along the banks, keep them as shallow as you can and keep the airspeed up. You don't want to risk a stall this close to the water.

River flying is challenging and rewarding, but it can be tricky. Even if you've had some experience with rivers, always try to get some advice from an experienced local pilot if you want to try a river you've never visited before. He or she will be able to point out the best places to land and what to watch out for. You might even consider taking the local pilot with you on your flight; not only will this help keep you out of trouble, but it might even get you to the best fishing spot on the river.

MOUNTAIN LAKES

Mountain lakes can offer some of the best fishing, hunting, and camping to be had, to say nothing of their spectacular settings, but a trip to the high country should not be taken lightly by an inexperienced floatplane pilot. The combination of small lakes and high altitudes excludes all but the highest performance floatplanes, and the tricky winds and unforgiving terrain can demand the utmost skill on the part of the pilot. Mountain flying itself is something of an art, and most flight schools located in, or near, a range of mountains offer courses specifically designed to introduce new pilots to the special techniques required to fly safely in the high country. There are also several excellent books on the subject. If you are seriously interested in someday flying to the high lakes, you would do well to read the books and invest some time and money in a mountain flying course.

One of the first things you'll learn is that distances are deceiving in the mountains. The massive size of the surrounding peaks and the clear air combine to upset your sense of proportion, and a lake that looks large enough to land on might in fact be much too small. Even worse, it might be large enough to land on but too small to take off from. The time to find this out is not when your floats touch down on the surface, but while you are still safely flying around it at altitude. The length of the water surface is not the only thing with which you need to be concerned. The surrounding slopes can make it impossible for you to climb straight ahead after you take off, so you'll need to determine if there is enough room for you to circle over the lake as you gain altitude.

The most difficult thing to cope with besides the physical size of a small mountain lake will be the wind. The wind does strange things in the mountains; it's not uncommon to have winds coming from several different directions on different parts of the same lake. Cold air sinks, and air from higher, colder elevations will come spilling down canyons and valleys and create local wind conditions that can be completely different from the primary wind direction and strength. If there is snow on the surrounding peaks, the downdrafts of cold air will be even more prevalent. Downdrafts can be extremely dangerous; if you fly into a downdraft while climbing out, you might be unable to clear the surrounding terrain. In addition to the downdrafts of cold air, a nearby ridge or peak can cause the prevailing wind to pour down onto the lake, thus adding to the problems already created by the local downdrafts. While there might be a corresponding updraft at the other end of the lake, the geography might not allow you to make use of it. If the surrounding terrain forces you to fly into the downdrafts, you might find it very difficult, if not impossible, to climb to altitude following takeoff.

The first thing to do when you arrive over a mountain lake is to determine the wind conditions. Define the direction of the prevailing wind, and try to locate any areas that might have local winds blowing in a different direction. These will often appear as dark patches on the surface of the water, similar to gusts. Identify the areas that might contain downdrafts, and mentally project your approach and departure routes to see if you can remain clear of these areas. When you have a good overall picture of the wind conditions, it's time to determine if the lake is big enough for you and your floatplane.

A method of roughly calculating the length of a lake by noting the time it takes to overfly it and relating this time to your ground speed is outlined in chapter 21. Another quick and practical way to determine if a lake is large enough to permit safe landings and takeoffs is to circle approximately 500 feet above the surface, terrain permitting. Reduce your airspeed until you are flying at your normal approach speed with the flap setting you normally use for takeoff. Fly down one side of the lake and then see how many 180-degree S-turns you can make before reaching the opposite side. This will give you an idea of the lake's width. Find out if you can make a 180-degree turn at each end of the lake while remaining over the water. If not, will the surrounding terrain allow you to make the turn over land? This information will help you determine if you can turn back and circle over the lake after you take off. If there isn't even enough room for you to do these preliminary maneuvers, the lake is not for you.

Once you've determined that the lake is large enough, give it the same inspection you would any other body of water. Look for shallow areas and underwater rocks or reefs, and locate the best place to beach your airplane.

Many mountain lakes are surrounded on three sides by mountains, while the fourth side is open (Fig. 16-3). If the wind is blowing in through the open end, you're in luck. If it's not too strong, you can make your approach through the open end for a downwind landing. When you leave, you'll be able to take off into the wind and climb out over the low terrain at the open end. If the wind is blowing from the other end of the lake, you'll have to take off toward the closed end and circle back toward the lake to gain altitude. The danger here is that your 180-degree turn can carry you into a downdraft area, and if it's severe enough, you might not be able to clear the rising ground around the lake. This is why it's so important to determine that there is sufficient room for you to

Fig. 16-3. *The best approach to this lake was to hug the side of the mountain while flying up the valley at pattern altitude. Upon reaching the far end of the lake, the power was pulled off, the flaps were lowered, and the Beaver was banked into a steep, 180-degree diving turn. Rolling out of the turn put us on final approach, into the wind, with an escape route out the open (near) end of the valley.*

leave the lake before you commit yourself to a landing. Even if the wind is blowing in through the open end of the valley, check out the amount of flying room at the closed end. Mountain winds have a habit of shifting suddenly, and you could find yourself looking at an entirely new situation when it's time to leave.

As you make your approach to the lake, keep a sharp lookout for the dark patches on the water caused by gusts. These gusts will often be the result of downdrafts, so be prepared to add power immediately if your plane starts to sink. The water in mountain lakes is often glassy, and you should always make a power-on landing to minimize your chances of misjudging your height above the water. Landing close to the shoreline will help you

judge your altitude. Don't forget that a power-on, glassy-water landing uses up a lot more room than a power-off landing, so make sure you don't run out of lake. If you've misjudged the length and find yourself running out of room, your only choice is to pull the power back and increase your sink rate. Don't give in to temptation and dive for the surface because you might find it sooner than you think. Keep those float tips up, because with the increased sink rate you'll probably hit the water pretty hard, and you don't want to dig in the floats.

Before you take off, calculate your plane's takeoff distance based on the density altitude. Your plane won't perform the way you're used to because of the high altitude, and if the day is warm, or if you have a heavy load, your takeoff and climb performance could be pretty miserable. I've talked to more than one pilot who told about spending an unplanned night on shore because the only way to successfully take off was to wait until morning when the air was cold. I've also talked to pilots who left half their load in the mountains and came back for it the next day because their planes refused to become airborne with everything on board.

When it's time to take off, taxi your plane all the way to the end of the lake before you turn around to start your takeoff run. The water behind you won't help you get off the lake, so use all of it. If the water is glassy, make your takeoff run close to shore so you'll have a way of estimating your height when you leave the water. Actually, it's a good idea to take off close to the shore whenever possible because you'll have more room to make a 180-degree turn if it becomes necessary. Remember to lean the engine for the best possible performance before you begin your takeoff. Even an extra 50 rpm could make the difference between clearing the trees and hiking out of the area.

If you have any doubts about your ability to take off and climb straight out, don't even try. Plan instead to take off and circle around to gain altitude. This way you won't hit a mountain in the process of discovering that a straightout departure won't work. Some pilots advocate taking off from a small lake using a circular takeoff run. This technique can work, but you need to be very familiar with your airplane's handling characteristics before you try it. Your chances of ever getting into trouble will be minimized if you take the attitude that any lake that's too small to let you land and take off in a straight line is too small, period, and stay off it.

On sunny mornings and afternoons, mountains and ridges will often throw deep shadows across the lakes, and the high contrast can make it difficult to see details in the shadow areas. Rather than risk flying into terrain you can't even see, it would be better to wait until the rising sun illuminates the entire lake or until the late afternoon shadows move over your entire takeoff and climbout area.

Not all floatplanes are suitable for operations in and out of high mountain lakes. Airplanes with low horsepower-to-weight ratios or high wing loadings do not make good mountain machines, regardless of their type of undercarriage: floats, wheels, or skis. A floatplane suitable for flights into mountain lakes should have a wing that will begin flying at a relatively slow speed and that will allow the plane to fly in slow, tight circles. The plane should have responsive slow-speed aileron and elevator control to make it easy to handle in the gusty wind conditions often encountered while landing or taking off in the mountains. It should also have a powerful engine to enable it to climb rapidly and at least hold its own in the downdrafts. Among the floatplanes that meet these requirements are the Piper Super Cub, the Aviat Husky, the Cessna 185, the higher horsepower Helio Couriers (Fig. 16-4), Maules, the Soloy Turbine 206, and the de Havilland Beaver. You should think twice about taking float-equipped Taylorcrafts, Cessna 172s, Piper Tri-Pacers, Cessna 206s, and piston-powered de Havilland Otters into the high country. Some people might not agree with my inclusion of the last two airplanes, but a fully loaded 206 on floats can be a real slug on takeoff, despite its 300 horse-

Fig. 16-4. *The Helio Model 800 is powered by a 400-horsepower eight-cylinder Lycoming engine, and the plane's short takeoff and landing (STOL) capabilities make it a good choice for operations in small, high lakes. This one is equipped with EDO Model 3500 amphibious floats.* EDO Corp.

power, and a piston Otter is too big and unwieldy, and has a very poor climb rate when loaded (the Vazar Dash-3 turbine Otter is another story).

Flying into mountain lakes is not easy. Like rivers, mountain lakes provide opportunities for flights into some spectacular country, but even more so than river flying, mountain flying requires the pilot to have a thorough knowledge of some very specialized techniques. The only way to obtain this knowledge is to receive expert instruction from an experienced mountain pilot, but even after you've received this instruction, don't take on something you're not sure you or your floatplane can handle. Like every other aspect of water flying, if you use good judgment and common sense, your trips to the high lakes will be rewarding ones.

ICE AND SNOW

A few pilots regularly land floatplanes on the frozen surfaces of lakes or the snow-covered slopes of glaciers. *Ice and snow operations are very specialized and are done only when there is no other alternative method available or in an emergency (Fig. 16-5).* Although the chances that you will ever have to take off or land on ice or snow are slim, I'm including a brief description of the basic techniques because they are interesting. And who knows? In the unlikely event that you are forced down someday onto a frozen lake or a snow-covered field, the information might come in handy.

Fig. 16-5. *One of Kenmore Air Harbor's first uses of a float-equipped Beaver for glacier work.* EDO Corp.

For the purpose of this book, I will confine my descriptions to include only operations made to and from low-altitude ice-covered lakes and areas of deep, soft snow. Sometime during each annual freeze up in the northern United States, Canada, and Alaska, there is a period when the presence of ice prevents normal float operations but isn't thick enough to support an airplane on skis.

If an occasion arises that requires an airplane to be flown under these conditions, the only option is to use a floatplane because it will at least remain on the surface as it crunches its way through the ice. The two main drawbacks of operating a floatplane in conditions of breakable ice are the noise—which is considerable and not unlike the continuous smashing of a large sheet of plate glass—and the wear and tear on the floats.

As a lake freezes up, ice first forms along the shoreline, while the deeper water in the main body of the lake remains clear. A takeoff should never be attempted through ice that is more than ½ inch

thick, so your problem will be to get to the open water through the ice that has formed in the shallow water along the shore (Fig. 16-6). As long as the plane is taxied straight ahead, the float keels will break through the ice, and the V-shaped bottom will push it out of the way. The danger lies in turning the plane. If the ice is very thin—no more than ½ to ¾ inch—gentle turns can be made with little danger of the broken ice ripping through the thin skin covering the sides of the floats. Once the ice reaches a thickness of ¾ inch, however, it will be much less yielding. While the keels will still break through this thicker ice, the jagged edges of the ice will tear easily through the float skins if a turn is attempted. In order to turn the plane under these conditions, you will have to shut down the engine, climb out on a float, and use a paddle, boat hook, or some other tool to clear a patch of water large enough for you to turn the plane by hand. After you have paddled or poled your airplane around to its new heading, you can restart the engine and continue on your way.

Fig. 16-6. *A Kenmore Cessna 180 sitting on the ice prior to departure. Open water is only a hundred yards away, but the plane faces a noisy taxi through the ice before it can take off.*

If your takeoff lane is covered with a thin sheet of ice, the drag generated as you break through it will lengthen your takeoff run. The only way a takeoff can be made through ice that is more than ½ inch thick is to taxi slowly up and down your takeoff lane several times to break up the ice and clear the larger pieces out of the way. *This is an emergency procedure only* because the pieces of floating ice will subject your floats to a severe pounding, and any severe damage might have to be repaired when you reach your destination.

You should not attempt to land on ice unless you already know how thick it is. There is no way of determining thickness from the air; you'll have to rely on information obtained beforehand from local residents or other pilots who have recently used the lake. The danger lies in breaking through thick ice and puncturing your floats. If the ice is relatively thin, you can perhaps arrange to have a path broken through it by a local operator before you arrive. This can be especially helpful if you need to taxi the plane to a ramp through shallow water covered with ice thick enough to damage your floats (Fig. 16-7).

Ice exceeding 2 inches in thickness will generally support a light floatplane, and the keels of the floats will act just like the runners on a pair of ice skates. Always land into the wind so your touchdown speed will be as slow as possible.

Fig. 16-7. *The same Cessna 180 in Fig. 16-6 returning through the channel cleared out by Kenmore's line crew. The ducks appreciated the channel, too.*

Make a power-on landing, and treat the surface as though it were glassy water. In other words, have the proper touchdown attitude set up well before you reach the surface, and control your rate of descent with power. The proper touchdown attitude for a landing on any surface other than water should be fairly flat with the bows of the floats only slightly elevated. An excessively nose-high attitude or a full-stall landing will result in the sterns of the floats striking the ground first, and your plane might be pitched violently forward onto its nose. The bows of the floats could be damaged, and if the surface of the ice is covered with snow, they could even dig in and flip the plane on its back.

If the surface of the ice is bare and smooth, you'll have another problem: trying to stop. With only the keels of the floats touching the ice, the likeness to a pair of ice skates will be exact. The weight of the plane will create a lubricating film of water under the floats, and you'll cover an amazing amount of distance before you stop. For this reason, always try to land toward the main body of the lake so you'll be in no danger of running into the shoreline before you come to a stop. There's not much you can do to slow your plane down if you're sliding on bare ice. Gently weaving the plane from side to side might generate enough friction to slow you down a little, and you can try applying some forward pressure on the stick or yoke to force as much of the forward keels against the ice as possible. This technique can also be used to shorten the runout after a water landing, but be careful! If you get too desperate to stop, you could force the bows too low and end up on your back.

Lack of braking is one drawback to operating a floatplane on ice. Lack of a shock absorber system is another. Unlike a skiplane, which has springs and shock absorbers to isolate the airframe from the vibration of the skis, a floatplane is rigidly connected to its floats. The shock and vibration of sliding over an uneven surface is transmitted directly to the airplane. Consequently, slightly rough surfaces or small pressure ridges that would pose no problem for a skiplane could completely destroy a floatplane if the shock of hitting these irregularities causes a major airframe component to fail. The lack of a shock absorber system effectively restricts a floatplane to takeoffs and landings on very smooth surfaces.

A floatplane is almost as effective as a skiplane when landing in deep, soft snow. The wide footprint of the floats provides adequate buoyancy, and because the V-shaped bottom creates a great deal more "wetted" surface than the relatively narrow, flat bottoms of a pair of skis, a floatplane will come to a stop very quickly. The problem occurs when you try to take off again. That same V-bottom that enabled you to stop so quickly can now cause enough drag to keep you from accelerating to flying speed. Lightening the load will help, as will employing the local residents to stamp out a runway for you. Your floats will ride higher on the packed snow, and you'll accelerate much faster. Be careful not to over-rotate the airplane when you lift off (Fig. 16-8). You don't want to slam the sterns of the floats onto the ground, possibly opening up some seams or damaging the water rudders.

Fig. 16-8. *A Fairchild 24 lifting off a snow-covered runway. It's important not to over-rotate a floatplane at liftoff. This could cause the sterns of the floats to strike the ground, resulting in possible damage to the floats or the water rudders.* EDO Corp.

Landing on flat snow is like landing on glassy water, only worse. The chances are the surrounding terrain will be white, and if the sky is white, too, things could get very tricky. Try to land close to a row of trees, a fence, or anything that will help you judge your height above the ground. This is one time when some evergreen branches, blankets, maps, or life vests thrown out onto the surface will really help. If you're in contact with someone on the ground, ask them to space some empty barrels or boxes along your landing lane. If there aren't any barrels or boxes around, ask the people to stand alongside your "runway" themselves. Any visual reference will be a help. Use a power-on glassy-water approach, and keep the nose up high enough to prevent the float tips from digging into the snow. When you touch down, expect the drag to pitch the plane forward and be ready to bring in some back pressure to maintain a flat attitude.

It will be difficult to turn the airplane once it's on the snow, and you'll probably have to get several people to help you do so when it's time to leave. If you fasten a long rope to the tiedown ring under the tail, your ground crew can get the leverage necessary to pull the rear of the plane around while you use the engine to move slowly forward through the snow. Do not lower the water rudders while you're on the ground. They won't make the plane any more maneuverable, and they'll probably be damaged.

Remember, operating a floatplane from ice or snow-covered surfaces is not a routine procedure. It's hard on the plane, and the opportunities for an accident are many. The fact that it can be done, however, is a good testimony to the floatplane's versatility and strength (Fig. 16-9).

Fig. 16-9. *Bob Munro, founder and president of Kenmore Air Harbor, standing beside one of his Noorduyn Norsemans. The company used the Norsemans for glacier flying before it acquired de Havilland Beavers.* Kenmore Air Harbor

17
The amphibious floatplane

ANYONE WHO HAS SEEN an amphibious floatplane towering storklike over everything else parked on the ramp has probably asked, "Why would anyone want to fly something that looks like that, let alone land it?" Amphibious floatplanes, normally called *amphibs*, are definitely not for everyone—not because they are difficult to fly, but because the privilege of landing a floatplane on dry land does not come without its sacrifices.

The main difference between straight (no wheels) and amphibious floats is weight. For example, a pair of EDO Model 3430 straight floats for a Cessna 185 weighs 469 pounds, but a set of EDO Model 3500 amphibious floats for the same airplane tips the scales at 750 pounds, a 281-pound difference. Add the weight of the hydraulic pump, manual extension pump, hoses, and other accessories, and you wind up with about a 300-pound reduction in useful load.

Amphibious floatplanes are at their best in commercial operations where the ability to operate off both land and water is more important than the ability to carry a heavy load. Commercial fish spotting, geological and mineral exploration, medical evacuation, and law enforcement are some of the areas in which the capabilities of the amphibious

floatplane are put to good use (Fig. 17-1). They are also becoming more popular for recreational uses, too. The owner of an amphibious floatplane can keep it at a convenient airport, fly to other airports, make cross-country flights in IFR conditions if the plane is so equipped, and still enjoy the ability to visit the remote lakes, rivers, and bays only accessible by seaplane.

Fig. 17-1. *A Cessna 180 equipped with EDO amphibious floats taxiing up a steel ramp in the oil fields of Louisiana.* EDO Corp.

An amphibious floatplane is easier to fly than its appearance indicates. On the water, it behaves just like its straight-float cousins. The only real difference is the slightly longer length of the amphibian's takeoff run. This is partly due to the fact that the floats are heavier, but also because with their main wheelwell cutouts behind the step, amphibious floats don't move across the water quite as efficiently as straight floats.

On land, however, an amphib displays some unique handling characteristics, and it's important that you receive a thorough checkout from a pilot well experienced with its sometimes strange behavior.

THE PREFLIGHT INSPECTION

When the amphib is on land, you'll have to add a thorough checkout of the landing gear and retraction system to the normal floatplane preflight inspection. Check all the tires for tread wear and proper inflation.

You'll be steering the plane on land with differential braking; the nosewheels are free-castering. Check the brakes carefully because they get a lot of hard use. Make sure the brake disks and pucks (pads) are in good shape and that there are no hydraulic leaks around the brake calipers. Some float manufacturers use a single main wheel on each float, and the brake components are on the outside and relatively easy to inspect. Other manufacturers prefer a dual wheel, and the brake components are mounted between the wheels. This makes them harder to inspect, but take the time to do it, anyway. There's a lot riding on those brakes, and you want to make sure they're in good shape before you start depending on them. The master cylinder for the wheel brakes is attached to the toe brakes on the rudder pedals, and the brake lines are routed down the float struts to the main wheels. Check underneath the rudder pedals in the cockpit for any signs of hydraulic fluid, and check the brake lines where they enter and emerge from the float struts.

The hydraulic pump that operates the landing gear might be located in the fuselage of the airplane or in one of the floats. Check the visible hydraulic lines and connections for leaks and make sure the lines are securely fastened to the airframe. Finally, check the hydraulic fluid level in the pump reservoir, and add fluid if necessary. If the level is very low, there's probably a leak somewhere in the system. Don't fly the plane until a mechanic has either located and fixed the leak or determined that there definitely isn't one. Don't forget to check the hydraulic lines leading to and from the manual extension pump in the cockpit. The manual pump itself contains rubber seals on the piston and in the cylinder, and if they are damaged or unseated, there will be traces of hydraulic fluid on the pump body.

Hydraulic fluid seen anywhere other than in the reservoir of the primary hydraulic pump should be reported. Hydraulic systems operate under high pressure, and if fluid is starting to leak from a hose coupling or a cylinder seal, it's just a matter of time before the faulty component fails completely.

Check the visible components of the retraction mechanism for any obvious signs of damage. The mainwheels of modern amphibious floats retract into a well immediately aft of the step, and the nosewheel strut either pivots up to lie flat against the underside of the bow or is drawn up and back into the float itself (Fig. 17-2). Some of the older retraction systems pivot the nosewheel strut up and back until it lies on top of the float deck, which contains a special recess to accommodate the nosewheel. De Havilland Beavers and Otters are sometimes equipped with floats of this type (Fig. 17-3).

WATER OPERATIONS

If the plane is already in the water, your preflight and departure procedures will be identical to those you would use if your floatplane were equipped with straight floats. Before you begin your takeoff run, however, check the position of the landing gear and verify that it's retracted.

If the amphib you're going to fly is kept in dry storage at a seaplane facility equipped with a ramp,

Fig. 17-2. *A Cessna 185 fitted with EDO Model 2790 amphibious floats. Note how the nose strut is drawn up flush against the underside of the bow.* EDO Corp.

Fig. 17-4. *Kenmore Air pilot Kevin Nelsen taxis a Cessna 185 down the ramp at Renton Airport into Lake Washington. The plane is fitted with EDO Model 3500 amphibious floats.*

Fig. 17-3. *De Havilland of Canada's Turbo Beaver on amphibious floats. The nose struts pivot up and back to lie on the float decks.* EDO Corp.

you can do your preflight inspection while the plane is sitting on its wheels in the parking area and then taxi over to the ramp. Because steering is by differential braking only, it might be necessary to build up some forward momentum with a brief burst of power before you can initiate a turn, especially if the turn is to be made from a full stop.

Be careful when you taxi down the ramp (Fig. 17-4). Ease the plane slowly over the top, and then let it roll freely down the slope. Holding the plane back with the brakes can cause the tires to skid on the boards, and if there are any nails, bolts, or large splinters projecting above the wood, the tires could be damaged. Obviously, if the ramp is a long one, you'll have to use some braking to avoid building up excessive speed, but normally you'll be able to let the plane roll down on its own. The

floatplane should roll straight into the water, and if you find you do need to use the brakes, apply them smoothly and evenly. Uneven braking could cause the plane to veer to one side, and if the ramp is narrow, you might drop a wheel off the edge and have a real problem on your hands.

The bows of the floats will submerge when you hit the water, but they will quickly surface again. Lower the water rudders, retract the landing gear, and you'll be ready to proceed with a normal water takeoff. It's important that you hold the yoke all the way back when taxiing in the water (unless you're taxiing downwind in a strong breeze). Most amphibious floats are bow-heavy, and in rough water or when displacement taxiing with the engine above idle, the bows of the floats could be driven under the surfaces unless full up-elevator is held at all times.

You can taxi an amphib up a ramp, too. After you've made your water landing, taxi toward the ramp and lower the gear. Make sure it's down and locked before you reach the ramp. Instead of adding power just before you hit the ramp, which is the correct procedure when ramping a plane on straight floats, wait until the nosewheels contact the ramp and then add enough power to pull you up the slope (Fig. 17-5). It will probably take a lot of power to taxi up the ramp, so be prepared to back off on the throttle when you go over the top. This procedure

Fig. 17-5. *Nelsen is taxiing the 185 back up the ramp. The turbulence on the water behind the plane gives an indication of the amount of power needed to pull the plane out of the water and up the slope.*

should only be used if you're going to taxi the plane to a parking area on shore. If you're going to leave the plane on the ramp itself, keep the wheels up and use the same ramping procedure you would if your plane were equipped with straight floats.

If you plan to leave your amphib in dry storage for some time and the facility has a forklift for moving floatplanes, have the operator raise your plane off its wheels so you can retract the gear. By storing the plane on the keels of its floats, you'll take the strain off the gear components and the tires.

LAND OPERATIONS

The view from the cockpit of an amphibious floatplane that's sitting on its wheels is impressive. You'll look down on every parked plane that is smaller than a Boeing 737, but the plane will not feel at all unstable. In fact, an amphibious floatplane has a more stable feel when taxiing than most low-slung tricycle-gear landplanes, thanks to the float's wide-track, quadricycle landing gear.

The quadricycle gear is stable and smooth-riding, but it's also responsible for the amphibious floatplane's strangest tendency. When taxiing on land in a crosswind, an amphib will weathercock *downwind*. In order to retain its efficiency in the water, the bottom of the float forward of the step

must be smooth, so the mainwheels and wheel-wells are placed aft of the step. As a result, there is more vertical sheet metal in front of the main-wheels than behind them. A crosswind will exert a sideways force on the upwind float and the side of the fuselage, and because the nosewheels are free-castering, the plane will pivot around the main-wheel under the downwind float.

When you're taxiing on land, your only means of steering will be the mainwheel braking system. If you are faced with a long crosswind taxi, the upwind brake will probably get quite hot and begin to fade, so be prepared to stop every now and then to let it cool down.

In a landplane, you are accustomed to using the rudder pedals and nosewheel steering to maintain directional control at the beginning of a takeoff roll. Amphibious floatplanes don't have nose-wheel steering, so you'll have to use the brakes. It will take several takeoffs before you develop just the right touch on the pedals. If you use too much brake, you'll keep the plane from accelerating, and if you use too little, you won't be able to stay on the centerline. As the speed increases, it will take less brake pressure to keep the plane in line, until eventually the air rudder will be all that's needed for directional control.

If a normal landplane takeoff technique is used, the amphibian might have a tendency to overrotate. This tendency isn't dangerous, but it can be a little startling and is probably the result of air getting under the bottoms of the floats as the nose is raised.

Smooth, professional takeoffs are best made by using a soft-field technique. Begin the takeoff roll with full up-elevator, and when the increasing speed lifts the nosewheels off the ground, ease off the back pressure to keep the nose from rising any farther. Continue the takeoff roll holding the nose-wheels just off the surface of the runway, and when the airplane is ready to fly, it will lift off smoothly with no overrotation.

Once you've established a positive rate of climb and there isn't enough runway left in front of you to land on, retract the wheels. The main gear is activated hydraulically, and the nose gear is operated by cables attached to the main gear retraction mechanism. The landing gear is raised by moving a wheel-shaped lever on the instrument panel to the up position. There are three ways you can determine the position of the gear. Indicator lights on the instrument panel show blue for up (water landing) and brown for down (runway landing). When the hydraulic pump is activated, a red light on a separate circuit illuminates to indicate that the gear is in transit.

There is also a mechanical gear-position indicator in the top of each float. EDO uses a metal tab fastened directly to the landing-gear activating mechanism. As the gear comes up, the tab slides into position under a window in the float deck labeled UP. When the gear is lowered, the tab slides under the window labeled DOWN. In addition, most amphibious floatplanes have small wide-angle mirrors mounted out on each wing that enable the pilot to actually see the gear under each float. The mirror on the right wing is used to check the gear under the left float, and the left-hand mirror is used to check the gear under the right float. Some amphib pilots paint the inside of their plane's wheels fluorescent orange to make them more visible against the terrain below.

LANDING PROCEDURES

If you're going to land on the water, you'll obviously leave the gear retracted; however, this does not mean that you can exclude a check of the landing gear from your prelanding checklist. If you should inadvertently land in the water with the gear down, your plane will slam over onto its back the instant it touches the water, so it's very important that you get in the habit of checking all the gear position indicators several times during the approach, regardless of the type of landing you're about to make.

If you're going to land on a runway, lower the gear before entering the traffic pattern and go through a "lever, lights, and visual" check of the gear on downwind, base, and final approach. Check the position of the gear lever on the instrument panel, confirm the gear's position with the indicator lights, and then make a visual check of the gear using the mechanical indicators in the floats and the mirrors underneath the wings. Have your passenger check the indicator in the top of the rightside float. There is no gear-up warning horn in an amphibian because normal water landings would set it off. While a gear-up landing on a runway is not terribly damaging, a gear-down landing on water is disastrous. The instant the nosewheels touch the surface, the plane will somersault. Make sure you know what position the gear is in at all times.

Another good habit you should develop is to mentally relate the type of landing you're about to make with the gear position. Tell yourself, "I'm landing on land, so the gear should be down," or, "I'm landing on water, so the gear should be up." Then visually check the gear *again*. A lot of amphib accidents seem to occur when the pilot takes off from a runway to make a short flight ending with a water landing. The pilot either forgets to raise the gear after takeoff or lowers it automatically before landing. Accidents also occur when a pilot is so tired after a long trip that he or she neglects to do a thorough prelanding systems check. *It's critically important that you get in the habit of repeating the landing gear checklist several times before every landing.*

When you move the gear selector to the DOWN position, the wheels in one float might begin to extend slightly in advance of the wheels in the other float. This will cause the plane to yaw to one side or the other, so be prepared to come in with some rudder pressure to keep the plane flying straight. As soon as both sets of gear are down and locked, the yawing tendency will disappear. Depending on the type of plane you are flying and the design of its floats, there might also be a slight pitch change as the wheels come out. The Cessna 185 pictured in this chapter is mounted on EDO Model

3500 amphibious floats, and while it displays no noticeable pitch change when the gear is lowered, it does yaw slightly to one side because the gear in one float precedes the gear in the other float.

A power-on approach and landing is the smoothest way to put an amphib on a runway. Think of it as a glassy-water landing with the transition to the touchdown attitude made right over the numbers. This method will ease the plane down onto its mainwheels while avoiding an extremely nose-high flare that could cause the tails of the floats to slam into the ground. After the mains touch, gently lower the nosewheels to the pavement and get ready to start steering with the brakes (Fig. 17-6).

You'll really have your hands (and feet) full, landing in a crosswind. Use the normal wing-low method to track straight down the runway and touch down on the upwind wheel. In addition to the normal gymnastics required on the ailerons and rudder, however, you'll have to start fighting that downwind weathercocking business with the upwind brake as soon as you touch down. It can be

Fig. 17-6. *A de Havilland Otter just prior to touchdown. Note the relatively flat attitude, which will keep the sterns of the floats from striking the ground.*

a real adventure and will certainly give you plenty to talk about in the next hangar-flying session.

Although the type of flying you do might not require the unique capabilities of an amphib, getting a checkout in one is a lot of fun. Not only will it give you some valuable experience in retractable gear procedures, but the challenge of mastering its steering system, and the opportunity to fly the tallest—if not the biggest—thing on the ramp will make it a flight you won't soon forget.

18
Turbines

LET'S FACE IT. The chances of your being ushered to the pilot's seat of a turbine when you show up for your floatplane lessons are just about nil, unless you happen to be incredibly wealthy. But if you *are* wealthy, or if you someday hope to fly floatplanes commercially, a basic overview of turbine operations is not out of order. If nothing else, you won't feel as though you're listening to a foreign language when a bunch of fogged-in air-taxi pilots clusters around the coffee pot and starts talking about gas generators and blade latches.

The introduction of the turbine engine to the floatplane world is a relatively recent phenomenon. Unlike commercial airliners whose speeds and carrying capacities justify their expense, floatplanes are by definition slow and small. Three to nine passengers per plane is the norm for most operations, and the resulting revenues rarely have been sufficient to warrant the purchase of a turbine. Just keeping a piston fleet running was expensive enough.

Then in the 1980s, things began to change. Increases in income and leisure time found more and more people demanding air service to waterside vacation spots. The number of cruise ships visiting the Caribbean and southeast Alaska doubled and doubled again as their popularity skyrocketed. Seaplane operators offering scenic flights taxed their aging piston fleets to the limit as passengers poured off the ships in droves and lined up for reef or glacier tours. With schedules demanding that every plane be available all day every day, a burnt valve or a blown gasket could be a costly repair in more ways than one. What the operators needed was a reliable, efficient floatplane, something that could haul a respectable load and fly day in and day out without any nasty little mechanical surprises. What they needed was a turbine.

Demand creates supply, and today there are several turbine floatplane packages on the market (Fig. 18-1). In real dollars, none of them are inexpensive, but like their commercial jetliner cousins, their efficiency, reliability, and hauling abilities more than make up for their initial cost. In the right hands, a turbine can be a real moneymaker.

THE PLANES

Some of the turbine floatplanes in service today are brand new and some of them are thirty or more years old, but they all possess certain similarities. To begin with, they all have long, pointy noses (Fig. 18-2). This was not an aesthetic choice, but one driven by necessity. Except for the Cessna

Fig. 18-1. *Removing the intake and exhaust plugs on one of Kenmore Air's Vazar Dash-3 turbine Otters. The large intake and exhaust ports of a turbine can be very tempting to birds, so it's important to keep the ports covered when the plane is not in use.*

Fig. 18-2. *This strange concoction was created for the Alaska Fish and Wildlife Department by combining a de Havilland Beaver with a Garrett turboprop. The plane is used to gather data on migratory bird flocks, a task that requires good forward visibility and lots of power to climb out of tight places.*

Caravan, all the turbine floatplanes on the market today are derivatives or conversions of piston designs. A turbine engine weighs considerably less than its piston equivalent. If the only thing you're going to change on an airplane is the engine, and the new engine is a lot lighter than the old one, you're going to have to hang the new one way out on the end of a long moment arm to preserve the airplane's center of gravity, which makes for the long noses.

Most of the turbines in commercial service today also use the same engine. The Pratt & Whitney PT6A has been around for a long time, and it's been produced in a variety of power ranges, from 550 shaft horsepower (shp) to over 1,000 shp. The power of a particular PT6A can be determined from the "dash" number following its main designator, as in PT6A-135.

Another thing most turbine floatplanes have in common is a reversing propeller. The reversing prop, or *Beta prop*, can give a pilot an enviable degree of control on the water. It can also get a pilot into an amazing amount of trouble, so if you're thinking reverse pitch will solve all your water handling problems, forget it.

As of this writing, the only turbine floatplanes you can buy new from the factory are the Caravan and the Turbine Maule. The nine-passenger Caravan uses a PT6A-114A, which develops 675 shp, while the four-place Maule rockets around behind a 420-shp Allison. The oldest turbine floatplanes you're likely to encounter are the Turbo Beavers that de Havilland began manufacturing in 1965 to replace the radial-engined original. They built 60 Turbo Beavers before shutting down the line forever, and most of them are still flyable. The Turbo Beaver is hampered somewhat by the outdated technology of its PT6A-20 engine, but there are several engine conversions available to enhance the airplane's performance and reliability. Kenmore Air Harbor's Super Turbine, for example, replaces the Dash-20 with a brand-new 750-shp PT6A-135 (Fig. 18-3). The factory tooling for the reciprocating and turbine versions of the Beaver

Fig. 18-3. *The PT6A-135 turbine installed on Kenmore's Super Turbine Beavers can put out almost twice the power of the piston Beaver's radial engine, yet it is less than half the size.*

was obtained by Viking Air in Victoria, British Columbia. Viking recently has begun using this tooling to convert piston Beavers into Turbo Beavers that are identical externally to the 60 airplanes made by de Havilland. The only difference is under the cowl, where Viking installs a 680-shp PT6A-27 instead of the old Dash-20.

At the same time de Havilland was putting a turbine into the Beaver, Pilatus was doing the same thing to its slightly larger PC-6 Porter over in Switzerland. Where de Havilland took advantage of the turbine's light weight to extend the Beaver's cockpit forward and gain an extra row of seats, Pilatus opted to leave the PC-6 fuselage unchanged. As a result, there's almost as much nose ahead of the Turbo-Porter's wing as there is fuselage behind it. Popular around the world for high-altitude mountain work, a few Turbo Porters have found their way into the fleets of United States and Canadian operators. The plane's dramatic STOL capabilities also attracted the attention of the Central Intelligence Agency, which ordered an undisclosed number of them for counterinsurgency operations.

Another CIA-inspired turbine was the eight-place Helio Stallion, a 550-shp derivative of the Helio Courier. The government bought most of the Stallions, but occasionally one shows up in civilian hands.

Two of the most recent turbine conversions originated in Washington state. The Soloy Corporation in Olympia replaces the six-cylinder Continental engine in the Cessna 206 with an Allison turbine, while up near the Canadian border in Bellingham, gold mining entrepreneur Dara Wilder came up with the most impressive turbine floatplane of all. The massive Vazar Dash-3 is a single-engine de Havilland Otter fitted with a PT6A-135 in place of the plane's original and notoriously unreliable R-1340 geared radial (Fig. 18-4).

Fig. 18-4. *One of the first Vazar Dash-3 Otter conversions was purchased by Irvin Olsen of Campbell River, British Columbia, to ferry crews to and from his logging camps along the coast. The turbine's reliability was the primary factor in his decision to get rid of the piston engine in his amphibious Otter.*

There is one other turbine that bears mentioning, although its operation is well outside the scope of this book. Where passenger loads warrant its expense, the de Havilland Twin Otter makes an outstanding floatplane, either on straight floats or the newer amphibious floats manufactured by Wipaire. I've watched Twin Otter pilots in Ketchikan, Alaska, jockey their reversing propellers and simultaneously park three planes in the same amount of space I need to coast up and stop in a piston Beaver. It's disgusting.

MENTAL PREPARATION

You would think that a high-tech turbine would be a complicated beast to run, but in fact just the opposite is true. Turbines are easy to start and easy to manage in flight. No more messing with mixture controls and cowl flaps. Learning to operate a Beta prop is easy, too, and it lets you make those precision stops that are the envy of every piston pilot on the dock. Best of all, turbines are so reliable you'll be tempted to delete the file in your brain that contains all the instructions for what to do when an engine quits. Assuming you're a competent floatplane pilot to begin with, you'll find the turbine transition one of the easiest things you've ever done. And therein lies the problem. It's almost too easy. But pilot beware! Reversing propellers can get you into as much trouble as they help you avoid. Turbine engines *can* quit, overspeed, or get stuck in idle, and you'd better have that mental emergency file close at hand when they do.

There's no denying that the turbine brings a degree of reliability and control to the floatplane world that the piston engine can't hope to achieve. But all that reliability and control mean nothing as far as the floatplane's environment is concerned. The wind can still blow from the wrong direction, the current can still foul up your docking plans, and boats and pilings and people will still get in your way. And don't forget that long, pointy nose. The first thing to arrive at your destination will be the propeller, not the rubber-cushioned bows of your floats. If you let that turbine whine lull you into a sense of complacency, if you relax in the belief that the engine will take care of itself and that you can solve all your water handling problems with a shot of reverse, you're going to make a mistake, and you're going to bend some metal—expensive metal. Replacing a Beta prop can run up a bill higher than the cost of new luxury car. Simply

tearing down and inspecting a turbine for damage costs tens of thousands of dollars, while replacing the engine altogether can cost half a million.

Don't let the ease of operating a turbine dull your state of mind. The moment you stop paying attention, it will reach around and take a very pricey bite out of your behind. Stay alert, plan ahead, and don't exceed your limitations. The mental vigilance that made you a good piston pilot is the key to becoming a good turbine pilot.

TURBINE BASICS

Dozens of books go into as much detail as you'd ever want on the principles of turbojet operation, so I'm going to give you just one sentence. Air entering the front of the engine is compressed, mixed with fuel, ignited in the combustion chamber, and blasted out the back of the engine through the turbine blades that spin and turn the compressor blades up front. Obviously there are starters and bleed air valves and fuel control units and a host of other components, but in a nutshell, that's how a turbojet works. The turboprop nestled in the nose of a floatplane works the same way, only the turbine drives a propeller as well as the compressor blades. Most of a turboprop's thrust comes from the propeller, although a certain amount of thrust is generated by the exhaust.

Turbine shafts spin at extremely high speeds, well over 30,000 rpm at full power in some models. These speeds would destroy a conventional propeller instantly if it was hooked directly to the engine, so a turboprop drives its propeller through a set of reduction gears. To keep the powerplant compact and to provide an uninterrupted flow of air into the engine, the gearbox is bolted to the rear (exhaust end) of the engine. The exhaust is directed out each side of the engine through two huge stacks, and the whole works is mounted in the airplane backward. Intakes under the nose or recessed into the cowl conduct air to the compressor inlet at the rear of the installation.

The engine controls in the cockpit are similar to what you're used to seeing in a piston airplane, although the names are somewhat different (Fig. 18-5). The throttle in a turbine is called a *power lever*, and in most cases it has two functions. From the idle position forward, the power lever works just like a regular throttle. The farther forward you push it, the more power you get. Aft of the idle position, however, the power lever becomes both a throttle and a propeller control. This is the so-called *Beta range*. Pulling the power lever back into Beta will first cause the propeller blades to twist or flatten out until they have no pitch at all. The engine will continue to idle, but the spinning propeller will produce zero thrust.

Fig. 18-5. *The power quadrant in a turbine Otter. The small lever mounted on the left side of the quadrant is the standby throttle. The spring-loaded catch on the power lever keeps the lever from being pulled inadvertently into Beta.*

Pulling the power lever back even more will cause the blades to twist farther, from zero pitch into reverse pitch. The power lever will now begin to do two things. It will continue to control the propeller, twisting the blades even farther into reverse pitch, and it will begin to act like a throttle again, giving you more power the more you pull it back. It's a lot like riding a horse. Pull back on the reins a little, and the horse will stop. Pull back

harder, and the horse will back up. In most of its applications, the PT6A is set up to generate as much power in reverse as it does in forward. Full reverse can be used to good effect in a landplane, but it will severely damage or even sink a floatplane. Used carefully and intelligently, however, reverse pitch can be a real blessing.

The prop control in a turbine does the same thing as the prop control in a piston plane, moving the propeller through its normal pitch range. The prop control is also the means by which you'll feather the propeller. It has no function when the power lever is in Beta.

The fuel feed to a turbine is regulated automatically by a fuel-control unit. The fuel-control unit uses outside air temperature, barometric pressure, propeller rpm, the position of the power lever, and a bunch of other stuff to determine what the optimum flow of fuel to the combustion chamber should be at any given moment. The good thing about the fuel control unit is that it doesn't need your help, so instead of a mixture control, you get a fuel lever with two positions, ON and OFF. Actually, most fuel levers have three positions, OFF, IDLE, and FLIGHT IDLE. Flight idle, sometimes called *high idle* or *approach idle*, sets the idle speed of the engine to a higher value. Turbines don't respond as quickly as piston engines to sudden power applications, so flight idle gives a pilot an extra margin of safety during descents and approaches by spooling up the engine ahead of time in case a rapid application of power is necessary to abort a landing or avoid an obstacle. De Havilland incorporated the high-idle setting in the Turbo Beaver as part of the plane's STOL system. The idea was for the pilot to control airspeed and rate of climb or descent by varying the propeller pitch during low-speed, STOL maneuvers while maintaining a high engine rpm for quick response.

The bad thing about the fuel control unit is that if it breaks, your engine won't run. Actually it will run, but probably only at idle rpm. The possibility of a busted fuel control unit is the reason for the standby throttle you'll find in the cockpit of every PT6-powered single-engine turbine. Normally left in the OFF position, the standby throttle is used to feed fuel to the engine in the event of a fuel-control unit failure. While the standby throttle can get you home, there are a couple of things you need to know about it. Its fuel metering is relatively crude compared to the automatic unit, so count on a reduction of your plane's range and endurance if you have to use it. The other thing to remember is that you won't have the luxury of Beta as you taxi up to the dock. Only the power lever can give you Beta, but the power lever won't work if the fuel control unit has failed. If you're docking on the standby throttle, you'll have to plan your moves as though you were at the controls of a piston-powered floatplane.

Unlike the engine controls, the gauges in a turbine are quite a bit different from what you're used to seeing. Instead of a tachometer and a manifold pressure gauge, you get a torque gauge, an interturbine temperature gauge, a flow meter, and a couple of rpm gauges usually calculated in percentage. The *interturbine temperature gauge* (ITT) tells you how hot or cold it is in the turbine section of the engine. It's a crucial gauge during starting, takeoff, and climb, and for determining the cause of a power loss during flight. The gauge labeled "Prop" tells you how fast the propeller is turning either in revolutions or as a percentage of its maximum speed. The gauge labeled "Gas Generator," or "Ng," indicates the speed of the turbine, and is also calibrated in percentage. The torque gauge tells you how much load is being put on the propeller and is calibrated in either pounds-per-square-inch (psi) or foot-pounds, depending on the airplane. The flow meter tells you how fast the fuel is disappearing from your tanks.

THE BETA PROPELLER

Piston and turboprop engines share the same basic operating principle: rapidly expanding gasses produce rotating power at the end of a shaft. It's a crankshaft in one and a turbine shaft in the other,

but in both cases you end up turning a propeller. But not the same propeller. The Beta prop brings a whole new set of rules to the table, and it's crucial that you understand how it works before you attempt to use it. First, let's look at the basics. Constant-speed, variable-pitch propellers work by balancing two opposing forces. Torsional forces on the blades, mechanical springs, or the action of centrifugal force on a set of counterweights try to twist the blades in one direction while oil pressure acts against a piston to twist the blades in the opposite direction. The pilot controls the oil pressure with the pitch control in the cockpit. The primary difference between the propeller on a single-engine plane and a prop on a twin is the direction the blades want to twist when the oil pressure goes away.

The propeller blades of a single-engine airplane will twist to their minimum setting, which is takeoff pitch, if the oil mechanism in the prop control should fail. This means the pilot can still get the maximum power out of the engine if necessary. On a twin, however, it's much more important to reduce the drag caused by a dead engine, so a combination of counterweights and springs is mounted on the blades to twist them the other way into alignment with the slipstream. When an engine on a twin quits or is shut down, the oil pressure that has been resisting the force of the springs and counterweights goes away, and the blades automatically begin to feather. The pilot is supposed to hasten the process by pulling the prop control back to the feather position, which eliminates any residual oil pressure that might hinder the springs and counterweights from doing their job.

Almost all the turbine installations in floatplanes today are derived from engine and propeller combinations used in twin-engine airplanes like the Beechcraft King Air. It's important that you remember this because it explains why a Beta prop wants to feather whenever oil pressure is lost, even if that loss occurs as a result of a normal engine shutdown (Fig. 18-6).

Fig. 18-6. *The Beta propeller on a Kenmore Air Super Turbine in its full-feather position.*

Actually, the ability to feather a propeller can be a useful tool. A turbine engine is just a bunch of spinning wheels attached to another spinning wheel, the propeller. Shutting off the fuel will turn off the fire in the combustion chamber, but it might take a minute or two for all those spinning wheels to come to a stop. Meanwhile, you're coasting up to the dock behind a propeller that's still generating forward thrust. Docking would be a lot easier to control if you could get the propeller to stop as soon as you shut off the engine, the way you do now in your piston floatplane. Feathering the propeller will maximize the air resistance of each blade, and they will slow to a stop very quickly. You can feather a propeller in one of two ways. The best way, and the one that gives you the most control, is to pull the prop control to feather while the engine is still running. This dumps the oil pressure in the pitch mechanism, and the blades will move rapidly to the feather position. A feathered propeller will continue to develop a small amount of forward thrust at idle rpm, something you can use to your advantage at times, but the main thing to remember is that once feathered, the blades will come to a rapid stop when you shut off the engine.

The other way to feather a Beta prop is to shut off the engine and do nothing. This will also cause the blades to feather, but at a much slower rate. In fact, and this is extremely important to remember,

if the propeller stops rotating before the blades have reached the feather position, the blades will continue to twist *even though the prop is stationary*. In this case, the twisting is being caused by the springs built into the pitch mechanism, but one way or the other, those blades are going to feather.

But what if you don't want the blades to feather when you shut down the engine? What if you have to back away from a piling or another floatplane as soon as you start up? A feathered propeller in this situation can present a real problem. Once the engine is up to idle speed, the feathered blades will have to twist through their full forward thrust range before they'll flatten out to the point where you can pull them into Beta. Unless you're tied to the dock during all of this, you're going to go a long way forward before you can begin to go back. To give you the option of starting the engine with the propeller already in Beta, most turbine floatplanes are equipped with blade latches. Blade latches prevent the blades from twisting into the feather position after the engine is shut off. The latches are held out by centrifugal force and are designed to drop into place the moment the propeller rpm falls below idle speed; however, the latches will engage and lock only if the blades are in zero or reverse pitch when the engine is shut down. If the blades are in forward pitch, even just a little, the blade latches will not engage, and the propeller eventually will feather.

Make it a habit always to check the position of the propeller blades before untying a turbine from the dock. Many a pilot has shut down thinking the blades were locked in Beta only to return later to find the propeller feathered. Perhaps the pilot had instinctively been holding a tiny bit of forward thrust to counter a wind or current, but whatever the reason, the blades had been far enough forward of zero pitch to keep the latches from engaging when the engine was shut off.

ENGINE MANAGEMENT

While this book never should be used in place of an operations manual, a brief overview of turbine engine management will put you that much farther ahead when you climb into that cockpit for the first time. You'll probably be surprised at how simple a turbine is to operate compared to the piston engines you're used to, especially if you've been flying around behind a radial. Forget about priming, pumping the throttle, judging the right moment to switch on the mags, and all the other tricks you sometimes have to use to get a piston engine to start promptly and without a backfire. A typical turbine start procedure involves turning on the master switch, building up fuel pressure with the electric pump, and hitting the start switch. Some planes such as the Turbo Beaver have *automatic igniters*, which are sparkpluglike devices in the combustion chamber that help get the fire going, while others such as the Vazar Dash-3 require you to switch on the igniters yourself. That click-click-click sound you hear as a turbine begins to spool up is the sound of the igniters firing.

As the engine spools up, watch the gas generator (turbine rpm) gauge until it indicates a specific percentage of rpm. In the case of the Vazar Dash-3, for example, you'll be looking for 16 percent. Move the fuel lever from off to idle and rivet your eyes to the interturbine temperature gauge. What you're watching for is a hot start, one of the few things that can destroy a turbine engine in short order. As the fuel ignites in the combustion chamber, the ITT will indicate a rapid rise in temperature. The temperature should peak quickly, however, and then drop back as the flow of air through the engine increases. If it doesn't drop back, or if the temperature continues to climb, you've got a *hot start*. If you see a hot start developing, all you can do is to shut off the fuel immediately and hope the owner has a good insurance policy.

When the gas generator gauge indicates the engine has reached idle speed, you can release the start switch and turn off the igniters. Don't let the dry roar of the engine lighting off fool you into releasing the start switch prematurely. Wait for the turbine to reach the correct speed. Unlike

the starter on a piston engine that disengages and stops when you release the start switch, the starter on a turbine keeps right on going, but in a different function. As soon as you release the start switch, the starter becomes a generator and begins charging the battery. It's a clever example of using one accessory to do two jobs while saving weight and reducing maintenance at the same time.

Although the start procedure is simple, it does take time, perhaps 20 to 30 seconds, for a turbine to spool up, ignite, and reach idle speed. A lot can happen in 20 or 30 seconds. If you've turned the plane out for a normal departure and your propeller is feathered, you're just going to sit there at the mercy of the wind and current while you wait for everything to come up to speed so you can unfeather your prop. A piston floatplane, on the other hand, will begin to move as soon as the engine fires, and you can begin steering it toward open water right away. As always, judgment and planning are the keys to staying out of trouble. If there's a wind or a current, figure out what effects they'll have on your plane before you untie it from the dock. If you think you might be blown into trouble before you can get the engine spooled up, have someone hold the tail, or consider using a different departure technique.

Taxiing a turbine is a little different from taxiing a piston floatplane. To begin with, the weathercocking tendency will be noticeably reduced thanks to that long nose, which means you might not be able to count on the wind to help spin you around in tight quarters. Another difference you'll notice right away is that your taxi speed is pretty high. A piston engine can be made to idle relatively slowly, well below 500 rpm in many cases. A turbine, on the other hand, has a fast idle speed, about 900 rpm at the propeller in the case of the PT6A-135. Recall from chapter 9 that most floatplanes reach their maximum safe displacement taxi speed at approximately 1,000 rpm, so even at a turbine's lowest power setting, you'll still be moving along at a pretty good clip. Taxiing slower is easy, however, thanks to that fancy propeller. Simply pull the prop into Beta and reduce the blade pitch until you're moving at the desired speed. Be careful of slowing down too much, however. You don't want the wind to overpower your water rudders and take control of your floatplane, something that can happen easily if you're in a plane with a lot of vertical surface area like the Vazar Dash-3 Otter.

You should be particularly wary of boat wakes while taxiing a turbine. The last thing you want to do is send a shot of cold water back through the compressor blades onto all that hot metal in the combustion and turbine sections of the engine. Even the suspicion that cold water might have entered the hot section is enough to warrant a teardown and inspection for thermal shock damage, an operation that is not only time consuming but expensive beyond belief. Fortunately, that long nose puts the propeller well ahead of any spray that might be kicked up by the floats, and the intake ducting is designed to keep water from reaching the compressor blades under normal conditions. If you're taxiing across very rough water, however, or are crossing a large boat wake, your plane could pitch up and down violently enough to enable the prop to pick up and fling more spray into the intake than it's designed to handle. If you find yourself having to taxi across rough water, slow down as much as you can without relinquishing control of your plane to the wind. If you see a boat wake bearing down on you, slow down before it gets to you or turn sideways so that the plane rolls from side to side instead of pitching nose-first over the top. Be mindful of what the wind's up to, however, and use common sense. You don't want to turn sideways to protect the engine only to have a gust get under your wing and flip you over.

Your before-takeoff checklist is likely to be pretty minimal: no magnetos to check, no carb-heat control to cycle. You will have used the propeller enough, either by unfeathering it after startup or using the Beta range to control your taxi speed, to know if it works or not. Other than checking the control surfaces for freedom of movement and setting the instruments, radios, flaps and trim, there's not all that much to do. You might need to check the function of an *inertial separator*, which is a device used to keep dirt particles and spray from reaching the engine, and an overspeed governor. You'll also probably have to turn on one or more electric fuel pumps as well as the igniters before takeoff.

Your primary visual indicators for setting takeoff power are the torque gauge and the ITT gauge. Like manifold pressure in a piston plane, there is a redline for the amount of torque that can be applied to the propeller. Most of the turbines you're likely to encounter are capable of being overtorqued at lower altitudes during takeoff and other high-power maneuvers, so monitor the gauge carefully.

The temperature limitations of a turbine are even more crucial, and it's essential that you never exceed the ITT redline. If you're flying one of the older turbines, you might find that the engine reaches its maximum temperature on a hot day before you've pushed the power lever up to maximum torque. If this happens, you'll simply have to live with the reduced takeoff power. Exceeding the temperature redline will ruin the engine.

Takeoffs in a turbine are downright exciting. In an airplane like a Turbine Maule, you'll be off the water almost before you're on the step. Even in a heavily loaded Vazar Dash-3 Otter, the acceleration and climb rates are impressive, especially when compared to the sluggish performance of the piston-powered original. But performance is not the only benefit. Turbine floatplanes are quiet. Instead of the staccato roar that blasts out the exhaust stacks of a piston plane, the turbine emits more of a whooshing whine. The fat-bladed Beta props turn slower than the slimmer piston-powered counterparts, so the tip snarl isn't nearly as ear shattering. Commercial operators who are forced to fly over residential areas or take off from lakes ringed with homes and apartments inevitably experience a significant reduction in noise complaints as they introduce turbines into their fleets.

Unlike a piston engine, a turbine can be operated at maximum rpm all day long, so there will be no need for you to reduce propeller rpm as soon as the plane is safely off the water. You will need to advance the power lever as you climb for the same reason you have to keep advancing the throttle on a piston airplane during climb to maintain manifold pressure. Don't forget to watch that ITT gauge as you go up; depending on the outside air temperature and the amount of work you're asking the engine to do, you might find yourself having to back off on the climb power in order to maintain the proper ITT reading.

You won't have much to do when it's time to level off and set your cruise power. As long as you don't force it to run harder or hotter than it's designed to, a turbine doesn't really care what you do with it. A turbine does love its fuel, however. A piston Beaver burns about 23 gallons of fuel an hour in cruise. A Turbo Beaver will burn almost twice that. Granted, you'll be going a whole lot faster in the turbine, but the Jet-A in the tanks will disappear at a prodigious rate if you're not careful.

Cruise power is set depending on what you want to do. You can go faster or you can burn less fuel. No matter which one you pick, it will be governed by what you do with the power lever. Some turbine floatplanes are capable of exceeding their maximum safe operating speeds. In the case of the Turbo Beaver and the Pilatus Porter, the maximum safe operating speed is the bottom of the yellow arc on the airspeed indicator. The Vazar Dash-3 Otter doesn't have a yellow arc, so the maximum safe operating speed is the redline. Anything below these limits is okay, weather and turbulence notwithstanding. If you're in a hurry, set the power lever for the maximum safe speed. If you're paying for the fuel, however, or if you have a long way to go between gas docks, set the cruise power for the most efficient fuel consumption as indicated by the flow meter. "Efficient fuel consumption" is a relative term; even at their most economic power settings, turbines consume a lot more fuel than the piston engines you fly now.

Once you've set the torque, you can reduce the propeller rpm if you want to. While not a requirement, most operators like to set their cruise rpm about 10 percent lower than maximum to increase the propeller's efficiency and reduce vibration and noise.

Turbine floatplanes are generally flown at higher altitudes than piston floatplanes. For any given indicated airspeed or fuel consumption rate, an increase in altitude will increase the airplane's true airspeed. This is true of any plane, but the higher fuel consumption of a turbine makes it even more important to get the most whine for the buck. Kenmore Air operates a mixed fleet of piston Beavers, Turbo-Beavers, and Vazar Dash-3 Otters. The piston Beavers generally are flown at altitudes below 5,000 feet. It's just not worth the time and wear on the engines to haul them up any higher. The turbines, on the other hand, often are taken clear up to 9,500 feet on an eastbound VFR flight or 8,500 feet westbound, which are the maximums that can be flown without oxygen equipment in the plane. The extra speed realized at these higher altitudes translates into very real savings at the fuel pump.

Depending on the type of turbine you're flying, fuel management can be very important. The engines in turbine-powered landplanes cannot be starved of fuel unless there is simply no more fuel on board the airplane. Their fuel systems are simple, and in the case of twins, each engine can draw fuel from any tank on the plane. This is not necessarily true of turbine floatplanes, particularly the de Havilland machines. A description of the fuel systems in turbine-equipped Beavers and Otters would require a separate chapter and a bunch of diagrams, but the bottom line is that their engines always draw fuel from the same tank. It's the pilot's responsibility to keep gas in that tank by transferring it from the other tanks. It's a crucial responsibility. According to the operator's manual, if the feed tank runs dry it will be impossible to restart the flow of fuel to the engine *even if the other tanks are still full*. So remember the price tag on that airplane you're about to fly and make sure you understand the operation of its fuel system.

Descents are easy. You don't need to worry about overcooling the engine by using a power setting that is too low as you head down, so the only limiting factors are the airplane's maximum safe speed and the tolerance you and your passengers have for a rapid increase of pressure. If you decide to pull the power back to idle for the descent, you might want to advance the fuel control to the flight idle setting. Not all pilots do this, but the higher idle setting will ensure that you'll get more power if you need it in a hurry.

If you're flying a Turbo Beaver and you want to come down really fast, you can pull the prop into Beta. The blades will flatten out and act like speed brakes, but be very careful if you try it. While Beta (but not reverse) is approved for use during flight in a Turbo Beaver, the operations manual warns that you can set up a rate of descent that is so high you won't be able to recover the airplane and flare for a landing. The use of Beta in flight is not approved for the Vazar Dash-3 Otter.

A turbine is shut down in the same manner as a piston engine. Simply move the fuel control lever into the OFF position and starve the engine into silence. Unlike a piston engine, however, you'll have to go through that 20- or 30-second spool-up sequence if you change your mind, so make sure you really do want to shut off the engine before you pull that lever.

PROPELLER MANAGEMENT

Now we get to the fun part. A good portion of your reputation as a turbine driver is going to be based on how effectively you use that Beta propeller. If you've managed to wade this far through the book, you're probably getting awfully tired of my constant reminders to plan ahead. Plan ahead before you untie the plane, plan ahead before you jump on and fire up, plan ahead before you take off, plan ahead before you land, and *definitely* plan ahead before you head for the dock. Well,

I'm sorry, but I'm going to say it again. Actually, with a turbine you have to plan even *farther* ahead because you'll often have to figure out your departure strategy first before you can decide on your best method of arrival.

Remember, you have two choices when you shut down the engine. You can feather the propeller, or you can lock it in zero pitch with the blade latches. Making the right choice can be crucial to the continued well-being of your airplane, to say nothing of your wallet (insurance never covers everything). Some pilots make it a practice to lock the blades in Beta every time they shut down, and they can cite plenty of plausible reasons to justify their preference. Other pilots try to feather the propeller whenever possible, shutting down in Beta only if they think they'll need zero or reverse pitch to make a safe departure. What you decide to do will depend on the nature of your flying and the handling qualities of your floatplane.

Because the way you arrive at a dock will often be determined by the way you anticipate leaving it, let's examine the departure phase first. If you have a line crew, you've got it made. If the prop is in Beta, you can start the engine right at the dock, and the line crew can turn you out whenever you want. If you're in a hurry, the crew can begin turning you out even as you hit the start switch. With the prop in zero pitch, there will be no danger of your taxiing into something while the crew swings you toward open water. If you feathered the prop deliberately when you shut down or find that the propeller has feathered itself while you were off eating lunch, wait until the crew has turned you safely toward open water before starting the engine (Fig. 18-7). Remember, a feathered propeller will develop some forward thrust, and it could be enough to pull the plane out of the line crew's grasp, not a good thing to have happen if you aren't turned out all the way and there's another airplane in front of you.

If the prop is feathered but you want the control afforded by the Beta range as soon as you're

Fig. 18-7. *If a line crewmember is available to help turn the plane out and hold the tail, a regular departure can be made with the engine being started after the plane is turned away from the dock.*

underway, you can start the engine at the dock and unfeather the propeller as soon as everything is spooled up to speed. Once the propeller is in Beta, the line crew can turn you out. A word of caution if you do this, however. Make sure there are at least two strong mooring lines holding the plane firmly to the dock, and DON'T LET ANYONE UNTIE THE PLANE until the engine is spooled up and you've pulled the prop into Beta. The high idle speed of the turbine combined with the big bites of air the blades are going to take as they twist from feather through maximum pitch to zero pitch will move your plane rapidly forward if it's not secured to the dock. If there's a floatplane docked ahead of you, your prop will be chewing through its tail in seconds, and the insurance company will be footing two huge repair bills instead of one.

If you have to turn the plane out yourself, you're probably better off having the prop in Beta to begin with. That way, you'll have full control of your forward or backward progress as soon as the engine lights off. If you don't have a wind or current to contend with, you can turn the plane out with the propeller feathered with no problems. As with a piston floatplane, make sure it's pointed well clear of any obstacles or other airplanes before you jump on board and start up.

I know a couple of high-time turbine pilots who routinely start the engines while their planes are tied to the dock, put the blades in zero pitch, and then step back to the dock to turn their planes out in the normal manner. I suppose this is okay if a wind or current dictates that you absolutely have to get moving the moment you leave the security of the dock, but I can't condone it as a regular practice. The risks are simply too great. There's the safety concern of running forward on a float and scrambling through a door only a few feet aft of a spinning propeller. And if that prop happens to be developing a little forward thrust, or if the pitch control slips, you could be left standing or treading water at the dock as your million-dollar airplane taxis into the rocks.

One of the big advantages of the reversing propeller is that it allows you to dock your float-plane in places you ordinarily wouldn't be able to get out of. Nosing into a narrow boat slip or up to a dock surrounded by pilings becomes a routine event because you can back out the same way you came in. At least that's the theory. Unfortunately, reverse isn't the panacea we aspiring turbine pilots tend to think it is. Assuming there is no wind, reverse works pretty much as advertised as long as you use it sparingly. The trick is to back up slowly and smoothly. You'll be able to steer with the water rudders as long as you're not going so fast as to overpower them. Remember that you're steering the tail, not the nose. Left rudder will swing the tail to the left as you back up, so don't let the fact that the nose swings right confuse you. If you're looking backward to see where you're going, it will all make sense.

If you suddenly find yourself unable to move the water rudders, you're backing up too fast. The rudders are designed to be trailed through the water, not pushed into it. At slow reverse speeds you can overpower the force of the water with your legs and hold the rudders in the position you want them. Go too fast, however, and the water pressure will quickly overpower your muscles. Letting the water rudders jam over against their stops is bad in two ways. First, the plane will begin to turn in the direction of the jammed rudders whether you want it to or not. Second, there's a good chance the rudders could be damaged or even torn off the floats. Incidentally, for those of you who are curious about such things, applying full reverse power to see what will happen will drive the tails of the floats under and sink the plane. Don't try it.

Your ability to steer while backing up will be affected by the wind and by the load you're carrying in the plane. A heavy load will push the floats deeper into the water and will affect the way they respond to the water rudders. Generally speaking, the more a float is submerged, the greater will be its resistance to turning, and the slower it will respond to your rudder inputs. A wind, of course, can mess everything up. Turbine-powered planes, with their large tails and long noses, present substantial surfaces to the wind. If you're lucky, the wind will be blowing in the direction you want to go and will actually help you get turned around as you back out. This almost never happens. Usually the wind is blowing in the opposite direction, so take this into account before committing yourself to a docking that will require you to back out with a reverse you might not be able to use.

The action of a wind blowing against the side of an airplane is pretty easy to figure out, but there is a more subtle effect that's almost impossible to predict. Under certain conditions, a wind can interact with the propeller, changing the symmetry of its thrust and causing the nose to swing to one side or the other. As there's no way to know when and if this is going to happen, your only defense when reversing on a breezy day is to stay alert and give yourself plenty of maneuvering room.

The greatest danger you're likely to encounter when using reverse is overconfidence. Get a few good experiences with reverse under your belt, a slick docking or two, and maybe a clever departure, and you might begin to think you've gotten this backing up business licked. You won't. I've had 20,000-hour floatplane pilots with thousands of hours of turbine time tell me about getting trapped between a pair of pilings or pinned against a dock because the plane didn't do what they thought it would do. They hadn't done anything wrong; they'd simply run into a situation they'd never encountered before. You have enough variables to deal with when you're flying a floatplane. Don't add overconfidence to the list because it will absolutely guarantee that you'll make a mistake sooner rather than later.

Now that we've looked at some of the ways to get away from a dock, let's examine your options when you arrive at the dock. You have two choices: You can feather the propeller or you can put it in Beta. Feathering has a psychological advantage as it won't scare the people on the dock half to death as you pull up. Take a listen to a pilot working the Beta range of a propeller and you'll know what I mean. You've never heard such an unnerving yowling and buzzing in all your life. If you feather the prop it will stop very quickly when you shut off the fuel. In fact, it will stop so quickly that if you need to walk forward to cushion the floats' arrival at the dock, you'll be able to stop the prop with your hand by the time you get to it. This is an accepted practice among experienced turbine pilots, but BE CAREFUL. Don't just rush blindly forward. The prop might still be moving fast enough to give you a nasty blow or boot you off the float, so pay attention to what it and you are doing.

Feathering the prop is the best thing to do if you have to nose up gently to a dock or the stern of a boat. The propeller still will be whizzing around at 900 rpm, but you will barely be creeping forward. In fact, most of your forward thrust will be from the exhaust coming out those big stacks. Remember, your water rudders will have very little authority at this speed, so even the slightest crosswind or adverse current might force you to use a different technique.

The downside of feathering the propeller is that you no longer have the advantage of reverse. You might not need reverse to dock, but if you think you'll need it to leave, you'll be better off leaving the prop in Beta as you come in. Don't forget those blade latches. Most pilots make it a practice to pull a tiny bit of reverse the instant before shutting down the engine to make sure the latches will drop into place.

Leave your prop in Beta if there's a possibility the wind might push you away from the dock before you or the line crew can secure the plane. Large floatplanes like the Otter are particularly susceptible to being pushed around by the wind, but if you're in Beta you can back off a safe distance and try again. If you have to put your plane on a beach, Beta can be a real help, especially if the wind is blowing toward shore. Turn your plane into the wind a short distance off the beach, retract the water rudders, and let the wind blow you back. If you were flying a piston plane, the idle speed of the engine might hold you in position or even move you forward; shutting off the engine might cause you to drift back a little too fast. This could be a problem if the beach is composed of gravel or small rocks. The advantage of Beta is that you can feed in just enough forward thrust to keep your backward drift slow and safe. If you have to take a group of fishermen to a lake with a rocky shoreline, you can back in and then hold the plane just off the beach while they walk to the rear of the floats and jump off. Presumably, they will have been smart enough to bring hip waders.

If the wind is blowing off the beach, you can use the Beta range to keep your approach slow and easy. If you suddenly see something in the water that might damage a float, you can instantly pull reverse and back away.

The greatest disadvantage of Beta is that the prop will continue to spin rapidly long after the fire has gone out in the engine. Up to two minutes isn't unusual, especially if there's a wind helping out. If outside the airplane, NEVER go forward on the floats if the blades are in Beta until they've come to a complete stop. Turbine propellers are heavy and sharp, and there's a tremendous amount of inertia behind them. Even at relatively slow speeds, they can cause serious injury or death if

someone gets in their way. If you think you might have to go forward and cushion the floats because a wind or current is forcing you to approach a dock faster than you'd like, don't leave the blades in Beta. Feather the propeller so it will be stopped or almost stopped by the time you get forward. The same thing is true if you're approaching a shoreline that will require you to jump off the front of the floats before or as soon as you touch. You don't want to run the risk of becoming so concerned with "saving" the plane that you dash forward into the whirling blades of an unfeathered prop.

Every situation will be different, of course, but a good rule of thumb is to feather the prop whenever safety is the prime concern, and leave it in Beta when the ability to maneuver is paramount (Fig. 18-8).

Fig 18-8. *The pilot of this Turbo Beaver is about to use some reverse to slow his plane and bring it to a stop alongside the dock in the foreground. Reverse is critical in this instance to keep the plane from coasting forward into the plane docked out of frame to the left.*

THINK SAFETY

Safety issues have been discussed throughout the chapter, but considering the cost and value of a turbine floatplane and the potential for serious damage or injury, I don't think a summary safety checklist is out of order.

- [ ] Always check the position of the propeller blades before you climb on board. You might *think* the blades are in Beta, but if you missed the latches, they're going to be feathered, and you'll run the risk of driving into something before you can stop or back up.
- [ ] Remember that you're driving a jet. Those exhaust gasses are hot, and they come out of the stacks with a lot of force. If you're going to fire up while alongside a dock, make sure everyone is safely clear of the exhaust path.
- [ ] Remember the time it takes to get a turbine spooled up. If you think a wind or current might carry you into trouble while you're starting up, have somebody hold the plane, or start up while you're still tied to the dock.
- [ ] Remember that for most turbines, the propeller will get there first. The floats won't protect it if you have to nose up to a dock. Even a little thing like a water faucet or an electrical conduit sticking up on a dock can ruin a multithousand-dollar propeller. Check that dock carefully before heading into it.
- [ ] Remember that the propeller won't stop right away as it does on a piston plane. Make sure you, your passengers, and the line crew stay well clear until it's come to a complete stop.
- [ ] If you find yourself thinking how easy turbine flying is, give yourself a mental slap in the face. Pilot complacency and inattention are the greatest causes of turbine accidents.

EMERGENCY PROCEDURES

Turbine engines are the most reliable powerplants that technology has come up with so far, so it stands to reason that there's not much to talk about in the way of emergency procedures. If your turbine suddenly stops running, there are only two probable causes, fuel starvation and flameout. A *flameout* is just what the word implies—the fire goes out in the combustion chamber. Several things can cause this: excessive moisture going through the engine and severe turbulence are the most likely reasons. If you encounter severe turbulence or visible moisture—rain, snow, or ice—the operations manuals of most turbine aircraft recommend switching on the igniters. This ensures that there will be a constant ignition source in the combustion chamber.

Fuel starvation can occur for a couple of reasons. If you let the plane run out of gas, or have mismanaged the fuel transfer process, the sudden silence under the cowl will be your fault. If the sudden silence is due to the failure of the fuel control unit, it won't be your fault, but you'll still be stuck with a powerless airplane. Fortunately, there's a quick way to evaluate why your plane is heading for Earth. If you've lost power and the ITT gauge indicates a radical loss of temperature, your engine has flamed out and you'll need to initiate the restart procedure outlined in the operating manual. If you've lost power but the ITT gauge is still indicating an ignition temperature, your fuel control unit has just died and your engine has dropped to idle. Advance the standby throttle and you should get your power back. Don't forget that you won't have any Beta control with the standby throttle.

If you're out of gas or if the engine has quit because of a catastrophic failure of some internal component, you're going to come down no matter what. Feather the propeller right away to get rid of the drag and set up the plane for best glide. From here on, the fact that you're flying a turbine is irrelevant. A powerless airplane is a powerless airplane, and you'll need to call up all the forced landing skills and procedures you learned in flight training and, I hope, have been practicing periodically.

One other problem can occur with a turbine, and that is an engine overspeed. This is caused by a failure of the engine's governing mechanism, and it's potentially quite dangerous. If an over-speed is allowed to continue unchecked, it could quickly lead to a violent failure of the engine's internal components. The operations manual will contain the proper procedures for dealing with an overspeed condition. In the case of a propeller overspeed, the overspeed governor will work with the fuel control unit to reduce the fuel flow to the engine, and you'll most likely end up with partial power. If the problem is a turbine over-speed, you'll have to shut down the engine immediately.

AFTER THE FLIGHT

The nice thing about a piston floatplane is that you can go home after you shut down the engine and secure the plane. You can do this with a turbine, too, if you're flying in fresh water, but if you're a saltwater seaplane pilot, you have an important chore to do before you can head for the sofa in front of the TV. There's no way to keep salt out of the engine. It either goes in as fine spray kicked up during takeoff, landing, or taxiing in rough water, or it goes in as particles suspended in the air itself, the "salt haze" that's so common along the coast. The salt gradually builds up on the compressor and turbine blades, as well as on the inner casing of the engine, where it immediately begins to corrode the metal. If left unchecked, the corrosion will first degrade the performance of the turbine by "roughing up" the blades and blade seals. Eventually, the damage will become so severe that a blade might actually separate or break during flight with catastrophic results.

It didn't take long for the engine manufacturers to figure out what was happening, so they began taking steps to combat the corrosion. New materials and alloys helped, but it was obvious that the best way to get rid of salt deposits was to flush them away with fresh water before they could begin to do their damage. So they fitted spray rings, which are circular tubes with tiny holes drilled in them, around the inlets of the engines. After a flight in salt water, a pilot could hook a hose to the ring and, while turning the engine over with the starter, shoot a spray of absolutely pure water into the engine. The use of pure water is essential because it actually attracts minerals off the engine parts. Spinning the engine ensured that all the blades were rinsed down along with the engine case. After the rinse-out process, which took about 30 seconds, the pilot would remove the hose, button the cowl back up, and start the engine in the normal manner to dry it out.

The spray ring was a good idea, and it was certainly better than doing nothing, but it left something to be desired. Operators of the original Turbo Beavers, for example, found that the performance of their planes still deteriorated despite their religious use of the spray rings, to the point where the Turbo Beavers were being outperformed by the piston Beavers the turbines were supposed to replace.

The problem was that while the pure water spray did a great job of removing the salt from the compressor blades and forward section of the engine, the spray had pretty much vaporized by the time it got back to the turbine section. There wasn't a sufficient volume of water left to do the job. The solution was obvious and simple. Newer turbines like the PT6A-135 used in the Vazar Dash-3 Otter have *two* spray points, the original ring around the inlet, and a special fitting that replaces one of the igniters for the flushing only.

At the end of a day's operations, and after the engine has thoroughly cooled, you'll need to open the cowl, remove the designated igniter, and install the spray fitting in its place. Run two hoses from an approved pure water filtration device and attach them to the spray ring and the spray fitting. Open the drains in the bottom of the engine and spin the turbine with the starter. Turn on the water and flush the engine for 30 seconds, which is long enough to ensure the removal of any salt deposits but not long enough to overheat the starter motor (Fig. 18-9).

Fig. 18-9. *Kenmore chief pilot Bill Whitney flushing the engine of one of the company's Super Turbines after a day's flying. Note the special filtration system in the foreground which ensures the purity of the water spraying into the engine.*

After you've flushed the engine and allowed the water to drain out, remove the hoses, replace the igniter, close the drains, and refasten the cowl. Start the engine and allow it to idle for a couple of minutes to ensure that any remaining moisture is blown out or evaporated. *Now* you can go home and watch TV.

When Kenmore Air Harbor began considering the acquisition and conversion of a pair of Turbo Beavers, they were very concerned about what ef-

fect their saltwater environment would have on the life of the expensive, new-generation turbines they were planning to install. Numerous telephone calls to operators in the Caribbean and along the Gulf of Mexico proved quite reassuring. As long as the engines are equipped with compressor and turbine spray fittings, they said, and as long as the engines are flushed every day, you should experience no performance loss due to internal corrosion. Kenmore went ahead with their conversions and arranged their maintenance schedule to make sure the engine of each plane was flushed out every day it flew. They have experienced no corrosion problems and have since added four more turbines to the fleet with great success.

There's no question that the process of flushing a turbine takes time, what with waiting for it to cool down, opening the cowl, hooking up the hoses, and so forth. For someone without a squad of mechanics to turn the job over to, it might be tempting to put the pure water flush off for a day or two. But corrosion doesn't care about your schedule—it's going to start eating the blades right now. Turbines are almost as expensive to repair as they are to buy. Take the time to flush away the salt, and the engine will reward you with thousands of hours of high-performance, trouble-free flight (Fig. 18-10).

Fig. 18-10. *A Vazar Dash-3 Otter on its scheduled run between Seattle, Washington, and Victoria, British Columbia.*

19
Emergencies

IF YOU HAVE TO HAVE an accident in an airplane, have it in a floatplane. I know this isn't a very positive statement, but it's true.

The addition of floats makes an airplane much more crashworthy, and statistics show that your chances of walking away from a controlled floatplane crash are excellent. The key word here is "controlled." Even if you experience a complete power failure over a dense forest, if you keep your wits about you and continue to fly the airplane all the way down to the trees, your biggest problem will most likely be figuring out how to climb down to the ground. (And you wondered why you were carrying around all that mooring line!)

There's more to surviving a crash than just making a good landing, however. If your accident occurs out in the bush someplace, you'll need adequate survival gear to keep you going until help arrives. If you end up in the water, you'll need to guard against hypothermia and revive any members of your party that succumb to it. And, if it's at all possible, you'll probably want to recover your airplane.

LANDINGS

There are two categories of emergency landings. The first one is the actual I-have-to-land-right-now emergency landing. This is the type of landing you're faced with in the event of a complete power loss or a failure of one of the airplane's crucial components. The second type of emergency landing is the precautionary landing. If the oil pressure starts a slow drop to zero, or if you suddenly realize you've miscalculated your fuel consumption and you shortly won't have any left to consume, or if you're running out of daylight and you don't want to risk a night landing at your destination, a precautionary landing is your ticket to survival.

The basic procedures for making an emergency landing are the same for floatplanes and landplanes. If a total power loss is experienced, first establish the maximum-distance glide speed for your particular airplane. Then pick the best possible landing site within reach and turn toward it. If you are in contact with a radio facility, advise him or her of your location and situation while you try to locate the source of the problem. If you are not in radio contact, switch to the emergency frequency (121.5 MHz) and broadcast MAYDAY together with your location and intentions. Don't let your radio broadcasts and troubleshooting efforts interfere with your flying. No one on the ground can help you at this point, and it's vital that you maintain control of the airplane as you head toward your landing site. As you prepare to land, follow the fire-prevention procedures outlined in your plane's flight manual.

The advantage of being in a floatplane now becomes apparent. Those same floats that enable the plane to land on ice or snow also work great on the ground. They are, in effect, two big skids. A freshly plowed field or soft, boggy meadow that would rip the gear off a landplane present no problems for a floatplane. Another advantage of being a floatplane pilot is that you are used to using something other than a windsock or a tower controller to determine the wind direction. Try to determine the wind direction by looking for rising smoke, blowing dust on the ground, or the direction the treetops are bending. This will not be easy to do under the pressure of the emergency, and is a good reason why you should always be looking for clues to the wind's direction during your flight. Then you'll be prepared in the unlikely event you have to make an emergency landing.

Pick the smoothest, most level landing site you can, and land into the wind. This will give you the slowest possible touchdown speed. Your landing attitude should be fairly flat, with the float tips raised just enough to avoid digging them into the ground. Try not to land in a full-stall attitude. The extreme nose-up angle could cause the sterns of the floats to strike the ground hard enough to pitch you forward onto the bows of the floats, which could then dig in and flip the plane. Even in a fairly flat attitude, the drag on the bottoms of the floats will tend to pitch the nose down anyway, so be prepared to pull the stick or yoke all the way back to keep the floats from digging in. The amount of drag exerted on the floats will vary with the type of surface you're landing on. A grass or crop-covered field will not create nearly as much friction on the float bottoms as a field covered with bare dirt or rocks.

If you're unable to find an obstacle-free touchdown site, the fact that you're in a floatplane will really pay off. Those big floats projecting out ahead of the plane with their struts and spreader bars

make wonderful energy-absorbers in the event of a crash. As long as you maintain control and touch down in a normal attitude, there will be an awful lot of sheet metal between you and whatever stops the plane to soak up the impact. While the plane might end up a total mess, you and your passengers have an excellent chance of walking away.

If you experience an engine failure over a forest, head into the wind and try to land in the thickest foliage you can find. Trees that are close together and have lots of branches will help cushion the impact, as will the floats and struts. It's better to come down on top of the trees than to try to land in a clear area that's too small and risk slamming into the tree trunks. Use full flaps and touch down at the slowest possible speed, but don't stall the plane. This will cause the nose to drop, and you might plummet down between the trees and hit the ground nose-first.

If you land in the trees and your plane comes to a stop before it reaches the ground, be very careful getting out. You don't want to come through the landing unscathed only to break a leg falling off a branch. Your mooring lines can come in handy if you're still some distance above the ground. Unless there's an immediate danger of fire, don't be in such a hurry to get out of the plane that you forget your survival gear. You'll just have to climb back up and get it later!

NIGHT LANDINGS

Some floatplane pilots make night landings on a routine basis, but to the average pilot, a night landing should be considered only as a last resort. In fact, if you have a choice between landing on an unfamiliar, unilluminated body of water on a moonless night or on a nearby lighted airport, choose the airport. You might have to replace the keels of your floats afterward, but landing on pavement you can see is a lot safer than landing on water you can't see.

One of the difficulties encountered when making a water landing at night is finding the water, especially if the night is a dark one. A lake I fly to on a regular basis has several acres of flat ground at one end. The area is covered with shrubs and blackberry bushes, crisscrossed with drainage ditches, and littered with rocks. It would not be a good place to land a floatplane. Yet at night, this patch of ground looks exactly like part of the lake. It's impossible to tell where the water ends and the ground begins. This is one reason you should plan to make night landings only on bodies of water with which you are very familiar.

The most dangerous thing about a night landing is the fact that it's difficult and often impossible to determine if the surface of the water is safe to land on. Moving boats are supposed to have their running lights illuminated, but some people forget to turn them on, or the lights might not work at all. Running lights seem to be the first things to quit on a new boat, and the canoes and outboard-powered skiffs normally encountered on lakes don't even have them to begin with. The only way to see all the boats, rafts, barges, and other large floating objects that might be out on the water is to position your airplane in such a way that whatever light is in the sky will reflect off the surface toward you. Any large objects will appear as black shapes against the gray or silver color of the water.

While you might be able to pick out large objects on the surface, there is no way you'll be able to spot deadheads, logs, and all the other types of floating debris that can do so much damage to your floats. Areas of shallow water and underwater obstructions also will be hidden from your view, so always land well out from shoreline if you are unfamiliar with the area.

Night landings are made much easier if there are lights along the shore of the lake. The light reflecting off the water will give you an idea of your height above the surface, and it will enable you to judge your distance from the shoreline. The reflections will also let you see how rough the surface of the water is, and whether or not there is an obstacle in your path.

Your landing should be made into the wind, but at night, this isn't as easy to do as it sounds. As a floatplane pilot, you will have learned to read the wind from all kinds of indicators: blowing smoke, bending trees, the sails on sailboats, and wind streaks—all of which are invisible at night. If the sky is luminescent enough to provide a good reflection off the water, you might be able to read the wind direction from the waves, but you'll probably have to rely on area weather reports and forecasts for a general idea of the wind conditions. If the lake or harbor is located near an airport with an operating control tower, you can get an approximate idea of the surface winds from a controller or the ATIS broadcasts. A nearby AWOS/ASOS broadcast might prove valuable.

If there are lights on the upwind shore of the lake, pick the brightest one and land straight toward it. Its reflection will make a runway of sorts, and if a boat should stray into your landing lane, you'll be able to spot it immediately. Even when you're at pattern altitude, lights along the shore will give you a good indication of the surface conditions. If the reflections extend a long way from shore and are sharp in definition, the water is glassy or very lightly rippled. If the reflections are blurred or indistinct and extend only a short distance from shore, the water is being ruffled by the wind. The fainter the reflection, the rougher the water and, presumably, the stronger the wind.

The procedure for landing at night is identical to the procedure for landing on glassy water, except you'll be more dependent upon your instruments. Unless the sky is very bright, you won't have a distinct horizon in front of you, so you'll have to use your plane's gyro horizon to keep the wings level and maintain the correct pitch angle during your descent. Remember, glassy-water landings use up a lot of space. Make sure you have enough lake in front of you to complete the landing. A light on shore will help, but make sure it's really a light. I've heard stories of pilots who ran out of lake because they mistook a bright star low on the horizon for a light on shore.

It's a strange and slightly scary feeling to be sitting there in the glow from the instrument panel, maintaining a constant attitude and descent rate through the blackness that surrounds you, heading toward what you hope is smooth, unobstructed water. The last 30 seconds or so will seem like an eternity, and you'll begin to wonder if you're ever going to land. About the time you decide that all your careful calculations were wrong and that you're going to run out of lake and crash, you'll feel the plane enter ground effect and then plunk down on the water. Believe me, it's a nice feeling.

Turning on your landing light won't make it any easier to find the water, but it will show you if the surface is covered with whitecaps. It will also warn any boaters in the area of your intentions to land. If your light is a powerful one, it might even pick out logs or other floating debris in time for you to take evasive action, but don't count on it. In this regard, night landings are always risky. Since it will be almost impossible to tell how rough the surface of the water is, you'll just have to wait until you actually touch down to find out. Be prepared to put in full power and go around because if you get bounced back high in the air as soon as you land, the water might be too rough for your plane. Whitecaps will be easy to see, but boat wakes, swells, and waves that aren't quite big enough to break will merge into the overall blackness of the water. If the water proves to be too rough for a safe landing, you'll have no other choice but to find somewhere else to land, and this could be very difficult on a dark night in unfamiliar territory.

As a general rule, you should avoid flying a floatplane at night. The risks are just too great. The Canadian government feels the same way, which is why it's illegal in that country to make a water takeoff or landing during the period between a half hour after sunset and a half hour before sunrise. The law does not prohibit seaplanes from *flying* at night, only from taking off or landing, so pilots can take off in Canada just before sunset and make a night flight to a destination in the United States if they want to. The regulation applies to water operations only; if you're flying an amphibious floatplane, you can operate from a runway after dark,

assuming your airplane is equipped to do so. For example, an amphib pilot could depart a remote lake before sunset and then make a night flight to a lighted airport for a wheels-down landing.

SURVIVAL GEAR

Much has been written about the type of survival gear that should be carried in an airplane, and there are several courses specifically designed to help people survive a plane crash in the wilderness. If you are planning a flight over sparsely settled country, it's essential that you carry at least a minimum of survival gear, regardless of the type of airplane you're flying. If you're going to be making the trip in a floatplane, there are some additional items you should carry. Let's look at the basics first.

A good place to start is the list of emergency equipment that the state of Alaska requires all aircraft to have on board while they are inside Alaska's borders. In the summer, from April to October, the following items are required:

- ☐ Food for each occupant sufficient to sustain life for two weeks.
- ☐ One ax or hatchet.
- ☐ One first aid kit.
- ☐ One pistol, shotgun, or rifle, and ammunition.
- ☐ One small gill net and an assortment of tackle, such as hooks, flies, lines, and sinkers.
- ☐ One knife.
- ☐ Two small boxes of matches.
- ☐ One mosquito headnet for each occupant.
- ☐ Two small signaling devices, such as colored smoke bombs, railroad fuses, or Very pistol shells in sealed metal containers. (A *Very light* is a pyrotechnic signal using white or colored balls fired from the Very pistol.)

From October to April, the following items must be carried in addition to the basic equipment listed above:

- ☐ One pair of snowshoes.
- ☐ One sleeping bag.

One wool blanket for each occupant over four years old.

Canada also has a list of required emergency equipment for aircraft operating within its borders, and while the list is similar to Alaska's, there are some additional items:

- Cooking utensils.
- A stove and a supply of fuel or a self-contained means of providing heat for cooking when you are operating north of the tree line.
- A portable compass.
- A flexible saw blade or equivalent cutting tool.
- Snare wire at least 30 feet (or 9 meters) in length, and instructions for its use.
- Tents or engine and wing covers—colored or with panels colored in international orange or other high-visibility color—of suitable design that are sufficient to accommodate all persons carried when operating north of the tree line.
- A suitable survival instruction manual.
- A large panel of fabric or plastic colored in international orange or other high-visibility color to mark the crash site.

Obviously, the contents of your survival kit will depend a lot on where you're flying. Float-plane pilots in Florida and Louisiana probably won't have much use for snowshoes, but most of the items listed here would be useful anywhere. If the requirement for two weeks worth of food conjures up images of stuffing several bulging grocery sacks into the back of your plane, relax. The human body can survive for two weeks on very little food, and you can pack a lot of freeze-dried foods, raisins, and candy bars into a very small container. For our camping flights into British Columbia and Southeast Alaska, my wife and I carry all our required emergency gear in one small duffel bag.

Make sure you include a good survival manual that covers the type of country you're going to

be flying over. The worse problem after a crash is recovering from the shock of the accident and organizing the survival efforts. A survival manual with step-by-step instructions will make it easier for you to begin constructing a shelter, making the site more visible from the air, organizing your food and water supplies, and so forth. Read through the manual before you pack it away in your emergency kit; you might decide there's additional emergency gear you'd like to take in addition to the items mentioned here.

A first-aid kit is vital. Aviation supply stores offer a number of ready-made kits complete with a container, or you can make up your own. If you choose to make your own, make sure it's packed in a waterproof container. Be prepared to deal with large and small cuts, sprains, diarrhea, headaches, and minor burns. Be sure to include disinfectant, and enough tape to fasten a makeshift splint to a broken arm or leg. If your passengers are prone to airsickness, include motion sickness pills in the kit as well. Be sure to include a good supply of water purification tablets. There are also special water filtering kits you can buy, although they tend to be rather expensive.

Handguns are illegal in Canada, so if you're going to be traveling in that country, you'll have to carry some other type of firearm. I don't think a handgun makes a very good survival weapon, anyway. In an actual survival situation, most people will have a better chance of bagging small game for food with a rifle or a shotgun. Personally, I feel the best survival weapon is a 12-gauge pump-action shotgun. I carry a police-type 12-gauge pump with an 18¼-inch barrel and a six-shot tubular magazine. The advantage of a shotgun is that you can use birdshot (for small game) and heavy, rifled slugs (in case a bear tries to participate in your survival efforts) in the same gun. The shotgun's disadvantage is that the gun itself is fairly heavy and the shells take up a fair amount of space in the emergency kit.

I used to carry a lightweight, single-shot shotgun, but after talking to people who deal with grizzly bears on a regular basis, I decided to switch to the six-shot pump. I've been told that at close range, the only thing that will stop a charging grizzly is a 12-gauge rifled slug—and it might take five or six of them to do it. I hope I never have to find out if I've been told right. (Incidentally, these same people also tell me that any handgun, even a powerful .44 Magnum, is pretty much worthless against a charging bear.)

If you're not flying in bear country, you won't need such a high-powered weapon. There is at least one .22-caliber rifle on the market, the Charter Arms AR-7 Explorer, that is designed specifically as a survival gun. The AR-7's barrel and receiver break down and store inside the gun's plastic stock. The disassembled gun is small, and it floats—both handy features to a floatplane pilot. Another good survival gun is the Savage Model 24. This over-and-under combination gun has a .22-caliber rifle barrel on top and a .410 or 20-gauge shotgun barrel on the bottom. All of the rifles and shotguns I've described comply with Canada's firearms regulations.

Insect protection is extremely important. Whether you're flying in Alaska, northeastern Canada, or Louisiana, the bugs can drive you nuts. Mosquitoes are not the only culprits. The northeastern United States and eastern Canada are home to the notorious blackfly, a small, biting fly that has been known to drive deer so insane that they literally run themselves to death. By comparison, mosquitoes are downright friendly. Blackflies are bad enough on a regular camping trip, but in a survival situation, they could easily disrupt all your efforts to remain calm and organized.

Another insect annoyance are the tiny, biting gnats called "no-see-ums." They got their name from their almost invisible presence, but skin that's been exposed to their microscopic bites will itch maddeningly for days. As far as I'm concerned, they're worse than mosquitoes. They can get inside the best of tents, and even a screened cabin can't offer complete protection.

Nothing is totally effective against insects, so the solution is to carry several forms of protection. Plenty of insect repellent is a must, and it's also a good idea to carry a headnet for each occupant of the airplane, even if it's not required by law. Choose your repellents carefully. The ingredients of some of the more popular brands have been known to cause dizziness and other problems, particularly in children. The past few years have seen the introduction of several new repellents based on natural ingredients, and you might want to consult your doctor before you make your decision.

If you're planning to wear short-sleeved shirts during your trip, carry a long-sleeved shirt with you anyway. It will help protect you from the bugs if you're forced down.

The Mylar "space blankets" available in many sporting goods stores take up very little room and can save the day if your sleeping bag gets soaked. A large plastic tarp doesn't take up much room either, and in the event of an emergency, it can be used to make a temporary shelter or a windbreak. Tarps are available in a variety of bright colors, and an orange or yellow tarp will make your location easier to spot from the air. Be sure to include several large plastic garbage bags in your survival kit. In an emergency, they make excellent rain ponchos, and they will be invaluable if you have to treat someone suffering from hypothermia.

Because you're flying a floatplane, you should have a life jacket on board for each occupant. As of this writing, the requirements for life jackets are getting stricter in both the United States and Canada. All aircraft operating in Canada farther than gliding distance from shore or taking off and landing on the water must carry approved life jackets meeting the Federal Aviation Administration Technical Standard Order (TSO) C13c. The life jacket must be equipped with a light and must have a buoyancy of at least 35 pounds. Older approved jackets had a buoyancy of anywhere from nine to 20 pounds and would not always right a wearer who was face-down in the water. An average adult has a buoyant weight of 10 to 12 pounds when immersed in water. Incidentally, Canadian law also requires that all aircraft operating more than 50 nautical miles from shore carry a life raft.

In January 1983, the FAA passed TSO C13d, which sets the standards for life jackets required in the United States. A jacket meeting the TSO C13d requirements must be able to be donned in 15 seconds, must have a 35-pound buoyancy, and must be able to right the wearer from a face-down position within five seconds. A light is not required unless the flight will take the aircraft more than 30 minutes flying time or 100 nautical miles from shore.

REQUIRED EMERGENCY EQUIPMENT

Federal Aviation Regulation (FAR) Part 91.509 spells out the survival equipment you are required to have on board for overwater flights in the United States; the regulation applies to landplanes as well as seaplanes. If your flight is going to take you more than 50 nautical miles from the nearest shoreline, you must have an approved life vest or flotation device on board for each occupant of the airplane. If you are never going to be more than 50 nautical miles from shore, you aren't legally required to carry life jackets, but you should anyway. A half-mile swim might be as impossible as a 50-mile swim for a child or someone who is out of shape. Store the life jackets where they will be easy to reach in a hurry (not in the baggage compartment), and periodically check the CO_2 bottles for leakage. If your life jackets have lights, make sure the batteries are good. Whenever you plan to conduct a flight at low altitude over water, you and your passengers should put on life jackets before you take off. An engine failure could put you in the water very quickly, and you might not have time to get a life jacket out of its pouch under the seat and put it on.

The airplanes I fly are equipped with life jackets, but I prefer to wear a flotation vest. The vest has a buoyancy of 15 pounds, and while it won't right me if I'm face-down in the water, it will support me if I right myself. Of course, in the event of an accident, I would put a life jacket on over the vest, but by already having the vest on, I'm that much better off. The advantage of wearing a flotation vest, or one of the long-sleeve flotation coats, is that it's comfortable, so you'll be more likely to wear it. It will also offer some protection against hypothermia should you end up in the water.

A word of caution: New materials and manufacturing techniques are making possible some extremely buoyant flotation garments that also offer warmth and protection from the wind. They are expensive, but well worth their cost in an actual survival situation. Be careful about wearing them in the plane, however. If your airplane should flip over on the water, the bulk and buoyancy of these garments could keep you pinned up against the floor of the plane, making it difficult, if not impossible, for you to swim out through the cabin door to safety. It would be better to keep the garment where you can reach it quickly in the event of an accident. Then, if you have to get out of the cabin in a hurry, you can push the garment ahead of you or pull it behind you as you leave. Either way, it won't impede your exit.

If you are going to be flying over water for more than 30 minutes, or if you are going to be more than 100 nautical miles from the nearest shoreline, you're required to carry additional emergency equipment. This equipment is also spelled out in FAR Part 91.509, and consists of:

☐ A life vest with an approved light for each occupant of the airplane.

☐ Enough life rafts to accommodate you and all your passengers. Each life raft must be equipped with an approved light.

☐ At least one pyrotechnic device (flare) per raft.

☐ One floating, water-resistant, battery-powered emergency locator transmitter (ELT).

☐ At least one lifeline.

☐ One survival kit per raft. The survival kit should be equipped for the route to be flown.

Air-taxi and commercial operators are governed by FAR Part 135. The list of required emergency equipment for extended over water commercial operations is found under Part 135.167. (An extended overwater operation is any flight that goes beyond 50 nautical miles from the nearest shoreline.) The equipment list for Part 135 operators includes:

☐ An approved life vest for each occupant of the airplane. Each vest must be equipped with a light.

☐ Enough life rafts to accommodate all the occupants of the airplane. Each raft must be equipped with the following items: canopy, radar reflector, bailing bucket, signal mirror, police whistle, knife, CO_2 bottle for emergency inflation, inflation pump, two oars, 75-foot lifeline, magnetic compass, dye marker, flashlight, at least one pyrotechnic signaling device (flare), two-day supply of emergency food rations, seawater desalting kit for every two people or two pints of fresh water per person, fishing kit, survival manual.

☐ At least one of the rafts must have attached to it an approved emergency locator transmitter meeting the requirements of TSO-C91.

This list was designed for commercial operators whose flights take them over large bodies of water such as the Great Lakes, the Caribbean, or the Gulf of Mexico; however, other items on it would certainly come in handy for any of us in an emergency, no matter what body of water we ended up in. The size and expense of the equipment are the limiting factors for those of us who fly only for recreation.

HYPOTHERMIA

If your floatplane flips over or sinks, the greatest threat to your life will not be the accident itself, but the danger of succumbing to hypothermia while you await rescue. *Hypothermia* is a subnormal body temperature, and many people don't realize how dangerous this can be. What's worse, many of the things we do to warm ourselves up only succeed in cooling us down even more.

Hypothermia is not as dangerous to people living in warmer, southern climates as it is to people living or traveling in the northern United States, Canada, and Alaska, but the fact that you're flying in Florida doesn't mean you can forget about hypothermia altogether. If your plane flips over on a southern lake some evening, and the night is cool, you can succumb to hypothermia as easily as the person who falls off a fishing boat in the Gulf of Alaska. The only difference will be in the amount of time it will take for hypothermia to set in. If the water temperature is less than 50 degrees, hypothermia will occur within minutes of immersion unless the body is somehow insulated from the cold.

The crucial factor in hypothermia is the temperature of the body's core, where the organs necessary to sustain life are located. The normal temperature of the human body averages around 98.6 degrees, and it doesn't have to drop very far before hypothermia sets in. A drop of only two or three degrees in core temperature will make a person extremely cold, and he or she will begin to shiver violently. This is the first stage of hypothermia. If the temperature of the body core continues to drop, but remains above 90 degrees, the victim will complain of being bitterly cold, will continue to shiver violently, and might be slightly uncoordinated; however, he or she will be able to move around fairly normally, will be coherent, and, with the proper rewarming techniques, will survive.

If the core temperature falls below 90 degrees, the victim will be uncoordinated and unable to walk. He or she will probably seem disoriented, be unable to speak coherently, and might also be very stiff. If the core temperature drops below 80 degrees, the victim will most likely lose consciousness. Statistics show that 65 percent of the victims whose core temperatures fall below 90 degrees will die if they are not treated properly during the rewarming process.

Prevention

If you find yourself in the water after an accident, there are several things you can do to delay the onslaught of hypothermia. First, try to get as much of your body out of the water as you can. When a floatplane flips over, it generally remains floating upside down if the floats have not been damaged. By climbing onto the bottom of a float, you won't lose body heat to the water. If the plane sinks, try to find some floating debris, such as a seat cushion, to help raise your body even a few extra inches out of the water.

Don't swim or thrash about in an effort to stay warm. While this activity will generate some heat, it will also speed up the pulse and increase the flow of warm blood to the arms and legs, where it will be cooled and returned to the heart, lowering the core temperature even faster. Unless the shore is very close, don't attempt to swim to it. Cold water can bring even an excellent swimmer to a stop within three quarters of a mile. Remain motionless in the water or on the float until help comes. This is one reason it's so important to be wearing a life jacket. If you're in the water, the jacket will buoy you up and you won't have to move your arms or legs to remain on the surface. If you are by yourself, bring your knees up to your chest. This will slow down the heat loss. If you're in the water with other people, group together to hold the heat in as long as possible. If you and your passengers are sitting on the bottoms of the floats, huddle close together to minimize the heat loss. These techniques can double your survival time in the water.

While it might be hard to force yourself to remain motionless and do nothing in the face of what seems like certain death, you will only hasten death by thrashing about or attempting to swim to a distant shore. If the water is 50 degrees, the survival time for an adult dressed in lightweight clothing and wearing a life jacket is 2.5 to 3.0 hours. Children succumb to hypothermia faster than adults because their smaller size affords less insulation against heat loss. The longer you can remain alive, the greater will be your chances of being rescued.

Obviously, your actions will be dependent upon the conditions in which you find yourself. The survival times and techniques described above are based upon the 50-degree water of Washington's Puget Sound. If you find yourself bobbing around in the Gulf of Mexico, your situation—from a temperature point of view, at least—won't be as serious, and if you're a good swimmer, you might be able to reach a shore you would have no hope of reaching if you were in the cold waters of Puget Sound.

Treatment

If you and your passengers have safely made it to shore after a capsizing or sinking, but you notice one or more members of your party showing signs of hypothermia, there are specific rules to follow when attempting to reverse the cooling process. First, do not allow the victim to exercise or move about, even if he or she wants to. This will only serve to move warm blood away from the vital organs to the extremities, where it will be cooled and returned to the heart. The victim should lie still until the body temperature begins to rise. It can take well over an hour before the victim begins to show signs of recovery.

Handle the victim gently. Most hypothermia victims die of heart failure, and rough handling might cause ventricular fibrillation. If it's necessary to move the victim, use a stretcher if there is one available. If there is no stretcher, carry the victim in such a way that he or she is not bumped or jostled and does not have to actively hold on to the rescuer. Do not rub or massage the victim. Massaging the chest area can cause the heart to fibrillate.

Remove all wet clothing immediately, but remember to handle the victim gently as you do so. If you roughly turn the victim over in your haste to remove the wet clothes, the movement could be enough to cause the victim's heart to fail. Replace the victim's wet clothing with dry clothing if possible because the moisture in the wet clothes will begin to evaporate and lower the body's temperature even more. If no dry clothes are available, wring out the wet clothes thoroughly and put them back on the victim. Wool garments are especially valuable in this situation because they will retain heat even when wet. Wrapping the victim in a plastic tarp or other nonporous material (i.e., the plastic garbage bag) will help prevent heat loss from evaporation and convection (wind chill). Try to place some sort of insulation between the victim and the ground. Even a plastic tarp or rain poncho will help slow the transfer of crucial body heat to the soil or sand beneath the victim.

Protect the victim from the wind by placing him or her behind a boulder, log, or other windbreak. The movement of air carries heat away from the skin, and as the body tries to replace this heat by increasing the flow of warm blood, the core temperature will begin to drop. In fact, loss of body heat from "wind chill" alone can bring on hypothermia, and it's important that hikers, backpackers, boaters, and bicyclists protect themselves from the cooling effects of the wind. Waterproof rain gear provides excellent wind protection, and if this type of clothing is available, it should be placed over the victim.

The appearance of a rescue helicopter brings another problem: The downwash from a hovering helicopter can exceed 100 miles per hour, and this could rapidly drive the victim's body temperature below the critical point. If the victim is going to be evacuated by helicopter, it's especially important to protect the head and neck from the rotor wash with plastic or some other nonporous fabric. Ideally, the victim's entire body should be wrapped in windproof garments or material before the rescue helicopter positions itself overhead, especially if the victim is going to be lifted directly from the water.

Rewarming

Contrary to popular belief, giving the victim warm liquids will not speed up the rewarming process. In fact, it will do just the opposite because the act of drinking sets up a reflex that moves blood to the extremities and skin. There, the blood will be cooled, and when it returns to the heart, the core temperature will drop some more. Do not give the victim alcoholic beverages. Alcohol makes people feel warmer because it causes an increase in the flow of warm blood to the skin, but this heat is easily lost through evaporation or convection, and the overall effect is to lower the temperature of the body's core.

The same three areas of the body that are so important to protect from the cold in the first place are also the areas where heat should be applied to begin rewarming a hypothermia victim. They are the head and neck, the sides of the chest, and the groin. There is little insulation on these parts of the body, and blood from these areas is quickly transferred back to the heart. Apply heat to these areas using hot water bottles, heating pads, stones warmed by a fire, or anything else you can think of. The warmed blood will quickly pass back to the heart, and the temperature of the body core will begin to rise.

Cover the entire body with blankets during the rewarming process. If no other heat source is available, place the victim in a sleeping bag with one or two other people. In this case, all clothing should be removed to facilitate the heat transfer from the rescuers to the victim; the contact must be skin-to-skin. If a fire is used to warm the victim, remove the victim's insulating clothing because it will prevent the heat from reaching the body. It's important that the victim be taken to a medical facility as soon as possible for further treatment and observation because further complications, such as pneumonia or heart trouble, could arise.

Hypothermia is a quiet killer. Most victims do not realize how serious their condition is. All they know is that they are cold. It does not take long for the condition to progress to the danger point, but by then, the victims will be unable to help themselves. By keeping your head after an accident, and following the basic guidelines outlined above, the chances are excellent that a real tragedy can be averted.

FLOATPLANE RECOVERY

Your first responsibility after an accident is for the health and safety of your passengers and yourself. Only after everyone has been safely returned to civilization should you turn your attention to your airplane. Unless it has been damaged beyond repair, you or your insurance company will probably want to get it back. If you managed to land on a flat piece of ground without damaging the plane, recovery will be a matter of transporting it to a facility where it can be repaired. This will probably involve a partial disassembly of the airplane so it can be moved by truck.

If you were lucky enough to land on a long, flat, grassy field, there might be a chance of flying the plane out once whatever broke has been fixed, but don't count on it unless you picked a field that's at least half again as long as the distance you require for a water takeoff. If you're in the vicinity of an airport, your floatplane can be taken there for repair, and then by using a special dolly, it can be flown off the runway (Fig. 19-1). The dolly will probably have to be constructed on the spot, or you might be able to locate an operator who will ship one to you.

If you went down in sparsely settled country, your plane will probably have to be recovered by helicopter. Here again, the plane will have to be partially disassembled so the helicopter can sling it out. This is an extremely expensive process, but if your plane is relatively undamaged, it probably will be worth it. In some parts of the world—Alaska and northern Canada, for example—airplane parts are so valuable that salvage companies often will purchase and recover a plane that is

Fig. 19-1. *A Cessna 180 using a specially constructed dolly to take off from a paved runway. When the plane lifts off, brakes on the dolly are automatically activated to bring it to a stop so it can be retrieved.* EDO Corp.

wrecked beyond repair just so they can strip off and sell all the undamaged parts. Our environmental laws are getting tougher, too, and in some areas of the country—national parks and wilderness areas, for example—it is now illegal to simply abandon a wrecked airplane, even if it's totally destroyed. The owner is responsible to see that all traces of the airplane are removed, regardless of the cost.

Floats are very strong for their weight, but they are thin-skinned and easily punctured. Depending on the severity of the damage, one of two things will happen if you rupture a float: The airplane will sink outright, or the float will take on so much water that you might not be able to get it into the air. Small punctures can often be temporarily fixed with a float repair kit. These kits are similar to the repair kits designed for aluminum canoes and generally consist of precut patches and a bonding agent.

A tear across one or more watertight compartments poses a stickier problem. If one compartment is flooding badly, you can drive most of the water out by stuffing a couple of air mattresses into the compartment and inflating them. There are also heavy-duty air bags designed specifically for this purpose available commercially, along with battery-powered pumps to inflate them. Air bags or mattresses can be used to reduce the water load of a holed float to the point where the plane is light enough to be flown, or they can be used to help raise a floatplane that has sunk.

Whether you use the air mattress method or one of the specially designed bags, there are a couple of precautions you have to take first. Since whatever ripped open the float was on the outside of the compartment, it stands to reason that the jagged edges of the tear will be bent up on the inside of the compartment. If you simply stick an air bag into the compartment and inflate it, the jagged edges of the cut might well deflate it in short order. Make sure you bend or hammer down any jagged edges that could press against and puncture the inflated air bag before you insert the bag into the compartment.

Once you've got a bag or a mattress into the compartment, take care to see that it won't be ripped or punctured by the sharp edge of a stringer or stiffener. Folded tarps or clothing can be used to protect the bag from potentially damaging sections of the float compartment's structure. Finally, try to arrange the air bag or mattress so it will displace the maximum amount of water when it's inflated. Remember, this is a very temporary fix designed to help you make it to the nearest repair facility only. Don't clear a flooded float compartment with an air bag and then expect it to get you through the rest of the season. Sooner or later, it will let you down—literally.

When a floatplane capsizes in the water, its floats will generally continue to support it even though the plane is upside down. If the plane went over onto its back because a wingtip or a float dug into the water while it was moving at high speed, it might have sustained some damage, but if the plane was simply blown over by a strong wind while at a mooring or taxiing slowly, it will probably be completely intact. The challenge is to return the plane to an upright position without causing any additional damage to the airframe. This is not an easy thing to do. An awful lot of un-

damaged, capsized floatplanes have been totally destroyed by inept salvage crews! If your plane should ever become inverted in the water for any reason, make sure the people you engage to recover it are experienced in the field of floatplane salvage.

If your plane capsizes, don't rush immediately to tow it into shallow water. Try to resist the frantic impulse to get the plane onto dry land right now, and take some time to thoroughly check out the situation. Of course, the best thing you can do is to hire an experienced floatplane salvage company that can approach the problem objectively, something you might not be able to do in your anxiety to save your plane.

Towing the plane to shallow water increases the risk of dragging it upside down across the bottom, which would result in substantial damage. If it is necessary to move the plane, tow it extremely slowly. The wing, tail, and control surfaces were designed to fly through air, not slide through water, and they can buckle easily if forced through the water at too great a speed.

Don't begin the recovery operation until you're prepared to deal with the airplane once it's lifted out of the water. Interior components, radios, and instruments will have to be removed immediately, cleaned, and dried in an attempt to prevent rust or corrosion from forming. The engine will have to be flushed out and dried as well.

If the plane has been immersed in saltwater, the situation is very serious. The water will work its way into every corner and crack of the airframe, and unless the entire plane is thoroughly flushed out with fresh water, corrosion could eventually render the plane unairworthy. A method often used to halt the spread of corrosion on a plane that has just been removed from saltwater is to quickly remove the wings and tail surfaces and immerse them, together with the fuselage, in a freshwater lake. As the fresh water permeates the entire airplane, all the salt will be flushed away.

If your plane has capsized near the end of the day, it would be better to leave it in the water overnight and begin the recovery operation in the morning because it is vital that the flushing and drying operations be carried out as soon as the plane is exposed to the air. Carefully move the plane to water deep enough to safely float the plane, but shallow enough to enable recovery if it should sink. If the plane is in tidal waters, make sure it won't hit the bottom when the tide goes out. Moor the plane to an anchored boat or barge, taking precautions to keep the plane from being damaged against the vessel during the night. If it's not practical to moor the plane to a boat, put out several anchors to keep the plane from drifting into shallow water and mark the spot with a separately anchored buoy. If the plane sinks during the night, the buoy will enable you to find it in the morning.

There are probably as many ways to right a capsized floatplane as there are ways to capsize it in the first place. The ingredients common to all of them are ingenuity, experience, and the right equipment. Jay J. Frey, the EDO Corporation's vice president in charge of their float operation, recommends the following technique in his book *How to Fly Floats*: "Position a salvage vessel equipped with a crane off the tail of the airplane and position the end of the boom so it is directly above the propeller. Place a lifting bridle around the propeller and slowly and gently raise the nose of the airplane out of the water. It's important to have plenty of extension on the boom so the plane will not be pulled back into the salvage vessel as it is being raised. Lift the plane in small increments, allowing time for the water to drain from the fuselage and wings between lifts. This is specially important if the floatplane is fabric-covered, as the weight of the water could easily rip the fabric off the airframe or bend the metal tubing. Some salvage experts cut small slits in the fabric along the trailing edge of the wings to help the water escape.

"When the lifting rings on the upper surfaces of the wings are exposed, secure the plane to the boom with a temporary line and reattach the lifting bridle to the rings. Remove the temporary line and continue lifting the plane until it's in a vertical position. After pumping the water out of the float compartments that are above the surface, attach a line to the tiedown ring on the tail and, using another boat, pull the tail of the floatplane away from the primary salvage vessel. This will restore the plane to an upright position, and it can be lifted into the air in a level attitude. Before lifting the plane clear of the water, be sure to pump out the remaining float compartments so the weight of the water trapped inside won't stress or break the float struts or their attach points.

"If the plane is structurally undamaged, it can be towed to shore on its own floats, but if you suspect it might have sustained damage—particularly to the float system—the plane should be set onto the deck of the salvage vessel or transported to shore while suspended from the crane. As soon as the floatplane is set on shore, begin the process of flushing, cleaning and drying immediately. Repairing the damage sustained during the accident is secondary to protecting the plane from corrosion. If you have an accident and are in doubt as to the best method of recovering your airplane, a long-distance call to a seaplane base experienced in the techniques of floatplane recovery and repair

Fig. 19-2. *Mechanics at Kenmore Air Harbor begin the long process of rebuilding a Beaver. This one was acquired from military surplus. The company specializes in taking old, worn-out, or wrecked Beavers and turning them into airplanes that are better than they were when they first rolled out of the factory.*

will be well worth the cost (Fig. 19-2). If you are unfamiliar with these facilities, a call to one of the float manufacturers or the national headquarters of the Seaplane Pilots Association can get you the names of qualified repair facilities in your area."

I hope you never have to put the survival and airplane recovery information contained in this chapter into use. The modern floatplane is a strong, reliable machine, and as long as you exercise good judgment while operating it, your flights will always end with both you and your plane on an even keel.

20
Floatplane maintenance

ACCORDING TO THE FAA, the average age of the general aviation fleet in this country hovers between 23 and 27 years. As of this writing, Cessna has announced plans to resume manufacturing some of its single-engine airplanes, but even if we begin seeing new 206s at the docks again, most of the seaplanes you're going to be flying will be several to many years old. Old does not have to mean worn out or unsafe. It's all a matter of maintenance, some of it mandated (i.e., the 100-hour inspection) and some of it plain, ordinary, common sense.

It's not my intention to teach you to be a mechanic. I'm not qualified, for one thing, and even if I was, it would take a book much larger than this one to do the job. But if you are aware of the problems that can affect a floatplane and know the danger signs, there are a lot of do-it-yourself tasks to prolong the life of your plane.

THE MAINTENANCE ATTITUDE

The single, most effective thing you can do to keep your floatplane in top condition is to have the desire to do it. If you don't want to take the time to keep corrosion at bay or prevent rust from ruining the door hinges, you won't. If being presented with a massive repair bill doesn't bother you, or if you find the idea of flying with the risk of an in-flight structural failure stimulating, okay. Ignore the plane. But if you're like most pilots and airplane owners, you probably want to do everything within your means to avoid either occurrence.

The secret of successful airplane maintenance isn't to do one big thing once or twice a year, but to do a whole lot of little things *all* year. An hour spent inspecting, cleaning, and greasing after every few flights can do wonders. A floatplane is a piece of machinery, and, like all pieces of machinery, it rusts, corrodes, sticks, jams, cracks, and breaks. And like all pieces of machinery, every part on a floatplane is attached to another part. (As we like to say at Boeing, "No one flies alone.") The corroded bracket you notice today might look like it can wait a while to be fixed, but if it fails before you get around to it, that cheap, busted bracket might cause the really expensive part that's attached to it to fail, as well (Fig. 20-1).

If you spot a problem that is beyond your ability or qualifications to remedy yourself, bring it to the attention of a reputable mechanic or shop that has experience with floatplanes. It's a little like going to the dentist. We'd much rather put it off, but if we don't take care of that cracked tooth now, it's a sure bet we'll be looking at a root canal later.

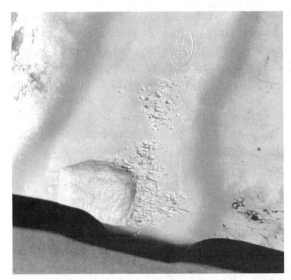

Fig. 20-1. *This float attachment fitting from a Cessna 185 is corroded to the point of no longer being airworthy. If it broke during a landing, the fuselage could drop down between the float struts. At best, a huge repair bill. At worst, a sinking and maybe even a wilderness survival situation.* EDO Corp.

I can't stress enough the importance of taking your plane to a shop that specializes in floatplane repair. A mechanic who tells you an airplane is an airplane is a mechanic who's never worked on a floatplane. True, the Cessna 185 that left the factory on wheels isn't any different mechanically from the Cessna 185 that ended up on floats, but the similarity ends there. Floatplane mechanics have to understand the sneaky nature of corrosion and know the out-of-the-way places to look for it. Once they find it, they have to know what to do about it. They have to be familiar with a whole range of corrosion-inhibiting liquids and sprays. They have to know about electrolysis and have some tricks up their sleeves to combat it. They have to be comfortable working with the extremely tight rivet pitch (rivet spacing) used on aluminum floats. They have to understand sealants and bonding agents. They have to know why the brightest, shiniest, and hardest paints aren't necessarily the right ones to use on a floatplane.

Aircraft repair is a competitive business. By all means, shop around for the best cost estimate. But if the landplane shop that gave you the lowest quote does the job incorrectly, getting its poor work corrected could cost you more than the higher quote you received from the shop that knows floatplanes backward and forward.

WHAT IS CORROSION?

The most persistent enemy you'll have to deal with in maintaining your floatplane is *corrosion*, which is the deterioration of metal as a result of its interaction with its environment. This interaction can take several forms. Many metals, when they come into contact with oxygen, will begin to deteriorate, or *oxidize*. In the case of iron and steel, we call it rust. On aluminum, we just call it corrosion. Some of these metals, iron and aluminum among them, protect themselves from corrosion by forming a thin layer of oxide on their surfaces. Oxygen cannot penetrate the oxide layer, and the metal underneath is protected from further corrosion. This works great when the surface is dry, but if the surface is wet, a chemical change occurs in the oxide layer that allows oxygen to penetrate through to the metal underneath, and the corrosion process continues. Given the floatplane's environment, it's obvious why we can't count on a metal's natural oxide layer to resist corrosion.

The aluminum used in everyday products like soda cans and airplanes is actually an *alloy* of aluminum and other metals. Alloys are better suited for structural use, and they're cheaper to use than pure aluminum, which is extremely expensive. Most of the nonaluminum metals used in the alloys are not as corrosion-resistant as pure aluminum, so a *cladding process* was developed that applies a thin coating of pure aluminum to the surface of the alloy sheets. The cladding does a great job of protecting the alloy sheet from corrosion unless it is damaged or penetrated in some way. Cutting aluminum-alloy sheets into fuselage panels or wing skins and drilling holes for fasteners compromises the cladding.

If an airplane is built properly with the skins fastened tightly, the rivets properly set, and the metal cleaned, treated, and finished at the appropriate stages in the manufacturing process, the opportunities for corrosion to spread into the core material underneath the cladding will be all but eliminated. But once that plane begins to fly, skins flex, rivets work loose, and gaps open up—all invitations for corrosion to come on in and have a party. If left unchecked, core corrosion can reduce aluminum alloy to powder. It's crucial that you keep an eye on the places where core corrosion can get a toehold; rivet heads and skin joints are two places to inspect carefully.

The key to holding surface corrosion at bay is to keep oxygen from touching the metal on your plane. Paint, corrosion-resistant plating, and spray- or brush-on chemical coatings are your weapons. Core corrosion, on the other hand, is like cancer. Once it's started, the only way to eliminate it is to cut it out and put new metal in its place.

Throwing salt into the equation just makes things worse. Anyone who has owned a car in a community that puts salt on the roads to remove ice knows what salt and moisture can do to metal. If you operate your floatplane in saltwater, your fight against corrosion is going to be a lot tougher than the person who flies in the lake country of Minnesota. Temperature is also a factor in the spread of corrosion. Warm climates and water are significantly more conducive to corrosion than cold climates. All other things being equal, the person who flies a floatplane in the Florida Keys is going to see corrosion develop a lot sooner and spread a lot faster than someone who operates in the cold, freshwater lakes of Ontario and Manitoba.

There's another cause of corrosion that's far more difficult to comprehend and deal with. *Electrolysis* is the decomposition into ions of a material in a solution by the action of an electric current passing through that solution. Let's talk about the solution, or "electrolyte," first. Put simply, the *electrolyte* is the water your floatplane is sitting in. Pure water doesn't conduct electricity, but I defy you to find anything resembling pure water where you fly your plane. Saltwater is out; even electric eels figured out how good a conductor it is, and they depend on that conductivity for lunch. But the fresh water in our lakes conducts electricity, too, thanks to pollutants, algae, acid rain, naturally occurring chemicals, and animal waste. As far as your floatplane is concerned, any water it comes in contact with is an electrolyte.

So where do we get the electricity? None of us are dumb enough to drop the bare end of an electrical cable into the water next to our floatplanes and turn the power on. Unfortunately, electrolysis doesn't need any help from us to eat away at the metal on our airplanes. The molecular makeup of a metal gives it an electrical characteristic all its own. When a piece of metal comes in contact with an electrolyte, an *electrochemical*, or *galvanic*, reaction occurs, and electricity is produced. If a piece of metal with a different molecular makeup is added to the same electrolyte, the electricity produced will flow from one piece to the other.

The farther apart the two metals are on the galvanic chart (Fig. 20-2), the greater will be the electrical current between them, and the faster that electrolysis will occur. As to which piece of metal will decompose, the material with the most negative, or *anodic*, potential will experience accelerated corrosion when it's electrically connected to a material with a more positive, or *noble*, potential. In other words, the metal farthest down the chart is the loser. If you put a piece of stainless steel into an electrolyte with a piece of zinc, the zinc will decompose while the stainless steel will remain untouched. Now let's drop a third piece of metal into the electrolyte, a piece of aircraft aluminum. Electricity will be running around all over the place, but the piece of zinc is still the lowest thing on the chart, so it's history.

But what happens if we take the piece of zinc out of the electrolyte? Without the zinc to beat up on, electrolysis will attack the next lowest metal on the chart, which in this case is the piece of air-

Positive potential

1. Graphite
2. Platinum
3. Titanium
4. Nickel-iron-chromium alloy 825
5. Alloy 70 stainless steels, cast and wrought
6. Stainless steel-types 310, 317
7. Nickel-copper alloys 400, K500
8. Stainless steel-types 302, 304, 321, 347
9. Silver
10. Nickel 700
11. Silver-bronze alloys
12. Nickel-chromium alloy 600
13. Nickel aluminum bronze
14. 70-30 copper nickel
15. Lead
16. Stainless steel-type 430
17. 80-20 copper nickel
18. 90-10 copper nickel
19. Nickel silver
20. Stainless steel-types 410, 416
21. Tin bronze
22. Silicon bronze
23. Manganese bronze
24. Admiralty brass, aluminum brass
25. Copper
26. Tin
27. Naval brass, yellow brass, red brass
28. Aluminum bronze
29. Austenitic nickel cast iron
30. Low alloy steel
31. Low carbon steel, cast iron
32. Cadmium
33. Aluminum alloys
34. Beryllium
35. Zinc
36. Magnesium

Negative potential

Fig. 20-2. *The Galvanic chart.*

craft aluminum. Now expand the picture. You moor your floatplane in a polluted lake to a dock held in place by steel pilings. You've got a hunk of steel in an electrolyte with a piece of aluminum. Look at the chart and figure out what will happen.

Now that I've thoroughly terrified you with an image of your floatplane dissolving away before your eyes because you happened to tie up to a steel dock, you should know that the electrical

currents we're talking about are pretty low, and they vary with the conductivity of the water and the physical distance between the metals involved. Electrolysis can do serious damage in a short time under ideal conditions, but you're going to be more concerned with preventing its effects over the long run.

WHERE CORROSION OCCURS

Any unprotected metal surface on your floatplane will be a target for corrosion. If the paint's worn thin and pitted on the leading edges of the wings and tail surfaces, surface corrosion will soon invade. If one of the floats has scraped hard enough against a dock to remove the paint and primer, expect to see corrosion there, especially if the scratch penetrated the cladding. Anyplace where water can collect is susceptible to corrosion. The unfortunate thing here is that most of these places are hidden away inside the structure of your plane (Fig. 20-3). The tailcone, stabilizer, and elevators are favorite spots for moisture

Fig. 20-3. *Severe corrosion on the metal surfaces of a Super Cub. The owner had no idea things had gotten this bad, as most of the damage was hidden behind the wing fairing.* EDO Corp.

to collect because they're drenched in spray every time you take off and land. Some planes have rubber strips cemented to the leading edges of wings and tail surfaces, while others use urethane foam to strengthen the trailing edges of ailerons and elevators. Both provide excellent places for moisture to collect, and as the glues attaching them break down, they might attack the paint underneath, aiding the spread of corrosion even more.

Many of the load-bearing bolts and fasteners on a floatplane are made of steel. To protect the steel from corrosion, a plating of *cadmium* often is applied during the manufacturing process. A quick glance at the galvanic chart will tell you what happens next. The floatplane's environment encourages electrolysis, the cad plating disappears, and the steel underneath rusts. This is not a screwup on the part of the bolt manufacturers. They know that an unprotected steel bolt will rust right away. They also know that painting the bolt won't do much good because the paint will come off the threads when the bolt is inserted, and it will probably chip off the head, too. Under normal usage, the cadmium won't chip off, and it will adhere to every part of the bolt, including the threads. Cad plating is a way of maximizing the life of a steel fastener in an environment that's very unfriendly to steel. The thing that's important for you to know is that an unprotected cad-plated fastener will eventually lose its cadmium plating, and the steel itself will begin to rust (Fig. 20-4).

Jay Frey, who runs EDO's float division and probably knows more about floats and float maintenance than anybody, told me about an owner who decided to replace all the cad-plated screws and bolts on his floatplane with stainless steel. He was fed up with replacing rusty fasteners, he said, and was going to solve the problem once and for all. The owner might have had an exasperating situation before, but after he installed the stainless steel fasteners, he had a disaster. The galvanic chart tells the story. Stainless steel and aluminum alloys are far apart on the chart, and the aluminum alloys are at the bottom. Electrolysis had a field

Fig. 20-4. *The attachment eyebolt of this float has lost its cad plating and has rusted over completely. The proper course of action in this case would be to install a new eyebolt.* EDO Corp.

day with the man's floatplane, and the repair bills were astronomical. Cadmium, on the other hand, is right next to aluminum alloys on the chart, and electrolysis is not a problem.

The tougher the aluminum alloy, the faster it will corrode. Attachment castings, float keels, chines, and other components that have to stand up under a load generally are made of 2024 or 7075 alloy. Skin panels, on the other hand, are made of softer 6061 alloy. Parts made of 2024 and 7075 are likely to show signs of corrosion first. The extrusion process that forms 2024 into stringers, keels, and chines renders the alloy even more susceptible to corrosion. And if that weren't bad enough, the extruded parts on a float are the ones that receive the most wear by rubbing against docks and grinding across beaches. The paint is the first thing to go, followed by the cladding, and corrosion has a new meal to munch on.

Algae attached to and growing on the submerged portions of an aluminum float can create a pH condition that pits the extruded keels and chines. The pitting then opens the door to corrosion. The conditions promoting the growth of algae are now so extensive across the United States that leaving an aluminum boat or seaplane in the water for more than a couple of days will see an accumulation of slime. If not cleaned off immediately, this slime rapidly develops into a full-blown crop of growing algae, and the attack on the aluminum begins. Brown algae lines below the waterline indicate a condition that could rapidly lead to a corrosion problem severe enough to compromise the strength of the float (Fig. 20-5).

FIGHTING CORROSION

Your primary defense against corrosion is to make sure there is no exposed metal on your floatplane. Your plane and floats should be painted, and the paint should be in good condition. Places where the paint has been chipped or scraped off should be cleaned, primed, and repainted immediately (Fig 20-6).

Interior surfaces where water tends to collect should be coated with a brush or spray-on inhibitor. When applied properly, products such as ACF-50, Corrosion-X, and Boeshield (a corrosion inhibitor developed by Boeing for use on commercial jetliners), all do an excellent job of sealing out moisture. While applying an inhibitor is not difficult, getting at all the places that need it is. This is one job where you'll probably need to enlist the help of a quali-

fied shop to ensure that the inhibitor completely covers the inner surfaces of the fuselage, tail, and control surfaces. Lightweight oils like WD-40 and LPS-1 can be useful for freeing stuck parts or inhibiting rust development on engines, but you shouldn't depend on them to provide long-term, heavy-duty corrosion protection on the structure of your plane. In fact, some floatplane owners claim light oils promote corrosion by migrating underneath rivet heads and loosening the fasteners.

All the different sprays and chemicals have different characteristics, and something that works well in the hot, humid climate of the Gulf of Mexico might not be as effective in the colder weather of the Pacific northwest. There are cases where owners living in dusty climates have sprayed light, sticky preservatives on the inside of their airplanes' wings, only to have it come back to haunt them as the whole thing degenerated into a filthy, gooey mess that fouled control cables and clogged the pulleys.

The first thing you should do is ask the local operators and mechanics which treatments they've found to be most effective in your area. The best treatments aren't always the newest or the most high-tech. Many floatplane operators like to coat the steel and cad-plated components on their planes with Black Bear Paralketone. The stuff's been

Fig. 20-5. *The dark patches around the chine of the floats on this Citabria are evidence of the damage being caused by algae buildup on the aluminum.* EDO Corp.

Fig. 20-6. *This Beaver float strut attachment fitting is showing severe corrosion around the attachment bolt holes. This normally would be hidden behind the lower end of the strut and could go unnoticed. The fitting also shows signs of stress corrosion, and there is no cad plating left on the bolts.* EDO Corp.

around forever, at least since World War II, but it does a very effective job of protecting bolts, nuts, fasteners, engine-mount fittings, turnbuckles, wires, cables, and any other bare metal parts you come across (Fig. 20-7). Paralketone is very sticky, and it can dry hard, so be careful not to get it on moving parts, or on cables where they run through guides or pulleys.

Fig. 20-7. *This is how the fittings on a float should look. The cad plating on the bolts is intact, and the entire fitting has been coated with Black Bear Paralketone.* EDO Corp.

Another product you can use to coat steel and cad-plated parts is LPS-3. It sprays on and dries to a waxy film. It's not as tough as paralketone, but it won't cement all the nuts and bolts on your plane together, either, which is a real plus if you switch from floats to wheels or skis each year.

The downside of applying corrosion inhibitors to the fittings on your airplane is that they promote dirt buildup. I regularly coat all the steel fittings on my galvanized boat trailer with LPS-3, and while I've managed to keep the rust to a minimum, the trailer looks pretty bad with dirty, dark blotches of road grime around every fitting. Floatplanes live in a cleaner environment, but there's still the dust that blows around the tiedown area and the carbon particles that come out of the exhaust stack. The only solution is to clean the stuff off periodically and reapply it.

Grease is an important corrosion fighter when it comes to moving parts. Put a generous coating on the aileron, elevator, rudder, trim tab, door, and window hinges. A lot of spray gets blown up under the wing by the propeller, so lower the flaps and liberally coat the flap tracks, rollers, and pushrods with grease. Grease the water-rudder hinges and pivots; also grease the pulleys that guide the steering and retraction cables. Admittedly, this can get a little messy. At the end of a day's flight you might have dirty streaks down the sides, wings, and tail of your airplane, but messy-looking grease is a lot easier to remove than corrosion.

It's very important that you use the proper type of grease. Don't be tempted to use automotive wheel-bearing grease, for example. Yes, it's inexpensive and readily available, but it breaks down badly when it comes in contact with water, particularly saltwater, and you'll end up doing more harm than good. Again, the answer is to talk to the local floatplane experts, and use the grease that they've found works best in the local environment.

If during the course of one of your inspections, you come across a steel bolt or screw that's starting to rust, have it replaced. The rust indicates that the cadmium plating is shot; you might be able to remove the rust with steel wool or a wire brush and then apply paint or a corrosion inhibitor, but that would be a temporary fix at best. You'll be better off replacing the fastener with a new one. But you must do *something*. Leaving a rusty fastener to be dealt with later could prove to be an expensive decision.

Combating electrolysis takes some skill and ingenuity. The best thing you can do is keep your plane out of the water when you aren't using it. This also solves the algae problem, by the way. Floatplane bases generally have railcars, elevators, or trailers to pull floatplanes out of the water so they can be moved to a tiedown area. If you keep your floatplane at home or docked at your vacation property, consider purchasing one of the small elevators that are designed to lift and hold a plane clear of the water. The Nyman Marine Corporation of Issaquah, Washington, for example, makes a line of boat and seaplane lifts that are powered by the water pressure from a garden hose.

If your plane is going to spend a lot of time in the water, however, you'll have to take specific steps to thwart electrolysis. Stay away from metal objects that are higher up the galvanic chart than your airplane. I've heard of one floatplane owner who kept his 206 tied to a chain that was in turn fastened to a submerged Caterpillar tractor. It wasn't long before the owner began to wonder why his float chines were dissolving.

There's only one way to ensure you won't be the victim in the electrolysis wars, and that's to make sure there's always something in the vicinity that's even lower on the galvanic chart than your airplane. The lowest thing on the chart is magnesium, but it's expensive. The next lowest thing is zinc. Zinc is cheap, and it's easily formed into bars that can be mounted to the underside of a float. The boat people have been doing this for years. Even wooden boats will have sacrificial zincs, or anodes, bolted to their bottoms to protect their bronze propellers and iron or steel rudder fittings. My Yamaha outboard has an easily replaced zinc trim tab to protect the aluminum lower unit and steel propeller. Zincs can disappear quite rapidly, depending on the conditions surrounding your moored plane, so include them in your periodic inspections. They're easy to forget about, but once they're gone, your floatplane becomes the target again.

If you have sacrificial zincs installed on your floats, keep in mind that they won't work unless there's a good, solid electrical contact between them and the aluminum they're attached to. Make sure the shop removes all paint and grease from the float where the zinc is to be mounted. After the zincs are attached, don't try to make them look nice by painting them. Painting will insulate the zinc from the water, and your floatplane will go back to the lowest spot on the electrolysis totem pole.

Wash your plane often. If you fly in a saltwater environment, wash it after every flight. Washing will remove the salt and chemical deposits that encourage corrosion and electrolysis. Make sure you flush out all those nooks and crannies where salt can hide, and don't forget to scrub away any slime or algae that might have accumulated on the floats. If it's not possible to get the plane out of the water, you can still wash it down if you can get a hose out to it. As for algae, buy yourself a long-handled mop, one with a head and handle that won't scratch the aluminum on your plane. Walk the length of each float and scrub down the inboard and outboard sides below the waterline—if you can reach underneath to scrub the bottoms, better yet.

It's a good idea to spray the inside of the engine cowl and the engine with a rust-preventing oil such as WD-40 or LPS-1. This will keep moisture and salt spray off the bare-metal parts of the engine. Painting an engine is a good way to protect it from rust and corrosion, but as the engine heats and cools during flight, some of the paint will crack and flake away, particularly on the cooling fins of the cylinders. Spraying on a light oil will prevent these areas from rusting and is particularly effective if your plane is going to be sitting around awhile before its next flight. The best time to spray the engine is while it's still warm after a flight. *Do not, however, spray oil on the engine when it's hot.*

To aid in your ongoing fight against corrosion, make up a chart listing all the items or areas on your plane that are particularly vulnerable. You should include cracks and crevices that can trap moisture, places where dissimilar metals are in contact with each other, castings and fittings made from 2024 or 7075 alloys, steel and cad-plated bolts and fasteners, and skin joints and rivet lines, particularly around the tail. Keep the chart with your airplane's operating manual, and use it each time you inspect the plane. It could help you find and fix a little inexpensive problem before it becomes a big expensive problem.

FIGHTING CORROSION WITH PAINT

All your corrosion-fighting efforts will come to naught if your plane and floats don't have the basic protection afforded by a good-quality, properly applied, paint job. Painting an airplane is a complex, exacting process that must be carried out in a carefully controlled environment. It is not a mask-it-off-and-hit-it-with-a-rented-spray-gun kind of operation. The old paint must be completely removed, the surfaces cleaned of all traces of corrosion, and the bare aluminum cleaned and chemically etched to receive the coats of primer and, finally, paint.

The kind of paint that's applied to your plane will have a great deal to do with how successful you are later in spotting and eliminating corrosion. Polyurethane paints have become very popular in aviation circles because of their toughness and lasting "wet" look. On a landplane, they're great. They're not so great on a floatplane. It's not that they don't look good. The problem is that polyurethane tends to hide any corrosion that might be building up underneath it. By the time

corrosion manages to make itself known underneath the tough polyurethane coating, it will have progressed far beyond the point of a simple repair.

A better paint to use on a floatplane is lacquer over an epoxy primer. True, it will fade over time, and it isn't as tough and scratch-resistant as polyurethane. The advantage lacquer brings to the floatplane owner is that it will bubble up and blister the moment corrosion begins to form beneath it. Spotting corrosion early is the key to treating it successfully, and you can't beat lacquer for waving a red flag the moment the aluminum on your plane is attacked.

The paint applied to the floats is just as important, if not more so, than the paint on the airplane. The silver floats you see under so many floatplanes are painted silver. They are not bare aluminum as many people believe. If your floats need painting, make sure you take them to a shop that knows how to paint floats. It's a different process than painting an airplane, and how well it's done will determine how resistant your floats are to corrosion. I'm not going to describe the entire process of stripping, cleaning, and preparing a float for painting, but there are a couple of steps in the painting process you should know about so you can judge a shop's ability to do the job. The descriptions are taken from the EDO Corporation's recommended painting process for aluminum floats.

After the float is stripped of all paint and corrosion, cleaned, alodined (etched), and cleaned again with solvent, apply a thin coat of wash coat primer. Immediately following the application of the wash coat, apply two covering coats of epoxy primer *or* two covering coats of zinc chromate primer. When the primer has dried, apply two coats of pigmented lacquer. When preparing the lacquer, it is recommended that 12 ounces of extra-fine aluminum paste be mixed with one gallon of clear lacquer. Mix the paste and lacquer thoroughly with the aid of lacquer thinner if necessary. The aluminum paste forms a protective scale that prevents water from penetrating. Another advantage of the aluminum lacquer is that it buffs out easily to hide minor scrapes or scuffs. Finally, EDO recommends spraying the inside of the float with one thin coat of whichever primer has been used on the outside followed by two heavy coats of the same primer. It should take approximately one and a half gallons of lacquer to cover one float.

LEAKS

Floats look a lot tougher than they are. While the structural members (the keels, chines, stringers, and bulkheads) are plenty strong, the skin panels covering them are extremely thin, not much thicker than a heavyweight beer can in some places. Rocks, nails sticking out of docks, even barnacles growing on the sides of tire bumpers can gouge a hole in a float in short order. But there are other, less obvious ways a float can take on water, and you should be on the lookout for them.

One of the most overlooked causes of water in a float is a missing or poorly fitting float ball. You wouldn't think something so obvious would go unnoticed, but there are cases on record of floatplanes sinking at their moorings because the float balls were missing. If you lose one of the float balls or notice that one of them keeps coming out in flight no matter how hard you jam it into its hole during the preflight, replace it immediately. They're not expensive, and the job they do is essential to your airplane's remaining on top of the water. If you take the attitude that your floatplane is not airworthy unless all the float balls are in place and *stay* in place, you'll eliminate a potential source of disaster.

While we're on the subject of float balls, you should regularly inspect each one of the down-tubes in the float compartments for cracks. The down-tubes transmit the vacuum you create with the bilge pump to the bottom of the float compartments to ensure that you remove all the accumulated water. If a tube is cracked halfway down, the vacuum from the pump will go to the crack, but no

farther. You'll pump out the water *above* the crack, but not below it. If one of the float compartments has a leak or a missing float ball and the down-tube has a crack three feet from the bottom, you could have three feet of water in the compartment and never know it.

The hull of an aluminum float is made up of panels that are riveted into place over a skeleton of stringers and bulkheads. To keep water from seeping in through the seams, the skin joints used to be sealed with a zinc chromate putty as the panels were riveted into place. The putty was a good sealant, but it had no adhesive properties. As long as the panels were held tightly in place, the sealant did its job. After awhile, however, twisting and flexing over waves and banging into docks begins to take its toll. Rivets stretch and loosen, and skin panels begin to move—not much, but enough to let the putty slip out. As the putty works its way out of the seams, water begins to work its way in. The loose rivets themselves can become a source of leaks. The strength of the float has not been compromised, but its buoyancy has.

Aluminum floats made today use a different sealant. Unlike the old zinc chromate putty, the new sealants contain an adhesive that, in effect, bonds the aluminum panels together. While he's never done it, Jay Frey of EDO believes that if you were to drill out and remove every single rivet from a pair of brand-new aluminum floats, nothing would happen. The float would remain intact thanks to the tremendous strength of the bonding agent in the sealing compound.

The two areas of a float most susceptible to leaks are around the step and the stern. The step takes quite a pounding during takeoffs and landings, and it is also the part of the float that takes the greatest beating at the dock, especially on the pilot's side. Seams around the stern of the float tend to work loose because of the action and stresses imposed on them by the water rudders.

While we tend to think of a leak in terms of water getting into a float, we can also have a leak within a float, between the watertight compartments. A slight seepage of water from one compartment to another is ordinarily okay unless the plane is going to be left unattended at a mooring for a long period of time. If you can actually see the water trickling between compartments, however, at the rate of a cupful or more every 10 minutes, you should take steps to have the leak repaired.

You can usually cure minor seam and rivet leaks by applying 8509 Slushing Compound. The compound is painted or poured into the seams and joints and onto the rivets from the inside of the float. It is generally put on in three coats over three days. For the first two coats, the compound should have the consistency of water, which can be achieved by mixing it with ethyl acetate. For the last coat, the compound should have the consistency of warm honey. This can be achieved by using it straight out of the can, or by leaving a portion of the compound in an open can overnight. Fumes from slushing compound are pretty strong, so make sure you work in a well-ventilated area.

If the floats are taking on water but the source is not obvious, you'll have to perform a leak test. There are a couple of ways of doing this. The first step in either process is to remove all the inspection plates in the top of the float compartments. The quick and dirty leak test method is to tie your floatplane securely to a trailer and back it down a ramp into the water (Fig. 20-8). Back it in until the floats are submerged deeper than they would normally sit with a full load in the plane, *but not completely submerged*. The reason for tying the plane down now becomes obvious; it will float away if you don't. Use a flashlight with a very bright beam and illumination to check each watertight compartment carefully for leaks. If you find a leak and can reach it with your hand, mark its location with a grease pencil. If you can't reach it, jot down as many references as you can to help you locate the spot when the plane is back on dry land: "25 rivets forward of the bulkhead and 10 rivets up from the chine," for instance.

The second method of finding a leak is more thorough, but it takes more preparation. You will

Fig. 20-8. *We thought we had a leak in one of the center compartments of this Cessna 180, so we decided to have it checked out at the Prince Rupert seaplane base. The plane was tied down to a transportation dolly to keep it from floating away while a mechanic checked each compartment with a flashlight for seam or rivet leaks.*

fill the float with water, but you have to make sure it will support the tremendous weight first. A shop that does this kind of work all the time should have wooden forms cut to fit the most common types of floats. These forms should be placed under each bulkhead, with additional forms supporting the floats between the bulkheads as well as the keel. If forms are unavailable, make sure the keel forward of the step is flat on the floor. Put supports under the keel at the bow and stern, and block up a number of points along the chine. Water weighs a lot. If you completely fill an EDO Model 2000 float, for example, you're asking that float to support one ton of water. Unless you have the proper and approved supporting equipment, the manufacturers recommend that you fill no more than two compartments at any one time, so keep that in mind as you read the following test procedure.

Fill every other compartment with water to check for leaks in the watertight bulkheads. Then fill the remaining compartments to check for exterior leaks. Unless the floats are very well braced, it's a good idea to only fill part of the compartments at any one time; otherwise, all compartments should be filled to the top. Mark any leaks you find with a grease pencil. Pump or siphon out the water; a portable electric pump would make the task much easier. You won't believe how much time and effort it takes to pump a completely flooded float dry with the plane's manual bilge pump.

If the leaks you find are minor, they can be repaired with the slushing compound. If the problem is a few loosened rivets, they can be tightened up or drilled out and replaced. If the float is leaking because a lot of rivets have worked loose and much of the zinc chromate putty is gone, you're probably better off having the floats rebuilt. This is a lot of work, and it's not cheap, but the good news is that if the job is done right, the floats will actually be more watertight and less susceptible to leaks over time than when they were new. The reason for this is the new sealing compounds that are being used today. If you decide to have the floats rebuilt, make sure the shop cleans away all traces of the old zinc chromate putty and reseals the floats with one of the new compounds. The floats will be leakfree for years.

Unless you hit something, of course. Holes and tears in a float should be patched immediately, even if the damage is above the waterline. A lot of water washes over a float during taxi, takeoff, landing, and even just sitting at a dock if there are waves or boat wakes present. You'd be surprised how much water can enter a float through even a three- or four-inch skin tear that is located up near the deck. If you can get at both sides of a tear through a float hatch or access plate, you can minimize the gap by pounding the curled aluminum flat from the inside. Make sure you have a heavy, smooth block to hold against the outside of the float while you're pounding away on the inside. Drying the skin around the tear and cleaning away any oil or slime might make it possible for you to cover the hole with strong tape, but don't think of this as a repair. It's just a way of minimizing the water intake until you can get the plane to someone who can fix it properly.

Most of the floats in service today are made of aluminum, but there are some older fiberglass floats around, and at least one manufacturer is making a new one. While loose rivets and missing seam sealant aren't causes for leaks in fiberglass or composite floats, there are other things to watch out for. Delamination of the composite layers can be a real problem. *Delamination* gets its start when cracks in the gel coat or holes drilled for fittings allow moisture to move by capillary action into voids in the fiberglass. If the outside air temperature falls below freezing, the moisture in the voids freezes and expands, separating the fiberglass layers even more, which in turn allows more moisture to collect. It's a vicious circle, and the only real solution is to cut out the delaminated section and replace it.

Blistering is a problem that might occur in fiberglass floats that are left in the water for long periods of time. The blisters are caused by the buildup of moisture under the gel coat. The frustrating thing is that the location of the blister is not necessarily the location of the moisture-admitting hole in the gel coat. Moisture seeping through the tiny hole can migrate quite a ways before collecting in a void in the fiberglass underneath. The only cure for blistering is to grind off the gel coat and then let the float dry out completely, usually in a heated room. Once all the traces of moisture are gone, the exposed fiberglass is given multiple coats of epoxy paint.

Fiberglass is heavier than aluminum, and it's somewhat more resistant to puncture and tear damage. Damage can occur, of course, and the same rule applies: Get it fixed right away. Repairing a fiberglass or composite float is a lot different than repairing an aluminum float, so make sure the shop that's doing the work understands resins and catalysts and knows how to use them.

AMPHIBIOUS FLOATS

Amphibious floats will require a lot more of your attention than straight floats if they're to remain troublefree. Everything that moves—wheel bearings, bushings, brake calipers, retraction cables, shock struts, gear latches, actuating levers, hydraulic pistons—is a potential source of trouble. The most important preventative maintenance you can perform on an amphibious float is to keep all moving parts greased and, where possible, painted.

If you operate your amphib in saltwater, the washdown becomes even more crucial. Thoroughly flush out the wheelwells behind the step and the slots in the bows that accommodate the nose struts. Keep a close eye on hydraulic fittings and electrical connections to microswitches to make sure they aren't compromised by corrosion. Moving parts wear out, so make it a practice to replace high-wear items like gear latches before they become a problem.

Jay Frey has begun to promote a concept he calls "demating." After examining dozens of maintenance records in the course of investigating problems customers have had with their aircraft or floats, Jay began to realize that at least two thirds of the components and assemblies in our aging general aviation fleet have never been taken apart since they left the factory. That's not to say they haven't been inspected or tested periodically, but the internal subcomponents and subassemblies have never been examined.

In the case of amphibious floats, "demating" means that the more sophisticated components such as pump motors, actuators, shock struts, and gear-retraction mechanisms that would normally be *inspected* for leaks and corrosion every 100 hours should be removed from the airplane and *completely disassembled* every 10 years. All the component's internal parts should be checked for corrosion and wear. Parts in poor condition should be replaced if possible, or if this is not practical, the entire component should be replaced.

Straight floats can benefit from the demating philosophy as well. Frey recommends the complete disassembly of the floats, spreaders, and attachment gear every 20 years. While the attachment gear must be examined as part of the 100-hour and annual inspections, there is no requirement to take it apart.

Frey has seen floats in Alaska with severely corroded spreader bar bolts, but because the attachment gear had never been taken apart, the owners had been totally unaware of how close they had come to losing their airplanes. From the outside, everything had appeared just fine.

When new airplanes were being manufactured, aircraft were being replaced on a 5-year to 10-year basis. With few new planes on the market, we're flying machines that are 20 to 30 years old or even older. Internal problems that we never would have seen before are beginning to surface. While demating a float and its major components can impose a considerable expense on the owner, it's certainly less expensive than having a major failure in a remote area with the potential loss of not only the floatplane but the lives of the occupants as well.

A BASIC MAINTENANCE CHECKLIST

The EDO Corporation has compiled a checklist of float inspections that it recommends be carried out every 100 hours (if your plane is on straight floats, you can ignore the items pertaining to landing gear):

- [ ] Hoist or jack up the airplane to remove all the weight from the landing gear. Shake the gear and wheels to check for looseness.
- [ ] Check the security of the float and fuselage attachment fittings, struts, and tie-rod connections. Tighten and resafety all bolts as required.
- [ ] Check float interiors with a flashlight for loose rivets, dents, or other damage. Check the bottoms. Flush out compartments one at a time with fresh water and watch for seepage between compartments as well as for external leakage.
- [ ] Examine tires for abnormal or excessive wear, cuts, blisters, and pressure. Check tire inflation.

- [ ] Operate brakes and check for sponginess. Bleed and refill system if necessary. Check brake linings for wear within permissible limits. Remove bow and main wheels, check bearings, clean and repack. Lubricate all grease fittings.
- [ ] Check static load positions of shock absorbers. Check torque on shimmy dampers.
- [ ] Check the control cables of the water rudder system and the landing gear retraction system for proper adjustment and rigging loads. Cycle gear and water rudders a minimum of two times. Check all pulleys for rotation.
- [ ] Coat all bare-steel parts (tie-rod terminals, wirepulls, bolt heads, nuts, and other hardware items) with Paralketone or grease over a thin coat of zinc chromate primer.

- [ ] Clean all terminals. Coat the terminals of all electrical parts (microswitches, their plunger actuators, and terminal strips) with Dow Corning No. 4 silicon insulating compound.
- [ ] Check the finish of the floats, struts, and airplane for corrosion. Clean and restore finish as necessary.
- [ ] Check foam gasket on float baggage compartment door for proper sealing.
- [ ] Check hydraulic system reservoir, and fill the reservoir to the proper level, if necessary. Inspect system for leaks.
- [ ] Clean slide tubes, main and bow, with clean oiled cloth. Coat the main gear latch mechanism on top with grease.
- [ ] Check the operation of the emergency hand pump in the three positions for ease of movement. Pump the system up and down, and record the number of strokes.

21
The cross-country floatplane

THE INSIDE PASSAGE to Alaska doesn't run south to north like it's supposed to. It runs east to west in some places and to the northwest in others. After pushing a clattering Beaver straight up the Passage for seven hours, I'm always surprised by the compass heading as I slide down final for the harbor at Ketchikan: 270 degrees. It doesn't seem right. "North to Alaska" should be just that, north.

The Passage is as unpredictable a place as you're likely to find. It can be the easiest flight you've ever made, or it can work you to the point of exhaustion. On a clear day, it's a highway: a narrow ribbon of water stretched taut and gleaming between gray-green walls of cedar, hemlock, and polished rock. A succession of broad arrows on the water below marks your route. They're the wakes of barges, fishing boats, and cruise ships, all of them using the Passage as protection from the heavy winds and swells that tear ceaselessly at the barren shores of the outer islands.

On a bad day, the Passage is a prison: walled by fog and rain, the rocky shoreline a ghostly smudge off the wingtip. The overcast hangs heavily overhead; you fly bent over in your seat, instinctively ducking the ceiling of solid gray above your plane. The altimeter quivers just above the zero mark. Water the color of slate slides by a few feet beneath your float keels. Your eyes dart between the hazy shoreline and the chart you're holding high beside the windscreen. The penciled line arcs around a narrow peninsula; up ahead a bony finger of land eases into focus through the rain-streaked Plexiglas, and you bank toward it. The rain slacks off a bit, and you find you can climb a little and still see. The altimeter hits 100 feet—it feels like 10,000 after what you've just been through—and you level off. The sky ahead seems lighter; perhaps you'll be able to go up another hundred feet.

The next day dawns clear. There's just the right amount of breeze in the harbor; the water is nicely ruffled, and your heavy plane gets off quickly. You've never been to the lake before, so when you get there you go in high, checking it out. There's the cabin, right where the map said it would be, and the aluminum skiff. The plane will go on the beach in front of the cabin. You circle over the saltwater fjord that runs in from the Passage, losing altitude. You're down between the rock walls now, but the wind is still light and there is little turbulence. Your final approach is over the stream that tumbles from the lake through the trees to the fjord, and as you settle off the step, you see two loons diving for fish near the jumble of logs across from the cabin. It's a good sign.

Cross-country in a floatplane—there's nothing like it! It's the payoff for all those hours you've spent practicing landings and dockings. "Cross-country" means many things in the world of water flying. The image that usually springs to mind is the one I've just painted: a long flight to a remote lake where the trout run upward of five pounds and the nearest person is a hundred miles away. I've taken trips like that, and although the trout didn't always live up to my expectations, everything else did. That's one kind of cross-country trip. Another is the flight made every weekday by the business executive who lives on a lake in Connecticut, or along the shore of Long Island, but who works in midtown Manhattan, in New York City. This chapter is aimed primarily at the person contemplating a recreational trip to that lake with the five-pound trout, but the business commuter might find some of the information useful, as well.

Whether you're flying for business or pleasure, a cross-country trip in a floatplane is uniquely different from a cross-country trip in a landplane. I rarely fly a landplane, but when I do, I always feel like an observer, an outsider looking down on the intricate pattern of life. When I fly a floatplane, I feel like a participant.

DESTINATIONS

The first thing you need to do in planning a cross-country trip is figure out where it is you want to go. Where you're going will determine, to large degree, what you have to take with you. For the purposes of description, I've come up with a three-tier classification system for destination categories: Type A, B, or C. There is nothing official about these classifications; if you start talking to another pilot about a "Type-A destination," don't expect much more than a puzzled stare in reply.

What I call a Type-A destination is a city or town with at least one developed seaplane facility. Seattle, Washington, and Prince Rupert, British Columbia, are good examples of Type-A destinations. Each has one or more seaplane bases with tire-lined docks, haul-out equipment, dry-land storage, and dockside fuel. Type A's also have the mechanics and tools necessary to perform just about any kind of maintenance or repair you might need, from an oil change to an engine rebuild.

A Type-A destination generally has established landing lanes for seaplanes. In Seattle, they're at the north and south ends of Lake Washington; Prince Rupert's seaplane landing area is inside the harbor. In the absence of a suitable lake or harbor, some communities built their own seaplane landing sites. One of these artificial seaplane "ponds" is in Juneau, Alaska, beside the runway at the airport. The pond was created when earth was excavated to create the runway, and it eliminated the need for a separate seaplane fueling facility. The same trucks that service the planes at the airport can drive over to fuel the seaplanes when requested. Seaplane ponds also are found in the southern United States, where floatplanes are sometimes used to support the oil-field activity in the swamps and along the coast (Fig. 21-1). Type-A destinations generally are in the vicinity of an FAA flight service station, where you can get weather and route information, and file a flight plan.

Type-B destinations are relatively remote towns or resorts with limited or no facilities. The towns of Wrangell, in southeast Alaska, and Dease Lake, in the northern interior of British Columbia, are good examples of Type-B destinations. Wrangell has a beautiful seaplane dock in the harbor, but no fuel (Fig. 21-2). The only way to get fuel in Wrangell is to carry it down from the airport in five-gallon cans. Unfortunately, the airport is a couple of miles away, on the other side of town.

At the time of this writing, Dease Lake has an operator who will sell you fuel at his dock (Fig. 21-3); however, his dock space is limited and can accommodate only one or two planes in addition to his own. This is typical of these remote loca-

Fig. 21-1. *A floatplane pond in Louisiana.* EDO Corp.

Fig. 21-2. *The big seaplane dock in Wrangell, Alaska, can accommodate three planes on ramps, and up to four more along the opposite side and on the end. Unfortunately, there is no avgas in the harbor; it has to be carried down from the airport in portable containers.*

tions; the local operators will be happy to sell you fuel or perform whatever maintenance is within their capabilities, but they might not have room for your plane if you want to stay awhile. I've always found them to be very friendly and helpful, so if you do want to stick around for a bit, they'll probably be able to point you to the safest spot along the shoreline to leave your plane.

The little towns and villages in this category rarely have flight service stations, but they do have telephone or radiophone service, so at least you can call the nearest FSS for whatever weather information is available for your location. Some of these towns have VHF repeater stations, so you can talk directly to flight service from your airplane; however, the people you're talking to might be hundreds of miles away. Wrangell, for example, is remoted to the flight service station in Sitka, Alaska.

Fly-in fishing or hunting lodges are other examples of Type-B destinations. Fuel might be unavailable (verify status when planning the trip), but they usually have a dock and a way to communicate with the outside world. You'll probably have to leave your plane in the water at a Type-B destination—a floatplane dock such as Wrangell's is a rarity—so make sure your floats are watertight, and be prepared to periodically check your plane.

Type-C destinations are places with no seaplane facilities whatsoever. The lake with the five-

Fig. 21-3. *The B.C.-Yukon Air Service dock on Dease Lake, British Columbia. Our Cessna Super 180 was dwarfed by B.C.-Yukon's Otter, but at least we had a place to tie up for the night. This is a typical northern seaplane base.*

pound trout, the clam beach nestled in a saltwater bay, and the lakeside forest-service cabin are all examples of Type-C destinations. The cabin might have a rudimentary dock, but most of the time you're going to have to figure out how to secure the plane yourself. There isn't any fuel, and there isn't a phone. Unless you have a portable ham-radio transceiver, you will be completely out of touch with civilization. Just about *everything* you'll need to survive will have to fit in the plane with you.

CHOOSING A ROUTE

Once you've chosen your destination, you have to figure out the best way to get there. There's a lot more to it than just drawing a line from where you are to where you want to go, although that's a good way to start. What you need is information, and it has to be current. You need to know how many seaplane facilities are located along or near your proposed route, where they are located, and if they have the type of fuel you require. The closure of just one seaplane base can leave a gap in your proposed route that's too large to cross. If that happens, you'll have to come up with an al-

ternate route that might take you hundreds of miles out of your way. You don't want to discover that a facility has closed as you're taxiing up to its abandoned dock with little more than fumes in your fuel tanks. It's vital that you have the most up-to-date facilities information you can get before you begin to plan your trip.

Fuel is easier to obtain in some areas than it is in others. The Pacific northwest, western and coastal British Columbia, the Yukon, and Alaska are all heavily dependent on floatplanes, so there are quite a few bases where fuel is available. The same is true of the lake country in Maine, Minnesota, Ontario, and Quebec. The central United States and Canada, on the other hand, have very few seaplane facilities, and you will have to do some careful planning if you want to fly through these areas in an airplane equipped with straight floats. In this regard, amphibious floatplanes give you the best of both worlds, for they allow you to use regular airports if seaplane bases are scarce, or if you want to keep your plane out of the saltwater. If you're going to be doing a lot of your flying in areas where seaplane facilities are few and far between, the versatility of an amphibious floatplane might well be worth its extra cost and reduced load-carrying ability.

If your floatplane is an older one that was designed to run on 80-octane fuel, it might be covered by one of the supplemental type certificates (STCs) that allow the use of automotive fuel. Airplanes ranging from the Piper Super Cub to the de Havilland Beaver can be powered legally by auto gas. Opinions are mixed on the advisability of using auto gas in an airplane, but if your plane qualifies and you feel comfortable doing it, every boat marina along your route becomes a potential fuel stop. The STCs don't help the pilots of new or high-performance floatplanes, all of which require high-octane aviation fuel.

The best single source of floatplane route information in the country is the Seaplane Pilots Association (SPA). The SPA staff has compiled a directory of the best routes along both coasts and across the country for pilots flying airplanes on straight floats. It's called the *SPA Water Landing Directory* and it's available by mail from the SPA. The directory also contains a listing of all the seaplane bases in the United States with information on the type of fuel they sell and the services each one has to offer (Fig. 21-4). Also included is a state-by-state listing of the rules and regulations governing the operation of seaplanes.

The SPA has regional field directors located throughout the United States and Canada. Their names, addresses, and telephone numbers are listed in each copy of the SPA's quarterly publication, *Water Flying*, and in the *Water Flying Annual*. A letter or phone call to the field directors in the regions along your proposed route can net you all sorts of valuable and current information.

If your destination lies in Canada, there is a publication put out every year by the government of Canada that is an absolute must. It's the *Water Aerodrome Supplement*, and it's available from:

Canada Map Office
Department of Energy, Mines and Resources
615 Booth Street
Ottawa, Ontario
Canada, K1A OE9

Fig. 21-4. *Kenmore Air Harbor, located at the north end of Seattle's Lake Washington, is the largest floatplane facility in the United States. This picture was taken during the summer. During the winter, the base is jammed with both private and commercial floatplanes, as well as de Havilland Beavers that are brought down from Alaska for overhaul or refurbishing.*

It contains information about every regularly used seaplane landing site in Canada, including location, fuel and service availability, communications, flight planning, and remarks of interest. Many of the entries include a little map of the landing site showing obstructions, beaches, channels, docks, and other details.

Once you've got all your information together, plotting your route is a matter of "connecting the dots" that represent the fueling stops closest to the straight line that connects your starting point to your destination. As soon as you've done this, go to the telephone and call every one of the "dots" on your route plan. Make sure each facility is still in business, and that they still sell the kind of fuel you need. A recent closure or change in fuel availability might not be reflected in the published guides you used for your initial information.

The closure of a facility is not the only thing that can adversely affect your fueling plans. Several seaplane bases have stopped selling fuel to the public because of mounting liability insurance costs. An aviation accident, no matter how obvious its cause, often results in lawsuits being filed against everyone from the aircraft manufacturer to the instructor who taught the pilot to fly. It doesn't seem right to hold a fuel supplier liable because a pilot neglected to check the tanks of his or her airplane for water, but that's the way it is these days. As of this writing, it is no longer possible to buy dockside fuel in Petersburg, Alaska, for example, thanks to the staggering cost of liability insurance. EDO's Jay Frey tells me that a number of operators in eastern Canada have stopped selling fuel to noncommercial buyers for the same reason. To avoid surprises, call ahead, and make sure the fuel you're going to need will be available when you need it.

If you're like me, you're going to have to stick to some kind of monetary budget during your trip. The phone calls to the seaplane bases also will give you a chance to find out how much your fuel is going to cost: the more remote the base, the more expensive the fuel. Back in 1985, I paid about $1.50 a gallon for 80-octane fuel in Petersburg, Alaska. Two hundred miles away, on the backside of the coast range, I paid $4 a gallon. The 55-gallon fuel drums in Telegraph Creek, British Columbia, had been trucked in over a washed-out gravel road that can destroy a vehicle—and sometimes its driver—within the first hundred miles. I hope the trucker who hauled that fuel got a good cut of the $4-a-gallon price; he or she deserved it. For my part, I was happy to pay it. I needed the gas. Ten years later, by the way, fuel in southeast Alaska was approaching $2 a gallon, with interior prices proportionately higher.

KNOW THE REGULATIONS

All the Federal Aviation Regulations (FARs) that apply to landplane pilots apply to those of us who fly floatplanes. The VFR visibility and cruising altitude requirements don't change just because we changed the undercarriage of our airplanes. The FARs that apply to general aviation pilots take a whole book to describe, and I'm certainly not going to bore you with them here. Floatplane pilots are governed by regulations in addition to the FARs, however, and you should be aware of them.

Water regulations

The phone calls you make to the facilities along your route will give you a chance to confirm that the bodies of water you're planning to land on are open from a legal point of view. The regulations governing the operation of seaplanes vary from state to state and between the United States and Canada. Some lakes, rivers, and coastal waters are closed to seaplanes, and landing on them can cost you hundreds of dollars in fines.

Finding out exactly which waters are open to seaplanes and which are closed can be a frustrating and time-consuming process because of the number of local, state, and federal agencies involved. Some lakes and rivers are under the jurisdiction of the Army Corps of Engineers, some are governed by state regulations, some by city ordinances, and some are privately controlled. If the body of water lies within the boundaries of an Indian nation, for example, regulations governing the operation of seaplanes will be determined by the tribal council. Sometimes a body of water falls under the jurisdiction of several agencies, and one agency's decision concerning seaplane operations might be overruled by another agency. It can get confusing, so the best solution is to contact the appropriate agencies directly.

It's not within the scope of this book to list all the different seaplane regulations currently in force in the United States, Canada, and elsewhere, but by way of illustration, here are some examples of the kind of regulations you will encounter. These particular regulations apply only to lakes in the Portland District of Oregon State that are under the jurisdiction of the U.S. Army Corps of Engineers, so do not assume that the bodies of water along your route or at your destination are covered by a similar set of regulations.

- Seaplanes may be operated seven days a week between sunrise and sunset at all Portland District Lakes with the exception of Big Cliff and Applegate Lakes.
- Once on the water, seaplanes shall be considered boats and must be operated in accordance with marine rules of the road. Seaplanes in the water may taxi to any area on the lake subject to the restrictions for those lakes described under Specific Provisions.
- Commercial operation of seaplanes at Corps lakes is prohibited unless authorized by the District Engineer.
- Seaplane operators planning to land on Corps lakes should notify the Project Manager's office beforehand. Fluctuating lake levels or heavy recreational activity may necessitate use of alternate landing areas.
- Seaplanes on project lands and waters in excess of 24 hours shall be securely

moored at mooring facilities and at locations permitted by the District Engineer. Seaplanes may be temporarily moored on project waters and lands, except in areas prohibited by the District Engineer, for periods less than 24 hours provided that (1) the mooring is safe, secure, and accomplished so as not to damage nor endanger the rights of the Government or members of the public and (2) the operator remains in the vicinity of the seaplane and reasonably available to relocate the seaplane if necessary.
- Seaplanes are prohibited within 500 feet of dam structures or as otherwise indicated under Specific Provisions.
- Seaplanes are prohibited within 200 feet of any marked swimming area.
- Seaplanes are prohibited within 200 feet of lake shorelines except when taxiing to and from the shoreline. Taxi speed shall not exceed five knots.
- Prior to using any designated public boat ramp, the seaplane operator must have permission from either the Corps Project Manager or the specific boat ramp manager if ramps are within areas managed by other entities.

The specific provisions that are mentioned in a few of these regulations include this example:
- Lake Bonneville—seaplanes are prohibited within 1,000 feet upstream and 2,000 feet downstream of the spillway and 500 feet upstream and 600 feet downstream of the powerhouses. Restricted areas are designated by signs placed at conspicuous places. CAUTION: Seaplane operators should be aware that Indian fishing nets throughout the lake could be a hazard during landing and takeoff.

As you can see, you'll need to know more about your route than you can learn from sectional and WAC charts. Besides a copy of the regulations themselves, you might need topographical maps or marine charts in order to locate the various points, bays, coves, creeks, islands, and bridges used to designate specific areas of operation.

Regulations vary from state to state, from city to city, and even from year to year. A lake or harbor that was open to seaplane operations last year might be closed this year and vice versa. The regulations address a multitude of issues. Because of local noise ordinances, some bodies of water are open only to seaplanes with three-bladed propellers, while on others, crowded conditions have resulted in regulations prohibiting step-taxiing. What's legal in one place might be illegal someplace else, so make sure you know all the current regulations in force along your route.

Canadian flight regulations

There are many similarities between Canadian and United States flight regulations; however, there are some differences, and you should know what they are before you cross the border. Transport Canada puts out a couple of handy booklets that are well worth the effort to obtain them. The first one is the *List of Civil Aviation Publications*. It lists every Canadian government publication that has anything to do with aviation, from *Flying the Weather VFR* to the *Water Aerodrome Supplement* that was previously mentioned in this chapter. The second booklet is titled *Air Tourist Information Canada*. It spells out some of the requirements for visiting pilots as well as flight procedures that are unique to Canada. Both publications are available from:

Transport Canada
Dept. AANDHD
Ottawa, Ontario
Canada, K1A 0N8

Following are some of the things you need to know before you take off for that remote Canadian waterfront. First of all, you must have in your possession an unrestricted certificate of airworthiness for your airplane and a valid pilot certificate for yourself.

Canadian airspace is divided into six classes, each designated by a single letter: A, B, C, D, E, or F. Class-A airspace is controlled high-altitude airspace, and requires an IFR clearance to enter. Class-B airspace is controlled airspace above 12,500 feet MSL. Only IFR and controlled VFR flights are permitted in Class-B airspace. Class-C airspace is controlled airspace in which both IFR and VFR flights are permitted; however, VFR flights must have a clearance from air traffic control before they can enter this airspace. Class-D airspace is controlled airspace in which both IFR and VFR flights are permitted: VFR flights do not require a clearance. Class-E airspace is uncontrolled airspace. Class-F airspace is special-use airspace.

The minimum visibility for VFR flight in controlled airspace (Classes B, C, and D) is 3 miles, and you must remain either 500 feet above, 500 feet below, or 1 mile horizontally from, the clouds. (The U.S. minimums are 3 miles of visibility, while remaining either 500 feet above, 1,000 feet below, or 2,000 feet horizontally from, the clouds.) The Canadian VFR minimums in uncontrolled airspace (Class E) less than 700 feet above ground level (AGL) are 1 mile of visibility while remaining clear of the clouds. (The U.S. minimums are the same, but they apply to any altitude up to 1,200 feet AGL.)

The VFR minimums in uncontrolled Canadian airspace (Class E) *above* 700 feet AGL are 1 mile of visibility, and you must remain 500 feet above or below, or 1 mile horizontally from, the clouds. (In the U.S., the VFR minimums in uncontrolled airspace above 1,200 feet AGL are 1 mile of visibility, and you must fly either 500 feet above, 1,000 feet below, or 2,000 feet horizontally from, the clouds.)

There is a special area—west from the coastal mountains in British Columbia extending out to and including Vancouver Island and the Queen Charlotte Island—within which the minimum VFR visibility in uncontrolled airspace is 2 miles instead of 1 mile. Flying "VFR-on-top" is an accepted practice in the United States (FAR 91.121a), but it is illegal in Canada. VFR cruising altitudes were formerly different in Canada, but several years ago the country adopted the same "odd-thousand-plus-500-feet eastbound" and "even-thousand-plus-500-feet westbound" system used in the United States.

If you're planning to fly VFR in Canada, you are required to carry enough fuel for the duration of your flight plus 45 minutes. (In the United States, you are only required to have 30 minutes worth of reserve fuel unless you're planning to fly at night, when you must have a 45-minute reserve.) Remember that water takeoffs and landings are prohibited in Canada between one half hour after sunset and one half hour before sunrise.

Flight plans are not required for VFR flight within the United States (although it's always a good idea to file one), but they are in Canada. Canada has two choices: a flight plan or a flight notification. *A flight plan is good for only one flight*, and if it has not been closed or amended within 30 minutes after your estimated time of arrival (ETA), search efforts are begun. A flight plan must be filed with a flight service station. *A flight notification, or "flight note," can cover several flights,* and search efforts are not begun until 24 hours after the ETA given for the last flight listed on the flight note. A flight note can be filed with a flight service station or any responsible party; the responsible party is anyone—family member, FBO, rental company—who is well aware of your travel plans, especially the conclusion of your trip, and is prepared to notify authorities if you don't show up on time. You are required to file a flight plan when crossing one of Canada's international borders.

PLANNING YOUR FLIGHT

When you're planning your itinerary and schedule, keep in mind the fact that floatplanes have slower cruise speeds and shorter ranges than landplanes. Don't try to cover too much distance in

one day, and make sure you can obtain and carry sufficient fuel for each leg of your trip. Allow time for weather delays. As a floatplane pilot, you're more dependent on the weather than a landplane pilot, who at least doesn't have to worry about high winds making a runway too rough for takeoffs and landings. If you're going to be flying in a coastal area, accept the fact that the often unpredictable marine weather can keep you tied to a dock for days. There's nothing more frustrating than pacing back and forth under a clear blue sky while you wait for a bank of fog out in the channel to lift so you can take off (Fig. 21-5).

Maps and charts

Make sure you have current sectional charts for your entire route. It's important that the charts be current because they'll show the latest obstructions. If low weather forces you to fly down between some islands or up a river valley, you'll want to know where all the power lines and radio towers are beforehand so you won't find them with a propeller. (Don't trust the charts completely, though; I've flown over power lines that weren't on the just-published chart my wife was holding.)

You're going to be referring to your charts continuously throughout your flight; most of your navigation is going to consist of comparing what you see on the chart to what you see out the window. Nothing is more frustrating than folding and unfolding a bunch of sectional charts in a cramped cockpit while flying through the rain in unfamiliar territory. Before my first flight up the Inside Passage to Alaska, I came up with a solution you might want to use for your longer cross-country flights. I purchased enough sectional charts so that I could see my entire route when the charts were laid out on the living room floor. Since the charts are printed on both sides, this meant I had to buy two of most of them. Sectional charts are printed with an overlap at the top and bottom, which I cut off. The end result was a single giant sectional

Fig. 21-5. *Waiting for the fog to burn off in Petersburg, Alaska. One of the frustrations of coastal float flying is to be grounded under clear skies by fog out in the channel.*

chart that covered the Pacific coast from Seattle, Washington, to Petersburg, Alaska—a distance of approximately 800 miles.

I cut some heavy cardboard into 11-×–14-inch panels, and laid them edge to edge on the charts, long edges touching, with each panel centered as much as possible over my penciled route of flight. I traced around each panel and cut the resulting rectangles out of the charts; I then taped each chart section to a cardboard panel. I ended up with nine panels, plus another two that covered the Stikine River country in British Columbia. All the panels fit in the pocket built into the back of the pilot's seat where my wife, who does most of the navigating, can reach them. Going north, we start with panel number one and work our way up to number nine. The panels lie flat in our laps, and we can pass them back and forth easily. We can concentrate on flying and navigating without the distraction of folding and unfolding a bunch of charts.

If you're going into unfamiliar territory, you might want to get the topographical maps covering the area around your destination. Sectional charts will give you a general idea of the terrain along your route, but if you want to know exactly what you're going to be dealing with, "topo" maps

will show you every ridge and valley. Most lakes large enough to accommodate a floatplane will show up on a sectional chart, but a sectional just isn't detailed enough to tell you if there's a little ridge you have to clear at one end of the lake or if there's enough room to turn around at the end of a box canyon. A topo map in combination with your floatplane's performance specifications (interpreted conservatively) will give you the answer. If you're going to make your own camp, the topo map of your destination will also give you some ideas of possible campsites, where the streams are, where there is likely to be a beach, and so forth.

The saltwater equivalent to the topo map is the marine chart. If your flight is to a beach or a bay, the marine chart covering the area will show you where the underwater obstructions are, the composition of the bottom, and the location of mud and sand flats that are above water at low tide. Don't forget your tide table, by the way.

Regardless of whether you use the charts as issued or mounted on boards, draw your route on them. Draw it exactly as you intend to fly it; if you want to fly outside a particular island and then inside the next one, draw it that way on the chart. Most of us fly pretty low because it's more interesting, and the weather often gives us no other choice. With the exception of Loran-C and GPS, navaids are relatively worthless at low altitudes in rugged terrain. Even if your floatplane has the performance to fly high, I doubt there's a VORTAC transmitter beside that lake with the five-pound trout. The pencil line you trace among the two-dimensional mountains, islands, and lakes on your charts is going to be your primary navaid through some very solid, three-dimensional scenery. Draw the line accurately, and when you're in your airplane, fly the line accurately (Fig. 21-6).

Fig. 21-6. *This is why it's so important to follow your route exactly as it's drawn on your charts. A wrong turn here in minimum visibility would put you into the side of a mountain or send you up a blind valley. This is Jervis Inlet, on the southwest coast of British Columbia, as seen from the cockpit of a Beaver.*

Radio frequencies, phone numbers, and flight plans

I like to print up a sheet with all the radio frequencies I'm going to use in the order that I'm going to use them. This eliminates fumbling through a bunch of flight plan forms, or squinting at the small print on a sectional chart while trying to keep the plane on an even keel in a windy valley. You might have to use a frequency that's not even listed on a chart—a blind channel for announcing your intentions at a seaplane base, for example.

Many of these frequencies are found only in flight supplements or in publications such as Canada's *Water Aerodrome Supplement*. It's a lot easier to look up frequencies and write them down in the comfort of your living room than while you're bouncing around in your airplane.

I also list all the telephone numbers I'm likely to need during my flight: flight service stations with which I'll file flight plans or notifications, seaplane facilities to buy fuel or obtain repairs if needed, fishing lodges I might visit, and so forth. I put the numbers on the same page as the radio frequencies.

I also print out flight plans ahead of time, mainly to eliminate wasted time and confusion if I have to airfile a flight plan. If you print your plans beforehand, you won't know all the required information (i.e., time of departure or cruising altitude), but you'll know most of it.

Try to file your flight plans by telephone or radiophone. You and the FSS person on the other end will understand each other clearly, and you won't tie up an aircraft radio frequency; however, floatplanes have a habit of taking you to remote places where the only way to file a plan is over the radio after you're airborne. By having your flight plans written out ahead of time, the FSS specialist won't have to keep prompting you for pieces of information you've forgotten to include. Incidentally, a Canadian flight plan form is a little different from the one used in the United States. Among other things, they're going to want your pilot's license number. If you don't know it by heart and you haven't written it down someplace convenient, flight service (and everyone else on the frequency or telephone) is going to have to wait while you dig out your wallet and paw through it in search of your license.

You might be wondering if it's really necessary to do all this preparation; after all, you're just going on a cross-country flight, not a voyage of discovery to uncharted lands. That might be, but I firmly believe that the success of a cross-country flight is directly proportional to the amount of preparation you do before you climb into your plane. One thing that will definitely benefit is your attitude; all this planning and preparation will put you in the right "frame of mind" for making a long flight. You'll be less likely to go off and leave a chart or flight supplement behind that contains vital information you'll need later during your flight.

If you've thoroughly organized your trip, an unexpected emergency won't be as potentially dangerous as it could be if you were already in a somewhat confused state, fumbling through your charts to find the radio frequencies you need or even worse trying to figure out what happened to the island you were supposed to fly over. If you've done your homework, the sudden appearance of a fog bank won't send you into a tailspin of panic as you frantically try to figure out exactly where you are, which is something that's good to know before you try to figure out where to go next. You won't have the distraction of fumbling through a bunch of charts trying to find the radio frequency for weather information. Instead, you'll be able to concentrate on flying your plane, confident of your location and knowing that your charts are in order and all the radio frequencies you'll need are on the piece of paper in front of you. You'll be able to figure out an alternate plan of action with a minimum of distraction.

You won't want to end up like an acquaintance of mine who became so engrossed with a chart that he flew into the water. Or like another pilot who ran out of fuel over an icy inlet in Alaska. He'd made the short flight dozens of times before. There were no reported problems with the plane, and the weather was fine, so we can only speculate that the cause must have been a fuel miscalculation before the flight—or perhaps no calculation at all. We'll never know.

FUELING CONSIDERATIONS

If your trip is going to take you to areas devoid of established seaplane bases, you might have to refuel your plane with gas that's been stored in five-gallon cans or 55-gallon drums. The fuel in these containers is often contaminated with water, dirt, and rust, so you will need to have some way of fil-

tering these contaminants out as you pour the fuel into the tanks. One of the most popular filters is a chamois skin, which not only filters out dirt and rust particles, but also absorbs water while allowing the fuel to pass through into the tank. It has been discovered, however, that the fine hairs from a chamois filter (particularly a brand-new one) can get into the fuel and subsequently plug the injectors of a fuel-injected engine. Although the instances of this actually happening have been few, the FAA considers it a potentially dangerous situation and has issued warnings about using chamois skins as fuel strainers. The only alternative is to carry synthetic or paper filters of some sort.

If you're going to an extremely remote area, you might have to arrange for fuel to be dropped off at your destination. The arrangements to do this will have to be made well in advance of your departure and can be quite costly. Back in the early 1970s, when aviation fuel was selling for about a dollar a gallon, Jay Frey paid $10 a gallon to have some drums of fuel air freighted to a remote village in the Canadian Arctic. He'd made the arrangements months in advance, but the DC-3 delivering his fuel was still three days late. He estimates that the same fuel would cost him at least $30 a gallon in the 1990s.

If the floats on your plane have been fitted with the optional baggage hatches described in chapter 3, you might consider caring a six-gallon plastic fuel container in each float. Twelve gallons of fuel are almost an hour's reserve if you're flying a Cessna 180. A single Beaver float will hold two six-gallon containers, so you can carry an extra 24 gallons, which again is almost an hour's reserve for the Beaver. If you think you'll need the reserve fuel, you can land, transfer the fuel to the airplane's tanks, and resume your flight.

CROSS-COUNTRY CAMPING EQUIPMENT

Humans need four things to survive: shelter, food, warmth, and water. If the destination is lacking any of these, you will have to supply the missing need or needs, which must be carried in the floatplane. There are as many theories about camping equipment as there are campers; the equipment I'm going to discuss has worked for me, but you will undoubtedly have your own ideas about what to take.

Take a good tent

If you're going to be staying in a cabin, the issue of shelter becomes a nonissue (Fig. 21-7). If you're going to be creating your own campsite, however, you'll need a tent. There are two kinds of tents: backpacking or expedition tents and what are often called "car-camping" tents. Expedition tents usually hold two or three people and stand about four feet tall. They come in a variety of shapes, from peaked rectangles to geodesic domes. Expedition tents generally fold and roll into a cylinder approximately 24 × 8 inches, and they rarely weigh more than five or six pounds. Their small size makes them easy to stow in a floatplane.

Their small size also makes them quite crowded, even for one person. You can't stand up in them, which can make it difficult to get dressed if you're not as flexible as you used to be. They can also get a bit claustrophobic if you have to spend an entire day crouched inside one waiting for the rain to stop.

I used an expedition tent for a long time, but several years ago I switched to a car tent (Fig. 21-8). Car-camping tents are heavier than expedi-

tion tents—the six-person tent pictured weighs 25 pounds—and when folded they occupy at least four times the space of a properly packed expedition tent; however, you can stand up in them, and there's plenty of room for several people to sit around playing cards while the rain ricochets off your beached floatplane. A big tent is not so good in the wind, though. Shortly after the picture in Fig. 21-8 was taken, the wind came up and blew nonstop for two days. I eventually had to run guy lines out to the trees to keep the tent from blowing away. I wouldn't have had this problem with a low-profile expedition tent.

If you buy a tent, buy a good one. Canvas tents are not well-suited for floatplane trips; they're heavy to begin with, and they get heavier when they get wet. Canvas doesn't "breathe" very well, and if you're camping in a rainy area, it won't be long before everything in your tent is damp from condensation. A good tent, large or small, uses a tough, waterproof material for the floor and lower walls, and a lightweight, "breathing" material for the upper walls and ceiling, usually ripstop nylon. Because ripstop nylon lets moisture out, it stands to reason that it will also let it in. To keep the top of the tent from getting wet and admitting moisture to the inside, a rain "fly" is used. The airspace between the top of the tent and the fly allows condensation to be drawn out of the tent while keeping rain or dew from being "wicked" into the tent.

Buy the best tent you can afford. In terms of comfort and security, it will pay for itself 10 times

Fig. 21-7. *The U.S. Forest Service cabin on Bakewell Lake in Alaska's Misty Fiords National Monument. These cabins can be rented for a nominal maintenance fee. Reservations are on a first-come, first-served basis, and they must be made with the appropriate Forest Service District Office.*

Fig. 21-8. *We had to make our own campsite at Tahltan Lake, in the western interior of British Columbia. The region is known for its winds, and while the top of the bluff had a great view, it proved to be a poor location for a tent when the wind picked up the next day.*

over when the weather goes to pot. Features to look for are an adequate rain fly, heavy-duty zippers, windows and ventilation openings completely protected with mosquito netting, entrances that zip completely closed so crawling things can't crawl in, and strong, damage-resistant poles strung together with elastic shock cord to help in their assembly. Finally, make sure it's easy to erect. The tent pictured here has almost seven feet of headroom in the center, but I can put it up by myself, if need be.

The size of tent you buy will depend on the number of people in your party and the amount of space you have in your floatplane. My wife and I have used a Cessna 180 for a week's worth of camping, and we found that even with the rest of our gear, we could still manage to squeeze our big tent into the plane. Of course, there were just two of us, so we were able to remove the 180's back seat. By comparison, when we use a Beaver, there's not only plenty of room for the tent, but for two more people, a full-sized cooler, and an outboard motor, as well!

Sleeping bags

The main question to ask when you're shopping for a sleeping bag for a floatplane trip is: "Will it stay warm when it gets wet?" Its ability to do so depends on the type of filling in the bag. It's pretty hard to beat natural goose down, which is lightweight and retains heat even when thoroughly soaked; however, goose down isn't perfect—when it gets wet, it gets heavy. Wet goose down tends to clump up, as well, although a well-designed bag will minimize this problem.

A high-quality polyester-fiber bag is almost the equal of a goose-down bag. Although it might be slightly heavier when dry, polyester fill gains little weight when it gets wet and doesn't clump up. As with a tent, buy the best sleeping bag you can afford. Look for well-sewn seams and heavy-duty zippers. You might want to replace the bag's original stuff-sack with one that's a couple of sizes larger. This makes it a lot easier to pack the bag, and the larger sack won't take up that much more room in the plane.

Pack the right clothes

The single greatest mistake most people make when selecting the clothes they're going to take on a camping trip is selecting too many. There's no way I'm going to attempt to suggest what clothes you should or shouldn't take; it depends on where you're going, what you're going to do when you get there, and what you like to wear. But be realistic when you're putting together your camping wardrobe. Believe me, if you're going to be gone for seven days, you won't need seven pairs of jeans.

You should carry some special items of clothing regardless of the climate or the time of year you're taking your trip. A good pair of boating or deck shoes are comfortable to wear during a long flight, and they'll keep you from slipping on wet docks and float decks. If you're going to be beaching your plane, take along a pair of hip waders. You rarely will be able to step directly from a float to the shore, and having a pair of waders will keep your feet and pants dry as you unload or maneuver the plane onto the beach (Fig. 21-9).

On the subject of staying dry, make sure each member of your party brings along a good set of rain gear. If all of you are well-prepared for rain, it

Fig. 21-9. *This is why you should carry hip waders in your plane. I didn't, and a gently sloping beach kept us from getting the plane any closer to dry land. The result was a pair of wet jeans and a pair of very cold feet.* Ruth Hustead-Faure

about these materials; some say they work great in light or intermittent rain, but they'll eventually leak if they're subjected to a driving rainstorm. Others claim they're every bit as waterproof as heavy, nonbreathing rain gear. Personally, I've not been impressed with the new stuff in heavy rain situations. I've never gotten wet in my old yellow rain gear, so I guess I'll stick with it.

Try to include a wool sweater in your gear. Yes, it will be bulky and a pain to pack, but nothing holds heat when it's wet like wool. Take along a couple of pairs of wool socks, too, for the same reason. Actually, it's a good idea to keep some warm clothes in your plane at all times. The winds off a lake or bay can be chilling, even in summer, and when the weather turns nasty, you'll be glad you stuck that old sweater or coat in the baggage compartment.

Duffel bags and other containers

It's amazing how quickly the gear for a camping trip adds up. If you were going in a car, it wouldn't matter; there always seems to be space for one more thing in a car. Not so in a plane, where space and weight are both prime considerations. Unless you've got a de Havilland Otter or a Cessna Caravan, you should forget about taking conventional luggage. Soft duffel bags that can mold their shape to the odd-size spaces you're going to be cramming them into are a better choice. If the bags are waterproof, so much the better. My wife and I use the kind of duffel bags used by white-water rafters; they open at the top only, and seal up to be virtually impervious to water.

probably won't, but if just one person leaves his or her rain gear behind, you can count on it raining nonstop for the duration of your trip. I have a set of that yellow rain gear you always see fishermen wearing, and while the bib-overall pants and hooded jacket are heavy and somewhat stiff, they keep me dry no matter how hard it rains. Also on the market are lighter and more fashionable garments made from materials like Gortex that are supposed to "breathe" moisture out while keeping you dry at the same time. I've heard mixed reports

We pack the rest of our camping gear—food, stove, cooking kit, utensils, paper towels, toilet paper, and so forth—in plastic crates. If we're taking a large floatplane such as a Beaver, we use crates about 2 feet by 18 inches. If we're going to be camping with a Cessna 180, we use a couple of those one-foot-square crates that are similar to what dairies use to transport milk. The plastic crates keep everything together, they sit flat on the floor of the plane, they can be stacked on top of each other, and they're easy to carry up to the campsite. If we're going to be camping in bear country, we pack our food in one or two small plastic garbage cans (clean ones, of course!) for reasons that are explained in a subsequent subsection of this chapter.

Food and food preparation

The kind and amount of food taken will depend on personal preferences, trip length, and available space in the airplane. A Beaver will have room for an ice chest, so my wife and I can take fresh meat, milk, cheese, and so forth. We also can take a supply of canned soup, vegetables, and fruit. In short, we can carry the same kind of food we eat at home. If we're using a Cessna 180, however, there's no room for the ice chest, and we can carry only a few items of canned food because of the weight. Instead we rely primarily on the freeze-dried packaged meals designed for backpackers. Add either hot or cold water to the package, and you have a nourishing meal. Most of the packages hold enough for two servings. There are a number of brands of freeze-dried food on the market, and they offer an impressive variety of entrees, side dishes, and desserts, so you don't have to eat the same thing day after day. The packages are very light, and they don't take up much room; we can carry a two-week supply of meals in a single plastic container the size of an office wastebasket.

We prepare our meals on that old standby, the Coleman two-burner stove. We also carry a tiny brass Svea Model 123 backpacking stove as a backup. Both stoves use the same kind of fuel (white gas), and the Svea is utterly reliable. Many of the newer stoves on the market use pressurized canisters of propane. I'm not a big fan of carrying pressurized canisters of anything in an airplane, but the safety record of propane stoves is excellent. Regardless of the type of stove you take, check it out thoroughly before you leave. Don't assume that because it worked on your last camping trip, it will work on this one. Our Coleman acted up once for no apparent reason; fortunately, I discovered the problem in our backyard instead of on the shore of the Alaskan lake we were departing for the following week, and I was able to get the replacement part I needed.

Like your food, the cooking equipment you take will be a matter of personal preference. We use a small cook set containing a frying pan, a couple of sizes of pots with lids, and a little teakettle. They all nest together and fit into a carrying sack about 4 inches deep by 8 inches in diameter. Whatever kind of cook set you select, I recommend that you get one made of stainless steel because it's much easier to clean than aluminum. We do carry a one-gallon aluminum pot for heating wash water or boiling drinking water. You also might want to add a grill for cooking fish over a fire and a full-sized frying pan or skillet.

We prefer to take a set of plastic dishes as opposed to paper plates. A one or two-week supply of paper plates can take up a fair amount of room, and even though you don't have to wash them, you'll be washing your pots and eating utensils anyway, so what's a couple of plates? Other kitchen items you should be sure to take are a can opener, a roll of aluminum foil, plastic zip-lock bags, and an adequate supply of fuel for your stove and lantern. Don't overlook the fact that the lake you're heading for will make a dandy refrigerator if it is located in northern latitudes. My wife puts drinks and sealed containers of butter, milk, and the like in a drawstring bag made of nylon netting and suspends the whole thing in the water on a line fastened to one of the bow cleats of our beached plane.

Your water supply

It's an unfortunate fact that we have finally managed to pollute every corner of the globe in one way or another. Even water tumbling down the side of a mountain hundreds of miles from the nearest human has been found to contain airborne bacteria that can cause illness. To be safe, you should plan on treating the water you drink, either by boiling or by the addition of purifying chemicals. You also can fill a 6-gallon plastic jerrican with water from home and carry the water-filled can in one of the float compartments. If you use this water for drinking and cooking only, it can fulfill the needs of four people for up to a week.

Odds and ends

Don't forget to take a pair of good sunglasses. Polaroid glasses are best because they cut the glare off the water and can help you see beneath the surface when you're checking for underwater obstacles. If you have room, take a pair of binoculars. If you're going to be camping in a remote area, the chances are good that you'll see some wildlife, and binoculars will make the experience that much more enjoyable. Don't forget a camera, and get a polarizing filter for it, if you can. After the filter is mounted on the camera lens, you can rotate it to eliminate all or most of the glare from the inside of your airplane's windshield and windows. Most of the pictures in this book that were taken from inside a plane were shot through a polarizing filter. It eliminated the reflection of the airplane's interior and increased the contrast.

One item on the list of emergency equipment discussed in chapter 18 was a knife. You can put one in your emergency kit if you like, but it's a good idea to wear one on your belt at all times. A knife is probably the most used item when you're in camp, and you don't want to be rummaging through your emergency kit every time you need one. I've found a folding knife with a single blade 4 inches in length to be the most versatile. The knife has a positive lock to hold the blade open so I can't inadvertently close it on my fingers while I'm using it. A 4-inch blade might not sound very long—there are knives with much longer blades on the market—but I've found that anything much larger begins to get a little bulky on my hip when I'm sitting in the plane. My hunting-guide acquaintances in Canada all carry knives with 4-inch blades, and they use them to skin and dress moose weighing up to 800 pounds. Blade quality and blade shape are more important than blade size. Don't forget to include a sharpening kit in your gear, too.

A second handy belt item is a Leatherman, which is a compact folding tool that contains pliers, wire cutters, slotted and Phillips screwdriver blades, saws, and files, in addition to a knife blade. The individual tools are strong and sized perfectly for a variety of chores, from tightening the screws on your plane to fixing your fishing reel.

Another thing I like to have along is a wind gauge. The one I use is a small, hand-held device that will read wind up to 50 knots. I'm something of a worrier, and to me, a floatplane tailed up on an unprotected beach represents a potential disaster. A 10-knot breeze begins to feel like a full gale, and suddenly I begin to envision our only link with the outside world being lifted into the air by the wind and smashed down on its back on the beach. The wind gauge calms my nerves somewhat by showing me that the wind is, in fact, only blowing 10 knots. If there really *was* some danger from the wind, the gauge would show that, too, and I would start thinking about adding more tiedown lines or moving the plane to a more protected spot. If the gusts started getting up around 35 knots or so, I'd start thinking seriously about filling the floats with water. Hand-held wind gauges are available through several mail-order marine-supply companies.

If your destination is in bear country, you might consider taking along a compressed-gas boat horn. They come in several sizes; the ones we carry have a gas cylinder about 6 inches long. Their purpose is not to scare off a bear that has wandered into camp; it might work, but it also could irritate a bear into charging, especially if it's a grizzly. The horn is to let the bears know you're around. Most bears, given the choice, will steer clear of humans. Blowing the horn periodically gives bears that choice long before they accidentally wander into camp, or before you stumble across them in the bush. Bears that are accustomed to the sounds and smells of humans might not be intimidated by the horn, and a grizzly that has a grudge against the world might even charge the sound. The chances of this happening are slim, but it is possible, and is the reason I carry that 12-gauge shotgun.

Don't forget to take an adequate supply of toilet paper. You'll need it for sure if you're making your own campsite, and Forest Service cabins rarely have a supply of paper on hand. The same holds true for paper towels; they weigh almost nothing, but they sure are handy to have in camp. Put a couple of your toilet paper rolls in waterproof plastic bags. Even if everything you own gets thoroughly soaked in a rainstorm, at least the toilet paper will be dry. We carry a small, folding shovel; the Army calls it an "entrenching tool." It has many uses, not the least important of which is to dig a latrine at those campsites that are not equipped with pit toilets.

Take a couple of flashlights, and make sure the batteries are new before you leave. We prefer the large square ones that use a single six-volt dry-cell battery. They throw a lot of light, they're waterproof, and they float. We also carry a Coleman lantern to illuminate the campsite at night. If you take one, make sure you have plenty of spare mantles; they're very fragile after they've been used, and the vibration of the plane can break them apart. Extra bulbs for the flashlights might prove worthwhile.

Finally, in addition to the matches in the emergency kit and the matches packed with our cooking equipment, I always carry a waterproof match case in my pocket. If by some strange twist of fate, I lose everything in the water, I'll still have some dry matches with which to light a fire.

Getting everything in the plane

My wife and I made our very first cross-country camping flight in a Beaver. What a luxury! We had room for everything but the kitchen sink, and we could have strapped *that* to the floats if we'd really needed it. Our second trip was made in a Cessna Super 180, which was a 180 equipped with a 270-horsepower engine. Even though we removed the rear seat, the amount of cargo space was less than half of what we'd had in the Beaver. Weight also was a much greater consideration with the 180. To determine if everything we wanted to take would fit in the plane, I first marked an outline of the 180's cabin floor on our dining room carpet with masking tape. The wall represented the backs of the front seats.

When we had all our gear packed, we tried to load it in our dining room "floatplane." It was soon obvious that we weren't going to be able to take everything we wanted to take. We unloaded the "plane" and began eliminating and consolidating. Then we tried loading again. Four or five tries later, we finally had our gear pared down to the point where it would all fit in the plane. My short-wave radio receiver and our large skillet got left behind, but at least we were able to make the decisions in a relatively calm manner, instead of hurriedly as we struggled to load the real plane the morning of our departure.

By the way, if your plane has float baggage compartments, they make ideal places to carry flammable liquids like Coleman fuel or propane for your stove and lantern, in addition to aviation fuel, engine oil, and drinking water.

Only plastic containers should be put in a float compartment. Metal containers have sharp edges and corners; if they start bouncing around, they could easily wear or punch a hole through the side or bottom of the float. Float compartments also make good storage places for tackle boxes and other items that won't get damaged if they get wet. If you decide to carry something in your floats, don't forget to include it in your weight and balance calculations.

We used our trusty bathroom scale to determine the weight of our little pile of gear. A quick weight and balance calculation showed we needed to shed a few pounds, so we eliminated some of the canned food we'd planned to take. By the end of the evening, we knew exactly what we were going to take with us and exactly how we were going to pack it into the plane. It saved a lot of time and aggravation the morning of our departure.

FILE A FLIGHT PLAN

The day you've eagerly been awaiting finally arrives, and it's time to head out on your trip. Your gear is loaded, your plane is fueled, your charts are in order. What's next? File a flight plan, that's what. You should always file a flight plan for anything other than a local flight, no matter what kind of plane you fly. Floatplane pilots have a habit of wandering off to some pretty remote places, which makes a flight plan all that much more important. Make sure you give a thorough description of your route, so if you are forced down, the search and rescue teams will know where to concentrate their efforts. Once you've filed your flight plan, stick to it. It doesn't do much good to file a detailed flight plan and then deviate from it. Your chances of being found in the event of an accident will be greatly reduced.

My wife and I were weathered in once, deep in the coastal mountains of British Columbia. We'd broken camp in the morning and flown down the narrow river valley that was our route out to the southeast Alaska coast and the town of Wrangell. Forty miles from the river's mouth, the valley was blocked by fog and low clouds forming in the cold air spilling off the glaciers. The ceiling was dropping, and it was starting to rain. I knew where I was—we'd flown the river before—but I lacked the local pilots' intimate knowledge of the area. My altimeter read 400 feet. On either side, rock walls tilted up into the overcast; they were the bases of mountains that I knew topped out at 8,000 feet. A local pilot might have been able to slip under the clouds to the mouth of the river. I knew *I* couldn't. We made a 180-degree turn and flew back to the campsite we'd left an hour before.

We sat beside that lake for two more days, out of touch and out of patience, waiting for the weather to break. Late in the afternoon of the second day, when our spirits were pretty low, the dreary hiss of the rain was interrupted by the whine and buzz of a jet helicopter. It appeared as a tiny orange dot at the far end of the lake, but it grew rapidly larger as it flew directly toward us. It circled once and then settled onto the beach. The man who stepped out was an officer in the Royal Canadian Mounted Police, and he was looking for us. Our flight note had expired, Canadian Flight Service had notified the RCMP, and they'd dispatched the helicopter to search for us. Their plan of action was to fly to the lake I'd named in my flight note and begin the search from there. It was an easy search; we were sitting right where we'd said we'd be.

The weather to the west was still bad, so the officer and his pilot helped us break camp, and we followed their orange Hughes 500 inland through the slanting rain showers to Dease Lake. We were a hundred miles farther from the coast, but Dease Lake had two things our campsite had lacked: fuel and a telephone.

The system works, but you have to do your part. Stick to your flight plan or flight note, and don't push yourself beyond your capabilities. Be prepared to sit for a few days beside a lake waiting for the weather to break. It's frustrating, and it might mess up your plans, but those guys in the orange helicopters would much rather find a frustrated pilot pacing the beach than have to dig through the remains of an airplane plastered against the side of a mountain.

CHECK THE WEATHER

Start checking the weather along your route a couple of weeks in advance of your trip. By studying the weather patterns between you and your destination, you'll be better prepared to make that go-no-go decision the day of your departure. Keeping track of the weather has become much easier lately with the advent of automated weather briefings, and the comprehensive weather information available on the Internet and other online services. Your home computer can be a real asset as you try to get a handle on the weather patterns along your proposed route.

Get a thorough weather briefing before you leave, and pay particular attention to the surface winds and visibility. Visibility is crucial to a float-plane pilot. If you can't see, you can't navigate. (It's certainly possible to fly IFR in a floatplane, but not to that lake with the five-pound trout.) The visibility briefing will give you advance warning of any haze, fog, or rain, and the surface winds will give you an idea of how rough the water will be along your route.

Make sure you get a weather forecast as well as a synopsis of the current weather. Conditions can change fast, especially along a coastline or in a mountain range. There's nothing worse than getting halfway to your destination only to find that an area that was reported clear in the morning has fogged in. Bear in mind, however, that the briefer in the flight service station is working with quite a handicap; it's difficult, and sometimes impossible, to forecast the weather for a remote area. There simply is no information to pass on. The best the briefer can do is look at information from the closest reporting points and add a large measure of conjecture. This is why it's helpful to study the overall weather patterns along your route well in advance of your trip. Regardless of what the briefer tells you, however, make it a practice to depart on a cross-country flight mentally prepared to turn around. Then if you do run into weather that's beyond your capabilities, you'll be more likely to turn around and go home, or at least land before things get too bad and wait it out. You'll be disappointed, but you'll be alive. If you try to force your way through, you might make it, but don't expect any of the folks who fly the orange helicopters to take the bet.

CLEARING CUSTOMS

If your trip takes you across an international border, you must file a flight plan to a designated port of entry so you can clear customs before continuing your journey. In some locations, Seattle, for example, it's sometimes possible to get customs to meet your plane at a seaplane facility that is not a designated port of entry. You can't count on this, however, so always call customs ahead of time to find out if this service is available.

The customs officials in the country you're entering must be advised of your flight in advance so they can meet and inspect your airplane. The easiest way to do this is to include a notification to advise customs when you file your flight plan. Generally, the phrase "Advise customs" is all that's needed, and it should be included in the "Remarks" box on the flight plan form. The flight service station will pass this information to the station at your destination, and the destination station will notify the local customs office of your flight and when you intend to arrive. Normally, customs requires at least one hour advance notice of your arrival. There is no charge for reporting to customs unless the official has to travel some distance to reach you, or if you arrive before or after normal working hours.

After you land at your specified port of entry, you as the pilot-in-command are responsible for keeping your passengers and cargo with the airplane until the customs official arrives. Don't let anyone wander off; it's a serious offense.

If you're entering Canada, the customs officer meeting your plane might want to conduct an inspection of both the plane and its contents. At the very least, the officer will ask you questions pertaining to your trip until he or she is satisfied that you will be using the plane for pleasure or health reasons only, and not for profit. You will then be issued a cruising permit, which will be valid for a specific period of time up to 12 months. Once you have this permit, you won't have to report to Canadian customs for the remainder of your trip. The cruising permit must be prominently displayed in one of your airplane's windows while you are in Canada.

Normally, you will not have to check in with Canadian customs prior to the start of your return flight to the United States; however, if you entered Canada with articles requiring a temporary permit, you will have to report to Canadian customs for completion of the permit documentation before you take off for the United States.

Both Canada and the United States prohibit the carrying of certain food items across their borders, and each country has laws governing the payment of duty on items purchased outside the country. A phone call to the appropriate agency will produce the information you need to be legal going in either direction.

If you take a floatplane outside the United States, a payment is required to bring it back in again. At the time of this writing, an *annual* fee of $25 is being levied against all noncommercial aircraft and boats as they pass through customs on their way back into the United States. When you pay the fee, you will be given a sticker to display on your airplane. The sticker is good for one calendar year. You can cross the border as many times as you like at no charge until the end of the year. The first time you pass through U.S. customs after one year has passed, you will be assessed the $25 fee, and you'll get a new sticker.

In the unlikely event that you experience a forced landing after you've crossed an international border, but before you've had a chance to clear customs, first secure your plane and then contact the authorities as soon as possible. Remain with your plane until the customs officials arrive.

If high winds or rough water conditions prohibit you from landing at the port of entry you specified in the flight plan, you'll have to select an alternate landing site. If you're in contact with a flight service station, keep them advised of your intentions. When you've located a safer landing site, have flight service notify customs of your new destination and arrival time. After you land and secure your plane, remain with it until a customs officer can reach you. Don't be surprised if you're charged a fee to cover the expense of sending the officer to your location.

NAVIGATION

If you learned to fly in a landplane, you've probably gotten used to relying on an array of electronics to assist you in your navigation chores. Even as basic an airplane as a Cessna 172 can have an instrument panel that looks like it came out of a commercial jetliner. By contrast, the panels of most working floatplanes are pretty stark. Until recently, the Beaver pictured throughout this book had a VHF communications radio and an HF company radio. That was it. Yet we took it 800 miles up the convoluted, island-strewn coastlines of British Columbia and Alaska, and as deep into the trackless coastal mountains as it's possible to get.

A finger on a chart is the primary instrument for navigating a floatplane. If what you see out the window is what you see next to your finger, you're in the right place. This is why that line you drew on your charts is so important. If you're flying in an area dotted with islands or lakes, it's easy to become confused. By carefully tracking every landmark along your course line, you'll always know where you are.

Finger-on-the-chart navigation is relatively easy in coastal areas or over country that has prominent landmarks. There are other areas, particularly in northern Canada, where the land is virtually featureless, or is dotted with innumerable lakes, each one identical to the next. It's virtually impossible to navigate by visual means alone in country like this, and radio aids are few. Unless you have a GPS on board, you'll have to rely on the time-proven navigation method known as dead reckoning. Dead reckoning can be very tricky in the far north. Variations in the Earth's magnetic field will do strange things to the airplane's compass, and calculating and holding accurate headings will become extremely difficult. Unless you plan to stick close to the area's obvious landmarks—rivers and roads, for example—talk first to the pilots who fly the region for a living. They'll be your best source for information about navigation, destinations, and hazards.

Finger-on-the-chart navigation won't work if your route takes you across a large body of water—one of the Great Lakes, or out over the Caribbean, for example. You can use dead reckoning for this portion of your trip, or radio navigation if the area is covered by VOR, ADF, or loran signals, and your plane is equipped to receive them.

After you receive your weather briefing and have a good idea of the winds you will encounter enroute, spend a few minutes with your flight computer making sure you'll be able to carry enough fuel for each leg of your trip. There are several hand-held electronic flight computers on the market, and they make short work of time-speed-distance-fuel consumption calculations. Personally, I prefer my old, round, manually-operated Jeppesen CR-3 computer because the batteries won't ever wear out and there aren't any metal or electronic components to corrode. Whatever kind of computer you use, make sure a strong headwind won't run the fuel tanks dry short of your destination.

Even if your route has VOR coverage, take the time to calculate the magnetic heading for each leg of your trip, and jot it down beside the enroute time you calculated during your fuel computations. A VOR depends on line-of-sight signals for position information, and if you're flying low, the signals might be blocked by the surrounding terrain. The only navigation instruments (other than your finger) that you can always depend on are the magnetic compass and the clock. If weather or beautiful scenery cause you to fly at a lower altitude, you'll have something to fall back on if the VOR quits working.

Actually, a VOR would be last on my list when selecting radio navigation equipment for a float-plane. I've found an automatic direction finder (ADF) receiver to be a much more useful instrument because it is not as altitude-dependent as a very-high-frequency omnidirectional range (VOR) receiver, and it can home in on commercial radio stations as well as low-frequency nondirectional beacons.

An even better navigation system to have on board is long-range navigation equipment (loran-C or simply called loran). Unlike VOR or ADF, loran does not fly you to or from fixed ground stations. Instead, it uses a group of low-frequency

transmitters, called a *chain*, to fix your current position. As your flight progresses, the loran unit in your plane will automatically switch from one chain to the next and will automatically select signals from the strongest stations within each chain.

Once the onboard computer has tuned in the closest chain and determined your plane's location, it can guide you to any destination or waypoint you choose. All you have to do is enter the latitude and longitude of the waypoint, and the computer does the rest. Besides the course-deviation display, loran receivers also can display current position (in terms of latitude and longitude), time and distance to the defined waypoint, current heading, and groundspeed. And because it depends upon low-frequency signals for its position information, a loran receiver can guide you along a course that is hundreds of miles long, regardless of your altitude. In fact, the set will display its information just as accurately when you're on the water as it will when you're at 10,000 feet.

Loran accomplishes all this by comparing the time differences between a signal from a master station and the signals from at least two secondary stations within each chain. When you enter the latitude and longitude of a waypoint, the computer compares this position with your current position, and determines the great-circle (shortest) route to the waypoint. The steering display then shows you whether you are to the right or left of this route. If you have entered the exact coordinates of a waypoint, loran often can guide you within 100 feet of the point.

As good as loran is, it's being replaced by the global positioning satellite (GPS) navigation system. GPS navigation is similar to loran in that it uses signals from several fixed transmitters to determine the precise location of the receiver. In this case, the transmitters are mounted on satellites in orbits around the Earth. The advantage of GPS is that its coverage is worldwide, unlike the loran chains that tend to be concentrated along the coasts. GPS is not affected by terrain, which can confuse or alter the timings of loran signals in some areas.

GPS is used commercially to guide helicopters to off-shore oil wells and by aerial fish-spotters to give accurate school locations to vessels on the surface. You can use GPS or loran to pinpoint a remote mountain lake or a seaplane base tucked away in a tiny coastal cove. By entering multiple waypoints, either system can guide you through a complex maze of islands, even if low weather forces you to fly right down on the deck. GPS signals are more reliable than loran signals, and it is fast becoming the navigation system of choice on everything from container ships to cross-country trucks to airliners. Loran is still a useful and valuable system, but if you're considering the purchase of a radio navigation unit for your plane, go with GPS.

FLYING FLOATS IN LOW WEATHER

Low-weather flying, or "scud running," is as potentially dangerous in a floatplane as it is in a landplane. Continued flight into marginal VFR or IFR weather conditions is the single greatest cause of general aviation accidents. Never allow yourself to be pressured into flying in weather you're not sure you can handle; however, there *are* times when low-weather flying can be accomplished in relative safety if you follow a few basic guidelines (Fig. 21-10).

Always fly within reach of a body of water large enough to land on. The protected waters of Washington's Puget Sound, the Inside Passage to Alaska, and the lake country of northern Minnesota, Manitoba, Ontario, and Quebec are examples of areas where your flight will probably carry you over more water than land. The advantage of being over or near water is that should the ceiling really start coming down, you'll be able to land quickly and wait until the situation improves. Obviously, the water you're flying over will have to be smooth enough to land on. Water covered with swells or the open ocean are as inhospitable to your floatplane as dry land, and you should think twice before attempting to cross them in marginal weather. The greatest hindrance to visibility along the coasts of British Columbia and southeast Alaska is fog. Fortunately, the presence of fog usually indicates an absence of wind, so the water is generally smooth enough to land on, unless it's exposed to ocean swells.

Fig. 21-10. *The clouds are full of rocks when the weather goes bad in the Stikine River valley. While the rain and low clouds haven't reduced visibility to the danger point yet, we were alert for any indication of worsening conditions. This time, we made it. The Stikine River flows from British Columbia through the coast range to saltwater in southeast Alaska.*

Don't fly over unfamiliar territory in low-weather conditions. Patches of fog or mist can hide the terrain around you, and if you don't have a good mental picture of the area, you can easily become disoriented. When flying over water, always keep the shoreline in sight, but leave yourself enough room to make a 180-degree turn toward it if the visibility ahead of you drops below minimums. By turning toward the shore, you always will have a visual reference to help you maintain altitude. If you turn *away* from the shoreline, you'll instantly be confronted with a featureless, gray void. You'll have nothing by which to judge your altitude or the airplane's attitude. The chances are good that you'll stall the plane or enter a spiral dive, but you'll have no idea what's happening until a wall of water suddenly explodes through the windshield.

If the visibility drops to less than two miles, slow down. Give yourself an additional margin above a stall by lowering the flaps to their normal takeoff position, and slow-flying along the shore. By reducing your speed, you'll have time to react if a rocky bluff suddenly looms out of the mist ahead of you or if you see that you're going to fly into a fog bank.

A very dangerous weather condition is created when rain starts falling in an area where the temperature and dewpoint are very close together. A mile or so in front of you, the rain might obscure the horizon, but you'll have no problem following the shoreline beside your airplane. The danger occurs when fog forms in the rain. The fog up ahead will look just like the rain, so you'll have no idea it's there. Then, bang! You'll be in it, and your visibility will drop instantly to zero. The shoreline you've been following will disappear, and you'll have no visual reference to help you turn the plane around. If the atmospheric conditions along your route are conducive to weather like this, be very, *very* careful. It might be better not to fly at all.

Low-ceiling weather tends to concentrate air traffic, so turn the landing lights on and keep a sharp eye out for other aircraft. You never know when someone might come barreling out of the mist toward you, so be prepared to take evasive action if another airplane should suddenly appear.

Keep an eye on what's going on behind you. I can't imagine a worse situation than being forced to turn around by fog or low clouds, only to find that it's socked in behind you, too. If you *do* find yourself in this situation, the best solution is to pull the power off and land, assuming the water beneath you will permit this. Once you're safely on the water, you can beach the plane and wait for the weather to improve, or you can shut the engine down and drift. Be careful that you don't drift right along with the bad weather.

If your problem is a local fog bank, and you know there is better weather on the other side, you can land and taxi your plane until the visibility improves to the point where you can take to the air once again; however, keep an eye on the engine temperature gauges. Some planes will overheat if they're taxied for a long time, so you might have to shut down occasionally to let the engine cool off. Also keep in mind that taxiing for long distances on the water will throw a monkey wrench into your fuel consumption calculations, and you might need to refuel sooner than you had planned. Unless the conditions are absolutely ideal, don't taxi on the step. You won't be able to stop or turn quickly enough to avoid a collision if a boat or a floating log appears suddenly in your path. If you do step-taxi, watch those temperature gauges.

If the water is too rough for a safe landing and you can't go back, the next alternative is to climb. As long as there is fuel in its tanks, your floatplane is safest in the air. If you've received sufficient training to allow you to climb, cruise, turn, and descend on instruments, you might be able to climb above the fog or low clouds to better visibility above. Once you're there, try to establish contact with a flight service station or an air route traffic control center for assistance in establishing your position and setting a course for an area with better visibility. This is an emergency situation, and it emphasizes the importance of sticking to familiar territory when flying in low weather. If you don't know exactly where you are, and you don't have a good mental picture of the terrain that surrounds you, you could climb blindly ahead into the side of a hill. You'd be better off trying to put the airplane down in the fog even if the water is rough. Your chances of surviving a capsizing are better than your chances of surviving a head-on collision with a mountain.

FLOAT FLYING
IN COLD WEATHER

If you fly your floatplane off the water when the air temperature is at or below freezing, the spray thrown onto the plane during takeoff can freeze, possibly immobilizing your plane's moving surfaces. While ice might form on the aileron, elevator, and trim tab hinges, you can exert enough leverage with the yoke and the trim mechanism to break the ice away. The air and water rudders are another story. If the steering cables for the water rudders are frozen into their guides and pulleys, the air rudder will be immobilized as well. The same thing applies to the water rudder retraction cables. If they are iced up solid after your takeoff, you might not be able to lower them after you land.

The solution is to seesaw the rudder back and forth after takeoff until you can visually determine that all the water on the floats has blown off or frozen. By moving the rudder back and forth, the water rudder cables will not stay still long enough to freeze. A tunnel of ice might form around the moving cables where they pass through their guides, but the cables themselves will not be immobilized. Do the same thing with the water rudder retraction system. After you lift off, keep lowering and retracting the water rudders until all the water on the floats has frozen.

If you take an amphibious floatplane off the water in freezing conditions, you'll be really busy. In addition to your gymnastics on the rudder pedals and the water rudder retraction handle, you'll also need to cycle the gear several times to keep ice from locking it in the retracted position. A lot of water will be thrown up into the wheelwells and over the nosewheel retraction system, so continue to cycle the gear until there's no doubt that all the water has either drained away or frozen solid. If you're planning to land on the water again, frozen landing gear is not really a problem, but if you intend to land on a runway, you could get a rude surprise when you go to lower the wheels and nothing happens. Don't forget, if the gear is frozen inside the float, the manual system won't bring it down, either.

Start cycling the gear as soon as you're safely off the water and have established a positive rate of climb, and don't stop cycling it until you're sure it will come down when you need it. If by some chance, it *does* become frozen in the retracted position, land in the water again and taxi slowly around until the ice weakens enough to break off when you operate the gear. Then take off and start the cycling procedure again.

CARBURETOR ICE

We've all been taught to watch for the symptoms of carburetor ice—a drop in rpm or manifold pressure with no corresponding reduction in throttle setting. We've also been taught the conditions under which to expect carburetor ice—low ambient air temperature and air with a high moisture content. Sometimes a high moisture content alone can cause carburetor ice; the rapid drop of pressure within the venturi can lower the air temperature to the freezing point or below. Carburetor ice is usually thought of as being an inflight occurrence, something to be watched for during cruise or a reduced-power descent to a landing. A few years ago, however, I had an experience with carburetor ice that took me totally by surprise because I was totally unprepared for it. I include it here so that those of you who, like me, have done most of your flying in relatively warm and dry climates can guard against the problem if you make a flight into a cooler and more moist environment.

My wife and I had spent almost a week camping in the coastal mountains of British Columbia. The plane we were using was a Cessna 180 equipped with a 270-hp carbureted engine. The weather fell in on us the day we were supposed to leave, and while it had not yet begun to rain, we could feel it coming. We broke camp early in the morning and loaded the plane. Everything seemed normal as I performed a quick runup. I took off and moments later was climbing out over the glacier valley that led to the river we were going to follow some 85 miles out to the coast.

We hadn't been airborne more than 30 seconds when the engine began to run rough. I immediately turned around and headed back for the lake. Not wanting to damage anything in the engine, I pulled the power back. It ran as smooth as silk. I eased the power back in, and the roughness resumed. Then the engine began to surge up and down. I was now faced with making a glassy water landing with erratic power from an engine I had little control over. I banked over near some cliffs so I would have a better idea of our height above the water, and my wife spotted some floating leaves that helped, too. My landing was okay, but I was still faced with the strange situation under the cowl. The engine would idle perfectly, but as soon as I tried to add power, it would miss and surge erratically. I became convinced something had broken in the fuel system, depriving the engine of all but idle fuel. The thought of carburetor ice crossed my mind, but I dismissed it. I couldn't believe it would form in an engine that was running at full power during takeoff.

I felt I ought to do *something*, however, so I pulled on the carburetor heat as we began the long taxi back across the lake to our campsite. Every now and then, I would add some power to see if anything had changed. Gradually, the engine began to put out more and more power until by the time we were almost back to the beach, the engine was revving up to full power without a hiccup. The application of carburetor heat apparently had fixed the problem, but I couldn't understand how

I could have picked up that much ice during a flight that had lasted barely 30 seconds.

When I described the incident to a mechanic friend in Petersburg a few days later, he had a ready explanation. The carburetor hadn't iced up during the flight, he told me, it had iced up during the taxi and run-up *before* the flight. He said it was a common occurrence in the cool moist air of southeast Alaska, especially in airplanes equipped with Continental engines. The carburetors on Continentals sit farther from the engine case than the carburetors on Lycomings, and it takes longer for the heat from the case to soak through to the carburetor body. When the engines are started after sitting all night in the cold, ice can build up quickly in the carburetor throat. If the runup is short, the carburetor body won't get a chance to warm up before takeoff power is applied, and the ice will continue to build up. At some point during the takeoff, the engine will begin to lose power.

The solution is simple. When you start your cold engine, taxi to the runup area with the carburetor heat on full. The hot air will cause your engine to run rich, so to prevent the plugs from fouling, lean the mixture, but not so much that the engine runs rough. Taxi around a few minutes longer than usual with the heat on to keep any ice from forming while you give the engine case a chance to warm up and radiate heat down into the carburetor body. Perform a normal runup and then put the heat back on while you taxi into position for takeoff. Don't forget to shut the heat off and return the mixture to rich before you start your takeoff run.

As a wheelplane pilot, I had been taught not to use carburetor heat on the ground because it is unfiltered and there was a risk of sucking debris into the engine. This is not a problem for the floatplane pilot because there is little chance of picking up grass clippings or dirt particles from the surface of the water. I started following my friend's advice the day he gave it to me, and I've never had a Cessna 180 ice up on me since. (This procedure is designed to prevent carburetor ice before takeoff only; it will not prevent ice from forming later on in the flight.)

OPERATING IN UNFAMILIAR WATERS

Unless you're duplicating a trip you've taken before, you'll be landing in some new—and possibly strange—places. The techniques described in chapters 12 and 13 apply no matter where you are, but a cross-country flight can present some situations you never encounter in your home waters.

Aerial inspections

Don't skimp on the aerial inspection, and make sure you thoroughly check out a shoreline before you commit to beaching your plane. If you're flying in a logging region, keep a sharp eye out for floating logs. They often break loose from rafts and booms, and their weight holds them low in the water. They're not hard to spot from the air, but if you're taxiing in after landing, they can be almost impossible to see, especially if the water is ruffled or choppy.

If you're landing on a lake for the first time, go in high enough to clear the surrounding terrain. You don't want to be trapped in a narrow valley and be forced to land before you're ready. Circle the lake and study the lay of the land. Which way is the wind blowing? What's the best approach path? If you have to go around, will there be a clear path ahead of you? If there's only one way in and out of the lake, is there enough room to make a 180-degree turn at the far end? Circle around at altitude until you've figured out exactly what you're going to do and how you're going to do it. Then drop down and make the approach (Fig. 21-11).

Measuring a lake from the air

It's easy to determine the length of a runway. It's either printed on your chart or listed in an airport directory. Even if you can't find it's exact length, it's a safe assumption that it's long enough for *something*, or it wouldn't have been built in the first place. It's a little harder to determine the length of an unfamiliar lake. The scale of a sectional chart is such that it's impossible to accurately measure the

Fig. 21-11. *Approaching Big Goat Lake in Misty Fiords National Monument. Before descending below the surrounding peaks, we circled the lake at altitude to check the wind direction and look for floating debris and other obstacles. Not until we had a clear plan of action did we drop down and begin our approach.*

length of a small lake. Topographical maps are more useful in this respect because their smaller scales make it possible to include greater and more accurate geographic detail. But what if you don't have a topographical map with you? What if you're beginning to run into bad weather and you decide to land and wait it out but you're not sure if the lake you've come across is long enough to take off from again? Is there any way to accurately determine the length of a lake from the air?

There is, and it's a relatively simple procedure. It's based on noting the time it takes you to overfly the lake and then comparing this time to a chart that relates ground speed and time to distance (Fig. 21-12). First, pick one of the ground speeds listed in the left column that best suits your floatplane. For instance, if you're flying a Super Cub, 80 knots would probably be your choice. If you're in a Cessna 185, you might prefer to use a ground speed of 90 or 100 knots. The ground speeds, times, and distances on the chart are based on true airspeeds at sea level on a standard day. True airspeed varies with temperature and pressure and increases approximately two percent per thousand feet of altitude gain. To maintain your chosen ground speed, you must subtract the additional airspeed you've "gained" by virtue of your altitude.

Let's say you want to determine the length of a lake that is at an elevation of 4,000 feet, and you want to use a ground speed of 90 knots. To obtain an accurate time, you should fly over the lake as low as possible while remaining safely clear of any obstacles. Let's say the surrounding terrain is fairly flat in this case, so your timing run will be made at an altitude a little more than 4,000 feet. First, use your flight computer to calculate a true airspeed based on your indicated altitude, the outside air temperature, and an indicated airspeed of 90 knots. (You really should use *pressure* altitude, which is the pressure recorded when your altimeter is set on 29.92 inches of mercury, and your *calibrated* airspeed, which is your indicated airspeed corrected for position and instrument error; however, in this scenario, indicated altitude and airspeed will be accurate enough.)

If the true airspeed calculates out to be 96 knots, subtract six knots from your indicated airspeed of 90 knots to find the airspeed you must maintain to yield true air and ground speeds of 90 knots. In this case, an airspeed of 84 knots will produce a ground speed of 90 knots (assuming there's no wind).

If you're mathematically inclined, you can make use of the fact that true airspeed increases about two percent per thousand feet of altitude gained. Using the same lake as an example, an altitude of 4,000 feet translates into an airspeed increase of approximately eight percent. Eight percent of 90 knots is 7.2 knots ($0.08 \times 90 = 7.2$).

Landing distance chart								
GROUND SPEED (Knots)				DISTANCE IN FEET				
	2,000	3,000	4,000	5,000	6,000	8,000	10,000	12,000
70	17	26	34	43	52	69	86	103
80	15	23	30	38	45	60	75	90
90	13	20	27	33	40	53	67	80
100	12	18	24	30	36	48	60	72

Elapsed time in seconds

Fig. 21-12. *This chart can be used to determine the approximate length of a lake or other landing area prior to the landing itself, so you can be sure that you'll be able to take off again.*

Round this off to seven knots and subtract it from the indicated airspeed of 90 knots, and you get 83 knots. This is the indicated airspeed you'll have to hold to maintain a true air and ground speed of 90 knots. This method isn't quite as accurate as actually computing your true airspeed because it's based on standard day and does not allow for temperature changes, but it will get you into the ballpark.

Once you've determined the indicated airspeed that will yield the target ground speed of 90 knots, set up your plane to fly at this speed. Overfly the lake at this speed, and note the elapsed time in seconds that it takes to go from one shoreline to the other. Find this time on the chart in the row labeled "90 Knots." The number directly above it in the "Distance" row is the length of the lake. If your measured time falls between two of the times on the chart, you'll have to interpolate the actual length. If it takes you 24 seconds to overfly a lake at a ground speed of 90 knots, the lake is 3,500 feet long. If there is a wind blowing, make a timed run at the same indicated airspeed in both directions and average the times or the distances to get the correct length of the lake.

Don't overlook the effect that the lake's altitude will have on the performance of your floatplane. A lake a couple of thousand feet long might be sufficient for your floatplane at sea level, but at an altitude of 4,000 feet, on a hot day, surrounded by hills, that same lake might be too short for your plane.

Dealing with currents

I approached the big seaplane dock at Wrangell, Alaska, one day in what appeared to be a perfectly executed docking. I shut off the engine as I neared the dock and prepared to step out and stop the plane. Much to my dismay, the Cessna 180 didn't slow down. We swooped up to the dock and continued down it quite at a brisk pace. Fortunately, there were no other planes there that day, and I had plenty of room to manhandle the plane to a stop,

although it took the entire length of the dock to do it. I was totally baffled until I noticed bits of bark and other debris sailing past our cleated-off plane. I'd completely forgotten about the current. The tide was coming in, and the water was flowing into the harbor at a remarkable speed.

If some of your stops are in saltwater, you'll want to know how fast the current is running and in which direction before you get to the dock (Fig. 21-13). A good way to do this is to turn and taxi toward the dock (or a portion of the shoreline that's parallel to the dock) at an angle of 90 degrees. Make sure you're still a good ways offshore when you do this; you don't want to end up so close in that you don't have any maneuvering room. Hold the heading and observe your sideways movement relative to the dock or the shoreline. This will tell you the direction of the current as well as its speed. There are times when it might be better to dock into the current even though it means docking downwind. The object is to reach the dock at the slowest possible speed (while maintaining directional control, of course). If the current is the stronger of the two elements, approach into the current.

PADDLES AND POLES

Like a plumber's helper, your paddle will be your salvation in all sorts of situations. You can fend yourself off a dock, pole yourself off a sandbar, extend it to steady a boarding passenger, and bury it in the sand for a tiedown. You can even use it to paddle your plane; however, it has some limitations, not the least of which is its (and your) lack of power. All floatplanes, even small ones, present relatively large surfaces to the wind. When you compare the area of your airplane's tail and fuselage to the area of your paddle blade, you can see that it won't take much of a breeze to overpower your best efforts with the paddle.

If your enemy happens to be an adverse current, you aren't much better off. Remember, you're trying to paddle *two* canoes, not just one,

Fig. 21-13. *It's important to know which way the current is running in the crowded harbors of southeast Alaska. With currents as fast as 10 knots, a miscalculation could cause you to miss the ramp, or worse, carry you out of control into a boat.*

and each "canoe" has a lot of underwater surface in the form of keels, chines, steps, and spray rails. When you compare the total area of your float-plane's underwater, "current-catching" surfaces to the area of your paddle blade, you come up the loser, even if you're a strong paddler.

However, there are many times when a paddle is worth its weight in gold. In calm conditions, a paddle is often the best means to carefully approach a rocky beach or maneuver through a crowded marina. If you misjudge your approach to a dock and come to a stop a bit too soon, a few strokes of the paddle will bring you alongside.

There's more to paddling a floatplane than you'd think. If you simply get out on the left float and start paddling, you will only succeed in going around in circles. This is because you are applying your paddling force to the left float only. In effect, you're applying a force to one end of a long moment-arm, the pivot point of which is the keel of the right float. Dropping the water rudders will help. The plane will still turn to the right, but not as sharply. If you are carrying a passenger, he or she can counter the right turn with pressure on the left rudder pedal. If your plane has a rudder trim control, you might be able to accomplish the same thing by dialing in a lot of left rudder.

I have found that the most effective way to make a floatplane go in a straight line is to position yourself toward the front of the left float and reach out ahead and to the left with the paddle before drawing it back toward you. (If you fly a Super Cub, a Citabria, or a Husky, you will have to reverse all the float directions I've given here because you normally step out on the right float instead of the left one.) To turn the plane to the left, reach straight out to the left with the paddle and draw it back in. You can also rotate the plane to the left by paddling backward on the outside of the left float.

Turning to the right is easy. Simply make your paddle strokes parallel with the outside edge of the left float. The harder you paddle, the tighter you'll turn. Another way to swing the nose to the right is to place the paddle as far out to the right between the floats as you can reach and pull it back in toward you.

Everything changes when the wind starts blowing. Even in a light breeze, it will be all you can do to keep the plane from weathercocking. If you let it point into the wind, you'll be able to make some forward headway, but if you try to swing the nose out of the wind, most of your paddling effort will go into holding the plane off the wind, and you'll make little forward progress.

In a stronger breeze, you won't be able to hold any kind of a crosswind heading at all, and your paddling efforts will serve only to slow your backward drift. If combined with the proper sailing techniques, this could be an effective method of backing up slowly to a downwind dock or beach. Obviously it will work best if there's a second person in the cockpit to manipulate the flight controls.

A current can foul up your paddling plans just as effectively as the wind. You won't be able to paddle you floatplane very fast to begin with, and if the current is moving you backward faster than you can paddle the plane forward, the net result will be a drift to the rear. On one of my first trips to southeast Alaska, I misjudged the current and stopped our Beaver five feet short of the Petersburg gas dock while the tide was going out. I was heading directly into the current, and it took several minutes of the fast and furious paddling to inch the airplane those last five feet to the dock. In this particular case, I could have let the plane drift back until I had enough room to restart the engine and try again, but things could have gotten very expensive very quickly if there had been a boat or another airplane behind me and the current had been just a bit stronger.

Maneuvering a floatplane with a paddle is not an exact science, and you'll have to experiment to find out just how responsive your plane is to your efforts. The time to learn how your floatplane handles under paddle-power is not when you suddenly find yourself in a tight situation. Instead, find a dock or a beach where you can practice paddling without the risk of running a wing into a piling, or grinding a float onto a rock. Then, on a nice

day, spend an hour or so maneuvering your floatplane around with the paddle and find out just how responsive your plane is. You'll be that much better prepared in the event a real docking or beaching problem requires you to paddle the plane correctly the first time.

If you're going to be flying regularly to lakes or bays with shallow water, you might find a pole more useful than a paddle. The first time I saw a pole in use was during a floatplane trip up the Stikine River in British Columbia. A Beaver belonging to one of the local air services landed on the lake one evening, and as it nosed up to the shore to pick up a couple of fishermen, I noticed a wooden pole about two inches in diameter and 12 feet long clipped to the top of the left float.

After the fishermen were aboard, the pilot slipped the pole from its mountings and poled the plane backward away from the bank. When he was well clear of the shoreline, he pushed sideways with the pole and turned the plane around until it was facing open water. After clipping the pole back onto the float, the pilot climbed into the cockpit, started the engine, and was on his way.

I thought this was pretty slick, and when I ran into the same pilot later in town, I asked him about the pole. He told me he found it far more effective than a paddle in shallow water because "You can jam it against the bottom and really reef down on it to move your plane around against the current or the wind."

He told me the lakes in his area are all susceptible to strong winds, which often make it difficult to maneuver a floatplane to and from the beach. The pole gave him the leverage he needed to keep the plane from drifting onto underwater rocks or into the trees and dense brush that line the shores. He often had to land on the Stikine River itself, which has a strong current and is filled with sandbars. He used the pole as a pry bar to lever the plane on and off the sandbars and turn it around against the current. And by jamming the pole into the bottom and leaning on it, he could hold the plane in position against the flow of the river, something that would be impossible to do with a paddle.

If you think a pole might be a handy thing to have, make sure you get a strong one. If you often operate over rocky bottoms, you might even consider having a metal cap made to fit over one end. This will keep the end from splitting and might help prevent the pole from becoming wedged between the rocks. You can simply lash the pole to the float struts, or you could rig up some sort of spring clip arrangement to hold the pole to the top of the float. The trick is to have it fastened securely while at the same time keeping it easily accessible. To my knowledge, there is no certified pole holder for floatplanes, so if you decide to carry a pole, you'll have to apply to the FAA for a special airworthiness certificate, restricted category, which functions as an external load permit.

External loads

It's not uncommon in Alaska to see a floatplane with a canoe or two strapped to the float struts, or a load of lumber, or even a snowmobile. I once saw a photograph of a Beaver carrying an entire two-place airplane (I believe it was a Taylorcraft). The small plane had been wrecked out in the bush, and it was being returned to town for repair. The fuselage was strapped to the Beaver's right float, the wings to the left float, while the engine, tail surfaces, and landing gear were inside the cabin. It was an air-to-air photo, so I know the whole thing got off the water!

Carrying an external load is something of a trial-and-error process, but the FAA has established some basic guidelines. First of all, you have to be in Alaska. If you want to carry an external load in the lower 48 states, you'll have to get a supplemental type certificate (STC) for your plane, a complex process that can be very expensive and time-consuming. To carry an external load in Alaska, you will have to obtain the aforementioned special airworthiness certificate, restricted category. To get it, you will have to have

logged at least the same number of flight hours required for a commercial certificate and a minimum of 50 hours of pilot-in-command time in the make and model of airplane on which you are proposing to carry the load. Then you'll have to demonstrate to an FAA maintenance inspector that you can carry the external load in a safe and secure manner.

Over the years, the FAA district office in Anchorage, Alaska, has compiled a list of external loads that have proven to be safe when carried on a specific model of floatplane. For example, pilots have been carrying canoes on Cessna 185s for years, so if this is what you want to do, you need only demonstrate to the FAA inspector that you know how to mount the canoe securely. The FAA's approved-loads list also places limitations on the weight and frontal area of the external load that can be carried on a particular model of floatplane. If the item you are proposing to carry is not on the approved-loads list, the inspector will require you to conduct a demonstration flight. If you crash, you won't get a certificate.

If you plan to carry an external load, make sure you don't load your plane outside its center of gravity envelope. A canoe that's safely within the CG envelope of one floatplane might knock you out of the envelope if you mount it in the same place on your plane. Pay careful attention to the ball in the turn coordinator when you're flying with an external load. A bulky load such as a canoe can have the same effect on your plane as the addition of the floats themselves; the additional vertical surface ahead of the plane's yaw axis can diminish the effectiveness of the vertical tail. Your canoe or load of lumber won't extend as far forward as the floats, so the directional stability of your plane might not be as dramatically affected, but you'll still have to stay on top of the ball. If you carry a load on one side of your plane only, you might have to apply pressure to the opposite rudder pedal throughout your entire flight. If you're flying a plane without rudder trim, this can get pretty tiring.

Surprisingly, an external load will not have as much effect on the cruising speed of your airplane as you might expect; a drop of five or six miles per hour is typical. On the other hand, the climb rate of your plane will be reduced dramatically. Small lakes and bays that normally would not present a problem for your plane might become off-limits when you're carrying an external load. Even if you managed to get your plane in the air before you hit the beach, you might not be able to climb fast enough to clear the trees along the shore or a nearby ridge. External loads also will affect your glide ratio; your plane will drop like a stone when you pull the power back. Long, shallow descents are the rule at an approach speed slightly higher than normal. This, too, will affect your ability to operate out of tight places.

The best advice concerning external loads comes from the Anchorage office of the FAA: Before you attempt to carry an external load, talk to pilots who are experienced in the practice. Many of the float operators on Anchorage's Lake Hood carry boats and other external loads on a routine basis. A call to one of them can get you all sorts of valuable information on how your own airplane will handle and perform with a particular load. Above all, don't experiment with external loads on your own. It's illegal, but legality becomes a minor issue when compared to the risk of injury or death if a load proves to be too much for you or your airplane to handle.

Here are a couple of tips on external loads that are well-known to Alaskan floatplane pilots. If you're going to carry 4-×-8-foot sheets of plywood on top of the spreader bars between the floats (the only place they'll fit), drill two or three holes through the leading edge of the stack and wire all the sheets firmly together. If you don't, the slipstream might cause them to fan out vertically, and the resulting drag could have dramatic, if not fatal, results.

Make sure that a long load like lumber or a canoe doesn't extend so far forward that it's in danger of being struck by the propeller. A good rule of thumb is to position the external load so that its weight is concentrated under the forward third of the wing. This location is the approximate midpoint of your airplane's center of gravity envelope.

If you carry a canoe, it should rest solidly against the top and bottom of the struts. If the canoe is so wide that it will not clear the lower end of the wing strut, don't carry it. (Special racks are available for some floatplanes that are designed to carry a wide canoe securely, while holding it clear of the wing strut.) If possible, carry your canoe on the right side of your plane. The drag of the canoe will help counteract the P-factor and slipstream effects, both of which cause an airplane to yaw to the left during takeoff and whenever it's at a higher than normal angle of attack. Finally, if you want to carry a square-stern canoe on the float struts of your plane, be sure to mount it with the flat stern facing forward. If you mount it the other way, it will look more streamlined, but the turbulence rolling off that square stern will buffet the daylights out of your airplane's horizontal stabilizer and elevator.

IN CAMP WITH A FLOATPLANE

You've made it! You've navigated your way into the back country without a hitch, and after a flawless landing and a perfectly executed beaching, you're ready to go after those five-pound trout. But before you pull on your waders and thread up your new graphite fly rod, take a few moments to make sure both your plane and your camp are in order.

Beaching in the bush

There is no way I can describe every beaching situation you are likely to run into on your cross-country flights, but I can point out some general guidelines to follow (Fig. 21-14). Try to anticipate everything bad that could happen to your plane so you can prevent it beforehand. Don't assume that the direction the wind was blowing when you beached the plane is the direction it will blow all

Fig. 21-14. *The shoreline of this lake was shallow and very muddy. Hip waders were a must, as it was impossible to get the plane anywhere near solid ground. Fortunately, the area was relatively protected from the wind, and we could run lines back to trees on shore to hold the plane in place.*

the time. After you've secured your plane on the beach, figure out every direction the wind could come from, and what effect it would have on your plane. If you think the wind could lift a wing, try to tie it down. If you think the plane could pivot and ram a wing into a tree, add whatever lines are necessary to keep it from doing so.

What will happen if the lake gets rough? Which way will the waves strike your plane? Is there a possibility that the floats could start pounding the bottom as the plane bobs up and down in the waves? The best way to prevent this is to beach the plane on a shore that drops off quickly into deep water. If this isn't possible, and you're pretty sure the plane will start pounding the bottom if the waves kick up, you could try holding your plane offshore with a couple of stout poles. Cut the poles from trees four or five inches in diameter, and cut them long enough to hold your plane offshore far enough to keep it from pounding on the bottom. Brace the poles securely against the shoreline, side by side and approximately the same distance apart

as the floats on your plane. Move the plane forward off the beach and lash the end of the left pole to the left end of the rear spreader bar. Lash the right pole to the right end of the bar. Hold the plane back against the poles, and against the beach, by running lines from the tail, floats, and wings back to the shore. Finally, if the wind does kick up, and the waves do start rolling in, stick around your campsite to make sure your plane stays put.

If the place you want to beach your plane doesn't have a beach, there are a couple of alternatives. One is to secure your plane to shore nose first (Fig. 21-15). The two requirements for this are water deep enough for your floats and something to butt the bows against without damaging them. What you are doing is no different from the nose-first docking described in chapter 13, only you won't have a dock. The best substitute is a log. You can run a line from each bow cleat to shore or wrap the lines around the log itself. Hold the plane firmly against the log with diagonal lines run in from the stern cleats and the wings.

Fig. 21-15. *The only way to get the plane up to the steep shore of Big Goat Lake was nose first. The log made a handy dock. Unlike many of the lakes in southeast Alaska, the water in Big Goat Lake is crystal clear and very cold. As a result, the lake supports a population of grayling, a fish rarely found outside arctic river systems.*

Don't forget to put bumpers between the bows of the floats and the log.

If the shoreline consists of a steep bank or bluff that drops into shallow water, you still might be able to tail the plane in normally. The trick here is to make sure the plane won't pound against the bottom, and that it won't be pushed back into the bank, where the water rudders or tail assembly could become damaged. The Beaver in the lower left of Fig. 21-8 is backed in against a steep bank. We were able to maneuver a small floating log up against the bank, upon which we supported the tails of the floats. We used the folding shovel from our emergency kit to dig two trenches into the

bank to house the water rudders. Finally, anticipating that waves might move the plane back a foot or two, we cleared away some stumps and brush that could have damaged the horizontal tail and the seaplane fins. There seemed to be sufficient water under the floats to keep them from pounding against the bottom.

Nightfall brought the wind and the waves, and as I lay in our rattling tent listening to the metallic slap of water on aluminum, I envisioned the float keels rising and falling, grinding into the gravel bottom until the thin skin wore away to admit a rush of black water into the ruptured compartments. Three times that night I made my way down the rocky bluff and into the frigid lake to make sure the floats were riding well clear of the bottom. They were, but two or three hours later, the hiss of the waves and that infernal, metallic slapping would convince me that the floats were pounding for sure now, and back down the bluff I would go.

Keep an eye on your plane

Once your plane is safely on the beach or tied to the dock, don't just forget about it. Make sure the control lock is installed. If your plane doesn't have a lock, make sure that the yoke or stick is tied back with a seat belt. Check the mooring lines every morning and evening. Make sure nothing is working loose and that your plane hasn't shifted. If it has, figure out why and fix it. Pump out the floats every morning—more often if you have a leaking compartment or if it's been raining heavily. Keep an eye on the weather. If it looks like it's going to turn nasty, double-check your plane and make sure it will weather the winds and the waves that are on the way.

Dealing with bears

This seems like a rather odd subject to include in a book about floatplanes, but I have good reason for doing so. That lake with the five-pound trout is going to be in relatively remote country; if that remote country lies within the northern United States or in Canada, there will likely be bears somewhere in the vicinity. You might never see one—most people who aren't out looking for them don't—but the possibility of a bear encounter still exists. Because a bear encounter can be dangerous, you should know how to avoid one. If an encounter is unavoidable, you should know how to ensure your safety and, if at all possible, the safety of the bear as well. Actually, you're more likely to have a problem with a bear in places that are frequented by people. Bears lose their natural fear of man as they learn to associate the presence of people with food, and that's when the problems begin. The bears that populate the back country retain their fear of man, and they'll generally go out of their way to avoid you.

There are three kinds of bears in North America: black bears, grizzly bears, and polar bears. If you have the guts to take a floatplane up among the grinding and shifting ice floes that polar bears call home, you are a braver person than me, and you'll have a lot more to worry about than bears. The bears the rest of us have to contend with are the *black*, which is widespread across the United States and Canada, and the *grizzly*, which has retreated to the more remote regions of western and north-central Canada, and Alaska. (The so-called Alaska brown bear is actually a grizzly.)

If you encounter a bear at all on your trip, it will most likely be a black bear, which, incidentally, can be black, brown, or cinnamon in color. They are smaller than a grizzly; adult black bears weigh from 200 up to as much as 600 pounds. They are relatively timid, and will generally avoid man *unless* they have gotten used to his presence and have come to associate it with food. Despite their relatively small size and somewhat humorous mannerisms, black bears can be very dangerous, and there are records of them attacking and mauling people. Generally speaking, however, black bears will run off when confronted by a human, although they might come back at the first opportunity. They can destroy a camp in short order in their search for food.

You shouldn't fool around with any bear, but never, *ever* mess with a grizzly. Weighing up to 1,500 pounds, grizzlies are unpredictable, and a mean-tempered one would just as soon kill you as look at you. Fortunately, they are quite wary of man, and they generally will avoid you if they know you are coming. The majority of grizzly maulings are the result of a surprise meeting between the victim and the bear.

If you're starting to think that maybe you shouldn't take that cross-country floatplane trip after all, relax. Your chances of having a bad experience with a bear are slim to begin with, and there are several things you can do to put the odds even more in your favor. First of all, keep a clean camp. Clean up promptly and thoroughly after every meal, and don't keep food in or anywhere near your tent. We don't even keep deodorant, soap, or toothpaste in the tent. If you're going to leave your camp for awhile, leave the front of your tent open. If a bear decides to investigate your tent, it will do so *whether the tent is open or not.* I'd rather have a bear wander in and out the front door than have it rip our tent to shreds trying to get in.

Previously in this chapter, I mentioned that my wife and I carried our food in little plastic garbage cans. We do this because the garbage cans are easy to hang in a tree away from the campsite. This gets our food somewhat out of the reach of any bears that might wander through to investigate the camp while we're not around. If you decide to do this, hang the cans at least 20 feet above the ground. Adult grizzlies can't climb trees (although they have been known to push them over), so even if they smell the food, they won't be able to get to it. Black bears, on the other hand, are very adept at climbing trees, so if possible, hang the food cans from a limb that extends some distance out from the trunk.

Even this is not a guarantee; I've heard of black bears first climbing a tree and then edging out on the branch to drop onto a suspended food container from above. The whole outfit—rope, container, and bear—comes crashing to the ground, which, of course, is what the bear had in mind all along. Fortunately, bears do not try to conduct these operations quietly, and the ensuing ruckus and general thrashing about will alert you to the fact that something out of the ordinary is going on, and you'd better investigate. I once was awakened early in the morning by a black bear that was hooking one of our food containers out of a tree, and I had to crawl out of our tent and fire a couple of rounds from the shotgun in the air before it would leave. I don't know which scared the bear more, the blast from the shotgun or the sight of me standing in the brush in my underwear, but it left and didn't come back.

You've probably heard that bears with cubs are dangerous. It's true. If, on your hikes away from your campsite, you come across a bear cub, turn around and go back the way you came. I know they're cute and cuddly, but their mothers aren't, and you can bet she's around, even if you can't see her.

If you're hiking in bear country, it's a good idea to make some sort of noise to let any bears in the area know you're around. Some people wear bells on their ankles, other people whistle, and still others carry the gas-powered boat horns that were previously mentioned in this chapter and beep them off periodically. Avoid walking through dense brushy areas; bears, especially grizzlies, like to bed down in them during the day. If you're walking along and catch a whiff of spoiled or rotten meat, turn around and go back. If you absolutely have to proceed, do so very cautiously and make a lot of noise. There's a good chance that what you're smelling is a dead animal that a bear has cached in the brush. Bears are very protective of their food, and they often bed down nearby to keep an eye or an ear on it. If you come wandering along, the owner of the carcass will immediately assume you're planning to steal his dinner, and he'll charge without warning.

If you carry a firearm for bear protection, keep it loaded and within reach if you're camping in grizzly country. *The gun is not an excuse to start blazing away at the first sight of a bear.* Besides the fines and other penalties for killing a bear out of season or without a hunting license, it's just not right to wound or kill a creature whose only crime was to stumble across your campsite. Ninety-nine percent of the time, the bear will leave as soon as it becomes aware of your presence. The gun should *only* be used against the bear as a last resort when the life of you or one of your companions is actually in danger. If you *should* be charged by a bear, wait until the bear is close enough to be sure of hitting it, and then aim for its chest. Don't try to stop a charging bear by aiming for its head; the skulls of bears are very tough and they're sloped back at a sharp angle. You're more likely to wound it than kill it with a head shot.

Bears have terrible eyesight. They rely on their acute hearing and remarkable sense of smell. A bear walking toward you does not constitute a charge. It constitutes a bear who senses something is around and wants to get close enough to actually see what it is. Once it gets a whiff of your scent or hears an unnatural sound, such as the banging of pots or a gun being discharged into the air, it will probably leave.

If you beach your plane only to step out and find bear tracks in the sand, don't panic. Any bears in the area will be much more apprehensive of your presence than you will be of theirs. Make plenty of noise to let them know you're around, and keep your camp absolutely clean.

If you do see a grizzly high on a mountainside or walking along the far shore of the lake, get out your binoculars and count yourself among the privileged; grizzlies are one of the most magnificent animals on Earth, and the opportunity to witness their power and grace in their natural habitat comes to few people.

NOISE ABATEMENT

Aircraft noise has become a major issue today. Every sector of the aviation world is affected, from international and municipal airports to heliports. Floatplanes are not exempt from the growing pressure to eliminate noise by eliminating aircraft operations altogether. In fact, they sometimes seem to draw more fire from residential communities and environmental groups than any other segment of aviation. Many lakes across the country that have been used by seaplanes for years have been closed to them as a result of pressure brought to bear on government agencies by various environmental or community groups.

The primary issue is noise. Ironically, many of the lakes that have been closed to seaplanes are still open to boaters, so while it's illegal to make noise for a few moments when you take off in a seaplane, it's perfectly legal to run around the lake all day in a boat with an unmuffled engine.

On the positive side, many lakes are being opened (or, in some cases, reopened) to seaplanes, thanks largely to the efforts of the Seaplane Pilots Association. The final steps toward opening a body of water to seaplane operations sometimes take place in a hearing room or courtroom, but the first and most important steps always take place in the cockpits of our airplanes. The image the public has of seaplanes and seaplane pilots is based upon our individual actions. It takes only *one* incident on the part of *one* inconsiderate pilot to taint a community's image of water flying in general. This is why it's so important that we all practice noise abatement techniques and procedures whenever possible, even when taking off from a remote wilderness lake. Some of the most vocal groups opposing the operation of seaplanes are wilderness preservation societies, and although there might be no one in sight when you take off, there could be backpackers or campers in the vicinity who don't like the sound of a seaplane prop at flat pitch echoing off the hills.

I can understand how they feel. I personally don't care for the sound of unmuffled trail bikes and snowmobiles. Their endless snarling somewhere in the distance can become very irritating as it reverberates around the mountains. At least seaplanes only make noise for a few minutes during takeoff, and then they're gone; however, the trail bike and snowmobile drivers have just as much right to be there as I do, and I know they are getting just as much pleasure from being in the back country as I am. And that's really the bottom line. It doesn't much matter *how* we choose to enjoy the things that nature has created. What's important is that we respect the environment around us and take care to leave it the way we found it.

I take issue with the more militant environmental groups and individuals who try to portray the seaplane community as a sort of aerial motorcycle gang that loves to roar around the wilderness with no regard for their surroundings, while making as much noise as possible with their machines. On the contrary, I think the reason most seaplane pilots get interested in water flying in the first place is because of their love and appreciation for the wilderness. All the seaplane pilots I know are just as concerned about the preservation of the wilderness as the groups that are trying to ban us from visiting it.

You can do several things to lessen the noise impact of your plane. First, reduce your engine rpm as soon as possible after takeoff. A reduction of a mere 200 rpm can make a dramatic difference in the noise output of the propeller. Of course, the safety of you and your passengers should be your first concern. If obstacles in your path dictate climbing with maximum power until they are cleared, then do so, but whenever possible, reduce your climb rpm. If you're taking off from a lake or harbor that's surrounded by residential areas, remain over the water until you have climbed to at least 1,000 feet AGL before crossing the shoreline, and avoid early morning or late evening takeoffs. If you want to practice takeoffs and landings, don't make more than one or two landings in the same place. The residents in the area might tolerate a couple of takeoffs, but after five or six, they'll be vowing to do whatever is necessary to ban seaplanes from their lake or bay altogether.

The airplane manufacturers are as aware of the noise problem as anybody else, so most of the high-performance floatplanes around today have been equipped with quieter, three-bladed propellers as standard equipment. The floatplanes that really have noise problems are Cessna 180s, older 185s, and 206s that are equipped with two-bladed propellers. The de Havilland Beaver was equipped originally with a two-bladed propeller, and it is very noisy during takeoff. All these planes can be equipped with three-bladed props, and while this can be an expensive conversion, it's worth it in terms of better relations with your neighbors (Fig. 21-16). If you're renting a floatplane equipped with a two-bladed propeller, or if the cost of converting your own floatplane to a three-bladed propeller is currently out of reach, you can still go a long way toward improving the public image of seaplanes by keeping your rpm as low as safely possible during takeoff and climbout.

Of course, the best way to improve relations with the community is to introduce as many people as possible to the joys of float flying. If you can get them into the plane, even the staunchest environmentalist can't help but be impressed by the frozen drama of a glacier-draped wall of rock rising vertically from the mirrorlike waters of a coastal fjord, or be impressed by the solemn, haunting beauty of a forested lake deep in the north woods, or by the brilliant sparkle of a transparent Caribbean lagoon.

The floatplane's world is indeed a beautiful one. In an age when most of man's machines are designed to physically change our environment, the floatplane is a welcome exception. I have a bumper sticker that reads: "Only seaplanes and canoes can visit a wilderness and leave no trace behind." It's a fact, but the proof rests with you and me. If we exercise good judgment in the operation of our floatplanes and show consideration for the other people who share and enjoy our world with us, that bumper sticker will continue to be true for a long time to come.

I hope you get your seaplane rating. You'll find it a challenging and enjoyable experience and one that will give a whole new meaning to the word "flying." The first time I saw a floatplane winging its lonely way through the silver skies of Alaska, I was hooked. I think you will be, too. Have fun and remember, *keep your float tips up!*

Fig. 21-16. *This Cessna 180 has been equipped with a more powerful engine (270-horsepower) and a three-bladed propeller. Increased performance is not the only benefit. The new propeller is not as noisy during take-off as the original two-bladed propeller. The engine and propeller modifications were developed by Kenmore Air Harbor.*

A de Havilland Beaver waits for its next assignment on a windy winter day on Lake Washington.

Resources

ORGANIZATION

Seaplane Pilots Association
421 Aviation Way
Frederick, Maryland 21701

The SPA publishes a quarterly magazine, *Water Flying*, as well as the *Water Flying Annual*. The association is constantly monitoring legislation that might or does affect seaplane operations. The group actively works to keep open any waters that are in danger of being closed and reopen waters that have already been closed.

SUPPLIERS AND MANUFACTURERS

Baumann Floats
45 East Pullman Avenue
St. Paul Park, Minnesota 55071

Manufactures floats for a variety of ultralights and kitplanes.

Canadian Aircraft Products, Ltd.
2611 Viscount Way
Richmond, British Columbia
Canada V6V 1M9

Manufactures floats for the Bellanca Scout and Citabria; Cessna models 170, 172, 175, 180 and 185; Maule models M-4 and M-5; the Piper PA-18 Super Cub; and the de Havilland DHC-6 Twin Otter.

Capre, Inc. (Aqua Floats)
P.O. Box 247
Brandon, Minnesota 56315

Manufactures floats for Taylorcraft models F-19 and F-21; the Piper J-3 Cub and the PA-18 Super Cub; Cessna models 172, 175, 180, 185, and 206; Maule models M-5, M-6, and M-7; and the Stinson 108.

DeVore Aviation Corporation (PK Floats)
6104B Kircher Boulevard, N.E.
Albuquerque, New Mexico 87109

Manufactures floats for the Bellanca Citabria and Scout; Piper PA-18 Super Cub; Cessna models 170, 172, Hawk XP, 180, 185, and 206; the Maule M-5; and the Soloy Turbine 206 and 207. The company also manufactures amphibious floats for Cessna models 185 and 206, and the Soloy Turbine 206 and 207.

EDO Corporation Float Operation
14-04 111 Street
College Point, New York 11356

Manufactures floats for the Bellanca Champion 7ECA, and the Bellanca Citabria and Scout; Piper PA-12 Super Cruiser, PA-18 Super Cub, PA-22 Tri-Pacer, PA-23 Aztec, PA-28 Cherokee 160, PA-28 Cherokee 180, PA-32 Cherokee Six; Cessna models 170, 172, Hawk XP, 180, 185, and 206; Maule models M-4, M-5, M-6, and M-7; Arctic Tern model S1B2; Aviat Husky; Helio Courier H-250, and Helio Super Courier H-295; de Havilland DHC-2 Beaver and Turbo Beaver; Pilatus Porter; and the Rockwell Thrush Commander. The company also makes amphibious floats for Cessna models 180, 185, and 206; Maule models M-5, M-6, and M-7; the Helio Super Courier H-295 and Helio models 700 and 800; and the Soloy Turbine 206.

Full Lotus Manufacturing, Inc.
No. 407-5940 North Road
Richmond, British Columbia
Canada V6V 1Z1

Manufactures straight and amphibious floats for a variety of ultralights and kitplanes.

Murphy Aircraft Manufacturing, Ltd.
Unit 1-8155 Aitken Road
Chilliwack, British Columbia
Canada V2R 4H5

Manufactures straight and amphibious float kits for a variety of kitplanes.

Wipaire, Incorporated (Wipline Floats)
South Doane Trail
Inver Grove Heights, Minnesota 55075

Manufactures floats for Cessna models 185, 206, and 208 Caravan; the de Havilland DHC-2 Beaver and Otter; the Piper PA-23 Aztec; the GAF N22B Nomad (Australia); and the Soloy Turbine 206. The company also manufactures amphibious floats for Cessna models 185, 206, and 208 Caravan; the Soloy Turbine 206; the de Havilland

DHC-2 Beaver, Turbo-Beaver, and Twin Otter; the Pilatus Porter; the Rockwell Thrush Commander; and the GAF N22B.

Zenair
Huronia Airport
Midland, Ontario
Canada L4R 4K8

Manufactures straight and amphibious floats for a variety of ultralights and kitplanes.

BIBLIOGRAPHY

Bruder, Gerry. *Northern Flights.* Boulder, Colorado: Pruett Publishing Company, 1988. Bush pilot technique and experiences, 161 pages.

Casey, Louis, and Batchelor, John. *The Illustrated History of Seaplanes and Flying Boats.* London: Phoebus Publishing Company/BPC Publishing Limited, 1980. History, 128 pages.

Fisk, William D. *Fundamentals of Float Flying, Seaplanes in the Mountain Lakes, and Glacier Flying.* Kenmore, Washington: William D. Fisk, 1964. Technique, 45 pages.

Frey, Jay J. *How to Fly Floats.* College Point, New York: EDO Corporation, 1972, revised 1988. Technique, 66 pages.

Hirsch, Robert S. *Schneider Trophy Racers.* Osceola, Wisconsin: Motorbooks International, 1993. History, 192 pages.

Hoffsommer, Alan. *Flying with Floats.* North Hollywood, California: Pan American Navigation Service, Inc., 1966. Technique, 146 pages.

Kurt, Franklin T. *Water Flying.* New York, New York: Macmillan Publishing Company, Inc., 1974. History and technique, 272 pages.

Newstrom, Gordon K. *Fly a Seaplane.* Grand Rapids, Minnesota: Gordon K. Newstrom, 1983. Technique, 53 pages.

Palmer, Henry R. *The Seaplanes.* Fallbrook, California: Aero Publishers, Inc., 1965. History, 52 pages.

Rivest, Pierre. *Bush Pilot*. Montreal, Quebec: Publications Aeroscope, 1988. Technique, 173 pages.

Vorderman, Don. *The Great Air Races*. Garden City, New York: Doubleday and Company, 1969. History, 288 pages.

Index

Illustrations are in **boldface**.